SPIRITUALITY THROUGH THE CENTURIES

SPIRITUALITY THROUGH THE CENTURIES

Ascetics and Mystics of the Western Church

Edited and Introduced by
JAMES WALSH, S.J.

LONDON
BURNS & OATES

CUM PERMISSU SUPERIORUM

Catalogue No.: 5/4996

MADE AND PRINTED IN GREAT BRITAIN BY
UNWIN BROTHERS, LIMITED, WOKING AND LONDON
FOR BURNS AND OATES LIMITED
25 ASHLEY PLACE, LONDON, S.W.1

CONTENTS

v

INTRODUCTION

One of the most encouraging and consoling aspects of the life of the Church in our century is the vast spiritual energy that appears to have been released through the movement that can be generally described as the lay apostolate. For the first two or three decades, this movement seemed to be almost entirely concerned with externals: with the way in which the laity could help the hierarchy and the clergy in carrying out the corporal, and some of the spiritual, works of mercy. Gradually, however, it became clear that this external apostolate demands participation in the interior life of·the Church beyond what had been considered to be ordinarily sufficient for lay people: that the stamina and selflessness which the active apostolate requires is only possible where there is a personal and conscious union with Christ in His Church. Lay people began to realize that they, as much as priests and religious, needed an interior formation and rule of life.

One result of these reflections on the nature and purpose of the lay apostolate has been a fresh emphasis on the Gospel truth that every Christian, by virtue of his baptism, is called to reproduce in his own life, according to his own place and circumstances, the perfection of Christ. And, naturally enough, it has become customary to define this perfection in terms of charity: that love of God which, according to St John, finds its reality and term in the love of one's neighbour.

However, this re-emphasis of the universal command "be ye perfect as your heavenly father is perfect" is not always in full accord with the Church's spiritual tradition. In the desire to make sanctity accessible to all, the distinction between the perfection required of a bishop, which stems from his obligation to lay down his life for his flock and is therefore related immediately to active charity, and the perfection required of religious, based on that interior surrender which effectively chooses God in place of all things, has been blurred; the teaching of the Council of Trent on the superiority of the celibate and virginal state of life has frequently been queried, so that recent popes have felt obliged to reiterate this teaching. There have also been attempts to narrow the gap between ordinary and heroic virtue: as when, for example, some modern hagiographers show undue eagerness to search out and portray in exaggerated detail the faults and defects of the subjects of their biographies. Again, when sanctity is defined in terms of the active charity of the apostolate, doubts are inevitably raised about the nature and worth of the contemplative vocation; and though lip-service is paid to the traditional priority of prayer in the life of active religious, it is often urged that action must take precedence over contemplation. Such a definition would seem to suggest that the traditional spirituality of the Church in the West, which, as this book makes clear, was for over a thousand years identified with monastic spirituality, needs radical adaptation to suit the needs of our time.

We need, therefore, a definition of sanctity which is a true reflection of the constant spiritual tradition of the Church, one which needs no radical adaptation to fit changing times, needs or circumstances. This sanctity must always be described in terms of a progressively more perfect union with and assimilation to Christ in His Church. This union has faith for its principle; it is begun in baptism and finds its growth in the frequent fruitful reception of the holy Eucharist: its essentials are prayer and mortification; in terms of daily living it consists in the imitation particularly of the suffering Christ, and in the practice of all the virtues.

Each Christian, then, will find his holiness in his own personal union with God in Christ according to the measure of his own particular vocation. And whoever fully corresponds to the constant graces which accompany his calling will be truly holy and perfect. But it is equally true that the diversity and variety of vocation within the Church will bring a similar diversity in holiness: a holiness not only of degree but of kind. The Lord Himself, when He said "if thou wouldst be perfect", made it plain that the perfect fulfilment of the commandments and the perfect following out of the evangelical counsels are different in kind. Underlying the teaching and practice of Christian perfection as it is portrayed in this book is the principle that the effective and whole-hearted practice of the counsels is alone compatible with the perfect following of and union with Christ in His Church. As a way of life it is this one alone that demands the total and exclusive consecration to God of the person; without this absolute commitment, the most perfect possible form of Christian charity is unattainable. While it not infrequently happens that the Holy Spirit leads a man or woman to the perfection of Christ's charity, even though they remain in the world, it is always through an approxima- tion to the spirit of the counsels. The effective practice of the counsels of itself demands that heroic practice of the many virtues which the life of Christ portrays; the same demands are not generally made on those who follow the counsels in spirit alone.

It is hardly surprising, then, that what gives this collection unity and continuity is that the figures treated are, almost without exception, monks or religious; and that they speak of the perfect union with Christ in terms of the celibate or virginal life. In spite of the interesting, and sometimes surprising, diversity, the essential similarities are inescapable. Whether it is the married Bishop Gregory of Nyssa speaking, or Venantius Fortunatus, who, as Dr Walsh disarmingly remarks, "has an appearance of incongruity amongst the formative figures of western spirituality", the story is the same: union through consecrated virginity and the cross of Christ.

Though some of the mystical writers here portrayed, such as Guigo the Angelic, Denys the Carthusian and Angela of Foligno, will be unfamiliar to most English readers; many others, such as Augustine and Bernard, are household names. Professor Knowles forestalls the objection of those who wonder whether yet another treatment of well-known figures can be of profit, when he says that "there is a never ending need to bring to the notice of every generation, again and again and in different places, the rich inheritance of the Catholic past, and to turn fresh eyes, perhaps as yet unfamiliar with the Master's words, back to a precious and venerable page of Catholic history". And this is sufficient apology for this kind of book, if apology is needed. Fr. Daniélou's quotation from St Basil is also appropriate: "he who strives to perfect himself in all the paths of virtue should turn his eyes to the life of the saints as to statues which move and act". As Paul VI said recently, the Church has never needed as much as she does now that public testimony which religious life makes manifest. "The more urgent the task of the laity in living and fostering the Christian life in the world, the greater the need for the shining example of those who have renounced the world effectively and who openly demonstrate that the Kingdom of Christ is not of this world." (Allocution to Heads of Religious Orders, 24 May 1964.)

One of the greater difficulties in editing a book of this nature is to find a suitable title: one which will neither exaggerate nor diminish its value. We hope that the sub-title will indicate sufficiently that it is in no sense offered as a history of the spirituality of the period that it covers: in substance, from the fifth to the seventeenth centuries. The two non-Western figures, Origen and Gregory of Nyssa, are included both because of the intrinsic value of the essays and also because of the influence that these two writers have had on the history of Western spirituality.

In conclusion, the editor would like to thank all the contributors to this volume; and also the publishers, who in their patience have overcome many incidental and irritating difficulties of reproduction. He would also like to thank Fr. Philip Caraman, editor of *The Month* during the years when these articles appeared in that publication, which is at present celebrating its centenary year.

JAMES WALSH, S.J.

1. ORIGEN

Henri Crouzel

ATTENTION has recently been drawn to the influence of Origen on medieval spirituality and exegesis.[1] His homilies were widely read in the western monasteries, and their effect on contemporary writers, on St. Bernard, for example, is manifest. This fact had been almost entirely ignored by the historians of the nineteenth and early twentieth centuries; in the Alexandrian they saw only a speculative theologian, or even a philosopher who concealed a pagan outlook under a veneer of Christianity—opinions indeed still quite widespread in Protestant circles. It was, however, a Lutheran, W. Völker, who, writing in 1931, first drew attention to the spiritual aspect of Origen's work.

One cannot read homilies and commentaries without becoming acutely aware of the spiritual feeling which informs them, and this, in the Middle Ages, was accessible in a particular way to monks and nuns, through their life of prayer and abnegation. The artificial character that some people attribute to "spiritual" or "allegorical" exegesis scarcely distracted them, attentive as they were, according to the Pauline precept, more to the spirit than to the letter. They knew that revelation is not primarily a mere text, but is the Incarnate Word, as a Person, His teaching and example, which the Holy Ghost explains interiorly to the Church, and in souls. For them the New Testament was already within this "tradition," in this climate of Faith which found expression in catechesis, prayer, liturgy and the organised Church even before it was written down. The Old Testament, read by Christ to His Church and by the Church to her children, became a New Testament; the water of the old covenant at Cana had been changed into the wine of the new. Origen's explanation of Scripture was based upon his spiritual insight as *ecclesiastikos*, as *man of the Church*. This is the reason the devout souls of the Middle Ages found in his work so much nourishment.[2]

[1] J. Leclerq, *L'amour des lettres et le désir de Dieu*, Paris, 1957; H. de Lubac, *Exégèse Médiévale: les quatre sens de l'Ecriture*, Paris, 1959, tome I, pp. 198–304.

[2] Cf. our judgment on R. P. C. Hanson's book, *Allegory and Event*, London, 1959, in the article "Origène devant l'incarnation et devant l'histoire," *Bulletin de Littérature Ecclésiastique*, Toulouse, 1960, pp. 81–110.

His thought is essentially scriptural and spiritual. From his childhood, according to Eusebius, his father Leonidas, an exceptional person both as a man and a Christian, had apprenticed him to the traditional culture of the Greeks and, at the same time, to the study of Holy Scripture. By the time he was seventeen his competence in profane learning enabled him, after the martyrdom of Leonidas and the confiscation of the family fortune, to provide for his mother and six younger brothers by giving lessons. Appointed official catechist of the Church at Alexandria, "he found teaching grammar incompatible with the exercise of religious asceticism and lost no time in breaking away from the grammar schools, which he considered unprofitable and in opposition to the sacred disciplines."

The young Origen stands out uncompromising in his zeal for the Kingdom of God; he is not of those who, having once put their hand to the plough, look back. He gave proof of this at the time of his father's martyrdom, and continued to give proof by a strictly ascetical life, and by the act prompted by his misinterpreting of Matt. xix. 12 in a literal sense. Later these excesses would be tempered by Christian prudence.

Soon the requirements of the apostolate were to make him return to the studies he had thought completed. It was the enquiries of men of learning, pagans or heretics, he had to answer. An immense profane as well as sacred erudition was to enable him to discover the "Will" of the Word of God, which was his essential purpose: he meant to use the "spoils of Egypt" to build the Tabernacle, the "divine philosophy" of Christianity.[1] So it was that the leader of the catechetical school could be seen, some years before Plotinus, attending regularly the lessons of the most famous philosopher of the period, Ammonius Saccas. Later, in his Didascaleion at·Caesarea, according to the fervent panegyric delivered by a pupil who was destined to become one of the great apostles of the Near East, St. Gregory Thaumaturgus, he taught all the Disciplines, recommended for reading philosophers of every school, with the exception of those who were atheist, insisting on an intellectual formation through dialectics and a moral formation through strict ascetical instruction, before proceeding to the study of Scripture.

[1] Cf. the letter of Origen to Gregory the Thaumaturge in the Philocalia, XIII: in J. A. Robinson, *The Philocalia of Origen*, Cambridge, 1893, pp. 64–7.

Platonism provides both the framework of his spiritual doctrine, and the means of expressing the symbolism essential to all knowledge of God; but it is adapted by Origen to fit into a Christian system. To the transcendental world of ideas corresponds the world of "mysteries," the divine realities which will be contemplated by the blessed participating in the "eternal gospel." The "intelligible world" of Platonic ideas, or of the "reasons" of the Stoics (principles of perceptible creatures), is contained in the Son, created from all eternity by the Father in the generation of His Word. In the Word is contained the totality of mysteries: they are represented by the members of the Paschal Lamb, whether they concern God or the Word, the angelic beings, the heavens above, or even those "mysteries of the abyss" observed by Samuel. Mystery, the end of knowledge, is in the final analysis a Divine Person. It includes the Bread which the High Priest, the Son, partakes of alone in the Holy of Holies, the divine nature He receives from the Father, the darkness which veils God from the eyes of creatures; but also that food which the Word shares with men and angels, allowing them communion with His own being.

The visible world is a symbol of these supernatural realities; the same is true of Scripture, which is an incarnation of the Word, and especially of the humanity of Our Lord, "the shadow of Christ the Lord under which we live among the nations."[1] But the nature of symbols requires that we go beyond them; like sign-posts they point to the mystery, by their own beauty they awaken in us the desire of it; but we must not stop short at the mere symbol itself.

A distinction, however, must here be made between the visible world or the Old Testament on the one hand, and, on the other, the New Testament and the humanity of Christ. In the first case, to stop short at the symbol, refusing to continue to what it symbolises, is the capital sin against truth, the sin of the idolater, of the Jew who sets up his law and cult as definitive realities, the sin of those who, in the passion of Christ, wished to destroy the truth and leave merely appearances. Their fault corresponds to that of the intemperate and the passion-seekers who look for, in creatures, the beatitude that is the gift of God alone. However, although one must go beyond the Gospel of

---

[1] According to *Lament*, iv, 20.

time to that of eternity, beyond the humanity of Christ to His divinity, in this case there is no fault in remaining, with simple faith, in the first stage: Christ the man, and the New Testament taken according to the letter offer means of salvation. Strictly speaking they are not to be transcended. The hypostatic union in which the Word is joined to His Body and Soul effects the union also of the two Gospels: the eternal Gospel, which is also the spiritual or intelligible Gospel, forms one *hypostasis*, a unique reality, with the temporal Gospel announced to the world in the "folly of preaching." They differ only through *epinoia*, the human way of considering things: as long as we remain in the state of knowing "through a glass, darkly," the only knowledge possible on earth, as long as we have not been granted the face-to-face knowledge of the blessed, the supernatural truths which patriarchs and prophets caught a glimpse of in hope, and which Christ brought to earth in their fullness, are indeed really within our reach, but covered by the veil of symbolism. This symbolism reveals the mysteries it contains in a degree corresponding to the stage we have reached in the ascent of the soul to God: the divinity becomes gradually more clear through the humanity of Christ, or the letter of the Scripture which is the other embodiment of the Word. In the contemplative and virtuous life allegorical exegesis becomes what dialectics were for Plato, the path which leads to the vision of true reality.

This progress is indicated by several images which set on foot a long tradition. There is the marriage of Christ and the soul, beginning in this life and reaching fulfilment after the resurrection of the body. The Alexandrian was the first to set this mystical exegesis side by side with the ecclesiastical interpretation of the spouse of the *Canticle* given in the New Testament and in the commentary of Hippolytus of Rome. Christ marries the Church by uniting Himself to each of her souls; Origen passes without transition from the collective meaning to the individual in his explanation of the *Canticle*. A further image is the ascent of the Mountain. Every ascent described in Scripture has a moral and mystical signification, and every descent expresses a falling-off. Those who, through their virtue, like Peter and the Sons of Thunder, climb the Mountain of Wisdom, contemplate at the summit the glory of the Divinity through the transfigured humanity of Christ, and the letter of Scripture becomes transparent. Finally there is the imagery of the birth and growth of Christ in the soul, a theme already developed by certain earlier Fathers. When the divine message is received by the catechumen, his soul conceives the Word, and at Baptism gives birth to it, as Mary gave birth to Jesus Christ. By the practice of virtue and meditation on the Bible the Word is nurtured, finds room to grow and produce fruit in the soul. The Word brings insight into the mysteries; without this the Incarnation would be valueless to us. After the Old Testament phase, and after that of the temporal Gospel, the *interiorisation* of Christ—"the imprint of the wounds produced in every soul that hears God's call, that is, Christ in each one, the expression of the Christ-Logos"—leads to "that Wisdom that is spoken of among the perfect," to Christ transfigured on the Mountain, the prelude to the beatific vision.[1]

Although it may contain certain speculative aspects, the "divine philosophy," the scope of which is outlined in the prologue to the *Commentary on the Canticle*, belongs to the sphere of mysticism, not speculation. Its whole system, its "logic" depends upon the understanding of Scripture as symbolical, as concealing the mysteries under its imagery. The first step in this philosophy is Ethics and deals with the asceticism essential to anyone who sets out in search of knowledge. For sin, and even simply sensuous attachments are obstacles in the way of knowledge; to the fallen angels, prisoners of their own malice, the order of salvation is unknown, while the prophet cannot be other than saintly. It is by the practice of virtue, purity of heart, humility, charity, that one climbs the Mountain. Expounded by Solomon in *Proverbs*, the ethical system becomes personified in Abraham with his heroic obedience. Next, "Physics" deals with the nature of creatures, showing how each must be used with due regard to the supernatural "reason" (the Stoic sense is maintained) in accord with which God created them; each proclaims itself an image and manifests the inadequacy of matter which represents merely a stage the seeker must go beyond. This is the lesson of *Ecclesiastes*, the moral to be learnt from the image of Isaac digging his wells, the Origenian symbol *par excellence* of knowledge, and searching among the hidden depths. The "divine philosophy"

---

[1] Con. Cels. VI 9: in H. Chadwick, *Origen: Contra Celsum*, Cambridge, 1953, pp. 322–3. Origen freely adapts the text of the Letter VII of Plato (342 AB) invoked by Celsus.

concludes in the "Enoptic" or "Insight," the science of contemplation and love, of vision and desire, the object of which is God, His Word, the next world, the angelic hosts, all mysteries. Represented in the *Canticle of Canticles* by the Bride and Bridegroom, it is further personified by Jacob who "was named Israel because of his contemplation of the divine realities, for he beheld the tents of heaven, the house of God, the going and coming of angels, and ladders between heaven and earth."[1]

It is this ardent desire to see into mysteries, to know the Word in whom they are contained, and God of whom the Word is the Image, that gives unity to the different facets of this man's personality, Origen, whom posterity (or possibly his own contemporaries)[2] also called "Adamantios," "the man of steel" or "of diamond." But this uncompromising person is also outstandingly *affective*, full of a tender love of Him whom he often calls "My Jesus."[3] His soul, pierced by the beauty of the Word as by an arrow, suffers from a sweet, incurable wound: this is in fact the first instance, supported by scriptural texts,[4] of that "transverberation" which St. Teresa of Jesus was to experience so forcibly. Here we must beware of an error which many historians have fallen into. The primacy of "knowledge"[5] over simple faith is not due to a certain esoteric tradition into which the perfect have become initiated. The object of knowledge is not of a different order from that of faith: faith is the necessary starting point of

---

[1] Cf. R. P. Lawson, *Origen: The Song of Songs, Commentary and Homilies*, Coll. *Ancient Christian Writers*, XXVI, Westminster (Maryland), 1957, pp. 39–46.

[2] This is what Eusebius seems to say: "Adamantios (for Origen bore also this name) . . ."

[3] Cf. Fr. Bertrand: *Mystique de Jésus chez Origène*, Coll. *Théologie* 23, Paris, 1951.

[4] *Cant.* "I am love-sick, etc.", ii, 5; and *Is.* xlix, 2: "He has chosen me out carefully as an arrow, hidden yet in His quiver."

[5] To designate the Origenian "knowledge" we have not employed the word "gnosis" which is the classic term in this context. Origen indeed uses "gnosis" but it is because this was the ordinary word for knowledge and is both scriptural and Pauline. Unlike Clement, however, Origen never uses the adjective *gnostikos* to refer to the "spiritual" or the "perfect," clearly intending to stand apart from the "so-called gnosticism" élite. This word "gnosticism" which the historians of religion use to designate a doctrine centred round knowledge characteristic of the "*spätantiker Geist,*" esoteric and exclusive, especially when used in the context of Christian gnosticism, very often heretical, would give Origenian knowledge a doubtful colour, and make it liable to be confused with the heterodox gnosticisms which Origen fought against all his life. There is no reason why Origen should be separated from the Christian mystical tradition.

knowledge, as knowledge is the perfection of faith, providing as
it does the evidence, as it were, of faith's affirmations. Mysteries,
it is clear, must not be approached rashly. To embrace a mystery
the soul must be attuned to it through personal progress. Otherwise the revelation would be ineffectual, or even do harm, like
food that is too rich for a man fever-stricken. Would we not
indeed be fortunate if such misunderstood instruction were not
used to divide the Church, as the heretics have done? But knowledge is not confined to a closed élite. How often does not Origen
exhort the Christians of Caesarea to but open themselves to it?
If at times he appears to attribute to the spiritual or the perfect,
as opposed to those who remain in simple faith, extraordinary
privileges and charismata, it is because he is thinking of the ideal
as it will be contemplated in the beatific vision, not of the incomplete realisations we admire in this life. He is very conscious of
the abyss that separates the highest possible earthly knowledge,
which is always "through a mirror, darkly," from that of the
vision "face to face." Compared to that of the blessed, the knowledge of St. John the Baptist, or Paul, for example, which marks
such heights in the story of human understanding, was but as the
knowledge of children; the difference, one might even say, is
like that between animals and rational man.

Knowledge, then, is evidence of the realities of faith. Its perfection is vision, or direct contact with the Word present in the
soul, without intermediary, conceptual, imaginative or discursive.
Here we enter upon the famous theme of the five spiritual senses,
which has a long history, recurring notably in the Ignatian method
of "application of the senses." This theme expresses strikingly the
directness of the contact between subject and object, a contact
much superior to that of the bodily senses. In this contact they
become associated with the joy of knowledge, with the delight, the
peace, the sweetness, the restfulness, the ardour which knowledge
confers upon the soul, with the "enthusiasm" which it inspires,
allowing the soul in some way to share the gift of prophecy; in a
word, with the headiness of the wine that comes from the true vine.
Like the organs of the bodily senses, those of the soul are informed
by their object through a sort of connaturality, which is an
expression of the charisma of wisdom. Like can be understood
only by like; knowledge presupposes participation, and increases
it. The soul can know the Divine Persons because it is made to

the image of the Word, to the image of God's Image. The more conformed the soul is to the Divine Persons, the more it tends to a "resemblance" of them, the greater does its aptitude for knowledge grow: knowledge is proportionate to affiliation. Conversely, the mysteries, and the Son in Whom they are contained, are nourishment. Pasturage for the soul that is still in the animal state, milk for the soul in its childhood, vegetable nourishment for the infirm, the Word becomes for the soul that is strong and adult, solid food, the flesh of the Lamb, the Bread of Heaven. The Word becomes the substance of the soul by changing it into its own substance, into the divine nature which it receives from the Father through His eternal and continuous generation. The duality of subject and object implied by this direct vision is finally resolved. Through His Word God "intermingles" with the soul. The Father and the Son, although they know the sinner "with that knowledge common to all," although they love him with a love that wishes his salvation, do not "know" him truly, because they cannot unite, "mingle" with him; his sinfulness belongs to non-being, to that "nothingness" which according to John i. 3, was made without the Word;[1] it is beyond God's embrace. The most profound definition of knowledge is given by this expression of Genesis: "Adam knew Eve."[2] Represented by this act of human love it coincides with love in union.

In this there is no pantheism. Adam and Eve remained two in one flesh. The Word and the soul are two in one spirit. Their unity does not abolish their duality; for knowledge remains the meeting together of two liberties. From one point of view knowledge is grace. Platonists of every age have held that God can be seen only in God's light. This light, for Origen, is the gift of love given by a free person. A divine or angelic being can only be seen if it allows itself to be seen. The Father is the supreme preceptor; from Him comes all doctrine through the Son, who is the mediator, and in the Spirit, who is the *milieu* of vision. The human teacher, in the bosom of the Church, leads his pupil to the divine Master, "to the source at which he himself has drunk," then

[1] Most of the early Fathers, Irenaeus, Tertullian, Origen separate verses 3 and 4 in this way: "It was through Him that all things came into being, and without Him came nothing. What was made in Him was life. . . ." Origen's interpretation is none the less strange. It comes from his conviction that Scripture contains no unnecessary words; thus the second part of verse 3 should have a different meaning from the first part.   [2] *Gen.* iv. 1.

he stands aside. The part played by the Son is wholly interior: modelling the Christian on Himself, to the extent of making him, like John, another Christ, the son of Mary, He gives him his "nous," his mentality, his vision of God and the world, He becomes in his soul the inexhaustible spring of living water, from which the Christian draws his understanding of the Scriptures. The Spirit, as He Who inspires the prophets, presides also over their exegesis, prompting the exegete with the true meaning. The theme of the light recapitulates these ideas. Its source is the Father; it is transmitted by the Son, the True Light, the Light of mankind, Light of the nations, Sun of Justice, He Whose name is Orient. It is reflected on the Church, the moon, on the saints, the stars, making of the contemplative a lamp, so that he must, like Moses, veil his face in order to speak with those who would be unable to bear its brightness. At the end of time, when Christ has set up His tent, the Church, in the Sun of Justice, all the saints will become, in Him, one single Sun. In opposition, Satan, the evil sun, has his mockery of light; he has his moon, the church of the evil, his stars, the hostile powers, he scatters around his false illuminations. In reality he is darkness, but darkness which is opposed to that "virtuous" darkness in which God hides Himself, and which is the expression of the divine mystery; that of Satan is the vicious darkness, the refusal of God, culpable ignorance, which persecutes the light.

The soul, then, has to accept God and His Word. The ecstasy produced by the wine of the true vine is not a sort of divine "possession": in it man transcends his humanity without going beyond his intelligence, that is, his "nous" or fine point of the soul. Far from dispelling the human *pneuma*, the touch of the Holy Spirit increases both consciousness and liberty in the prophet. It safeguards the basic possibility of falling in with God's good pleasure, of being open to illumination. Contrarily, the devil alienates and obscures the personality, as is to be seen in the possessed and in those governed by passions; such is Origen's golden rule for the "discernment of spirits." This refusal of "unconscious" ecstasy marks a reaction against certain "mystery" cults, and was to be ratified by the later tradition of the Church.[1]

[1] Further support of the preceding pages is to be found in H. Crouzel, *Origène et la connaissance mystique*, coll. Museum Lessianum, Bruges–Paris, 1961.

In this rapid sketch we have fallen far short of a complete exposé of Origen's spiritual doctrine. It would be particularly incomplete if we were to omit to mention one of its most attractive features, its mystique of martyrdom. Origen was both the son of a martyr and the master of others, such as Plutarch whom he assisted in his agony, ignoring the reproaches shouted at him by the crowd who held him responsible for the martyr's death, and he himself confessed the faith, suffering imprisonment and torture in the persecution of Decius. Many homilies deal with this subject, and particularly the famous *Exhortation* which he addressed from Caesarea in Cappadocia to his friend Ambrose, who had been arrested at Caesarea in Palestine under Maximin the Thracian. No consideration, not even that of his family, must deter the martyr from his confession, since this it is that identifies him with Christ in the most complete manner possible. Baptism of blood should be the Christian's fondest desire; it is much superior to the baptism of water, since it brings with it, in act and not through a sacramental sign, conformity with the death and resurrection of the Saviour, conformity that is perfect and not merely progressive. Like Christ, the martyr triumphs over sin and the powers of darkness, so that he has a redemptive value for the world. During the few years of peace and relative favour under Philip the Arabian, a brief respite before the first general persecution, that of Decius, certain sermons even reveal, one might say, a nostalgia for the days when the fervour of the Church was maintained by the blood of martyrs.

To his pupils Origen was more than a professor; he was, in addition, a spiritual director. The unbounded admiration of St. Gregory the Thaumaturge, the touching love which he compares to that of Jonathan for David, were inspired, not primarily by the pedagogue or the man of universal learning, but by the man of God; the *Panegyric* abounds in passages that testify to this. The master was at times severe, and the young Gregory confesses frankly that at the beginning he often felt tempted to run away. The "philosophy" expounded to him was that of self-knowledge, without which it is impossible to be dutiful towards God of the Universe. We must recognise the motives of our actions, avoid the cult of the body and the pursuit of exterior goods preached by Aristotle, and seek only what profits the soul. This self-knowledge is entirely religious; man

finds in himself a reflection of that divine intelligence which is an
intimate part of his being, and by its light he is led to God.
Origen did not give merely theoretical lessons on the virtues; he
formed his pupils by his example, his exhortations and the standards he set. On the intellectual as well as on the moral plane it is
formation he aims at much more than instruction, and in his
instruction an important place is given to dialectical exercises,
practised with socratic method. These in St. Gregory's exposé
appear curiously mixed with the ascetical exercises, mortification
of the passions, the eradication of false convictions, prejudices,
insufficiently examined opinions, all that is dull or illegitimate in
the soul, that it may be enabled to see truth in its fullness. He
does not limit himself to the authors of any one school of philosophy, intending as he does to develop his pupil's critical faculty,
to accustom him to distinguish for himself between the true and
the false. At the same time he has an end in view that is more
properly Christian. Attaching oneself to any one system would
mean accepting it idolatrously, like the philosophers,[1] as the
absolute truth. The Christian may only bow to the word of God,
contained in Scripture, of which Origen is, in the eyes of Gregory,
the divinely inspired interpreter. But the essential task of the
Christian teacher is to awaken in his pupil's soul that desire of
God by which he himself is consumed. "Like a spark struck
alight in our inmost souls, the love of the most sacred, the most
amiable Word which draws to itself all beings by its ineffable
beauty, became flame in us, together with the love of this man,
the friend and witness of the Word."[2] Mary visited Elizabeth that
the Voice that would cry in the wilderness might receive its form
from the Word, that John might receive the spirit of prophecy.[3]
The "spiritual" according to Origen, for whom she is a particular
model, transmits to others the Word and the Spirit, the light
which he carries in him, the interior fire lit by Christ, the living
water springing in his soul where God dwells.

A page of Eusebius, the influence of which can be seen on

---

[1] In his homilies Origen often levels this reproach at the philosophers. Heretics
incur the same censures, for they set up their doctrinal idols on the mountain of
the Scriptures, like the golden calf in Bethel, the house of God. Cf. Origen's letter
to Gregory, footnote [1] on p. 231.

[2] *St. Gregory's Prosphonetic and Panegyric discourse addressed to Origen* is edited
in Vol. X of Migne's *Patrologia Graeca*: the two quotations given here can be
found in columns 1076 B and 1072 B.   [3] *Commentary on John*, vi. 46.

(

early monasticism, describes the "philosophic life" that is the austere practice of poverty and corporal mortification to which the young teacher of Alexandria had recourse. His ascetic doctrine is diverse: unfortunately it remains almost entirely unexplored. It is centred, apparently, on the idea of the spiritual combat which was to be given so much emphasis by the early anchorites.[1] In this struggle it is the soul itself, the seat of free will and of the personality, that is at stake. Each camp has a foothold in it, for the soul is made up of two zones; the higher one, the realm of the contemplative and virtuous life, called the intelligence (*nous*), reason (*logos*) or hegemonic faculty (*hegemonikon*)—according to Rufinus and St. Jerome the "*principale cordis*" or "*principale animae*"—is opposed by another dark zone that is the ally of the flesh, the principle of passions, fantasies, instincts. Being created to the image of God the soul must become the bride of Christ, the adopted son of the Father; but it can elect to follow diabolical and bestial images, the adulterous love of Satan, and choose sonship of the evil father, the Devil. God has granted the soul an interior mentor, the spirit (*pneuma*) which shares in the divine Spirit, acts as the moral conscience, guides the soul to prayer, contemplation and the virtues, and is the first movement of every good act. It strives to rescue the soul from the influence of the flesh and turn it towards God. This does not mean that the body is evil. Created by God it contains, to use the language of the Stoics, the "seminal principle" or the "corporal form" of the Platonists, the grain destined to germinate the glorified body. For those who co-operate with the spirit it becomes the tabernacle of the Holy Ghost, the sanctuary of God, who is present therein by His image. In this case it can be seen by the "spiritual eyes" in transfiguration, almost as Christ was seen on the mountain. But sin has made the body a source of temptations. Every tangible thing is ambiguous, and fraught with danger; instead of directing the intelligence towards the mystery, its ideal, there is the danger that it may cause the intelligence to stop short in idolatrous worship of itself, so that the soul's *élan* is broken. Side by side with the spirit and the flesh numerous auxiliaries join in the struggle, good and evil guardian angels, angels appointed over virtues and vices, angels and demons in charge of nations, a whole invisible world,

---

[1] For example, in the life of St. Anthony by St. Athanasius.

drawn up as two armies in the soul, under their respective leaders, Christ, the Angel of the Great Council, and Satan, Prince of this world. But they cannot do more than incite to action; the soul alone has the power of decision.

Finally Origen is the first great exponent of the spirituality of virginity, the meaning of which he developed at length. The marriage of Christ and the Church, symbolised on earth by the marriage between a man and a woman, becomes concrete in the union of the Word and the soul, and made even more perfect by consecrated celibacy. Thus those who remain virgins are the first fruits of the Church; already close to heaven, they foretoken the unique and eternal marriage of the resurrection of the body. Virginity is a gift of God, the work of the Word—which is the sword that cuts off the passions—a charisma of the spirit, and can be preserved only through prayer. It is also a gift of man to God, a gift over and above that which is required; by mortification, purity of heart, custody of the senses, and avoidance of the occasion of sin, the soul, like the priest, offers to God in sacrifice the natural love it has for its body. Virginity, however, is valueless unless it is practised for God's sake only, with a pure faith, and unless it is accompanied by the other virtues. Chastity of the soul is both the source and the end for chastity of the body; by chastity the soul is freed from worldly anxieties and from the tumult of the flesh, in order to serve God. Like Esdras, whoever remains a virgin builds Jerusalem, the Church; the virgin, like Daniel, receives divine revelations, and like Mary, gives birth to Christ, for virginity is fertile. Against the Marcionists and Montanists Origen defended the sanctity of marriage as the image of a supernatural mystery. The love of husband for wife has as model the love of Christ for the Church. The fundamental virtue of this state is the agreement or harmony of the partners, which may be the sign of the Holy Ghost's presence. But the married person is inevitably the slave of his partner, while the one who remains a virgin serves God in complete freedom. Origen manifests a heavy pessimism in regard to conjugal relations, which is explained by his view of the ambiguity and danger of all things tangible. The couple may not habitually withhold themselves from one another; a rash desire for purity would make each responsible for the other's faults; besides it would be against right order to prefer this virtue to charity.

But the Holy Spirit does not preside over the sexual act; the married couple must temporarily abstain from it, by mutual agreement, whenever they wish to give themselves over to prayer, to receive the Eucharist, or practise the liturgical fasts. It brings with it in fact a certain blemish, which only affects the couple at the time of their relationship, as opposed to sin which endures. The impurity of the new-born child, shown from the necessity of Baptism, is linked with the carnal union of which it is the issue. This is why the soul of Christ, exempt from concupiscence by its union with the Word, could take a body only in the womb of a virgin. Ideas such as these still prevented some of the most highly-considered theologians in the Middle Ages from accepting the Immaculate Conception.

Today the abundance of Origenian studies has restored both the exegete and the spiritual writer, ill-understood by earlier generations, to his rightful place of honour. Desire of a theology more explicitly in contact with its scriptural sources and the interior life has doubtless been a contributory factor in this. Numerous translations of the Alexandrian's works have appeared in the most important modern languages. If the *Commentaries on St. John* and *St. Matthew*, and to a greater extent the *De Principiis* and the *Contra Celsum* are perhaps less accessible, on the other hand an informed public would find in the homilies and opuscules such as the treatise *On Prayer* and the *Exhortation to Martyrdom* excellent spiritual reading. Doubtless the allegorical exegesis may appear strange to our habits of thought, but if we try to understand we cannot fail to appreciate the wealth of deep experience expressed in Origen's symbolism. He scarcely ever speaks of himself, and personal confidences are rare. He explains simply what he believes to be the "will" of the Word of God, in all modesty, his aim being to make other souls disposed to hear it. The link that joins his interpretation to the letter is no artificial one; it is his personal consciousness of the operations of the Word and the Spirit together in his Christian soul.

2. ST. AUGUSTINE

Charles Boyer

THE SPIRITUAL TEACHING of St. Augustine has its roots deep in Holy Scripture: its framework is a profound philosophical and theological synthesis; it is expressed in a multitude of unforgettable formulae and epigrams. Above all, it was intensely lived by the saint himself. Yet it is woven so closely into the very texture of Christian thought that we are in danger of taking it for granted, of losing sight of its originality and grandeur. My purpose here is to review briefly the saint's leading ideas on the spiritual life, and their internal cohesion.

Augustine never lost sight of the ultimate meaning and purpose of the interior life. For him, the term of all human activity is the possession of God. From the age of nineteen, when he first read Cicero's *Hortensius*, he had understood that we are made for a happiness that is above the pleasures of sense. The sermons of St. Ambrose revealed to him that our promised destiny is the vision of God; and the *Enneads* of Plotinus helped him to understand that no good, other than the supreme Good, can fully satisfy the human heart. We are spiritually alive just in so far as we are capable of uniting ourselves to God in the possession of Him. This, for Augustine, is the fundamental truth.

Yet man is so placed that he needs the Divine help to come to that possession of God which is his destiny. This was so, even before the Fall. Adam, even before his sin, was the recipient of a Divine gift without which he could persevere in good, but which did not guarantee him that perseverance. For fallen man this Divine help is indispensable, as well for his initiation into his supernatural vocation, as child of God, as for his progress in the way; and also to give him the strength to overcome concupiscence. Against the Pelagians, Augustine defended the absolute necessity of this grace; and, against the semi-Pelagians, he showed that, without it, even to begin anything useful for salvation is beyond our power. Without Divine grace the spiritual life is impossible.

The Holy Trinity, in its love for humanity, decreed the Incarnation of the Word, so that by virtue of the redemptive work of Christ the grace which we had lost should be restored to us. Consequently, the person of Jesus Christ, His example, His words, His merits are the sources of the ·spiritual life. Everything is summed up in Jesus Christ. As God, He is the term, the promised land, our destiny; as man, He is the way which leads us to life: *Deus Christus patria est quo imus, homo Christus via est qua imus.*[1]

Here, then, is man as he is: his concrete situation delineated by these fundamental theological theses. He is created to find God through the grace which comes to him from Jesus Christ.

Against this theological background, we can pick out the structure, the outline of the spiritual life. Love is the head of all virtue, and the measure of all perfection: "Where love burgeons, there burgeons righteousness; where charity blossoms, there blossoms righteousness; abundance of love is abundance of righteousness."[2] Love means, first of all, love of God. To love the sovereign Good is the most rational of pursuits. To love Him as we ought is to love Him for Himself, or gratuitously, as St. Augustine says. It is this gratuitous love of God, precisely, which is our true good; and which is, therefore, true love of ourselves. To love God for His sake, not for our own, is to love ourselves in the best possible way. Everything then, even the love of self, is borne back upon the love of God. "Nemo, nisi Deum diligendo, diligit seipsum;"[3] and again: "In some mysterious way, the man who loves himself and not God, does not truly love himself; and he truly loves himself who loves God and not himself;"[4] so it is that our happiness consists in loving God, with the pure love to which Augustine refers in the famous text: "Thou hast made us for Thyself, and our hearts are restless until they find rest in Thee."[5] Love of self, then, is not a commandment distinct from the first; but love of one's neighbour is.

To love one's neighbour is a second commandment, but it follows from the first, and this for several reasons. First, it is willed by God, and to love God without doing His will is impossible. Again we are united to the rest of men by nature and by grace, and with them we are drawn towards the same sovereign Good,

---

1 *Sermo* 123, n.3; PL 38, 685   4 *In Ioannis evangelium*, tract 123, n.5.
2 *De natura et gratia*, c.70, n. 84.   5 *Confessions*, 1.I, n.1.
3 Epist. 155, n. 15.

our God. And most important of all, all the faithful are one in the unity of the Mystical Body of Christ. It would be difficult to over-emphasise the importance of this last conception in the thought of St. Augustine. The union of the members with their Head is for him so real that he does not hesitate to attribute to Christ what properly belongs only to the faithful, and to predicate of the faithful what belongs only to Christ. To wound one of the members is to inflict suffering on the Head, who is Christ. Augustine speaks of Christ in His Church as of a giant with his head in the clouds and his feet on the ground:

> Now you do not find Christ speaking on earth; you find him speaking from heaven. Why does he speak from heaven? Because his members stand on earth. He spoke from heaven to Saul his persecutor: "Saul, Saul, why dost thou persecute me? I have ascended into heaven, but I am still on earth. Though I sit here at the right hand of the Father, I am still there, hungry, thirsty, and a stranger."[1]

What you do to your neighbour you do to Christ; and what is done to one member is done to the whole body. Since the Christian is *in* the Body of Christ, this charity is in some sort natural to him; it is this charity which cements the members in the Mystical Body each to other. Now and then he becomes lyrical on the subject:

> The bond of charity, my brethren, is the stout strength of the tree, its blossom and its fruit; it is all that is fair and lovely; it is the food and the drink, the kiss that never palls. If it is such a delight to us in our exile, what joy shall we find therein when we come home at last![2]

The man who is carried along by charity inevitably does all things well: "Love, and do as you like."[3] Hence, though all true virtue proceeds from a good will, it is charity which makes the will good: *voluntas bona esse non potest, ubi charitas non est.*

Charity, of course, presupposes the other theological virtues, faith and hope; and Augustine does not underestimate the importance of faith in the interior life. With St. Paul, he repeats again and again the text of Habacuc: "the just man lives by faith." Faith it is which rescues a man from a state of ignorance concerning his final end and the life of virtue. Once faith is given, there is room for purification, which brings some understanding of the truths of faith itself. It is by faith that the objects of our hope and of our love are revealed to us. A gift so precious can come to us

---

1 *Tract in Ep. Joann. ad Parthos*, 10, c.5, n.9.   3 *Ibid.*, c.7, n.8.
2 *Ibid.* n.7.

only from God, nor can we receive it without the inspiration of divine grace. The saint defends this doctrine against the Manicheans, who say that they can understand without having to believe,[1] and also against the semi-Pelagians, who would have it that free will alone is enough for the beginnings of faith. And faith begets hope, which is rooted in the all-powerful, loving God. Our hope is centred on the graces we need to accomplish good works in this life, and on the reward which shall follow them. The object of our hope is summed up in the petitions of the Lord's Prayer. The blessing of the name of God, the coming of His kingdom, the fulfilling of His will; these are the good things which shall not pass away. In our hope we find their beginning in this life; their full flowering in the life to come.[2]

To come to the fullness of charity, which is the fullness of all virtue, we need Christ our Lord. He is the mediator, the one means which comprehends all the rest. He is the Way. In Him is the truth which enlightens, the example which draws, the strength which upholds. His purifying action prepares the way for charity, and according to the measure of our readiness, He communicates to us the Holy Spirit, who pours forth the love of God in our hearts.

The Neo-Platonists had taught the need for purification in order to arrive at the contemplation of the Godhead. Augustine rounds out their teaching with that of Christian tradition. The things of sense fascinate the soul by their variety—the *fascinatio nugacitatis*; but they deceive it in a thousand ways, and, at the last, leave it unsatisfied. It is from these things that the soul needs to be detached. In giving itself over to these objects of sense, the soul is turning away from what is truly good, debasing itself, defiling itself. The harm done to the soul by attachment to the objects of sense is described by the Bishop of Hippo, in the same terms as St. John of the Cross will later describe it in *The Ascent of Mount Carmel*. But this detachment is a hard task: the objects of our desire are so close to us and the soul so feeble in her powers. In the tenth book of the *Confessions*, Augustine subjects himself to a searching examination of his own inclinations, and finds a variety of subtle imperfections. For example, eating is a necessity, but it is also a pleasure; there comes a moment when it is no longer obvious whether we are eating because we need to or

---

[1] Cf. *De Utilitate Credendi*, c.9, n.21.   [2] Cf. *Enchiridion*. cc. 14-15.

merely for pleasure; and we are glad of this uncertainty which allows us to continue the meal in peace.[1] Or again, he no longer frequents the public games; but all the same, curiosity is still sufficiently alive in him to force him to stop, in the middle of his meditations, to watch a dog chasing a hare.[2] And the difficulty of achieving the right disposition, whenever we hear ourselves praised![3]

There is a further purification, not of command, but of counsel, which will bring the soul to true liberty and suppleness of spirit in the way of God. Voluntary poverty, spiritual virginity or chastity, religious obedience, constitute a privileged state of detachment with regard to the good things of this world. It was a state of life that Augustine never ceased to recommend, uncompromisingly. While still a layman, he wanted to live as a monk and with monks; and afterwards, as a bishop, he turned his palace into a religious house for clerics vowed to the evangelical counsels.

When he writes in praise of virginity, especially the virginity of the Mother of Christ and the virginity of the Church, St. Augustine reveals a lyrical quality. The Church is a virgin in the chaste purity of her faith, and as the spiritual mother of the faithful she is the reflection of Mary. As for Mary:

> . . . as an example to all holy virgins, she consecrated her virginity to God before she knew of her future motherhood, lest she alone be considered a virgin, who was found worthy to conceive without concupiscence. So she, a mortal woman, chose to imitate the heavenly life, without being commanded, through love and not through necessity.[4]

Mary is mother of all the faithful. She is mother, physically, of Christ, and she co-operates with Him in bringing forth, spiritually, by her love, the members of the Mystical Body. Virginity is of inestimable value because of the love with which the virgin is consecrated to God for life without end. Because marriage is itself a high good, virginity is not obligatory, in spite of its being a higher good. It is with this essential qualification in mind that Augustine exhorts so boldly to virginity. Only virgins may follow the Lamb wherever He goes, for He walked the way of virginity. Virginity is a privilege far higher than any worldly honour, a glory beyond the glory of being a parent.[5]

1 *Conf.* 10, C.31, n.44.
2 *Ibid.* C.35, n. 57.
3 *Ibid.* C.37, n.61.

4 *De Sancta Virginitate.* 6.
5 *Epist.* 150.

The high purification of virginity and the other evangelical counsels cannot be achieved without special grace. So Augustine prays repeatedly to his God: *Da quod iubes et iube quod vis.* The necessity of grace, and consequently of prayer, is never out of Augustine's thought. It is true that God can give these graces without their being sought. But ordinarily He first inspires the prayer which disposes the recipient for further gifts: "He gives only to him who asks, lest His gift be spurned."[1] Though one must set aside special hours for prayer, the foundation of all prayer, which is desire for God, is a constant, an habitual direction of the will, not limited to fixed intervals. In this desire everything becomes a prayer: "You praise not only with the tongue, but by taking up the Psalter of good works. Thus you praise God in your business, you praise him at mealtimes, you praise him when you go to bed, you praise him when you are asleep. There is no moment when you do not praise him."[2]

True prayer is impossible without humility; in humility we recognise our own destitution. Charity and humility: these are the virtues on which St. Augustine lays most stress. Humility is becoming to a man, no matter how well off he may be; but to us wretched sons of Adam, it is a fundamental necessity. This is the reason why Christ gave us, in His own Person, such a vivid example of humility. The Incarnation itself is an act of incredible humility, carried beyond all our imagining by the conditions of poverty, of suffering and of humiliation which Christ accepted. The humility of the Word made flesh had affected Augustine deeply while he was still professor of rhetoric at Milan; it drew him, little by little to embrace the Evangelical Counsels.[3] Man's pride, the root of all sin, is healed by the stooping down of God. So he writes to the young Dioscorus:

It is to Him, Dioscorus, that I would have you submit yourself in all reverence. Nor would I have you follow any other way to the truth than that which He chose—He, who as God saw the feebleness of our going. This way is first of all humility. Secondly, it is humility. And thirdly, it is humility. And as often as you asked me I would give you the same answer. This is not because there are no other commandments; but unless humility precedes, accompanies and follows all our good actions; unless we have it steadily before our eyes, cling to it and rule ourselves by it, pride will snatch everything from our grasp, even in the very moment when we are rejoicing in some good deed.[4]

[1] *Enarrat. in Ps.* 102, n.10.
[2] *Enarrat. in Ps.* 146, n.2.
[3] *Conf.* 1.7, n.26; 1.8, n.29.
[4] *Epist.* 118, n.22.

Humility is a specifically Christian virtue. It comes from Christ, and it grows as we grow in our attachment to Christ.

Augustine distinguishes seven degrees of the spiritual life. In an ascending order, these correspond to the seven Beatitudes; and, in the inverse order, to the seven gifts of the Holy Ghost enumerated by Isaias (xi, 2). We begin with "conversion"— abiding sorrow which is poverty of spirit; the second degree is piety or docility to the Commandments and to Holy Scripture (blessed are the meek); the third is knowledge, or awareness of one's own insufficiency (blessed are the mourners). In the fourth degree begins the movement towards contemplation, with that courage which proceeds from the love of the eternal good and the thirst for the divine justice. In the fifth degree, of counsel, we are purified of our minor faults through an abundance of charity towards our neighbour, through mercy and forgiveness (blessed are the merciful). In the sixth degree, of understanding, we turn our gaze towards God with our hearts ever more pure. And finally one comes to the contemplation of the divine perfections, the seventh degree of wisdom, in a soul at peace, the final Beatitude.[1]

The spiritual life, then, tends to contemplation, as to its term: to be reached, normally, even in this life. A few privileged souls— Augustine, drawing his arguments from Holy Scripture, names Moses and St. Paul—have enjoyed the vision of the Divine essence whilst on earth.[2] There are also some few (perpauci) who arrive at a limited vision of the Immutable Truth—as it were a confused reflection in a mirror.[3] The rest of the faithful, whose knowledge of God is confined to the limits of faith, are nevertheless preparing themselves for the contemplation face to face in the life to come.

For Augustine, contemplation, as the name implies, is primarily an intellectual act. It is a vision of the things of God, an understanding of the divine; but it is accompanied by love and joy. It can be achieved on three distinct levels: firstly, it may be the result of a purely philosophical search. Then again, it may be specifically religious and supernatural, achieved through the workings of ordinary graces. It is this level of contemplation

---

1 De Quantitate Animae, C.33.
2 De genesi ad litteram, 1.12, nn.55-56.
3 Per speculum in aenigmate. De Consensu evangelistarum. 1.5.8.

which has been given the name "acquired." Finally, it may be the result of extraordinary graces, under whose influence the faculties of the soul are passive rather than active. This level is called infused contemplation. The texts which deal with contemplation have to be examined one by one and assigned to these different levels according to their content. There are some which scarcely go beyond what may be achieved by philosophical reflection; for example, the demonstration of the existence of God in the second book of the *De Libero Arbitrio*. But more usually in this context, Augustine is speaking of the religious approach, and specifically of that loving desire for God which is itself a prayer. And it is not always easy to decide whether he is speaking of acquired or infused contemplation.

With regard to Augustine's own experience, Dom Cuthbert Butler has called him the Prince of mystics;[1] whereas Fr. Endriks is unwilling to grant that he was a mystic at all.[2] But we must, surely, recognise a high degree of infused contemplation in some, at least, of his experiences. He writes, for example, after an account of one of his ways of finding God:

> And sometimes, O my God, You plunge me into a state of mind quite out of the ordinary, which carries me into the depths of a sweetness beyond description; were this once perfected in me, it would be I know not what, but it would no longer be this present life.[3]

Whether the saint is dealing simply with rational speculation or with a religious exercise, the way to God is always the same; but he allows for the fact that the soul will pass through a variety of different states along that way. Take his account of the experience which he shared with his mother at Ostia, whilst they were waiting to begin their journey home to Africa:

> We were talking together, we two alone, in a sweet joy; and forgetting these things that were behind and reaching out to those that lay ahead, we were discussing, in the presence of the Truth—Thyself—what the eternal life of the saints would be like ... But with the palate of the heart we yearned to savour the heavenly waters of Thy fountain, the fountain of that life which is Thee: that our thirst might be quenched according to our capacity—that we might come to some measure of contemplation. ... and as we soared with longing towards that Selfsame, we passed through all the levels of material creation, and through the heavens themselves, whence sun, moon and stars shine forth upon this earth. And leaving these, we began a more inward

[1] *Western Mysticism*, 2nd edition, London 1951, p.20.
[2] *Augustins Verhaltnis zur Mystik*, Wurzburg, 1936, p.176.
[3] *Conf.* 10, n.65.

ascent, in our thoughts and our speech, as we wondered at the marvel of Thy works. And so we came to these souls of ours; yea, and passed above these also, that we might at the last reach that land of unfailing plenty, where Thou feedest Israel for ever with the food of truth; where Life is that Wisdom by which are made all these things both that have been and are still to be; but Itself is not made, but so is as It always was, and shall be ever . . . And as we talked and yearned after this Wisdom, with the whole effort of the heart lifted towards It—we got one touch. And we sighed, and left the first-fruits of our heart fastened there, and relapsed again into our former manner of speech—where a word has its beginning and end.[1]

This was not, in all probability, the highest contemplation he enjoyed, but it is the most careful description of a contemplative experience; or rather, the most detailed description of the normal way to it. First, the period of immediate preparation: he seeks God by means of creatures, mounting up through their degrees, from the lowest to the highest, marvelling at them, reflections of God as they are, and passing beyond their limitations, he comes to the bounds of the human spirit; and beyond and above it, finds the source of truth, uncreated, unchangeable, eternal. For an instant, his gaze dazzled and his heart burning, he reaches that source; and then, slowly, returning again to his normal thinking, he finds words to savour the memory of the summit to which he had attained.

This general scheme allows for a great variety of content. The Created good which serves as a stepping-stone on the way to God may be some enjoyment on the level of sense,[2] or an awareness of the beauty of a soul,[3] or the image of the divine Trinity in the human intellect.[4] Whilst the action of grace in the ascent towards God and at the highest point of contemplation may be gradual or rapid, delicate or imperious, gentle or intense.

Contemplation is a precious aid to the spiritual life; it is the strength which enables us to bear our earthly trials, it gives us a yearning for the happiness of the life to come; it prepares the pastors of souls for their work: "No one should be so much at leisure that in his leisure he never thinks of his neighbour's needs; no one should be so active that he cannot find time for contemplation."[5]

The contemplation of God is the fulfilment of man's desire, for it reveals God as supremely worthy of love. All through his

1 Conf. 9, 23-24.
2 Ibid. 10, 8.
3 Enarratio in Ps. 41, n.9.
4 De Trinitate, 14, n.15.
5 De Civitate Dei, 1.19, c.19.

writings Augustine proclaims the lovableness of God with a great eagerness and profundity. Sometimes he reflects on the divine perfections, already glimpsed by the light of reason, but better known through Revelation. And one sees how God is in Himself the supreme Good, desirable above all else. Sometimes he dilates upon the greatness of the love of God for men, how He invites them to love Him with the love of a friend and of a son. Augustine manifests the love of God for man in all its aspects, as the source of all God's gifts to us. By a free, gratuitous act, the All-Powerful has given us being;[1] the entire Trinity has decreed, for our salvation, the Incarnation of the Word;[2] the Word in His humanity has humbled Himself to the depths for us; He has poured out for us His words, His example, and finally His blood and His life.[3] His grace is with each of us, individually, in a most marvellous way.[4] No matter how we love, our love for God can never equal His love for us: *Maior est caritas Dei in nos quam nostra in Deum.*[5] So speaks the Augustine who loved God with an overpassing love. "Late have I loved thee, O Beauty ever old and ever new: late have I loved thee . . . I have tasted thee, and now I hunger for thee, thirst for thee."[6]

The spirituality of St. Augustine is set firmly upon the first truths of the Christian faith; it is the common heritage of all spiritual families. His writings have an unfading appeal because in them, in their simplicity and sublimity, their clarity and ardour, their sincerity and true charity, we learn to read the soul of a great Doctor and a great Saint.

[1] Cf. Enarr. in Ps.70: in Ps.134.
[2] De Trinitate, 13, n.15.
[3] Cf. Enarr in Ps.44, n.3.
[4] Cf. Conf. 11, n.19.
[5] Enarr. in Ps. 103, n.3.
[6] Conf. 10, n.38.

3. JOHN CASSIAN[1]

Bede Griffiths

"FOR HIM who would hasten to the perfection of the monastic life," wrote St. Benedict at the end of his Rule, "there are the teachings of the holy Fathers, by observing which a man is led to the summit of perfection"; and among the teachings of the holy Fathers he gives the first place to the *Conferences* of Cassian and his *Institutes*. There can be no doubt of the place which the writings of Cassian held in the actual composition of the Rule. "St. Benedict," writes Abbot Butler, "was familiar with Cassian's writings and was saturated with their thought and language, in a greater measure than with any other, save only the Holy Scriptures."[2] Thus through the Rule of St. Benedict the writings of Cassian entered into the tradition of monastic life in the West, and that not only indirectly but directly, because in another part of the Rule St. Benedict had recommended that the "*Conferences* of Cassian or the Lives of the Fathers" should be read every day after supper before the office of Compline. Thus the teaching of Cassian was woven into the very structure of the monastic life and formed, one may say, the basis of monastic spirituality. But not only this. We find that even at a later date, when new Orders began to arise in the Church, the *Conferences* of Cassian still held their place. We are told that they were one of the two books which St. Thomas Aquinas always kept on his desk (the other being the Commentary of Chrysostom on St. Matthew's Gospel). In this way this ideal of monastic

[1] The best book on Cassian in English is that of Mr. Owen Chadwick, *John Cassian, A Study in Primitive Monasticism* (Cambridge 1950). This is a scholarly work, but it needs to be read in the light of the criticism made of it by Dom Aelred Sillem in an article in *The Downside Review* (Summer 1951).

The works of Cassian in Latin are published in Migne, *Patrologia Latina*, vols. XLIX and L, and in the *Corpus Scriptorum Ecclesiasticorum Latinorum*, vols. XIII–XIV (Vienna 1886–8).

The quotations are taken from the English translation of Cassian's works in the Oxford Library of the Fathers, vol. XI (1894).

[2] *Benedictine Monachism*, p. 46.

spirituality, coming originally from the East, penetrated into the
heart of Western tradition, and it may be said to underlie the
doctrine of such a supremely popular work as *The Imitation of
Christ*.

Yet when we come to study this doctrine today, whether
from a monastic or a more general point of view, we are immediately faced with some grave difficulties. The very basis of this
doctrine seems to be that Christian perfection can only be found
in a complete renunciation of the "world." In the very first
book of the *Institutes* we read that a monk is one who has "cut
off all the deeds and works of this world" and is "dead to all
earthly conversation." It may be said that this is good advice for
a monk (though I think that this needs many reservations),
but when it is constantly held up, as it has been, as the ideal of
Christian perfection, it presents, as I have said, a grave problem.
The ideal of Christian perfection was set by the Fathers of the
Desert, and the very first condition of it was "flight from the
world"; and yet today we see the goal of the Christian life more
and more in terms of an apostolic life, penetrating the world in
all its forms of activity. How are we to reconcile these conflicting
ideas? That is the problem, and it is only by studying the work
of Cassian in its historical setting that we can begin to find an
answer to it.

Cassian was born at an unknown date towards the beginning
of the second half of the fourth century, probably in what is now
Yugoslavia, which was then a province of the Roman Empire
in which both Greek and Latin were spoken. This, no doubt,
helped him in his task of translating the teaching of the Greek
Fathers into Latin. At an early age he left his native land to
become a monk in a monastery at Bethlehem, near to that of
St. Jerome. But some years later he obtained permission, together
with another monk of his community, to visit Egypt, where he
remained for twelve years. It was this visit to Egypt which determined the course of his life. He spent his time there going round
from monastery to monastery and visiting the cells of the solitaries, studying the life and teaching of the Fathers of the Desert,
and later embodied all that he had been able to learn in the two
books of his *Institutes* and *Conferences*. The books were not written
till twenty-five years later, when Cassian had become the abbot
of a monastery in Marseilles. It was thus that the teaching of the

Fathers of the Desert came to be translated into Latin and given to the western world.

The monastic life in the Egyptian desert was then at its height, and Cassian regarded these monks of the desert as the embodiment of Christian perfection. He writes of them with the naïve enthusiasm of hero-worship, which reminds one sometimes of the attitude of Boswell to Dr. Johnson. Yet there can be no doubt of the grandeur of this ideal. The monastic life had begun in the third century with St. Antony, and it was his life and teaching, which was made known to the West in the Life of St. Antony by St. Athanasius, which set the ideal for the monastic life. The movement which followed arose spontaneously at the end of the period of persecution, when those Christians who sought to follow the example of the martyrs left the world and all that they possessed in order to follow Christ. The reasons for this movement are, no doubt, complex. Behind it all there lay without question the call of the Gospel, which Antony had heard: "Go, sell all that thou hast and give to the poor, and thou shalt have treasure in heaven, and come follow me." There was also the example of the martyrs who had given their lives for Christ, and the monk was seen as one who gave his life for Christ by "dying" to the world. But behind these motives there lay also the longing for "perfection," which lies so deep in the human soul, the desire for union with God, for "contemplation," for solitude, for self-conquest.

Now this desire has nothing specifically Christian in it. A similar movement took place in India five hundred years before the birth of Christ, which was marked by exactly the same characteristics. There was the same ideal of total renunciation (*sannyasa*), the same desire for union with God (or the absolute—Brahman), apart from all earthly ties, the same labour of asceticism (*yoga*) which developed into a positive science of perfection, the same goal of "contemplation" (*jnana* or knowledge, like the Greek *gnosis*). We can trace the beginning of a similar movement in Greece at the same time with Pythagoras and his followers, which developed through Plato into the fully-developed doctrine of contemplation in Plotinus. Nor can there be any doubt of the influence of this doctrine on Christian thought. We find the vocabulary of the Greek philosophers already in Clement of Alexandria, and with Origen a Christian philosophy has already begun to take shape, which was to be perfected by St. Gregory of Nyssa. But it was Evagrius of Pontus (the importance of whose work has only recently been discovered), who was responsible for giving this doctrine the shape which it took among the Fathers of the Desert. We find in him all the fundamental ideas of Greek philosophy, of virtue and perfection, of contemplation and gnosis, fused into a fully-developed Christian doctrine of asceticism and contemplation.

There can be no question but that this was a genuine "integration" of Greek philosophy in Christian thought and practice. The Greek ideal is fundamentally transformed by the Christian genius: the Greek stem is grafted into the Christian stock and becomes a new thing. Fr. Daniélou has shown the wonderfully subtle nature of this process in his study of the work of St. Gregory of Nyssa.[1] It is a work of incalculable importance because it is a model of the kind of work which has yet to be done with the Indian doctrines of Yoga and Advaita. But it is important to notice that both the language and the ideas of this philosophy are Greek and not Christian in their origin. The words for asceticism (*ascesis*) and contemplation (*theoria*) are not to be found in the New Testament. Thus, though one may hold that the new doctrine was a genuine "development" of the Gospel, yet it cannot be denied that it gave the teaching and practice of the Gospel a new direction. Whereas in the New Testament the ideal of the Gospel is seen in terms of Charity, the love of God with all one's heart and soul and strength, and the love of one's neighbour as oneself, in the Greek view "perfection" (the word is significant, because, though it is found in the New Testament, it has quite a different emphasis) is seen in terms of contemplation, that is, the perfection of the intellect rather than of the will, and means to perfection is seen as asceticism, that is, the practice of virtue with a view to one's own spiritual perfection rather than to the good of one's neigbour.

These ideals are by no means incompatible, but it is essential that the Greek ideal of virtue and contemplation should be kept always in subordination to the Christian ideal of charity. In Evagrius, there is a tendency to subordinate charity to contemplation and to see charity as a means to the ultimate goal of gnosis, in which perfection consists. When this is done it is

[1] *Platonisme et Théologie Mystique.*

almost inevitable that an artificial division between the "active" and the "contemplative" life should be created. The active life of "virtue" is seen as simply a means for the ultimate end of contemplation, and Christian perfection is regarded as consisting in the perfection of the individual in solitary communion with God. Thus separation from the "world" and the "flesh," considered not so much under their aspect of the sinful condition of fallen man, as the condition of all created things, comes to be regarded as the necessary condition of Christian perfection. The ideal is found in the monk living totally cut off not only from the "world" but even from,his fellow monks, taking the absolute minimum of food which is necessary to sustain life, and occupied in ceaseless meditation, free from all earthly thoughts.

There can be no doubt of the influence of Evagrius on Cassian's thought, or that it was this ideal of the monastic life which he sought and found in the teaching and practice of the Fathers of of the Desert. Yet there were also other influences at work. Not all the monks of the desert were "Origenists"; the majority perhaps were simple Egyptians who knew no Greek, and who followed a simpler path, though their ideal may have been much the same. Cassian was also influenced by the more moderate ideas of St. Basil, St. Jerome and St. John Chrysostom. But still more we must consider that Cassian was concerned to present this ideal of the monastic life to the West and to adapt it to the needs of "Gallic souls and Gallic bodies," which were very different from those of Egyptians. It has indeed been questioned how much Cassian was actually representing the teaching of the Fathers to whom he attributes the Conferences and how much he was reinterpreting it in the light of his own experience. There can be little doubt that after twenty-five years he can hardly have reproduced the actual words of the Egyptian monks and it is evident that he has reflected deeply on it himself. It seems probable that we have in his writings an authentic representation of the teaching of the Desert Fathers, yet reflected through Cassian's own mind and interpreted in the light of his own experience.

When one turns to the actual writings of Cassian, one is surprised by the balance and moderation which he displays. Anyone who expects from him stories of miracles or of feats of asceticism in the manner of Palladius will be disappointed.

Cassian has his stories which enliven the conferences, but they tell not so much of miracles of fasting and asceticism as of examples of humility, obedience and the perfection of chastity or of prayer. It is true that he sometimes shocks us by judgment on these matters. There is the well-known story of the monk who watered a dry stick for a whole year because he was told to do so by his superior, which is held up as an example of the perfection of obedience[1]; and there is the really shocking inhumanity of the story of the father who entered a monastery with his little son, and consented to see his son beaten daily before his eyes without any reason and was finally given the command to throw him into the river, which he was proceeding to do, when some of the brethren, "who had been purposely set to watch the banks of the river very carefully," mercifully stopped him.[2] There is the still more serious story of the monk who tried to persuade his wife to renounce the world with him and, when he was not successful, deliberately abandoned her and defended himself on the ground of the gospel saying that a man must "hate" his wife and children.[3] It is true that Cassian himself has some doubts about the morality of this proceeding, and on the whole we must say that these examples serve only to remind us that Cassian was writing about a movement of tremendous power, in which men were carried to extremes and only gradually was it possible to find a true balance and to work out a valid system of morality.

Cassian's own attitude can be most clearly seen in the admirable conference of Abbot Moses on the "grace of discretion." We are inclined to regard discretion as the supreme merit of the Rule of St. Benedict, but it is interesting to find that this is precisely one of those principles which St. Benedict derived from Cassian, and which Cassian traces to no less a person than St. Antony. We are told that the "elders" of the Thebaid, the region in which St. Antony lived, had met together one day to inquire about perfection. And when many had given their opinion as to the surest way of reaching perfection, one placing it in fasting and vigils, others in withdrawal from the world into solitude, others (and this is of special interest to us) in the duties of charity; St. Antony at last arose and declared that after all his experience of life in the desert he was convinced that, though all these things

---

[1] *Inst.*, IV. 24.   [2] *Ibid.*, IV. 27.   [3] *Conf.*, XXL. 8–10.

were good and useful, yet none of them was of any value without the grace of discretion.[1] Here we have the considered judgment of the Father of all monks, the man whose example had set the world afire with the ideal of the ascetic life, and we find him affirming the very principle which St. Benedict was to place at the basis of his Rule.

In fact, when one examines the *Institutes* of Cassian, as distinct from the *Conferences*, one is surprised to find how closely St. Benedict has modelled his Rule on them. Now the *Institutes* give the ideal of the ascetic or "practical" life as it was called, while the *Conferences* are concerned with the contemplative life or the way of "perfection." It is worth noting at the outset that St. Benedict takes over from Cassian the conception that the monastery, or coenobium, with its common life of prayer and discipline, is a training ground for the solitary life of the anchorite, who is engaged in ceaseless contemplation, to which St. Benedict refers, following Cassian, as the "lofty heights of perfection." St. Benedict makes it clear that his Rule is a "little rule for beginners" and is concerned, like Cassian's Institutes, with the "practical" life. It is not so surprising, therefore, that he should have followed the plan of the *Institutes* so closely.

Cassian begins his *Institutes* with an account of the dress of the monks, which is not of much practical value as the dress of the Egyptian monks could not be very closely followed in the West: but Cassian shows his practical sense by saying at the end, in words which St. Benedict was to echo: "So much we have said that we may not appear to have left out any article of the dress of the Egyptians. But we need only keep to those customs which the situation of the place and the customs of the district permit." In the next two books he describes the system of the canonical prayers of the monks, which is of great interest to us, as it gives us one of the fullest descriptions of the liturgy at this very early date. On the whole it is very close to the system which St. Benedict adopted and which has become traditional in the Church. He mentions the venerable tradition according to which an angel had revealed that no more than twelve psalms should be said at Matins, so that the office should not become a burden. But it is noticeable that Cassian goes on to say that after the night office the brethren are wont to return

[1] *Conf.*, II. 2.

to their cells and "there they offer with great earnestness the same service of prayer, as their special sacrifice, as it were; nor do any of them give themselves up to any further rest and sleep, till the brightness of the day comes and the labours of the day succeed the labours and meditations of the night."

Already one begins to discern the place which the liturgy of the Church, the divine office in common, holds in the mind of Cassian. This is one of the most crucial questions we have to consider in regard to the conception of prayer which we find in Cassian and the Fathers of the Desert. It seems to be clear that the common prayer of the liturgy is regarded, like the common life in general, as a kind of preparation or training ground for the "private sacrifice" of prayer which is the real "work" of the monk. This is one of the ideas which St. Benedict was to modify profoundly and which is of vital importance for us today.

In the fourth book of the *Institutes*, Cassian describes the monastic training of the Egyptian monks, and it is here that we find the most striking resemblances with the Rule of St. Benedict. The monastic life is firmly grounded on the fundamental principles of poverty, humility and obedience. One is struck by the severity of the rules with regard to what St. Benedict was to call the "vice of private ownership" and which he reproduces almost verbatim. It is obvious that this was felt to be the very basis of the renunciation, the response to the "go sell all that thou hast" of the Gospel, which marks a monk. But external poverty can only be the setting for a training in poverty of spirit, and it is humility and obedience which therefore constitute the essential training of a monk. Here St. Benedict follows Cassian very closely and the Twelve Degrees of Humility, which form the core of the ascetic discipline of the Rule, are already outlined in Cassian, though St. Benedict has expanded and enriched them. In this respect Cassian's teaching lies behind the ascetic teaching of all later religious life in the West.

The last eight books of the *Institutes* deal with the "eight principal faults," gluttony, fornication, covetousness, anger, dejection, "accidie" or sloth, vainglory, and pride. It is the struggle with these sins which constitutes the essence of the "practical" life in Cassian's eyes. A monk is for him an "athlete of Christ" or a "soldier of Christ ever ready for battle." The battle in question is fundamentally that between the "flesh and the spirit." It is here that the Greek character of Cassian's view of life comes out most clearly. Yet it must be recognised that the basis for this view is found in St. Paul, and Cassian is fond of quoting St. Paul: "I run yet not aimlessly, I fight not as one beating the air" (I Cor. ix. 26). But the spiritual warfare in question goes beyond that of the flesh and the spirit; it is ultimately a battle with evil spirits. This "conflict with demons" undoubtedly played a very large part in the spirituality of the Fathers of the Desert. Yet here again we must recognise its scriptural basis. It is not only that St. Paul declares that "our wrestling is not with flesh and blood but with spiritual wickedness in high places" (Eph. vi. 12), but that this idea of a conflict with the powers of darkness lies behind the whole Gospel, especially in the account of Our Lord's temptation in the wilderness, which was the model for the monk's life in the desert.

Fr. Bouyer in his *Meaning of the Monastic Life* has insisted that this "conflict with demons" was the essential purpose of the monk's retirement to the desert, but this is surely to exaggerate. There is no doubt that it played a very important part in the primitive conception of the monastic life, but in Cassian at least it nowhere takes the first place. This is one of those points in which modern psychology is most inclined to question the motives of the monks of the desert. It must surely be admitted that the motive of conflict and warfare in the monastic life, whether against the flesh or against evil spirits, was exaggerated. Perhaps there is a trace here of the "semi-Pelagianism" of which Cassian was accused. In the relations between grace and the freewill there is certainly a strong emphasis on the part of the free will and there are one or two statements by Cassian which would now be considered incorrect. But on the whole it must be said that Cassian's position was very balanced and, considering the heated atmosphere of the time, he showed remarkable moderation. Yet nowadays we should be inclined to see the monastic life less in terms of war and conflict with evil and more in terms of grace and co-operation with the action of the Holy Spirit. This is one of those points where we must recognise the need of a change of emphasis in our conception of the monastic life.

But if we would find the real purpose of the monastic life in

Cassian's eyes, we must turn to the *Conferences*. The *Institutes* are comparatively short and serve merely as an introduction to the main part of his work, which is to describe the way of "perfection" according to the teaching of the Fathers of the Desert. The tone of the *Conferences* is more intimate and we feel more closely in touch with the actual words of the Fathers whom Cassian consulted. He describes vividly the burning enthusiasm which filled him and his companion, Germanus, when they approached these heroes of the monastic life, and it is difficult not to believe that we have here the very substance of those talks which must have become engraven on Cassian's mind. Each of the great Fathers to whom he talks is described with loving devotion and some of the circumstances of their life and character are given. Cassian leaves us in no doubt as to what he was seeking and of the answer which he received. In the first Conference of Abbot Moses we are given a description of the aim or goal (the *skopos*) of the monastic life. From this there can be no doubt that what the monks of the desert set out to find was the way to attain to perpetual prayer. The question they sought to answer was how can one attain to "continual and unceasing perseverance in prayer" so that Our Lord's command to "pray without ceasing" could be fulfilled.

The terms in which Abbot Moses answers this question are of great interest. He replies that the aim of the monastic life in general is "the kingdom of God," but the immediate aim or goal is "purity of heart." "Everything," he says, "should be done and sought after for the sake of this. For this we must seek solitude, for this we know that we ought to submit to fastings, vigils, toils, bodily nakedness, reading and all other virtues, that through them we may prepare our heart and to keep it unharmed by all evil passions, and resting on these steps to mount to the perfection of charity."[1] And again: "This then should be our main effort, and this steadfastness of purpose of heart we should constantly aspire after, *viz.*, that the soul may ever cleave to God and to heavenly things."[2] It is this way of envisaging Christian perfection which determines Cassian's whole conception of the monastic life. It is to be noticed in the first place that Cassian uses only evangelical terms. The aim of the monastic life is the "kingdom of heaven" and the means is

---

[1] *Conf.*, I. 7.   [2] *Ibid.*, I. 8.

"purity of heart." This is of particular interest, because what Cassian calls "purity of heart" comes very close to what Evagrius and the Greek school of thought called "passionlessness" (*apatheia*) or freedom from all disturbance (*ataraxia*). Now these were originally Stoic terms and it seems that we have here an example of Cassian's transposing the language of Greek philosophy into that of the Gospel. Cassian further goes on to equate this "purity of heart" with that charity which St. Paul describes in the Epistle to the Corinthians. For, Abbot Moses goes on, "it clearly follows that perfection is not arrived at simply by self-denial, and the giving up of all our goods, and the casting away of honours, unless there is that charity which the Apostle describes, which consists in purity of heart alone."[1]

It can be seen how profoundly Christian is Cassian's point of view, and no doubt that of the Fathers whose teaching he reproduces. Yet at the same time one cannot help noticing that charity and purity of heart have been given a definitely new direction. The emphasis all the time is on tranquillity of mind and freedom from passion; for what, he asks, is all this (that is, the perfection of charity) "but to offer to God a perfect and clean heart and to keep it free from all disturbances."[2] It is here that we can detect the direction given to the monastic life by Evagrius and the Greek tradition. Though the terms are Christian and the whole conception of the monastic life is steeped in the tradition of the Gospel, yet it has received a new direction. The goal of life is "contemplation," an "immovable tranquillity of mind and a perpetual purity." Once Christian perfection is seen in terms of "tranquillity of mind" (*apatheia*) and "freedom from disturbances" (*ataraxia*), it is inevitable that solitude and separation from the world should be regarded as its necessary conditions. We shall see how this view dominates Cassian's conception of the monastic life.

Cassian's teaching on prayer itself is found in the two conferences of Abbot Isaac on Prayer, which are justly regarded as the most memorable of all the Conferences. It remains one of the most profound and at the same time one of the most practical treatises on prayer which has ever been written. Cassian divides prayer into four kinds, following St. Paul's description in the first epistle to Timothy, "I exhort therefore that supplications,

[1] *Conf.*, I. 6.   [2] *Ibid.*, I. 6.

prayers, intercessions, and thanksgivings be made" (I Tim. ii. 1). This division of prayer is derived from Origen and by a skilful interpretation of these four kinds of prayer Cassian is able to construct a ladder of prayer, leading from the first stage of beginners, "who are still troubled by the stings and recollection of their sins," through the intermediate stages of "those who have already attained some loftiness of mind in their spiritual progress," to the final stage of those who "have already torn from their hearts the guilty thorns of conscience, and thus being free from care can contemplate with a pure mind the beneficence of God."[1] Thus the three stages of the purgative, illuminative and unitive way are indicated, but the terms are not yet to be found. Cassian then gives an exposition of the Lord's Prayer, which as in all early treatises on prayer remains a model of Christian prayer. Thus we see once again how firmly Cassian's teaching is grounded in the doctrine of the Gospel. At the same time we see that he is constantly moving towards that supreme type of prayer which he regards as the ultimate perfection. For, he says, the Lord's Prayer itself will ultimately lead the monk to that higher stage,

> which is known and tried by few and which to speak the truth is ineffable, which transcends all human thoughts, and is distinguished, I will not say by any sound of the voice, but by no movement of the tongue, or utterance of words but which the mind, enlightened by the effusion of that heavenly light describes in no human and confined language, but pours forth richly as from copious fountains in an accumulation of thoughts, and ineffably utters to God, expressing in the shortest space of time such great things that the mind when it returns to its usual condition cannot easily utter or relate.[2]

This rather involved description of the perfection of prayer nevertheless shows us very clearly the kind of perfection at which the monks of the desert were aiming. It is a prayer which transcends both speech and thought, and is, therefore, properly mystical. At the same time in another passage Cassian says that in this state we "offer to God inexpressible prayers of the purest force, which the Spirit itself, intervening with groanings which cannot be uttered, while we ourselves understand not, utters to God."[3] We can see, therefore, that this prayer goes beyond human powers and is the work of the Holy Spirit in the soul.

[1] *Conf.*, IX. 15.   [2] *Ibid.*, IX. 25.   [3] *Ibid.*, IX. 15.

Thus Cassian in the highest ascent of prayer keeps firmly within the Christian tradition and in a beautiful passage goes on to say that by this prayer there will be fulfilled in us that prayer of our Saviour, "that they all may be one, as Thou, Father, in me and I in thee, that they also may be one in us."[1] "And this will come to pass, when God shall be all our love, and every desire and wish and effort, every thought of ours and all our life and words and breath, and that unity which exists between the Father and the Son, and the Son and the Father, has been shed abroad in our hearts and minds."[2] Thus the ultimate goal of Christian perfection is seen to be the participation of the soul in the life and love of the Holy Trinity.

It is impossible to describe the goal of Christian prayer more accurately than this. Cassian is here making use not merely of the language but the innermost thought of the Scriptures. Indeed it is of special importance to notice how Scriptural is Cassian's whole method of prayer. The Fathers of the Desert knew no method of prayer but that of the Psalms. Many of them were accustomed, as St. Benedict tells us in the Rule, to recite the whole Psalter each day and this was no mechanical recitation but a deep meditation which led them to the height of prayer. Cassian describes this method of using the Psalms and says: "Thriving on this pasture continually, he will take into himself all the thoughts of the Psalms and will begin to sing them in such a way that he will utter them with the deepest emotion of heart not as if they were the composition of the Psalmist, but rather as if they were his own utterances and his very own prayer."[3] This way of reading the Psalms was derived from the habit of meditating on the spiritual meaning of the Scriptures, which was one of the chief occupations of the monks and corresponds with what St. Benedict called "lectio divina." Perhaps there is nothing which we more need to recover in our life of prayer than this understanding of the inner meaning, or what is sometimes called the "theological" sense, of the Scriptures, especially of the Psalms. It is the sense which St. Augustine expounded so profoundly, but which was the common inheritance of the early Church.

Thus it is impossible to deny that we find in Cassian a method of prayer which is not only authentically Christian, but which

[1] Conf., IX. 15.   [2] Ibid., X. 7.   [3] Ibid., X. 11.

is, one may say, the authentic Christian tradition based on meditation on the Scriptures and making use of the Psalms continually, which leads to the highest goal of mystical prayer and yet remains centred in Christ and finds its perfection in a union with God in charity. Yet we are still faced with the problem which we encountered in the beginning. It remains true that for Cassian this perfection of prayer normally involves a complete withdrawal from the world and a life of solitude. This comes out most clearly in the last two or three Conferences. In the third Conference of Abbot Theonas, for instance, we are squarely faced with the problem, how can perfect prayer, that is, continuous attention to God, be reconciled with the duties of charity? "For who," says Abbot Theonas, "when ministering support to the poor, or when receiving with benevolent kindness the crowds that come to him can at that very moment, when he is perplexed for the wants of his brethren, contemplate the vastness of the bliss on high, and while he is shaken by the troubles and cares of the present life, look forward to the state of the world to come with a heart raised above the stains of earth?"[1] The problem could hardly be put more decisively. The answer of Abbot Theonas is that it is definitely impossible, and therefore the monk who seeks perfection must withdraw from all concern with this world and fix his thoughts on God alone.[2]

But this will hardly satisfy us. We think of St. Vincent de Paul and so many other saints who have learned to find Christ in the poor and to contemplate the image of God in their brethren. This is surely where we encounter the weakness of the Greek view of life. The terms in which Abbot Theonas expresses himself are in themselves significant. "Because," he says, "there is nothing of itself enduring, nothing unchangeable, nothing good but deity alone, while every creature to obtain the blessing of eternity and immutability, aims at it not by its own nature but by participation of its creator."[3] We are here in the full stream of Platonism. We are in the presence of the "eternal and immutable deity" for a participation in whose unchanging nature the Greek soul had always yearned. But it is surely the message of the Gospel that this eternal and unchanging Being has made Himself known in this world of time and change; that He has

[1] Conf., XXIII. 3.   [2] Ibid., XXIII. 4, cf. XXIV. 3.   [3] Ibid., XXIII. 3.

entered into human life and human history and revealed Himself
in the common life of men. But this was something which the
Greek genius, even when it had come under the influence of the
Gospel, found it difficult to grasp. Even the Latin mind, in so
far as it was affected by the Greek view of life, found it difficult to
reconcile the contemplative and the active life. Abbot Butler in
his *Western Mysticism* has shown how the problem presented
itself in the work of St. Augustine, St. Gregory and St. Bernard,
and in all of them the conflict between the two ideals is felt,
though St. Bernard, perhaps, came near to resolving it.

As long as Christian perfection is seen in terms of "contemplation," that is, of the perfection of the "mind," there is indeed
no way in which the conflict can be resolved, and St. Thomas's
conception of the relation between the two ways remains un-
satisfactory for this reason. The problem can only be resolved
if perfection is seen in terms of charity, that is, of the love of
God with all one's heart and soul and strength, and of one's
neighbour as oneself. But in this respect also we have to go deeper
than Cassian was inclined to go. In all his writing one is conscious
of an emphasis on the active energy of the will in the ascetic life
and of the intellect in the contemplative life, which is typically
Greek. But a truly Christian view must go beyond the activity
both of the mind and the will and find the perfection of charity
in a total surrender of the person to God by which the Holy
Spirit comes to dwell in the heart, and the activity of the Holy
Spirit takes the place of our human activity. It is not by any
effort of concentration of mind, so that the thoughts are not
allowed to wander, that the perfection of charity is found, but
in a total surrender of the will by which the whole of our being
is transformed, and both mind and will are moved no longer by
their own energy but by the power of the Holy Spirit dwelling
in us.

But we have now to carry this a step further. When the soul
is filled with the Holy Spirit, it is transformed into the likeness of
Christ; it is then that we can begin to say, "it is not I that live
but Christ that lives in me." But to have Christ living in us is
to enter into the heart of Christ, and this is the heart both of the
Church and of humanity. This transformation in charity does
not take us away from our fellow men, it draws us to them as
Christ was drawn to share the suffering and also the joys of

D

mankind. There can be no conflict here between the contemplation of God and the service of one's brethren. It is God who is manifested in our fellow men and it is the love of God in us which drives us to serve them. This conception of charity will also radically affect one's prayer. There can be no question of prayer drawing us apart from this world, but rather of our learning to find God in the world and the world in God. We come here upon the profound paradox that as we enter more deeply into ourselves, we come into closer contact with our fellow men. It is by their external activities that men tend to be divided; it is the depth of our being, in the heart of Christ, that the only true union of mankind can take place.

It is here, perhaps, that we can find the final resolution of our problem. The Church today is called, more than ever before, to enter into human life to be "present" in everything which concerns the life of man. We have to enter into the economic, the political and the cultural world, to bear witness to Christ, not so much by preaching as by charity, that is, by the witness of the Holy Spirit. But if this mission is to be effective, we have to be "filled with the Holy Spirit." No mere human activity of love is adequate; there must be a renewal in the depths of the spirit. This means that we have to enter deeply into the interior life of the Church. We have to go to the sources of that life, to the Scriptures and the liturgy and to the teaching of the Fathers in which the tradition of the Church is contained. It is here that we can find the value of Cassian's writings. He is one of the great sources, to which St. Benedict refers, through which a man is "led to the summit of perfection." We need the discipline of repentance and of the ascetic life which Cassian describes, if we are to be capable of selfless love. We need also the habit of meditation on the Scriptures and the use of the Psalms as our prayer, which Cassian makes the basis of the contemplative life. But this "asceticism" and "contemplation" will not necessarily lead us to withdraw from the world. There is indeed a sense in which we all need the "solitary" life. There is a solitude within the heart which everyone who seeks God has to find. There is a place of meeting with God "face to face" where no creature can enter, and in this sense every Christian is called to the solitary life. But this solitude need not always be found in the desert; it can be found in the crowded city, at every time and in every place.

No doubt, there will always be some who are drawn to the actual solitude of the desert; others will be drawn to the monastic community. But there will be many who will be drawn to the life of the world, to a married life, to a profession, a life of labour or of service to the poor. All these constitute differences of vocation; but it is the same Spirit, as St. Paul says, who distributes His gifts to each as He wills. To each there will be a call to solitude and silence and discipline, to poverty, chastity and obedience, but these virtues will be realised in different ways. No doubt there will always be a certain tension in a Christian life; until we have reached the perfection of charity we shall always feel the pull either towards activity or towards contemplation. But the goal is the same for all; it is to be found in the words of St. Paul: "to comprehend with all the saints what is the length and the breadth and the height and the depth, to know the charity of Christ which surpasses knowledge" and to be "filled with all the fullness of God" (Eph. iii. 18–19).

4 · ST. CAESARIUS OF ARLES

Mother Maria Caritas

THE VIGOROUS, capable archbishop who shepherded Arles from 502 to 542 and was papal vicar for Gaul and Spain, has been recognised more and more for his influence on the shaping of Western Christendom as the Roman Empire fell to ruins. As an administrator and legislator he is well known for reforming, developing and extending the Church in Gaul, and for strengthening its bonds with the Holy See. He is noted, too, not only for his own indefatigable devotion to preaching, but also for his successful programme for better and more frequent sermons in an era, when, though Christian instruction was a vital need in the face of semi-barbarism and heresy, only bishops were allowed to preach. His zeal for the cultivation of the supernatural life in souls shows clearly in his exhortations to bishops to preach at least on Sundays and great feasts, and in his legislation allowing the priests and deacons of his diocese to preach the homilies of the Fathers from sermon collections he himself provided. These collections were made up of his own sermons and those of the Fathers before him, compiled, edited and spread abroad by the enterprising bishop with the help of his clerics of Arles.[1]

Just over twenty years ago Dom Morin completed his monumental life's work of seeking out and editing the extant works of Caesarius, the major portion of which are two hundred and thirty-eight vigorous sermons. These and the saint's rules for monks and nuns, his canonical legislation and a few short doctrinal treatises[2] reveal that his spiritual heritage lies as much in what he thought and said as in what he did. Although no claim can be made for him as a speculative theologian, recent studies

[1] G. de Plinval, "Césaire d'Arles," *Dictionnaire d'histoire et de géographie ecclésiastiques*, XII (Paris, 1953), 186–96.

[2] Sancti Caesarii *Opera omnia* (2 vols. Maredsous, 1937–42). The sermons have been reprinted as vols. CIII and CIV of *Corpus Christianorum*, Series Latina (Turnhout, 1953).

have shown him a faithful transmitter of patristic doctrine on the great mysteries of Faith;[1] and he has long been renowned for his formulation of the Augustinian doctrine of grace at the Council of Orange (529), a formulation confirmed shortly afterwards for the universal Church.[2] Not only has his active work in firmly establishing convent life for women religious in the West been given increased attention, but also his spiritual teachings on the religious state. These embody the monastic tradition of the Fathers before him, but they are made Caesarius' own by his personal emphases and inimitable enthusiasm for the truths and practice of the spiritual life.[3] He had been a monk at Lérins from the ages of about twenty to twenty-seven (c. 490–97). There he had endeavoured, amid a then tepid community, to emulate the spiritual fervour of the renowned "Fathers" of the island monastery, Honoratus, Hilary and Faustus, all of whom became Gallic bishops. He had so weakened his health that his abbot Porcarius sent him to Arles for medical treatment where, his worth being recognised, he was soon ordained a priest. Upon the death of Bishop Eonius a few years later, he was elected to the episcopacy of Arles. Although his biographers could record at the end of his forty years as bishop that he had "remained a monk in humility, in charity, in submission, in the cross,"[4] they could also tell of exterior accomplishments of lasting influence on the ecclesiastical and even the secular life of southern Gaul.

Monk, ecclesiastical legislator and administrator, moralist, preacher, even diplomat, Caesarius is all of these, but none of these pre-eminently to those who come to know him well. He is, above all, as he often said, a spiritual father: "We admonish you with the words of a shepherd, but with the affection of a father."[5] And it is here proposed that he is a spiritual father who can lead one to the fullness of the Christian life, to a faith that sees the

---

[1] M. Dorenkemper, *The Trinitarian Doctrine and Sources of St. Caesarius of Arles* (Fribourg, 1953); J. Riviére, "La doctrine de la Rédemption chez saint Césaire d'Arles." *Bulletin de littérature ecclésiastique*, XLIV (1944), 3–20.

[2] de Plinval, *op. cit.* cols. 191–92.

[3] M. M. Caritas McCarthy, *The Rule for Nuns of St. Caesarius of Arles: A Translation with a Critical Introduction. C.U.A. Studies in Mediaeval History*, New Series, vol. XVI (Washington, D.C., 1960).

[4] Vita Sancti Caesarii ed. G. Morin in *Opera omnia*, vol. II.

[5] Sermon 68, p. 277. All the sermons are edited in *Opera omnia*, vol. I. Hereafter "Sermon" will be cited as "S."

supernatural as the only real life, that encompasses in one sweep the whole story of God and man, from Creation through Redemption to eternal union in heaven; and to a love and devotion that joyfully accept God's gifts, and manfully fight the battle of the spirit, considering no labour too great for those who are destined to reign with Christ.

Before Caesarius' simple yet richly developed spiritual teachings are presented, mention should be made of a value they have beyond their worth in themselves. They serve to introduce us to the spirituality of the Fathers in general, not to the richness, variety, subtlety, and peculiar nuances of each individually, but to the core that was central and basic to all, to the atmosphere and climate of their spiritual thinking. Caesarius had reverently nourished his soul on many of the Fathers and could make no prouder claim than "we do not speak out of our own presumption, but according to that which is read in the canonical Scriptures and which abounds in the books of the ancient Fathers."[1] Augustine was by far his preferred source; among others from whom he borrowed or to whom he referred were Ambrose, Origen, Faustus of Riez, a certain Pseudo-Eusebius associated with the Lérins tradition, Cassian, Maximus of Turin, Jerome, Cyprian, and Hilary of Poitiers.[2] For all the Fathers, Scripture was the great fount of inspiration and devotion. Other marked characteristics of their devotion have been summarised by Dom Wilmart:

> It is contemplative, that is, turned toward God for whose Presence, veiled here below, it seeks and hopes in patient faith and by means of liturgical prayer. It is at the same time . . . Christocentric in the sense that Christ is the necessary Mediator. . . . It does not attach itself to Christ on earth and it does not pursue Him here below, but . . . it is the God-Man whom it adores and to whom it adheres humbly, in the mystery of the Incarnation and the works of Redemption. Faith is its dominant note; . . . it rejects ordinarily too vivid emotions of the heart. . . . The liturgy suffices habitually to nourish it, and, imposing on it a discipline, continues to act on it when it abandons itself to greater freedom in prayer.[3]

[1] Regula sanctarum virginum, ch. 63, ed. in Opera omnia, vol. II.
[2] See Morin's indices in Opera omnia, vol. II.
[3] A. Wilmart, Le "Jubilus" dit de saint Bernard (Rome, 1944), p. 227.

Within a common climate of patristic thought Caesarius loses nothing of his individuality. What are most characteristic and most winning in his spiritual teachings are his never-flagging enthusiasm for the spiritual life and his simplicity and directness, reinforced rather than weakened by his homely, popular speech. One best grasps the strength of the faith underlying these characteristics when one meets them persistently throughout all his works, but it is hoped that by letting Caesarius speak for himself as much as possible in the following pages some of the force of his inspiration will be apparent.

The fact of the possession of God's word in Sacred Scripture, with its message of Christ redeeming and bestowing eternal life, was the springboard of Caesarius' faith and devotion, inspiring him with an evangelical joy. Meditation on any passage of Scripture seemed to take this shepherd of souls back in spirit to the hill outside Bethlehem to hear the angel, for surely he had the "good tidings of great joy." And meditation always led to action—response to the message so warmly welcomed:

Through the goodness of Christ, dearest brethren, may you so receive the sacred text with an eager and thirsting heart that you may give us spiritual joy as a result of your faithful obedience. If you want the sacred writings to become sweet to you, . . . withdraw from worldly occupations for several hours to reread the divine words in your homes and to dedicate yourselves entirely to God's mercy. . . .

Notice carefully, beloved brethren, that the Sacred Scriptures have been transmitted to us like letters from our heavenly country. Our homeland is paradise, and our parents are the patriarchs, prophets, apostles, and martyrs; the angels are its citizens, Christ is our King. When Adam sinned, we were all as though thrown into the exile of this world. However, since our King is more kind and merciful than can be imagined or expressed, He deigned to send us through the patriarchs and prophets, sacred writings as letters of invitation summoning us to the eternal and excellent country. . . .

What do servants think of themselves when they dare to despise the Lord's precepts, not even condescending to reread the letters of invitation whereby He asks them to the blessedness of His kingdom? If anyone of us sends a letter to his procurator, and he in turn not only fails to do what is commanded, but even refuses to read over the orders, that man deserves to receive punishment. . . .

Similarly, one who refuses to read the Sacred Scriptures which have been transmitted from the eternal country should fear that he perhaps will not receive eternal rewards and not even escape endless punishment. . . . Doubtless if a man fails to seek God in this world through the sacred lessons, God will refuse to recognise him in eternal bliss.[1]

I beg and exhort you, dearly beloved, if any of you are educated, read the Sacred Scriptures frequently; those of you who are not, should listen attentively when others read it. The light and eternal food of the soul is nothing else but the word of God, without which the soul can neither see nor live. Just as our body dies if it does not receive food, so too, our soul is killed if it does not receive the word of God.[2]

So vital a message as Scripture from so high a personage as God must be understood rightly and in its fullness: thus Caesarius reiterates frequently an admonition to seek the spiritual meaning of the Sacred text:

. . . as I have often admonished you, you ought to note most carefully not only what is meant in word, but what is meant to be understood and savoured in spirit; so the Apostle admonishes us saying: "the letter kills but the spirit gives life."[3] Truly, all these things which are read in the Old Testament, as the Apostle says, "happened to them as a type, and they were written for our correction."[4] For what good would it be for the Christian people, when they came to church faithfully, to hear how the holy prophets took to themselves their wives and how they begot their children, unless that they might perceive in a spiritual sense why these things were done and what things they typified?[5]

With a keen aptitude for teaching, Caesarius did not miss the instructions of the Divine Teacher on the value of images and figures in imparting truth and driving home lessons. He produced his own extensive fund of figures and parables from the life about him to give variety, freshness, and vitality to the few great truths he was always repeating about Christ incarnate and redeeming, about paradise to which He calls, and about the "good fight" here below to attain it. Many of his figures are drawn from the rural life in which large portions of his flock were engaged. One of the most picturesque of these returns to

---

[1] S 7, 40 f.   [2] S 6, 33.   [3] 2 Cor. iii. 6.   [4] 1 Cor. x. 11.   [5] S 89, 350.

his ever-present realisation of the joy and urgency of the Scriptural message:

> Now, in the Church, priests seem to bear a likeness to cows, while the Christian people fulfil the type of calves. Cows run about through fields and meadows, go around the vineyard and olive gardens, to prepare the food of milk for their calves by eating grasses and leaves. So priests, by continually reading the word of God, ought to pick flowers from the various mountains of Holy Scripture. As a result they will be able to offer spiritual milk to their children, so as to be able to have a part with the Apostle Paul, who said: "I fed you with milk, not with solid food."[1] Not unfittingly, most dear brethren, do priests seem to bear a likeness to cows. Just as a cow has two udders to nurse her calf, so also priests ought to feed the Christian people with the two udders of the Old and New Testaments. Moreover, consider, brethren and see that not only do carnal cows come to their calves, but the calves also go to meet them. They strike the udders of their mother with their heads so that, if the calves are rather large, they seem to lift the bodies of their mothers from the ground. However, the cows willingly accept this injury, for they desire to see the growth of their calves. Good priests, too, should devoutly desire and long for their sons to disturb them by continual questions concerning the salvation of their souls. While divine grace is bestowed upon the sons who are knocking, an eternal reward is prepared for the priests who reveal the secrets of Holy Scripture.[2]

To our modern and mostly urban ears, this is perhaps naïve, but the picture remains long after the hearing, and as a picture it is not too different from the Divine portrayals of the hen with her chicks, the birds and their nests, the foxes and their holes.

What are the "secrets of Holy Scripture"? What gave Caesarius such an integrated view of life, of the supernatural informing the natural? What made life so full of purpose as to make its struggles just what a vigorous man might expect? It is rather a single secret for Caesarius: that life is wholly a journey toward the deep realities of judgment, heaven or hell, and God—the God-Man and Redeemer who prepares eternal espousals for every soul. The reality is in some way already with us in Christ, in His Mystical Body, in the types of the Old Testament, in His own words in the New, in the life of grace and in the Eucharist; but the soul must never lose sight of the end, and in consequence,

---

[1] I Cor. iii. 2.   [2] S 4, 25–27.

life's whole earnest business becomes a cultivation of the interior life and its overflow in the practice of justice and charity.

A striking repetition of this outline of Caesarius' spiritual teaching occurs in Fr. Daniélou's meditation on the heavenly Temple. It seems significant that a twentieth-century reflection of the patristic synthesis such as Fr. Daniélou can give, should so precisely catch not only the doctrinal emphasis, but even the devotional appeal of Caesarius. The coincidence substantiates the value of this saint as an introduction to the spirituality of the Fathers, and the appropriateness of his teachings for contemporary spiritual trends.

> Christ is the high priest, that is to say, He is the representative of total Humanity—and with Him the whole of "human nature" is finally brought into the heavenly Temple. . . . Henceforth, Humanity's place is in heaven; it is there that man dwells already through Christ, the head of the mystical Body, and through the glorified Church. . . . But . . . this entry of mankind into the heavenly Temple, if it is achieved for all men, if it is already real for every member, must nevertheless be gained by each of them. . . . Every present economy, if it is a reality in relation to the Mosaic figure, is itself a figure in relation to the consummation of all things. It is prophecy, waiting. The real life, the real dwellings are elsewhere. . . .
>
> Thus the Christian life is altogether an act of waiting. The Christian knows that he is made for greater things. He feels acutely the misery of his present condition. He aspires to be relieved of the weight of animal life and its servitude. . . . Whilst carnal man grasps desperately at his pleasures and possessions, the Christian lives already in the order of being detached, free, making use of time so long as it is given, to perform works of charity towards all. . . . This does not mean, all the same, that the Christian is not interested in the world, but he sees it only as a beginning, only a crucible where immortal souls are in the making. The only work that interests him is, at every moment, making the life of Christ grow in himself and others. The world is indeed for him "a machine for making gods." But it is in this world that gods are made; so he takes part eagerly in temporal struggles, not for their own sake, and without believing in the establishment of a perfect human city, . . . but because the salvation of many souls is bound up with the temporal conditions of life.
>
> This is not to say that there is for him, as it were, a devaluing of earthly realities, a weakening of the instinct for life, a desire to escape from the wicked world, a morbid taste for death. . . . But it

remains true that the human act by which the free soul ratifies his detachment from mortality and adheres to eternal life is the most serious of all. . . . It is to prepare himself for this solemn act, which is the entry of every man into the heavenly Temple, through the veil that still conceals it, that a man's whole life must be devoted.[1]

Caesarius peers into the dim reaches of the Old Testament and sees the Redeemer approach nearer and nearer to fallen man in an ever-increasing succession of figures. His Spouse, the Church, is there too, not so luminous as the Bridegroom, but clearly perceptible with her life-giving fount of Baptism. Isaac journeying with Abraham as a victim and carrying the wood for sacrifice, is the Saviour sent by the Father and carrying His cross for sacrifice.[2] Isaac, in turn, sending his son Jacob to a far country for a wife, becomes God the Father sending His Son into the world to espouse the Church. Jacob's ladder reaching from earth to heaven is the cross upon which Christ hangs. As Head of the Church He is in heaven, in His Body the Church He is on earth.[3] Joseph typifies Christ in many details of His Passion: as Joseph's descent into Egypt saved it from famine, so Christ's descent to earth saved it from damnation. Joseph's mistreatment at the hands of his brothers prefigures Christ sold, stripped, descending into Limbo after His death. Joseph returning good for evil to his brethren is the Redeemer saving the men who crucified Him.[4]

Type follows upon type for Caesarius: "As Isaac and Joseph and Jacob, so we understand Moses to have typified Christ," he says, and explains how Moses' staff reminds one of the cross of the Saviour.[5] Elias persecuted by the Jews and leaving his own people is Christ persecuted and setting aside the synagogue.[6] Eliseus shows forth many aspects of Christ's mission: his sweetening of the bitter waters with a vessel of salt is Christ with the vessel of His human flesh sweetening the bitterness of fallen man. Eliseus mocked is Christ mocked; Eliseus saving the widow from her creditors is Christ saving the Church; Eliseus restoring life to the son of the Sunamitess is Christ restoring the Gentiles to their mother the Church.[7]

Caesarius' exegesis was no sterile scholarship, but a fount of

---

[1] J. Daniélou, *The Presence of God*, trans. W. Roberts (Baltimore, 1959), pp. 51–57 *passim*.

[2] S 84, 330–33; Gen. xxii. 1–14. [3] S 87, 342–44; Gen. xxviii. 1–15.

[4] Ss 89, 90, 350–60; Gen. xxxvii–xlv. *passim*. [5] S 95, 373–74; Exod. iv. 2–5.

[6] S 124, 492; 3 Kings 18–22. [7] Ss 126, 127, 489–505; 4 Kings 2–4.

living devotion, and each interpretation of a figure is followed
by a call to prayer and action worthy of the mystery revealed:

> Truly, brethren, we who have seen all things which werę typified
> in the Old Testament, fulfilled in the New, should as much as is
> in our power, give thanks to God who has deigned to bestow such
> great gifts without any antecedent merits of ours; with His help
> we should labour with all our strength that so many and such
> great benefits may beget for us not judgment but gain. Yes, we
> should indeed so strive to live by the spirit and to persist always in
> good works, that the day of judgment will find us chaste, temperate,
> merciful and holy, and that we shall not be punished with the
> impious and sinful; but, with the just and God-fearing, we shall
> deserve to attain to eternal beatitude.[1]

Caesarius continues to find devotional inspiration in figures
abounding in the New Testament where Christ, now united
with human nature, shows Himself with greater familiarity and
tenderness. Thus in the parable of the Prodigal Son He is both
the arm of the Father embracing the repentant sinner, and the
fatted calf sacrificed by the Father for the sinner.[2] With Augustine,
from whom the previous interpretation is also borrowed,
Caesarius sees Christ in the Good Samaritan, and the Church in
the inn to which the injured man—the sinner—was taken.[3]

The mere sampling given here of Caesarius' use of Scriptural
figures shows how inseparable for him were Christ and the
Church. He sees her at the dawn of Revelation, in Eve coming
forth from the side of the sleeping Adam, as the Church will
come forth from the side of Christ, when, "having bowed down
His head, He died on the cross."[4] Following Augustine closely,
Caesarius is devoted to the Church not only as the virginal Bride
of Christ, but to the Church as the members of Christ, especially
the poor, the suffering, the weak, the sinful members who have
their Saviour's own claim to the charity of the stronger members.[5]

If, in the tradition of the Fathers, Caesarius does not dwell at
length on the intimate relations of the individual soul with God,
he had the deepest awareness of the personal and sacred character
of the adoration and love of the Christian in the presence of his
Creator and Redeemer. His penchant for the notion of espousals

---

[1] S 87, 345.   [2] S 163, 633-34; Luke xv. 11-31.
[3] S 161, 625-27; Luke x. 30-36.   [4] S 169, 653-54; Gen. ii. 21-24.
[5] See *e.g.* S 24, 102-106, for a theme that recurs frequently throughout the
sermons.

in describing the relations of the soul and God shows that, although he is not in the affective tradition, he knows of what it speaks. His most frequent references to spiritual espousals are in his writings for religious, for consecrated virginity is of the essence of their state. They are invited to full participation in the dignity and delights of the wise virgin with her lamp, the bride of the Canticle, and the spouses of the heavenly Lamb:

> ... consecrated virgins and souls dedicated to God, who with your lamps burning await with secure consciences the coming of the Lord, ... as you ... shine forth among the most precious gems of the Church, ... afterwards you can say with confidence: "We have found Him whom our soul has sought."[1]

The holy soul should strive constantly to adorn herself with the flowers of paradise, that is, with thoughts from Holy Scripture; from them she should unceasingly hang precious pearls from her ears; from these she should make rings and bracelets while she performs good works. ... You who wish to show forth the apostolic virgin in body, prepare your lamp burning with the oil of good works, for the meeting with the Spouse, thinking always on the things of the Lord.[2]

But further, Caesarius rejoices that the spiritual nuptials are for every Christian soul—all can be of the number of wise virgins, of those who follow the Lamb:

> Because the blessed Apostle has called the whole Catholic Church a virgin, considering in it not only those virgin in body, but desiring uncorrupted minds in all, saying thus: "I have espoused you to one husband that I may present you as a chaste virgin to Christ,"[3] the souls not only of nuns but also of all men and women, if they will guard chastity of the body and virginity of heart in the five senses discussed above, should not doubt that they may be espoused to Christ. For Christ is to be understood as the Spouse, not of bodies, but of souls. And therefore, beloved brethren, both men and women, both boys and girls, if they have preserved virginity to the time of their marriage and have not corrupted their souls through the five senses, ... provided that they have used them rightly, will happily deserve to enter on judgment day through the wide open doors into the bridal chamber of the Spouse.[4]

Although Caesarius' primary orientation is toward the perfect fulfilment of the spiritual nuptials in heaven, he can, on occasion,

[1] Reg. sanc. virg., ch. 1; Cant. 3, 4.
[2] Letter of Caesarius to nuns of Arles in Opera omnia II, 143–47 passim.
[3] 2 Cor. xi. 2.   [4] S 155, 599.

give vivid reminders of heaven begun here on earth in the
indwelling Presence through grace, in Christ in His Revealed
Word, and in the Eucharist:

On Christmas, most dear brethren, Christ is united as in spiritual
nuptials to His Spouse the Church: then "truth shall spring out of
the earth," then "justice shall look down from heaven," then there
has come forth "the Spouse from His bridal chamber,"[1] that is, the
Word of God from the virginal womb. In truth He has come forth
with His Spouse, for He has taken on human flesh. Having been
invited to the holy nuptials, and about to go into the banquet of
the Father, Son, and Holy Spirit, behold, with what kind of
clothing we ought to be adorned. . . . For we have been invited to
a wedding feast where, if we conduct ourselves worthily, we shall
be the bride. Let us reflect on what kind of a wedding, to how great
a Spouse, to how great a feast we have been invited. Indeed we
have been invited to a table, where is found, not the food of men,
but where the Bread of angels is set out. Therefore, let us take care,
lest perchance within our souls, where we ought to be adorned
with the pearls of good works, we find ourselves covered with
shabby old rags.[2]

Heaven is found here, despite suffering, in Christ with us.
Caesarius borrows from Augustine to show the sweetness brought
by the Incarnate Word to the fallen world:

What He has said is true: "For My yoke is easy and My burden
light."[3] In truth, what is harsh in precept love makes light. We
know this to be so. . . . There are many who for the love of Christ
undergo many labours not only patiently but willingly. Why do
you marvel if he who loves Christ and wishes to follow Christ,
denies himself in loving Him? Just as man was lost by loving himself,
so he is recovered by denying himself. . . . He who desires to follow
Christ should hear the Apostle saying: "He who says that he abides
in Him, ought himself to walk just as He walked."[4] Do you wish
to follow Christ? Be humble where He was humble. . . . The way
indeed was made rough when man sinned; but it was made smooth
when Christ conquered it by His resurrection; and from a very
narrow path He made it a regal road. One runs along that way by
two feet, that is humility and charity. . . . For Christ you ought to
hold all things as nothing, that you may deserve to attain to fellowship with Him. The world is loved, but much preferred to it, He
by whom the world was made. The world is beautiful, but much

---

[1] Ps. lxxxiv. 12, and Ps. xviii. 6.   [2] S 188, 727–28.
[3] Matt. xi. 30.   [4] 1 John ii. 6.

more beautiful He by whom the world was made. The world is alluring, but much sweeter He by whom the world was made.[1]

Always Caesarius comes back to the end which will be the true beginning. That is why the parable of the virgins with their lamps summed up so much for him. Over a hundred times throughout his sermons he recalls the Gospel parable which spoke even more vividly to him—Christ's "Come, blessed of my Father!" Almost fifty times he repeats the very sentence. And with the "Come" of his Lord ever-ringing in his heart, how else could Caesarius view life but as a journey?

In truth, beloved brethren, we who are strangers and foreigners in this world, ought to understand that we are still on the way, not yet in the homeland. For life is that journey. When a man is born he sets out on the way; when he dies he is known to have completed the journey. Those who are wise, and are solicitous for the salvation of their souls, do not love the journey, but, running along the way, they eagerly seek for the homeland. The lovers of luxurious living, who for fleeting delights love the present more than the future, prefer the journey; and since they want to have their joy on the way, they will not merit to attain it in the eternal homeland. . . . What are those two feet by which we run to the heavenly Jerusalem, unless the two commandments of love. . . . If you love God and do not love your neighbour, you have only one foot, and you will remain on the way, and will not be able to attain to the homeland. Again, if you love your neighbour and do not love God, you will be a cripple and you will not be able to run at all.[2]

Skilful teacher that he was, Caesarius gives a preview of the journey's end to spur the travellers on their way:

When by a happy exchange, that most long-awaited and most blessed moment is transformed into eternal life, the Lord's word will be fulfilled: "Men will be as angels." And again: "Then the just will shine forth like the sun in the kingdom of their Father."[3]

Do you realise what the splendour of souls will be when the light of the body will possess the brightness of the sun? . . . There will be no sadness or fear or infirmity or death . . . no human weakness to keep us from serving God, no opposition of the miserable flesh to contradict us, no further need to fight. There will come that time, I say, when no refreshment of food or sleep will be desired, no weariness from fasting felt, no restlessness of the flesh or temptation of the enemy feared. . . . When sin and misery and grief are ended,

[1] S 159, 616–18.   [2] S 186, 718.   [3] Matt. xxii. 30; Matt. xiii. 43.

innocence and joy and happiness will completely hold sway. . . .
Among the immense benefits of our God, we will enjoy perfect
happiness, so that we will never tire of giving thanks to Him for
having made us His co-heirs when He said: "Come blessed, take
possession of the kingdom prepared for you from the foundation
of the world."[1]

With the realism of the saints, Caesarius never separates the
"Come, blessed" from "Depart from Me, accursed ones." He
never forgets that the Eternal Bridegroom must also be the Eternal
Judge. But the salutary fear evoked by this remembrance is
mingled with confidence, for behold what kind of Judge we have!

> We have heard the Lord saying:, "Come blessed, take possession
> of the kingdom prepared for you from the foundation of the world."
> In order that you may hear that most desirable utterance and escape
> hearing the dreadful one, strive with all your strength by the aid
> of God to read frequently this divine lesson in your homes, and to
> hear it in Church with a willing and obedient spirit. For as that
> word is most desirable which is said to the merciful, . . . so, on the
> contrary, that is greatly to be feared, and is most terrible which will
> be heard by the unmerciful and those unfruitful in good works, to
> whom it must be said: "Depart from me, accursed ones, into (the)
> everlasting fire." May God keep us from this, most dear brethren,
> and may He deign to save us from an evil report. . . . Irrevocable will
> be the sentence! Therefore is it proclaimed beforehand by the most
> benevolent God, that we may be warned in the strongest terms. . . .
> Truly He does not wish to slay you, who calls out to you "Watch
> out!"[2]

The final aspect of Caesarius' spiritual teachings is the logical
corollary of the eschatological character of his devotion. The
cultivation of the interior life is, in co-operation with grace, *the
responsibility of the Christian*, his response to Redemption and
the promise of paradise:

> You ought to know, brethren, that we have become Christians in
> order to reflect always upon the future life and an eternal reward,
> and to labour more in the interests of the soul than of the body.[3]

To the task of portraying the life of the soul, its need of
purgation, cultivation, protection, nourishment, inspiration,
Caesarius applies all his energies, utilises every figure his imagina-

[1] S 58, 246–47; Matt. xxv. 34.   [2] S 157, 606–07.   [3] S 16, 75.

tion can construct. Some of his best spiritual teaching is here in extended parables which can only be sampled in these pages:

Who is ignorant of the fact that everyone has an interior and an exterior man? For this reason, whenever we invite people to a banquet it is proper for us to read over a divine lesson or strive to say something holy to sustain the soul, just as we arrange the service of food to refresh the body. For, since the soul ought to be the mistress and the body like her servant, it is not right for the maid to be satiated with many dainties even to the point of surfeit, while the mistress is not fed with the sweetness of the word of God.[1]

The care of our soul, beloved brethren, is very much like earthly cultivation. Just as in land which is tilled some things are torn out and others are completely uprooted in order that what is good may be sown, so this should also be the case in our soul. . . . Pride should be torn out, humility planted; avarice thrown away, mercy kept; dissipation despised, chastity loved. . . .

I beseech you to notice, brethren, that there are two kinds of fields; one belongs to God, the other to man. You possess your farm and God has His; yours is your land, God's is your soul. Is it right for you to cultivate your farm and leave God's deserted? Is this just, brethren? Does God deserve this from us, that we should neglect our soul which He loved so much?[2]

It is within the framework of his solicitude for the growth of the supernatural life in every soul, no matter how weak, that Caesarius' numerous and detailed passages of admonition against sin of every kind must be placed. Many of his people had very recently come from paganism and semi-barbarism, and he had of necessity to preach frequently in what might appear to be a very negative fashion. Yet his spiritual teachings taken as a whole show that he is most positive, that, acutely aware of the abyss of evil and the wiles of the devil, he is supremely confident in the Redemptive grace of Christ. He holds out before the most depraved of sinners, not only the necessity of rooting out vice, but the immediate promise of cultivating the seeds of virtue which would blossom in eternity. He has the sensitiveness of the holy to the war of the carnal against the spiritual, the ceaseless struggle ever present in this life. Ever influenced by Augustine he represents this most graphically by the two cities: the city of this world and the city of paradise, the Babylon of confusion and the Jerusalem of peace, the city of the devil and the city of

[1] S 1, 15.   [2] S 6, 34-35.

E

Christ.[1] Caesarius also has the common sense of the holy. Pithy admonitions punctuating his writings reveal a very sane spirituality: "Much better is humble married life than proud virginity" and "Let no one think that he must speak the truth to a Christian but not to a pagan."[2]

The modern Christian who turns to Caesarius as a spiritual father will find his teachings very simple yet forceful in the richness with which they are illustrated, the vigour with which they are presented. He may feel the absence of familiar and frequent devotion to the Blessed Sacrament and to Our Lady, and to the Humanity of Christ—devotions which have enriched our spiritual heritage since the Fathers wrote. But he cannot fail to be inspired by the great lesson which the Fathers, and Caesarius not the least of these, have to teach—Faith. The Bishop of Arles possessed a belief in the great mysteries of Revelation which generated joy and confidence throughout his life. The overwhelming truth of what he believed made love of God and fellow-man inescapable and completely desirable. And faith made heaven very real. His faith has evoked a portrait of him, of a shepherd striding vigorously at the head of an immense flock with his gaze fixed on something above and ahead. One feels he sees something more than those behind him and that he sees it very surely:

> No one can get around it, dearly beloved, the homeland of Christians is in heaven, it is not here. The city of Christians, the beatitude of Christians, the true and eternal happiness of Christians is not here. . . . Our homeland is paradise, our city the heavenly Jerusalem. Our citizens are the angels, our parents are the patriarchs and prophets, apostles and martyrs; Christ is our King.[3]

[1] Ss 151, 618; 186, 717; 233, 880.   [2] Ss 237, 901; 23, 100.   [3] S 151, 618.

5. ST. BENEDICT

David Knowles

Some years ago, the late Pope Pius XII, in one of his allocutions, referred to St. Benedict as "the Father of Europe." His Holiness was addressing a company of Benedictine abbots, who were not likely to cavil at a touch of rhetoric of which their Patriarch was the beneficiary, but the title was not a mere compliment. For more than five centuries, and those the formative centuries of western European civilisation and religious sentiment, the vast majority of influential churchmen—abbots, missionaries, bishops and even popes—and almost a totality of the theologians, preachers and educators of Europe, were monks: and from the days of St. Gregory the Great onwards to be a monk was, in western Europe short of Ireland and the western isles, to be one familiar with the Rule of St. Benedict either as a norm of life or at least as an influential part of the monastic formation. For five hundred years, therefore, the Rule of St. Benedict was, to the religious world of western Europe, a document more widely known and revered than any other save Holy Scripture. Its phrases and precepts, memorised in the noviciate and heard daily in chapter, must have sunk so deeply into the mind of those who ruled and judged and taught, as to become part of the framework of daily life and action throughout the western church, and to remain for centuries more as a kind of basic dye, colouring all subsequent thought.

To attempt a description or an analysis of the spiritual teaching of St. Benedict might well appear both unnecessary and futile: unnecessary, because some of the greatest saints and spiritual writers have been its expositors and commentators: futile, because no individual can hope or wish to add anything of value. This is true, but it is also true that there is a never-ending need to bring to the notice of every generation, again and again and in different places, the rich inheritance of the Catholic past, and to turn fresh eyes, perhaps as yet unfamiliar with a master's words, back to a precious and venerable page of Catholic history.

St. Benedict was born *circa* 480 in Nursia, in central Italy to the north of Rome. He was sent for education to the capital, but while still young escaped from the schools to become a hermit at Enfide. His fame spread after some years and he became a trusted leader and ultimately abbot of twelve small monasteries in the neighbourhood of Subiaco, in the Abruzzi to the east of Rome. His monks, however, proved intractable, and he migrated to Monte Cassino, on one of the routes to Capua and Naples, south of Rome. Here he ruled a single monastery for the rest of his life. He died *circa* 547. The Rule, which he may have begun to put together at Subiaco, was finished at Monte Cassino *circa* 530–540. We owe all that we know of his life and character to St. Gregory the Great, who devoted the second book of his Dialogues to the subject. St. Benedict founded no Order and wrote no book. He lives and has lived in virtue of his Rule alone. But before looking at this Rule a word must be said of two controversies which have been agitating monastic historians in recent years.

The first concerns the so-called *Rule of the Master*, a long and wandering monastic code dating probably from the sixth century, that is, from the century of St. Benedict. This code contains embedded in it, either verbally or in paraphrase, almost the whole of the Rule of St. Benedict, and until very recently it had been universally accepted that the unknown Master was an unskilful plagiarist. Recently, however, a series of competent scholars have maintained that the Master's work preceded St. Benedict's, and that the latter was little more than a selective copyist, albeit a copyist of genius. The debate, which turns largely upon very fine points of palaeography and stylistic and linguistic analysis, continues, and will probably never be settled unless or until it can be proved to demonstration that a manuscript of the Master's Rule was in existence many years before the death of St. Benedict. At the moment, indeed, the purely technical and critical evidence in favour of the debt of St. Benedict to the Master seems very strong. Yet to the present writer, at least, arguments of another kind are still stronger. Even after reading most of the literature on the subject he still feels that literary and spiritual considerations stand in the way of supposing that the Master's Rule was the original, and St. Benedict's the derivative; he feels also, even more strongly, that the Rule of St. Benedict reflects a single, distinctive, and saintly personality, which is not that of the Master.

The second controversy, still more recent but probably less durable, is concerned with the identity of the author of the Benedictine Rule. It has been argued, with great ingenuity and learning, that he was not Benedict of Monte Cassino, but another legislator whose work was subsequently fathered upon the great abbot. Here again the debate continues, though in this case the conservatives seem to be the winning party.

These controversies do not essentially affect the purpose of this essay, for no one denies that the document traditionally known as the Rule of St. Benedict existed in the late sixth century, and that it was this document, whatever its provenance and authorship, that has come down the centuries as the monastic code. Nevertheless, it is perhaps worth saying that the assumption to be made in these pages, that the Rule was the original work of St. Benedict of Monte Cassino, is not merely an assumption of convenience, but reflects the conviction of the writer. St. Gregory the Great, himself a monk, was a man of great intelligence, of spiritual wisdom, and of wide experience in the Italy of his day. His words, written some fifty years after the death of St. Benedict of Monte Cassino, are perhaps still valid as a judgment on the controversies to which we have just now alluded. "I would not," he says to his interlocutor, "have you ignorant of this, that Benedict was eminent, not only for the many miracles that made him famous, but also for his teaching. For he wrote a Rule for monks, which is of conspicuous discretion and is written in a lucid style. If anyone wishes to know Benedict's character and life more precisely, he may find a complete account of his principles and practice in the ordinances of that Rule; for the saint cannot have taught otherwise than as he lived."[1] Can we, acting upon St. Gregory's words, discover that character and its principles of action?

The Rule is a short document of some nine thousand words in length, of which a thousand or so are merely the numbers of psalms to be said and other purely liturgical directions. There were many orders and rules in the medieval church, but of these

[1] St. Gregory, *Dialogues*, II, 36.

only three have any claim to be mature spiritual documents as opposed to disciplinary, constitutional or liturgical codes. These three are the so-called Rule of St. Augustine, the Rule of St. Benedict and the Rule of St. Francis, and of the three that of St. Benedict is unique in its combination of firm legislation with humane and spiritual instruction over a wide range of subjects. As has been shown by editors, especially Abbot Cuthbert Butler, St. Benedict knew the early monastic literature well, together with certain writings of the Fathers, and he borrows freely from them, but in the most characteristic passages, where we feel that he is speaking from the ripeness of his experience, his debt to others is almost non-existent.

It has been said, and said truly, that St. Benedict domesticated Eastern monachism in the West, and rendered it viable by tempering its austerity. It has also been truly said that he gave order and stability to the disorderly, individualistic monachism of the Italy of his day. These were certainly two long-term effects of his work. It is not so certain, however, that they were, historically speaking, the objects at which he aimed. Paradoxically as it may seem to those conscious of the strongly authoritarian, monarchical tone of the Rule, St. Benedict's principal short-term achievement was to limit the abbot's freedom and thus to temper the rigours and the vagaries of contemporary monastic life by making the Rule the norm and the code by which all, even the abbot, were to be bound, and from which even the abbot might only depart in the purely material, day-to-day ordering of the life. Hitherto, in Italy and in Gaul, as also in the Celtic lands, the only alternative to individualism and indiscipline had been the authority of an acknowledged leader applying a disciplinary code. St. Benedict, with the hand of genius, gave in outline a complete rule for the government, administration, recruitment and daily life of a monastic family, adding thereto the elements of a spiritual directory, and chapters of wise human advice on the conduct of affairs for his officials.

St. Benedict, we are often told, wrote at the moment when all ordered life and organisation was going to pieces in the West, and that therefore he belongs to that important group of men who, during the gradual break-up of the Empire, made their own a part of the heritage of the past and adapted it, consciously or unconsciously, to the capacities of their contemporaries and

of posterity. In the case of St. Benedict, the heritage he saved
would have been that of Egyptian monachism, both in its original
form in the rules and writings of the Fathers of the Desert, and
in its more detailed and schematic form as presented to the West
by John Cassian. Before accepting this reading of his life, it is
perhaps worth noting, when we are seeking to grasp his personality, what parts of the ancient heritage he did not preserve.

Though his age, and especially the later decades of his life,
was a time of rapid decline of civilised government, he was
nevertheless the contemporary of Boethius and Cassiodorus,
and of more than one exceptionally vigorous pope such as
Gelasius I and Hormisdas, and it is a remarkable circumstance
that two of the best known documents of the Middle Ages, the
Rule of St. Benedict and the *Consolation of Philosophy* of Boethius,
should have been written by two Italians of pure blood who
were contemporaries, and that one of these should have lived so
wholly in the spirit and literature of the classical past that we still
find it hard to believe that he was a devout Catholic Christian,
while the other displays an utter disregard and ignorance of the
heritage of Greece and Rome. Here again we may remember
St. Gregory, with his well-known oxymoron when he describes
the boy Benedict flying from the schools of Rome *scienter nescius
et sapienter indoctus*—deliberately ignorant and wisely uneducated.
All these terms can carry their full weight: Benedict's ignorance
and disregard affected not only the literary projects of Cassiodorus
and the philosophy of Boethius: he knew indeed some of the
sermons and letters of St. Augustine, but he shows no familiarity
with the autobiographical or theological treatises. This of itself
is perhaps not remarkable, but when we remember on the one
hand how Augustinian doctrine had agitated the monasteries of
Gaul and Cassian himself, a century earlier, and on the other
how powerfully Augustine was to influence Benedictine thought
from St. Gregory onwards, we may think it worth while to
record that Benedict himself was neither theologically nor
spiritually an Augustinian. His view of human nature and grace
shows no trace of Augustine's influence, and his description of
the spiritual life has no hint of the half-intellectual, half-mystical
scheme of Augustine. More surprising still is the absence of any
direct echo of the doctrine of Egypt, as elaborated by Cassian,
upon the life of prayer and contemplation. True, St. Benedict

has a global reference to Cassian and the relative conferences may have formed part of the regular reading at Monte Cassino, but it is nevertheless significant, in view of the preoccupation of earlier and later writers with the problem of the active and contemplative lives, that there is no reference, not even the most distant, to the topic in the Rule. Is it also significant that St. Benedict has thirty citations from St. Matthew and not a single one from the discourses of Christ in St. John? Not all saints are mystics, nor are all mystics self-revealing, but the absence of any specifically "contemplative" element must be noted as a principal negative characteristic of the Rule. True, one does not expect a reference to such matters in a Rule, but the Rule of St. Benedict is no ordinary Rule.

What, then, is the personality that emerges from its pages? First and foremost, perhaps, there is the impression of authority. From the first words of the Prologue—"Hearken, my son, to the commands of thy master"—to the last words of the original Rule—"we wish this Rule to be read often"—we are aware that we are listening to one who speaks with the quiet and confident authority of a man who has long been used to command. It has indeed been said, with only slight exaggeration, that the abbot of the Rule is specifically different from his monks in all spiritual qualities—he is wise and all but perfect, an ideal figure; they are a scramble of good, bad and indifferent, capable of every kind of fault and folly. It is certainly true, as we have seen and shall again notice, that it was the achievement of St. Benedict to put the Rule above the abbot in the daily life of the community, but this does not affect the question we are considering, for after all the Rule and the abbot at Monte Cassino were twin barrels of a single gun: the Rule *is* Abbot Benedict. There could be no more striking proof of the self-confidence of the legislator than his references to the Rule as the *Master* and the *Holy* Rule.[1] And even though this insistence on the supremacy of the Rule, which even the abbot—or should we say, which the abbot above all—must recognise and obey, is very real, and is in fact the master

[1] *Magistra regula* (ch. 3); *Sancta regula* (ch. 23, 65). The most convenient edition of the Rule, with translation and notes, is that by the late Abbot Justin McCann (Burns and Oates; Orchard Books, 1952). For a critical Latin edition, with valuable appendices, see that of Abbot Cuthbert Butler (Freiburg-im-Breisgau, latest impression 1936).

key of Benedictine monachism, yet every reader must feel that
an enormous weight of responsibility rests upon the abbot of
the Rule. He is much more than the linch pin; we may almost
say that no one who is not a saint could fill the bill drawn up for
him by the legislator. Perhaps no stronger proof than this could
be given of the sanctity of the writer of the Rule.

Yet, having said so much, we must immediately add that the
second impression that emerges from the Rule is one of immense
loving-kindness—the benevolence and considerate charity of an
entirely selfless man. This is apparent not only in the well-known
instructions which St. Benedict makes for the peculiar needs and
claims of the young, the aged, the delicate, the sick and even of
the ignorant, the slow-moving and the timid, but also in the
positive decrees against all narrow rigidity and mechanical
measurement in the physical and psychological arrangements of
things in a monastery. Allied to this is a note peculiarly characteristic of the Rule. This is 'its humanity, which undoubtedly
had an incalculable influence for good upon the new and uncul-
tured peoples of the West. Whatever may have been the faults
and limitations of Benedictine monasticism, cruelty and barbarity
were certainly not among them. St. Benedict, indeed, has an
almost Aristotelian attitude in his common-sense, benevolent
approach to the problems of daily life. His appeal to the goodness
of human nature itself, though certainly devoid of direct theological implication, must be almost unique in the literature of
monastic codes. Equally revealing of the humble and sensitive
personality of the author are his advice to the abbot to desire to
be loved rather than feared, his description of his office as the
condescending service of every manner of man, and his hesitation,
remarkable in such a bold and decisive legislator, in allotting the
measures of food, drink and clothing. Indeed, we should not be
far wrong in considering the Rule simply as a guide to the human
relationships of a Christian family, where all are to be patient of
the weaknesses of body and character of others, where mercy is
to take precedence of justice, where every kind of inconsiderate
word and action is to be avoided, and where all are to be more
concerned with another's interests than with their own.

A second characteristic of the Rule is the simplicity and directness of the writer's approach. A perfect instance, noted by many
in the course of the centuries, is the instruction on prayer: "if

anyone wishes to pray by himself, let him just enter the oratory and pray."[1] Another is his instruction on the care of the sick: "Before all things and above all things must come the care of the sick." The Rule abounds in short, concrete, practical statements and precepts of this kind, that can be understood at once by every reader, not excepting the blockheads, tough guys and simpletons to whom St. Benedict alludes,[2] and that remain imprinted in the memory of his sons to serve as armour in a crisis. Whether consciously and by design or (more probably) unconsciously and by nature, St. Benedict speaks always in terms of action and behaviour rather than in those of principles and motives. This has always been a great source of strength to the Rule. A tendency to analysis, introversion and schematisation has always been a great fault in most spiritual and theological writing. Of this there is not a trace in the Rule, and the one apparent exception to this general statement—the long seventh chapter on the twelve degrees of humility—would appear, to judge from the acrobatics of the commentators, to have failed signally as a piece of analysis, while remaining unforgettable as a series of ascetical and moral precepts.

Along with this simplicity in St. Benedict went a great gift of economy in words and of lapidary precision of expression. This, to a judge of the finest hearing, Dom Germain Morin, was the hall-mark and touchstone of the Rule, and if, as happens in some passages, the idea or precept is drawn from an earlier writer, it will be seen almost invariably that St. Benedict, with a deft transposition or excision, has given the old saying an altogether new point and drive. Such phrases as the following are characteristic and unforgettable: *Obedientia quae majoribus praebetur, Deo exhibetur; Primus humilitatis gradus est obedientia sine mora; Nihil operi Dei praeponatur; Oratorium hoc sit quod dicitur, nec ibi quicquid aliud geratur vel condatur; Tunc vere monachi sunt si labore manuum suarum vivunt:*[3]

[1] *Simpliciter intret et oret* (ch. 52).
[2] *Duris corde et simplicioribus . . . indisciplinati et inquieti . . . negligentes et contempnentes . . . improbi, duri, superbi, inobedientes* (all these adjectives applied to the community occur in a single chapter, the second, on the duties of the abbot).
[3] One who obeys a superior obeys God (ch. 5). The first degree of obedience is instant obedience (ch. 5). Let nothing be put before the Work of God (ch. 43). Let the oratory be what it is called, *oratorium* = a place of prayer, and let nothing else be done or kept there (ch. 52). Then are they truly monks, when they live by the labour of their hands (ch. 48).

St. Benedict is one of the last of the Romans. The piety of his sons has attempted to insert him into one of the great families of republican Rome, but it is enough to remark that in Nursia the ancient stock had been very little contaminated during the late Republic and Empire. St. Benedict certainly had by nature the quality of rulership seen by the poet as typical of his race. *Tu regere imperio populos, Romane, memento.*[1] It is remarkable how often, in this short document of which a great part is made up of formal and liturgical directions, the great Roman words recur: *Imperium* and *imperare* (eight times); *gravitas* (five times); *stabilitas* (five times); *rationabiles* and *rationabiliter* (five times); *mensura* and *mensurate* (eight times). Indeed the sense of firm government, reason, moderation, just reckoning, love of tradition, all bound together by the paternal, patriarchal rule of a single authority, pervades the Rule from beginning to end.

Upon this foundation of firm, just, humane government St. Benedict built the Christian, evangelical fabric. He is probably the most evangelical of all religious founders and legislators. He does not view human nature primarily as depraved, nor life as a struggle against corruption. Absolute chastity is of course assumed throughout, but the word is never used in the Rule itself, and there is no vestige of that preoccupation with temptations and phantoms of the mind which had found such a large place in early monastic literature. Nor is there any mention of the struggle for recollection and indifference, or of the perils of *accidie*, that find such copious mention in the writings of the desert. For St. Benedict the monastic life is the return of a disobedient servant or son to perfect obedience, and a gradual bending of the hard self-will to reverence and humility. Abbot Cuthbert Butler, in the excellent series of extracts from the Rule which he entitles "*Medulla doctrinae S. Benedicti*," is unquestionably right in placing humility and obedience as the principal—one might almost say the sole and all-sufficing—virtues in the monastic ascesis.

All those who have written of the Rule from St. Gregory's time to the present day have remarked upon its discretion and its moderation. The modern reader or novice may feel at a first glance that too much has been made of this, but careful reflection will show that what seems most harsh in the Rule, whether an

[1] "Do thou, O Roman, remember thy task, to rule the world with authority." Vergil, *Aeneid*, vi, 851.

important feature such as corporal punishment, or a trifling one such as the prohibition of frequent baths, is a matter of custom and manners rather than of purely physical severity. There is a world of difference between the methods of St. Benedict and those of Peter Damian in his young days or those of Armand de Rancé. The Rule, as its author hoped, contains nothing that is repellent or unbearable, and even within its four corners the wind is to be tempered to the shorn lamb. Yet there is need of caution here. There is a great gulf between the evangelical spirit of ardent charity and the purely human spirit of good nature and easy going, between the honest man of the poet and the saint of God; but one who has his spiritual eye uncleansed may easily blur the distinction. The great danger throughout Benedictine history has been to read the Rule with the natural, and not with the supernatural, goal of life in mind, and to apply to the essentials of the life of perfection the same economy and latitude that St. Benedict applies to means and methods. Let us therefore consider for a moment the matters on which St. Benedict is strict.

And first, as to poverty. Ownership of any kind, and particularly the sense of ownership, is the most evil of vices; it is to be cut out of the monastery by the roots. No one is to possess, receive or give the very smallest or most necessary thing without permission; he is not to receive a letter or the smallest present even from a parent or one of his brethren. Nor should we suppose that the abbot's permission would be a mere formality. The examples of articles so allowed are few and extremely simple, and the brethren are to regard all things, even their clothes, as really and truly common property. St. Benedict was a realist, and while he hoped that his monks would be supported by their field and craft work he did not forbid his monastery to receive and to own land, but the spirit and often the letter of the Rule suggest that the living and the equipment of the individual monk were to be of the simplest. The necessities allowed by the abbot, including articles of clothing, are a dozen or so all told, and we may surely apply to all else what St. Benedict applies to the necessary matter of clothes. If a monk has anything above two tunics and two cowls, it is superfluous and should be cut out. Modern commentators have differed in their attempts to apply this doctrine to the circumstances of to-day, but any interpretation

that wishes to remain true to the spirit of the Rule must be able
to face the two questions of the Rule itself: is it absolutely necessary? and is it truly held as common, and not as personal,
property? Much has been made, especially during the later
Middle Ages, of the distinction between the "possessioners"
and the "mendicants," and between the Benedictine and Franciscan "ideals of poverty," but the careful reader of the Rule will
find little difference between the practice there laid down and
the *usus pauper* of the Franciscan Rule as interpreted by St.
Bonaventure.

And secondly, as to seclusion from the world. There was no
"perpetual silence" in St. Benedict's monastery, save for the
hours between Compline and Prime (about half of the twenty-
four hour span). Here, as elsewhere, St. Benedict was a human
being and a realist, and if speech were necessary, the monk might
speak. But there is no allowance for merely "recreative" conversation: permission to talk is to be given but rarely; there is a
virtue and a beauty in an absence of words. Similarly there is
strength in a lack of contact with others outside the monastery.
Monks are rarely to receive letters, and never to retail news on
their return from an unavoidable journey, nor are they to leave
the monastic precinct, for it is utterly ruinous for the life of their
souls.

These two examples may have shown that St. Benedict was
inflexible in essential matters. Above all, perhaps, we may
remember the round of regular duties and discipline year in,
year out, for a life-time. The willing acceptance of that changeless
round was to the mind of St. Benedict, and it remains to-day,
the clearest sign of a desire to seek God to the end of the road.

What, then, was this round of life that was to lead the monk,
by daily exercise over the years, to the perfect love that casteth
out fear, and to the unspeakable delight of ensuing, as of second
nature, the commands of God? St. Benedict found all the elements
of the monastic life in the writings of his predecessors, but his
celebrated tripartite division of the day was a clearer and more
decisive programme than anything that had gone before. According to this, the hours of the day, after allowance for sleep, meals
and toilet, were allotted to three occupations in almost equal
measure: the divine office, spiritual (or in St. Benedict's phrase
"divine") reading, and work.

The "divine" office, which already had a long history of
growth both in the monasteries of the East and in the liturgy of
cathedral churches, was to be regarded as the monk's primary
task, the praise of God at regularly recurring hours of the day
and night. It was to take precedence of all other duties, which
were to be abandoned when the signal for it was heard. *Nihil
operi Dei praeponatur.* So far as we know, it consisted simply of
the hours, much as they are said now after the recent reform of
the breviary, without any of the accretions that came in so rapidly,
and without the fuller list of festal days that developed from the
Carolingian age. The psalmody, hymns and responds would
have been chanted to simple tones and melodies, and the lessons
were longer than those now in use at Matins. To the office must
be added the Mass on Sundays and feast days; the daily Mass,
though not unknown in the Church at large, was not as yet
celebrated in the monasteries, and few of the monks were in
orders. Apart from a short period of silent prayer after certain
parts of the office there were, so far as the Rule goes, no further
devotions in public.

Spiritual reading, *lectio divina,* was also already a feature of
western monastic life, but whereas the psalmody was a legacy
from Egypt, the set periods of reading are first mentioned in
the instructions of Jerome and Augustine. The monastic reading
of the Rule may be thought of as combining three practices that
were later separated: meditative prayer, what we now call
spiritual reading, and doctrinal instruction. St. Benedict himself
gives a summary reading-list: the Bible, the Fathers, and the
classics of the monastic East. The space of time allotted to this
reading is ample, and we have no means of knowing how the
miscellaneous community of young and old, intelligent and
simple, actually employed their time. St. Benedict himself,
though not a man of letters, clearly knew much of the literature
that he recommended, and in particular the Scriptures.

Finally, there is the work. This was of various kinds; house
work, craft work, garden labour and, not infrequently, work
in field and olive yard. While the doctrine of the early Cistercians,
that heavy agricultural labour was a normal employment of all
under the Rule, cannot be maintained as historically accurate,
it is certain, both from the Rule itself and from St. Gregory's
life of St. Benedict, that some of the community were normally,

and that all were occasionally, employed in the basic tasks of the countryman's year. St. Benedict's monastery, it must be remembered, was economically almost entirely self-contained. It existed to provide a home and a framework for a family of men who desired to serve Christ alone, apart from the world. It had no task or mission towards the fellow-Christians outside, save the tasks of Christian charity to neighbours and strangers, and of intercession for all men, and anyone who entered its walls was called upon to abandon all ambition to develop or to employ any gifts that nature or training might have given him. He was expected, therefore, to take his share in all that affected the livelihood of the community, including the provision of means of subsistence. St. Benedict even added, in a sentence that has already been quoted, that monks were deserving of their name, when they lived by the work of their hands.

Wisely ordered, with an elastic and yet firm regularity, this threefold division of the day is for body and spirit the most health-giving régime that can be devised for a community of moderate size, living in rural surroundings and depending upon the neighbouring fields and fruits for its subsistence. Its balance was quickly shaken, and has only been restored from time to time in certain places and as a result of set programmes of reform. In the course of the centuries the solemn performance of the liturgy, and a devotion to educational or literary work, have come to be regarded as characteristic tasks of Benedictine monks. The Rule, like all wise spiritual documents, is broad and capacious in its designs. In the words of the quaint medieval saying, a lamb can bathe in it without drowning, while an elephant can swim in it; and there are many legitimate developments which the legislator did not intend or foresee, but which he would not have refused to accept. But time and again it has been found that when the threefold division of the day can be preserved, the moral and spiritual characteristics of the monastery of the Rule are most clearly seen.

In studying the Rule we are apt to consider it as the beginning and end of St. Benedict's teaching for his monks. There were, however, two other important sources, quite apart from the one presupposed above all—the unseen guidance of the Holy Spirit. The one has been mentioned already: it is the personal instruction and direction of the abbot. The monastery and the monk of the Rule could not have existed or prospered without the daily and hourly contact and teaching of the father of the community. It is a notable and in many ways a lamentable circumstance that throughout the Middle Ages the abbot steadily became less and less the loving, chastening shepherd and father, and more and more the dignified, wealthy and independent prelate, even if he did not in the end disappear altogether into a commendatory bishop or layman. Yet nothing in the Rule is clearer than the absolute co-relationship of the abbot and his monks. The abbot of the Rule has no right to exist, still less to occupy any position of dignity or receive any honour whatsoever, save in so far as he holds and fills the place of Christ to his monks. As the relations and duties of sonship cannot exist without a father, so the name of father implies relations and responsibilities towards a son. By a comprehensible, but in some ways regrettable, process of change the abbot, who is still the sole source of spiritual jurisdiction within the monastery, is canonically disabled from standing normally in the relationship of sacramental father to his monks, but the abbot who regarded himself as solely or principally the manager or the commanding officer of his monastery would throw the whole of St. Benedict's scheme of things out of gear.

The other additional source of doctrine can be more easily overlooked, but it is embodied in the Rule: the corpus of spiritual teaching to which the legislator refers in the last chapter of the existing Rule. In this last chapter, St. Benedict speaks of his work as "a little Rule for beginners" which guarantees "the rudiments of monastic virtues," and opposes these to "the perfection of the monastic life." This passage has always presented something of a difficulty to the commentators. Benedictines have not unnaturally felt loath to admit that their Rule, even if kept to perfection, was only a rudimentary beginning, and some have tacitly taken these words as a *façon de parler*, or a sign of humility on the part of a saint. Others have connected this passage with the equally enigmatic phrases of the first chapter, which contains a passing reference to the eremitic life as a better way for those long exercised in the virtues of a community life. Others again, and among them, it would seem, Abbot Cuthbert Butler, while strenuously rejecting a charge of false humility, have contrasted the Rule with other contemporary codes and with the Lives of the Fathers. Yet surely St. Benedict would not have regarded greater physical austerity as necessarily a spiritual advance upon his own programme. Are we then to suppose that the writer has a purely spiritual doctrine and practice in mind, and that he expects a monk to find in Cassian and the Fathers what is unsaid in the Rule? And if so, are we to see here, what we look for in vain elsewhere, an invitation to a doctrine that invites more explicitly to the higher degrees of the spiritual life as outlined by the desert saints and by St. Augustine? The reader must answer the enigma as best he may.

The spiritual teaching of St. Benedict has now for more than fourteen hundred years influenced in greater or less measure the religious life of western Europe. It is as fresh and living to-day as it was in the days of St. Gregory the Great: clear, simple and wise; the rule of life for a family whose only aim is to seek God by following the precepts and example of Christ. It is still well calculated to lead souls to a life of perfection, if it is followed in its full ascetic and spiritual rigour, under conditions of monastic observance and poverty and seclusion such as the legislator himself assumed as the framework of his doctrine.

6. VENANTIUS FORTUNATUS

P. G. Walsh

A<small>T FIRST SIGHT</small>, the inclusion of the sixth-century Italian poet Venantius Fortunatus in a series with such formative figures of Western spirituality as St. Augustine and St. Bernard has an appearance of incongruity. It is hard to disregard the stern criticisms[1] passed on his personal life as a result of the evidence of his own poems. To present Venantius as an unswerving exemplar of saintly self-denial and austerity would in fact be impossible. He himself recounts, for example, his leisurely pilgrimage from Ravenna to St. Martin's tomb at Tours, a journey embarked upon in thanksgiving after he was cured of an eye-ailment. But the journey was scarcely a sober pilgrimage. He describes his trek amongst the barbarians, "wearied with journeying or with drunkenness," and his frequent halts to accept the hospitality of the bishops and princes of Merovingian Gaul. "C'est plus le voyage d'un touriste que celui d'un pèlerin."[2]

Then again, his critics claim, the verses which describe his daily round, after he had settled to live in Gaul, hardly betray a life of intense spirituality and Christian devotion. He had become the estate-manager of the Convent of the Holy Cross at Poitiers. The trivial compositions addressed to its foundress, St. Radegund, and to its abbess, Agnes, allegedly present a damning self-portrait of a pietistic dilettante, excessively preoccupied with the stomach's delights.

Nor have his poems been greeted with conspicuous enthusiasm. Because his verses were, stylistically speaking, modelled on Vergil and Ovid, he was labelled by Ampère the "last and feeble representative of Classical poetry." From the purely literary standpoint, indeed, it is easy to condemn his egregious errors of syntax and prosody; Venantius himself is the first to concede

---

[1] As, for example, in Sir Samuel Dill's *Roman Society in Merovingian Gaul* (1926).
[2] P. Godet in *Dict. Théol. Cath.*

such deficiencies.[1] These failures reflect acutely the literary poverty of Merovingian Gaul. Writing to Gregory of Tours, Venantius states that he has no fear of judgment, no applause from friends, no correction from readers; he writes amongst "revelling drunkards," "who cannot tell the swan's song from the cackle of a goose." And it was the same Gregory who, in the Preface to his *History of the Franks*, lamented the disappearance of literary studies in Gaul: "vae diebus nostris, quia periit studium litterarum a nobis!"

Such condemnations of Venantius's life and poetry are, however, largely beside the point. For Venantius's central significance is not as a Classical but as a medieval poet—perhaps the first of major stature. In particular, his religious poems mark the effective beginning of the great tradition of liturgical poetry in Latin. It is true that earlier Christian poets, notably Prudentius and St. Ambrose, had already pointed the way. There is frequently a remarkable correspondence of content and poetic technique between the sacred hymns designated Ambrosian and the religious poems of Fortunatus. But Venantius has deservedly achieved the greater eminence in the public worship of the Western Church. Until the recent reform, two of his hymns formed part of the Good Friday liturgy, and this prominence indicates the veneration which the medieval Church felt for these compositions, which were widely studied and for long imitated.

Of primary relevance in this religious poetry is not so much the extent of his own spiritual formation as his understanding and his interpretation of the Church's spirituality. These poems reflect above all a close acquaintance with the Old and New Testaments, and with the teaching of St. Paul, who is quoted on innumerable occasions. Venantius did not, however, claim to be a learned philosopher or theologian. His Greek was rudimentary and he could not have read Plato or Aristotle. And though his further admission[2] that he had not studied the works of Hilary or Gregory, Ambrose or Augustine may characteristically err on the side of modesty, his acquaintance with the Fathers can only have been superficial.

[1] *Vita S. Mart.*, I, 29 f.
[2] V. 1.7. (The best and most accessible text of the poems is that edited by F. Leo in *Monumenta Germaniae Historica: Auctorum Antiquissimorum*, IV, 1.)

It was at school at Aquileia that his knowledge of the Bible was firmly implanted. He attended the monastery where, two centuries before, St. Jerome had gathered his ascetic circle, and where Rufinus had taught. St. Jerome's Vulgate was the main version studied by Venantius, for there are many verbal reminiscences of this translation in his poems.[1] Such studies did not, however, at that stage decisively shape his vocation. When his mentor Paul, later Bishop of Aquileia, invited him to become a novice in the monastery, he rejected this invitation, and preferred to extend his literary education by taking up residence at Ravenna.

This solid foundation did, however, assist him when in his later years at Poitiers he studied the Scriptures and the central mysteries of Christianity more deeply. After his poetry was written, he was ordained priest, and finally in 599 consecrated bishop. There is a very fine sermon on the Our Father which is almost certainly attributable to these final years, and which testifies to his heightened knowledge and devotion.

This *Expositio Orationis Dominicae* is a series of meditations on the phrases of the *Pater Noster*. It begins with an inspiring account of the doctrine of the Mystical Body. We pray *Pater noster* and not *Pater meus* because "all who assemble in the Church are contained in the one Body of Christ, though there are many limbs; and so those who are joined together in the temple ought not to be separated in prayer." And when we pray *sanctificetur nomen tuum*, we speak in the name of all mankind—not only of ourselves, but also of those who have not yet merited the grace of baptism. There follows a fine meditation on the kingship of Christ (*adveniat regnum tuum . . .*). Throughout this first half of the sermon the numerous quotations from Scripture and from St. Paul attest Venantius's close and continuous reading of them. Next, "after the eternal elements have been cited, the temporal things are sought." But *panem nostrum quotidianum* implies more than bodily sustenance. "It seems to infer that every day, if it is possible, we should reverently take communion of His Body; for since He, our Life, is our nourishment, we make ourselves strangers if we are slow to approach the Eucharist." Unfortunately the final sections of this sermon are lost.[2]

[1] There is a list in Ch. 2 of the Abbé Tardi's *Fortunat* (1927), a useful and sympathetic study with a systematic bibliography.
[2] Leo prints the *Expositio* at the beginning of Book X of the poems.

It has seemed useful to quote this sermon at some length to demonstrate the religious development in Fortunatus from steady belief and solid lay piety to sanctity and pastoral diligence. This spiritual progress was conspicuously furthered by the influence of the saintly Radegund and Agnes, and also by St. Gregory of Tours, whose intimacy with Venantius is demonstrated by the dedication of the poems to him.

Amongst these poems those with religious themes are our sole concern. Venantius's most important and influential contribution is his group of hymns on the Holy Cross. They were written in honour of a signal event at Poitiers. About A.D. 567 Radegund had despatched to the emperor Justin II a plea for a relic of the True Cross, which was preserved at Constantinople. Justin graciously acceded to the request, and on the occasion of the solemn translation of this relic to Poitiers, Venantius composed the *Vexilla regis* and the *Pange, lingua, gloriosi proelium certaminis*. At about the same time he wrote the splendid poem *Crux benedicta nitet*.

In all these compositions one can see clearly how the central Christian mysteries have furnished Latin letters with new inspiration. In *Crux benedicta* the new series of themes is admirably served by the elegiac verse-form. Ovid had developed this form in Augustan Rome to consummate his predilection for neat contrast, and for him antithesis was almost all. How suited then is this Ovidian vehicle for the presentation of the great antithetic truths of Christianity as propounded by St. John and more especially by St. Paul! The first Adam and the new Adam: Death and Resurrection: the Tree in the Garden and the Tree of Calvary: Christ's birth and His second coming—the list is well-nigh inexhaustible.

This antithetical effect is reinforced by the vigour of the scriptural symbolism. The poem *Crux benedicta*[1] reveals this with particular force. The Cross "where Our Lord hung, washing our wounds with His Blood," is not merely the instrument of Christ's death. It is also the means of regeneration and rebirth; it is the fruitful tree whose leaves protect the world. "And between thine arms" (here Venantius unites Christ with His Cross) "there hangs a vine, from which flows sweet wine with the redness of blood." It is this symbolism of the Cross as a

[1] II, 1.

verdant, fruitful tree which is Venantius's main contribution to
Catholic mysticism:

Fertilitate potens, o dulce et nobile lignum,
quando tuis ramis tam nova poma geris!

"Sweet and noble wood, so strong in thy fecundity, for on thy
branches such new fruit dost thou bear!"

In the hymn *Pange lingua*[1] Venantius fittingly exploited the
rhythm of the trochaic tetrameter. Just as triumphing Roman
generals had entered Rome to this measure, so the relic of the
True Cross was greeted at Poitiers. These are the exultant lines
of triumph still sung on Good Friday during the Veneration of
the Holy Cross. The poem begins with the statement of its
theme—the supreme conflict between God and Satan, and the
noble triumph held over the trophy of the Cross (for in ancient
warfare the *tropaeum*, the memorial of victory, was a tree hung
with spoils). Two stanzas are devoted to each of the three inter-
locked themes—First Fall, Incarnation, Redemption; and in the
final three stanzas the Cross itself is celebrated.

First came Satan's victory. The Creator of the world, grieved
at the error of Adam, "marked out the Tree which would repair
the losses of that earlier tree." For our salvation demanded that
He should "by guile deceive the guile of the Destroyer who
assumes many shapes, and seek a remedy from that source from
which the enemy had wrought harm."

Then, in the fullness of sacred time, the Son was sent forth,
becoming Flesh from the womb of a virgin. In a notably tender
stanza, Venantius lays emphasis on the helplessness of the Child,
confined in His narrow crib, His limbs closely bound by the cord
drawn tight. It is this helpless Child who thirty years later becomes
the sacrificial Lamb, hoisted on the trunk of the Cross. Here is
found the symbolism already noted in the poem *Crux benedicta*:

mite corpus perforatur; sanguis, unda profluit
terra pontus astra mundus quo lavantur flumine.

"His gentle Body is pierced; blood and water flow forth, and by

[1] II, 2. Not, of course, to be confused with the better-known *Pange lingua* of
St. Thomas, which deliberately echoes the first three words in acknowledgment
of the liturgical line of descent.

this river, the universe—earth, sea, and stars—is washed." The
blood flowing from the Body of Christ heals the whole of
creation.

Finally, Venantius hails the Cross, and repeating the mystical
concept of fertility already observed in *Crux benedicta*, calls it the
one noble tree, unique in its blossom, foliage and fruit. "Thou
alone wert worthy to sustain the world's Ransom"; this tree is
the place of safe-keeping for that ship-wrecked world. It is here
above all that Fortunatus's personal devotion for the Person of
Our Lord shines out: "Sweet wood, with sweet nails bearing
that sweet weight. . . . Bend thy branches, lofty tree, relieve
that distended Flesh. Relax thy native rigidity, and stretch gently
on thy trunk the limbs of the heavenly King."

So too in the *Vexilla regis*, now no longer part of the Good
Friday liturgy but still one of the best-known hymns in the
Breviary,[1] there is an emotional intensity which provides a
marked contrast to the theological precision of a Prudentius.
The hymn celebrates the mystery of the Cross (*Fulget crucis
mysterium*) which is the liberation of man by the Blood of the
Redemption. The structure is simpler than that of *Pange lingua*;
the first four stanzas describe Christ's crucifixion, the second four
are devoted to the Cross itself.

In the earlier section, emphasis is first laid on the mental
humiliation and the physical suffering undergone by the sacrificial
Victim. "He hung from a gibbet in the flesh, the Creator of all
flesh; His body pinned by nails, hands and feet extended, the
Victim here was sacrificed to achieve Redemption." Venantius
then brings out the purpose of the Sacrifice in the symbolism
familiar to us from the other hymns: "Wounded too by the
savage tip of the lance, He streamed forth water and blood to
cleanse us of our crimes." The fourth stanza lays stress on the
Crucifixion as the fulfilment of the prophecies of the Old Testament. David's prophecies are fulfilled: *regnavit a ligno deus*. It is
interesting to note here a correspondence with Jerome's first
revision of an older Latin translation of Psalm 95.10: *dicite in
gentibus quia dominus regnavit a ligno*. This clearly reveals itself
as a Christian addition to the Septuagint, where no "kingship

[1] The version in the Breviary differs from the hymn as originally composed.
The second stanza has fallen out; and the final two have been replaced by later
(? eleventh century) compositions.

from the Cross" is to be found. Fortunatus's dependence on Jerome is manifest here, and perhaps also elsewhere.[1]

The praise of the Cross in the second half of the poem develops at greater length the motifs observable in the other hymns. The tree was "marked out (*electa*) by reason of its worthy trunk to touch such sacred limbs": it was blessed, for "on its arms hung the Ransom of the world." Its bark is fragrant, its taste excels that of nectar. It is fecund in its harvest (*iucunda fructu fertili*). And in the final stanza, Venantius emphasises that God used the Cross to enact the supreme Christian mystery:

> . . . *qua vita mortem pertulit*
> *et morte vitam reddidit.*

Although these hymns on the Holy Cross are deservedly the best known of Venantius's writings, there are others which are worthy of study. One of these is a composition of about a hundred lines celebrating the festival of Easter.[2] It begins with the description (content and style are highly Vergilian) of the regeneration of the earth—the stars shining forth their joy, the flowers and trees renewing their splendour, the return of birds and bees, the whole universe combining in praise of the Creator:

> *laudant rite deum lux polus arva fretum.*

"Light, heavens, fields, deep render to God due praise." This is the victory of Christ the crucified, "who as God reigns over all"; the Saviour and Redeemer who "became a man to deliver man," who "the source of life and of the world, endures the rites of burial, and who, in granting the riches of salvation, enters upon the path of death." There follows an apostrophe to Christ, an eloquent appeal to the *pretium mundi*, the Ransom of the world, to leave the tomb, and to bring back to the world the light that shuns us when He is dead.

But Christ not merely renews the face of the earth, He also snatches "the countless throng" from the prison of death and from Satan: "From the jaws of the wolf the Lamb delivers his sheep." (This Biblical image of the sacrificial Lamb, lent an Ovidian

---

[1] See F. J. E. Raby, *Oxford Book of Medieval Latin Verse* (1959), p. 460. This excellent new edition, however, wrongly states that the hymns on the Holy Cross "are sung in the Roman Church on Maundy Thursday." This has never been the case, and now only the *Pange lingua* is sung (on Good Friday).

[2] III, 9.

paradox by the deliverance of the sheep, is also observable in *Crux benedicta*.) The souls of the dead are cleansed, and emerge a glistening army in splendid garments. The Shepherd takes joy in His snow-white flock.

Another theme in which Venantius takes a characteristic interest (for it is one of the most prominent features of pastoral teaching in this era) is the splendour of dedicated virginity. Here he was stimulated by the example of St. Radegund and the saintly Agnes, who had founded the double monastery of the Holy Cross, which was one of the first to insist upon strict and permanent enclosure. They had adopted the Rule of St. Caesarius of Arles, by which nuns had to spend two hours every day in study; and when St. Caesaria sent a copy of the Rule from the Convent of St. John at Arles, where she was Abbess, she recommended that every nun learn the psalter by heart, and be able to read. Holy Cross thus became a centre of vigorous spiritual and intellectual life; and when St. Gregory of Tours visited Poitiers after the death of Radegund, he found no fewer than two hundred nuns living the enclosed life.

The ideal of consecrated virginity was thus daily before Venantius's eyes to inspire his compositions on this theme, and in particular Radegund (whose life of piety, studious application, humility and charity shines out from his poems and from the biography written by her fellow-nun, Baudonivia) and Agnes, to whom his major poem on virginity is dedicated, were his exemplars. For Venantius the virgin's heavenly glory approximates to that of the martyr: "Amongst the lines of apostles and sacred prophets, the virgin gains rewards next to those of the martyrs," and she is adorned with jewels and splendid garments. She joins Mary in joyful celebration, as *virgo dei, fructus caeli, victoria mundi*.[1]

One of his longest poems, specifically called *De Virginitate*, is perhaps his most original in conception.[2] The scene is set in the hall of Heaven, where all await to applaud the entry of a consecrated virgin, and her reception by the heavenly Bridegroom. The patriarchs, headed by Abraham, are drawn up below the angels: Moses comes next leading the prophets: then the ranks of the apostles with Peter at their head, and the martyrs, who obtain equal reward, with Stephen in the place of honour.

[1] VIII, 4.   [2] VIII, 3.

"Next, the mother of God, Mary the goodly virgin shines forth, and leads the sheep of the Lamb's virgin flock. Surrounded in the midst of the maiden throng, she leads on her army gleaming with the light of chastity." Amongst them are Euphemia, Agatha and Agnes. Also there is Caesaria, "the glory of Arles in our own day, who through the advice of Caesarius shares undying glory by the resources of her virginity."

Venantius now digresses, at mention of Caesarius, to state that it was his Rule which Radegund was now imbibing:

> *cuius pontificis refluentia pectore mella*
> *colligit et rivos insatiata bibit.*

"She stores in her heart the honey of that Bishop in its abundant flow, and ever thirsty drinks his streams." And again, Venantius advises Radegund: "Follow Caesaria and Caesarius in heart, and fulfil their commands in body: imitate these bees that you may gain the flowers."

Next follows a splendid passage which celebrates the Virgin Birth. "Look to Him who willed to be born from a maiden's womb, and see from what flesh comes the flesh of our highest Lord. The Holy Spirit approached the virgin womb, desirous to live in a maiden's dwelling. God entered her who had no knowledge of men—a maiden who knew man only in her own Son." Though Sarah and Rebecca, Judith and Anna have gained their glory in heaven, "yet none of them deserved to beget the Father of the world. Mary who begot the Lord remains inviolate." There is a refreshing humanity in the portrait of Mary the virgin mother, which obviously draws inspiration from the Classical poets, yet at the same time the Biblical symbolism is never far away:

> *Intemerata deum suspendit ad ubera natum*
> *et panem coeli munere lactis alit.*

"Mary inviolate holds her divine Son to her breast, and with her gift of milk nourishes the Bread of heaven."

This glorification of Mary has a direct relevance to the next topic. Just as God chose a virgin to be His mother, so He is the Bridegroom of the consecrated virgin, for "He believes that the limbs which no violence stains, and which have been shared by no other, belong to Him. . . . Although God desires His kingdom to be for all alike, yet Christ is averse to sharing this as common possession—*virgineam solus vult habitare domum.*"

The Bridegroom is depicted as the warrior who goes forth in armour to rout the foe before returning to His bride to "implant chaste kisses on those consecrated cheeks." Fortunatus is pre-eminently a poet of two worlds, the Classical and the Christian, and here he has clearly adapted a Greek epic treatment to develop this theme. The assembly now gathers to celebrate the marriage; angels, prophets, apostles[1] bring their gifts. Every land sends its saint to represent it—Greece despatches Andrew, India Bartholomew, Africa Cyprian, "fruitful Britain sends the noble Alban." Thus "the nobility of heaven, rich with the Cross and the Blood of Christ, hastens to celebrate in union the future marriage."

There follows a most interesting and original section of seventy lines, in which God addresses His princes in praise of the unflinching constancy of His bride. "This maiden preserved the chastity which she had pledged to me. . . . Following with scrupulous mind her Bridegroom's steps, she comes undefiled in quest of my marriage-vows." He relates her griefs and perils in life—thorns, snakes, flying arrows, swords—through which she held her undeviating course. "Only love could have endured such hardships." "She hid her griefs from others, confessing them to none. . . . Whenever she saw My face in representation, she routed the tears from her eyes by implanting kisses with her lips. . . . Stiff with cold, she preserved My fire in her bones; in her frigid body her heart is warm with love."

God then recounts the prayers addressed to Him by the suffering virgin; here the Classical student notes the influence of Ovid's *Heroides*, a book of imaginary letters addressed by deserted women of legend to their lovers. The criticism has been made that the yearnings of the bride are drawn in a hypersensual way,[2] but this perhaps reveals a failure to comprehend the attraction exercised by such allegory under the influence of Biblical and Classical exemplars. "Tell me where You are, in what city I shall seek You. . . . Would that I could come if my poised foot could maintain its starry path amongst the constellations. . . . I wish to

[1] Including Peter and Paul, *hi quorum cineres urbs caput orbis habet*, reflecting the tradition that Peter was buried at Rome.
[2] See, for example, the comment of Tardi: "Peut-être le poète peint-il parfois avec des couleurs trop sensuelles l'amour des religieuses pour le fiancé céleste."

wash the stones before your feet, to wipe your shrines with my hair. Let me endure whatever will be; all hardships are sweet." God tells how He often lay with her to offer consolation, and to wipe away her floods of tears. "Now therefore let her reign and enjoy pleasing love, for she has long been joined to Me in heart." As God ends His proclamation, Heaven resounds with applause as her name is written in the eternal book.

One could wish that Fortunatus had decided to end his poem at this point. Instead, the final section of it is devoted to a comparison between the glories of virginity and the miseries of the married state. Here there is an unsubtlety of treatment, a bogus rhetoric in the description of the woes of motherhood which is reminiscent of the worst Ovidian excesses. But the poem as a whole is a remarkable and original achievement, casting a flood of light on the importance attached to the concept of the consecrated virgin in sixth-century Gaul. *Non veto coniugium, sed praefero virginis alvum* is Fortunatus's free adaptation of the Pauline dictum.

St. Augustine's exhortation to Christians to "bear off the gold and silver vessels" of pagan antiquity, and to employ them for Christian purposes, is met in a pleasingly literal way by the religious poetry of Venantius. His techniques of versification, his conceptions of rhetorical presentation owe much to the Augustans Vergil and Ovid. These "vessels" Venantius filled with new and potent inspiration; in particular, the compositions commemorating the Holy Cross play a decisive part in the creation of a new poetic tradition. From Rhaban Maur's *De laudibus sanctae crucis* to the *Pange lingua* of St. Thomas and beyond, Venantius's influence can be directly traced.

There is a remarkable picture of El Greco's which depicts St. Jerome in his cave. His Bible lies closed before him, and he trains his gaze steadfastly on the crucifix grasped in his left hand; the impression of concentrated devotion to Christ crucified is overwhelming. It is no idle *pietas* to attribute to St. Jerome much of the credit of Venantius's achievement. In the monastery of Jerome's foundation, through study of St. Jerome's translations and other writings, Venantius became animated by the same central passion. For him too, overshadowing all else, *Crux benedicta nitet.*

7. JOHN SCOTUS ERIGENA

Jean-Marie Déchanet

IN THE YEAR 850, an Irishman appeared at the court of Charles the Bald. His name was John, but he was called Scotus Eriugena[1]—a pleonasm, for the first name means Irish as well as Scottish, and the second, native of Erin or Eriu. John was a member of the Palatine School, the title given to the Emperor's academy of scholars. Charlemagne had gathered together at Aachen, Peter of Pisa, Paul the Deacon, Paulinus of Aquileia, and Eginpard; and Louis the Pious, his son, added Claudius and Clement the Irishman. It is during the reign of Charles the Bald, who held court at Quierzy-sur-Oise, in the Ile-de-France, that we come upon John Scotus in this galaxy. Whether he came of his own accord, or because the Emperor sent for him, we do not know; but very probably he had previously been a member of the Irish colony at Laon. At any rate, Ireland remained true to her custom of sending her choicest spirits to Gaul.

John at once made a name for himself, and was spoken of as "the famous Irishman at court." Then and afterwards he had many disciples—Martin the Irishman, "Master of the Schools of Laon," Heiric d'Auxerre, Remi d'Auxerre. At the beginning of his career he was a layman; later he became a deacon, and perhaps was ordained priest, though we do not know for certain. He began by teaching "grammar," the medieval term for profane learning, and his *Annotatio in Martianum Capellam* has come down to us, as well as a few commentaries (probably not authentic) and some poems on the Life and Passion of Christ, dedicated to Charles the Bald.

In 851, Scotus became involved in a controversy concerning Predestination. A wandering monk, Godescalc, had written a treatise in which he maintained that God predisposed men to

<hr/>

[1] Cf. Dom M. Cappuyns, *John Scot Erigène sa vie, son oeuvre, sa pensée.* Louvain, 1933.

A. Forest, *La Synthèse de Jean Scot Erigène*, in *Historie de l'Eglise* (Fliche et Martin), Paris, t. XIII, pp. 9 *et seq.*

evil and to hell, as well as to good and to heaven. At the request of Hincmar, Archbishop of Rheims, Scotus replied with a formal refutation. But the extreme position he adopted shocked the theologians; he ended by denying that there was any such thing as predestination at all. He insisted on a metaphorical interpretation of any texts in Scripture or the Fathers which affirmed either predestination to good, or a divine justice that punished the guilty. It is only the feebleness of human language which leads us to talk of prescience and predestination; in God, these two activities are not distinct. The book was condemned, and Hincmar did not seek credit for inspiring it; even though, compared with Ratramnus, Loup de Ferrière, Prudentius de Troyes, Florus and Remi de Lyon, the Archbishop of Rheims was in favour of some degree of emancipation from the more sombre formulas of St. Augustine. Indeed, Godescalc had been only too logical in their application.

This was no more than a passing episode in Scotus's life. He acquired his following not as a controversialist but as a translator. From his pen we have a Latin version of the writings of the Pseudo-Denys, translated from the Greek at the instance of Charles the Bald; a translation of the *Ambigua* of St. Maximus the Confessor; and of *De Structura Hominis* of St. Gregory of Nyssa. These translations had great influence in the Middle Ages, for John Scotus did more than merely translate his favourite authors; he became their champion. Through his lengthy studies of their works, the Greek Fathers became something of an obsession with him; and he set himself the task of showing how useful it would be to have recourse to their writings in defending and expounding the faith. This was his precise aim in his commentaries on the Pseudo-Denys,[1] and the Gospel of St. John, which survives only in fragments,[2] and in his masterpiece, *De divisione naturae*, which we shall discuss later on.

Erigena's was an age when St. Augustine, through countless popularisations, reigned supreme, when this contact with the Greek Fathers was in the nature of a revelation for Erigena. We can understand his enthusiasm when we think of the narrow confines of sacred science in his day, reduced to interpretations of St. Augustine that were one-sided when they were not down-right exaggerated, like Godescalc's.

[1] Migne, *Patres Latini*, cxxii, 126–284.   [2] *Ibid.*, 283–348.

To discover another and more optimistic anthropology than Augustine's, above all to discover the negative theology of the Pseudo-Denys, which opened up fresh perspectives on the mystery of God; all this was highly exhilarating for a mind as inquiring and open as Erigena's. He set about doing for the West what the Greek Fathers and the Pseudo-Denys had done for the East— providing a synthesis of Neo-Platonism and Christian thought. Audacious though the project was, Erigena was partially success- ful. But he was ahead of his time. His contemporaries were not equal to understanding what he was trying to do, and his system, as such, was disregarded. Yet in spite of his having no immediate successors, his ideas did have a profound influence, especially in the twelfth century, before they became so distorted that *De divisione naturae* was unreservedly condemned. It would be out of place here to analyse this work, condensed as it is and full of digressions, or to outline in any detail Erigena's system. I should like better to concentrate on a few of his ideas, and show how they constantly recur in the monastic writings of the twelfth century, restated, developed, and sometimes embellished.

But first, a word about the fate of the *De divisione naturae*. Before the twelfth century there was no word of criticism; rather, the book had a wide circulation and is to be found in many monasteries. "Numerous monks and scholastics," Honorius was to write in the bull of condemnation, "more interested in novelties than is expedient, are given to close study of this book." Of course, the dangers of such study did not go unrecognised. We quite often find marginalia in the manuscripts warning the reader to be on his guard for "there are some very obscure passages which could lead to confusion and error." But the main criticism made against Erigena from the beginning of the twelfth century is his undisguised preference for the Greek Fathers. Some of his critics cannot forgive him for it. As early as the ninth century Florus of Lyons calls him "an abominable heretic," simply because he resolutely avoided, in his treatise on predestina- tion, the use of certain Augustinian formulae and propositions. In the twelfth century, sinister rumours began to circulate against the author of *De divisione naturae*. In a work refuting Peter Abelard, a Norman Abbot wrote: "This passage is borrowed, if I am not mistaken, from Maximus, a Greek, whom John Scotus copied to the point of heresy." Elsewhere, William of Malmesbury, one of Erigena's defenders, says of him: "He has written a book which is certainly very useful in solving thorny problems. But he must be forgiven for what he says in some passages, because he is following the Greeks too closely and forsakes the path trodden by the Latins. This, incidentally, is the reason why he has been suspected of heresy."[1] William of St. Thierry, who quotes him several times, never dares to mention him by name, but says simply: *dixit quidam servus tuus, Domine* . . .

The storm broke in the thirteenth century, when Amaury de Bene took up certain propositions from the *De divisione* which, torn from their context, were clearly unorthodox. Amaury's disciples went further. They drew from Erigena's work conclusions which he had certainly never thought of himself. For them, "Everything was God" and "God was everything." The reign of the Father (incarnated in Abraham) had given way to the reign of the Son (incarnated in Jesus); now the Kingdom of the Holy Spirit had come, the reign of love. The Amauricians were going the way of the Albigensians. They were condemned in 1210 at the Council of Paris, which ordered the burning of their books. Among these was a much-vaunted treatise on the nature of man; it was none other than the *De divisione*. In 1215, Pope Honorius III, without naming Erigena, ordered a thorough search to be made for copies of this book; they were all to be sent to Rome for burning. Erigena was suffering for the sin of another. Very few copies of the book escaped; its author's name was long coupled with that of Amaury. Erigena's system and ideas passed into oblivion. He had tried to bring about a marriage between Plotinus and the Gospel. The masters who succeeded him were less daring, perhaps, but they succeeded where he failed. The union of Aristotle and the Gospel is with us to-day.

Until comparatively recently, the name of Erigena was hardly ever mentioned except to draw attention to his errors—his rationalism, pantheism, agnosticism, and others; although several more impartial studies had appeared. Dom M. Cappuyns' work, while not strictly a rehabilitation, does show that Erigena's thought can be given a perfectly orthodox interpretation so long as it is read with sympathy, as was the case with many monastic writers and scholastic theologians in the twelfth century. What Erigena did was to broaden the horizons of Christian thought.

[1] P.L. clxxix, 1652.

His attempt to harmonise the Latin and Greek Fathers was a real service to the Church. He was indeed a bridge between East and West, and the literature of mysticism owes much to him. If he did not leave his stamp on theology proper, he did exercise a profound influence on the thought of certain theologians and spiritual writers. Unhappily, no study as yet exists which would enable us to assess the precise effect of Erigenism on the medieval Spirituals. The following pages are an attempt to fill this gap.

One of the most important facets of Erigena's system is his intellectualism. It enables us to see how Erigena and those he influenced differ from the Latin Fathers, at the same time professing the highest regard for them, and claiming to follow their spirit as well as their thought. The chief aim of the Latin Fathers in their search after truth was a pastoral one—to minister to souls and to combat heresy. Their teaching was intimately bound up with morals. Their disciples, during the first eight centuries of the Church, were less concerned with overcoming their own ignorance and arriving at Christ's Truth, sought after for its own sake, as an object of contemplation, than with finding a rule of life, a direct and certain way to salvation and eternal life. Erigena's aims are very different—the result, no doubt, of his long contact with the Greek Fathers; and in his expression of them he has no equal amongst the Contemplatives of the West, with the possible exception of Augustine in his rare neo-Platonic moments. His "Hymn to Truth" explains to us at length the nature of these "intellectualist" tendencies:

I cannot deny that in the past I have been led into error by the false reasonings of human opinion, so far from Truth. I did indeed accept these positions, seduced by an appearance of Truth and, as often happens, by the senses. But nowadays I am coming back little by little, guided by the Holy Fathers. I have been called back from my own errors and those of others and led along the straight way by the rays of divine light. God's goodness never permits those who follow the Truth with humility and reverence to lose their way in the darkness of ignorance. He will not allow them to fall into the snares of wrong opinions, there to perish. There is no worse death than not to know the truth, no deeper abyss than to mistake the false for the true. Here is the very essence of error; from this source flow forth in man's mind shameful and abominable figments, which the soul, a prisoner to the bodily sense, desires and pursues as if they were true. She turns her back on the light and

G

vainly tries to clutch fleeting shades. Thus she falls headlong into a gulf of misery. For this reason we must pray without ceasing: O God our Salvation and our Redemption, Thou hast given us our nature, give us also Thy grace. Guide with Thy light those who grope for Thee in the night of ignorance. Draw us away from error. Stretch out Thy right hand to those who are weak, those who cannot, without Thee, advance towards Thee. Show Thyself to those who ask for nothing besides Thee. Sweep away the clouds of vain imaginings which prevent the spirit from seeing Thee, though invisible, in the way in which Thou dost deign to reveal Thyself to those who wish to gaze upon Thee face to face. These are they who seek their rest and goal, and beyond this have no desire; since nothing lies beyond the supreme and superessential good.[1]

Erigena is consumed, if one may use the phrase, by a thirst for knowledge, for strengthening his hold on reality, especially on God in the purity and simplicity of His Being, for advancing beyond imagination and conceptual knowledge. His intellectualism is emphatically not the kind which demands that faith should be dominated by reason. It is rather an aspiration for a higher order of knowledge, one that is itself sustained by faith. He wishes to make the fullest possible use of reason, with the aid of a special illumination from God, a divine gift which is never wanting to those who seek Him, in order to arrive at what he calls *Theoria, Altior ratio, Altior theoria, Contemplatio Theologica.* What does Erigena mean by these terms? To understand him, we have to take notice of his own system of psychology and the three distinct degrees of man's knowledge here below—from faith to the highest contemplation.

Here below, all true knowledge of the true God begins with faith. "Faith, in my opinion," he says, "is none other than the principle, a certain principle, from which knowledge of the Creator takes its rise in our rational nature."[2] It is first of all a sense knowledge, then a rational science and, finally, wisdom. Man is so constituted (and this for Erigena is an effect of sin) that he must have recourse to *sensus*, then to *ratio*, and at last to *intellectus*, which receives the divine illumination.

Simple faith has its beginnings in sense knowledge: *fides ex auditu.* For God, who is Truth, has enshrined Himself first and foremost in Sacred Scripture. It is there, by reading and hearing,

[1] P.L. cxxii, 649–50.   [2] Ibid., 516.

that we must humbly look for Him, and find Him. In the following prayer which corresponds to his invocation to Truth, cited
above, Erigena asks for grace to penetrate the meaning of the
Scriptures:

> O Lord Jesus, I ask for no other reward, no other blessing, no
> other joy, than to understand in a pure manner, without any error
> due to false speculation, Thy words inspired by Thy Holy Spirit.
> There indeed lies the summit of my happiness, the goal of perfect
> contemplation. Beyond that, even the most pure among rational
> souls will find nothing, since nothing is beyond. There is no place
> more fitting to seek Thee than in Thy Words; nowhere art Thou
> found more clearly than in them. There is Thy dwelling place,
> where Thou biddest those enter who seek Thee and love Thee.
> There will they find the spiritual banquet of true knowledge which
> Thou hast prepared for them; and going in before them, there Thou
> Thyself shalt serve them.[1]

Of course, to find God it is not enough merely to read the
Scriptures, or hear them read. The reason (*sensus interior*) must
work on what the *sensus exterior* has taken in. But it remains true
that everything must begin with the *sensus exterior*. This, for
Erigena, as well as for a number of twelfth-century Spirituals
who followed him, is an effect of original sin. If Adam had not
fallen he would have known God and Truth directly, without
having to pass through the deceiving world of sense. And if God
had not foreseen the Fall, He would not have given man the
gift of sense knowledge. This is a weakness which makes manifest
the inferiority of man's status compared with that of the angels;
it is also the cause of many errors.

Sacred Scripture is like a field; we must till it and sow it, a
laborious and difficult task. God has willed it so, and the Holy
Spirit has thus disposed it:

> Man must eat his bread in the sweat of his brow, the bread of
> God's word, and till the ground of Holy Scripture, covered with
> thorns and briars, that is, with a subtle complex of divine thoughts.
> Though there are no paths marked out, reason must stalk after
> wisdom with the steady tread of investigation, till she come upon
> the Lord's dwelling, the tabernacle of the God of Jacob. By constant
> and laborious study of Holy Scripture, under the guidance of divine
> grace, with its aid, co-operation and impetus, reason will recover

[1] P.L. cxxii, 1010.

that contemplation of Truth which was lost in the fall of the first man: and when she has found it again, she will delight in it, cherish it, dwell in it, and so find true repose.[1]

If we are to find the hidden God, we must ponder over all the various senses of Sacred Scripture. But we may hope to understand, and to arrive one day at wisdom, only if we start from simple faith (*simplicitas fidei*), which is based on the first, the literal meaning of Scripture: that is, on sense knowledge.

Erigena recognises another source of the knowledge of God besides the Scriptures—visible creation. He would hardly be a good Platonist if he did not apply himself to the text of St. Paul, "His invisible nature—His eternal power and divinity—has been clearly perceived in the things that have been made." The created world is a great book which man is invited to read. Abraham did not have the Scriptures—yet he knew God through looking at the world and the heavens. One must not look askance at philosophical reasonings; for by this means—by way of cause and effect—man can arrive at a knowledge of the Invisible through the visible. This was Plato's method; St. Paul does not accuse him of having erred concerning the reasons for visible creation, but of not having searched sufficiently beyond creation to the author of all creation Himself. Here again Erigena sees a consequence of sin—in the fact that man cannot arrive at a knowledge of God and His infinite perfections except through creatures. The danger of error is even greater than it is where the Scriptures are concerned, because man is always liable to lose his way by attributing to God qualities He does not possess, by thinking of Him as an inferior nature, whereas there is nothing visible, nothing tangible about God, nothing strictly that can be thought of at all. God is not just *more* beautiful than the fairest body, *larger* than the greatest bulk. There is a complete *dissimilarity*, a complete disparity between God and bodies which occupy space. For us then, the danger will always be to attribute to God qualities which He does not possess. But in this very danger Erigena sees a means offered to man of getting outside himself. Even though he risks losing his way, remaining below the level of reality (in the thorns and briars mentioned above), man is invited to raise himself, with God's help, towards an ever higher, ever purer, ever simpler form of knowledge. For man, to know is to be made

[1] *De divisione naturae*, I, c. 744.

pure, to be stripped of everything which has shackled and encumbered him since the Fall, and through the Fall. To know is the return to Paradise, to that mode of knowing "face to face," which once was his. To know is a religious act, an ascent to God—in Erigena's own words a *reversio*, a return.

The second stage in this ascent is the work of reason. Reason carries us back to first causes, penetrating the mysterious world of "ideas," of creative "energies," making use of "theophanies" or manifestations of God. Reason's task is to apply various names to God, or rather to learn how to tell the meaning of the different names we apply to God. Reason must interpret Biblical metaphors correctly, and discern what is there expressed, under the cloak of human language.

Nothing can be said worthily about God. Hardly a single noun, verb, or any other part of speech can be used appropriately of God, in the strict sense. How indeed could visible signs, intimately dependent as they are on the material, manage to express exactly this Invisible Nature which has nothing to do with any bodily sense? Indeed, It so far surpasses all understanding, that the purest spirit can scarcely attain to it. And yet, ever since the Fall, poverty-stricken human reason has been labouring with these words, these visible signs, to suggest and give some sort of a hint of the sublime richness of the Creator.[1]

Human reason, then, has to apply to God whatever is most appropriate. Some words are adequate in part: the verb "to be," for example—God *is*. Indeed this is the only thing we can say about Him with complete truth. It is what He says of Himself: *Ego sum qui sum.* There are other words which express God's reality, but only to some extent: *essentia, veritas, bonitas, virtus, sapientia, scientia.* God is all these, certainly—so long as we remember that whilst He is all these, He is far more than all of them, infinitely more than all that these expressions convey to us.

Many words and symbols, words transposed from the human order to the divine, are foreign to the Divine Nature. This is the case with many metaphors in the Bible. The role of reason is to see and see clearly whatever can, in some way or other, reveal God or something that has to do with God. One if its resources is to apply to God "whatever is best in us, most essential to our nature: being, essence, truth, virtue, wisdom, and so on"; whilst

[1] P.L. cxxii, 390.

at the same time making it quite clear that God surpasses them all infinitely. He is these things in a way that we are not. He is goodness, wisdom, love, infinitely more and infinitely better than we can ever conceive. Above all, He *is* these things in a quite different way from us.[1] At the end of this task of purification, the reason perceives that God absolutely surpasses everything, and that whatever we can and must affirm of Him, He is something still better. It is at this point that reason reaches Wisdom..

Above sense and reason is the intellect. It is the upper chamber where God comes to meet man, who is moving towards Him by means of sense-knowledge and reason. Here is a terrace which opens on Heaven and the world of divine things, bathed in the rays of eternal light; here the mind is illumined; here the man of desire finds the true contemplation of God. According to Erigena, this contemplation is "a completely simple and supernatural knowledge." It does not consist in an effort to reach a definition of God, nor in reasoning which carries us back through a series of effects to the First Cause of all things. It is a knowledge which apprehends the divine Excellence itself; ordinary knowledge conceives of this Excellence only by limiting it.

> This knowledge, simple beyond the nature of the soul itself, cannot be expressed in words (*interpellatione caret*); for the simple reason that no words can suffice adequately to represent God as He is, in His transcendence. He is not found in any essence, any substance, anything whatsoever which can be uttered or thought. He is above everything that exists, and above everything that does not exist. What He is cannot be defined in any way at all.[2]

Evidently, the soul does not arrive at this special knowledge all at once, but ascends to God by degrees. Its progress in this ascent is dependent on the purification which the knowledge of God itself effects, in proportion as the soul discards its former representations of God, based on sense and imagination. It gradually comes to realise that all its previous ideas of God were utterly inadequate. And yet such ideas contain in them something of God. Erigena called them "theophanies"—manifestations of God, a term which he inherited from the Pseudo-Denys, and one much in vogue in the twelfth century. It is because these theophanies have something of God in them, just as the created universe

[1] P.L. cxxii, 390-2.   [2] P.L. clxxxii, 572.

has, that visible things can lead us to Him who is Invisible. The precise purpose of visible creation is to reveal to us the majesty and immensity of the Divine Goodness, that this Goodness might receive the praise which is Its due.[1]

Physical creatures, then, are theophanies; and ideas, the manifestations in the intellect of eternal reasons and prime causes, these are more excellent theophanies. And when the special illumination is vouchsafed, as will ordinarily be the case with those who seek God with a pure heart, there are further divine manifestations, progressively higher and more simple.

It should be noted that this progress in purification takes place in the context of the life of faith. The most sublime idea of God which the human mind, illuminated by grace, can conceive, will still coincide in content with what faith and the Scriptures reveal to us of God's mystery. "I am who am," "My Father and I are one," all that is taught in the Prologue of St. John, all this the soul will see and grasp with an ineffable clarity. But before reaching this wisdom, this supernatural knowledge directly infused by God in a theophany differing in kind from the rest, the soul must have passed through the discursive, logical processes of "science," and the laborious, humble way of faith, *simplicitas fidei*. "It is through faith that one begins to understand"—Erigena brings new lights to this teaching in affirming strongly the continuity and the intimate connection between *fides* and *intellectus*. This is not to say that there is not a considerable distance between them which only divine grace can bridge.

The summit of contemplation—the gift of wisdom—lies in the awareness that God effectively surpasses all science; that, in His transcendence, He is absolutely none of those things which we affirm of Him. There are two theologies, both true, both exact, both of them necessary. The first proceeds from effects to causes, and to the Cause of all things. It applies to God the best of what it has found in His handiwork. It says of God that He is Essence, Truth, Goodness, Wisdom, Justice, Light, etc., and that *quasi proprie;* for even while it is so affirming, theological reason knows that nothing can, properly speaking, be affirmed of God, since He surpasses all intellect and all expression, whether of sense or intellect. The same theological reason applies a host of images to God. Erigena thinks that the simpler, cruder metaphors—like

[1] P.L. cxxii, 952.

those of the Bible—are the more fitting. Why? Because simple
souls are less likely to be led astray by them. They are less tempted
to mistake these representations for reality than if they had to
deal with loftier comparisons. It is quite clear that one and the
same theological reason, while affirming with all its strength,
must in the very same breath vigorously deny. When it says that
God is Goodness, essential goodness, it means the word to be
taken in an infinitely loftier sense than the one we normally give
to it. We have an idea of goodness; but however pure and lofty
that notion of ours may be it must fall short of grasping the
reality of God. Hence we must deny that God is goodness, truth,
justice.

When you have got hold of reason's way of looking at things,
you will see clearly that these two theologies which seem to be so
contrary, far from being opposed in any way, are in the most perfect harmony. Let us give an example which will make this clear.
Positive theology says "God is Truth"; negative theology says "God
is not Truth." The first does not say that the divine substance is,
properly speaking, truth, but only that one can use this metaphor
drawn from creatures to speak of the Creator. The second says that
God is not truth. It recognises, quite correctly, that the divine
nature is incomprehensible and ineffable, and so denies that He is,
properly speaking, truth. Negative theology despoils the Godhead
of all the attributes with which It is clothed by positive theology.
The one says "We can speak of God in this way," but what it does
not say is "God really is like this." The other says "God is not like
this," though it is possible for us to speak of Him in this way.[1]

Negative theology does not destroy positive theology, nor
vice versa. When the one attributes a quality to God, the other
refines on its meaning and bearing. When the one denies a quality,
the other limits the negation. But this refining, this limiting, is
only possible by the simultaneous use of both theologies, for
both are true.

We should note that the whole purpose of denial is to affirm
more strongly. What is denied is that God is "goodness" in our
narrow meaning of the word. But thereby God is affirmed as
superessential goodness. "Super"—a formula dear to Erigena,
expressing (in his own eyes, most happily) the exact nuance, the
precise measure of our knowledge of God. It suggests not
"nothing," but excellence.

[1] P.L. cxxii, 461.

All intellects seek after You, and always at one and the same time they both find You and are hindered from finding You. They find You in these theophanies where You appear in multiple guises, as if in mirrors; in the way that You permit us to know You, not as You are, but as You are not, and in Your existence. They cannot find You in your superessential nature, through which You surpass and exceed any intellect that moves and raises itself up to know You. To these You grant, in an ineffable way, the presence of Your apparitions. You leave them far behind because of Your excellence, beyond compare, and the infinity of Your essence.[1]

We must notice, however, that negative theology, just like positive theology, can be the product of reason. On careful reflection, we recognise that God must necessarily out-distance all we can think of Him. But usually negative theology is a grace, a form of that wisdom from on high of which we spoke earlier. It is something from heaven which imposes itself, and silences the reasonings of reason. "Never," writes William of St. Thierry in his *Enigma Fidei*, which seems to owe so much to the great Irishman, "never in this life does the human intelligence understand the Divinity better than when it recognises that it passes all grasp of our understanding. Silence is the attitude in which we ought to honour the reality of God."[2]

What has been said here is not intended as a résumé of Erigena's system, but simply to draw attention to the religious and mystical content of the work of a theologian too much ignored, and a thinker too little known and hard to get to know. If the truth be told, to grasp the full interest of Erigena's system one must have pored over the spiritual writings of men like St. Bernard (who has intellectual moments which recall Erigena), William of St. Thierry and Isaac de Stella.[3] In our familiarity with the *docta ignorantia* and the *Cloud of Unknowing*, it would be easy for us to dismiss Erigena's theory of mystical knowledge, as outlined above, as a banal rehash of old ideas; it is so easy for us to go back to the Pseudo-Denys. And certainly the Dionysian citations of Thomas Aquinas, and his commentary on the *De nominibus divinis* put Erigena completely in the shade. But he

[1] P.L. cxxii, 1010.   [2] P.L. clxxx, 426, 423.
[3] It will be enough to refer to Hourlier's edition of William of St. Thierry's *Traité de la Contemplation*, Sources Chrétiennes, Vol. 61, Paris 1959, pp. 41-6 and *passim*.

still remains the pioneer of strictly Dionysian ideas and formulae in our Christian West. Erigena was discredited; and this is another factor which has closed the eyes of many to the undeniable influence he had on the Middle Ages. A bold, somewhat subtle theologian, he was a servant of the Lord with a burning thirst for God and His Truth. And we are moved when we come across his powerful impact in the pages of the great saints and spiritual writers three centuries later. It is proper to invoke his memory.

8. ST. BRUNO

Humphrey Pawsey

" About St. Bruno we know very little." So wrote a recent
Benedictine savant who liked to delve into the Carthusians' past. Though he deplored the dearth of documentation, he pointed out that reserve has always been natural to
Carthusians: they speak about themselves and are spoken about
as little as possible. St. Anthelm and St. Hugh of Lincoln are
exceptions to this rule, because their elevation to the episcopacy
brought their virtues to light. They were obliged to live in the
world where biographers are to be found.[1]

Benedict XIV spoke in similar terms when he beatified the
cardinal Nicolas Albergati; Carthusian life, he said, was calculated
to make a man holy, not to make his holiness known. It is one
of the marks of all true greatness, and therefore of holiness, that
it should tend to be nameless; of every great deed and therefore
of heroic self-denial, that its doer strive to remain unknown.
"When thou dost an alms let not thy left hand know what thy
right hand doth, that thy alms may be in secret."

Guy I, Bruno's fourth successor as head of his hermits of
Chartreuse, wrote the first account about him, a short unbiased
monastic chronicle:

> Master Bruno, of German origin, from the renowned city of
> Cologne; of good family and of great culture, both secular and
> divine; a canon and master of a church second to none, in Rheims,
> Gaul; he gave up the world and founded and ruled for six years
> the desert of Chartreuse. He was obliged by Pope Urban, whose
> tutor he had been, to join the Roman Curia, to counsel and sustain
> the Holy Father in ecclesiastical affairs. Unable to endure the turmoil
> and procedure of the Curia, and longing keenly for the solitude
> and tranquillity he had left, he resigned his post. He refused to
> accept the archbishopric of Reggio to which he had been elected

[1] André Wilmart: *Chronique des Premiers Chartreux*, Revue Mabillon, Mars
1926.

at the Pope's bidding. He then retired to a hermitage in Calabria, called La Torre. Here he died and was buried about ten years after leaving Chartreuse.[1]

That was all, and during centuries Bruno remained as nameless to the world as the plain wooden cross over the grave of any one of his sons. A true hermit's desire is to be hidden not only in life but in death. If Bruno is now remembered, it is not for his remarkable culture and high ecclesiastical offices, but because he renounced all this for the solitary life, the life of pure prayer. There are books about him, and they reveal local colour as varied as his portraits: Le Sueur's in the Louvre, Zurbarán's at Cadiz. One day, perhaps, a St. Bruno whom no one knows, not even his biographers, will be revealed. But this revelation is not a task for a Carthusian, whose solitary life hardly affords the facilities for the necessary research, correspondence and conversation which the writing of a definitive biography would demand.

Bruno is acknowledged by his contemporaries to be an outstanding theologian—"a doctor of doctors." There is a commentary in the Psalms of this period, almost certainly his,[2] which may be taken as representative of his spiritual teaching. It marks him out as learned in all the sacred sciences and filled with the Holy Spirit. In it we catch a glimpse of the Seminary Professor teaching his young students; but with a richness of methodology and a spiritual fervour so often absent from the treatises of the later Scholastics.

No one can attain to eternal happiness by morality alone. They are the blessed ones who walk in the law of God and keep themselves undefiled on their journey, who do not make idle enquiries but examine His testimony closely, who strive in all sincerity after a spiritual understanding of His decrees which are secret, set forth in parable and mystery . . . and rise thence to find Him in contemplation, with all their hearts' affection set on Him. Blessed indeed are they who turn from this world's cares, and gaze longingly upon Him, seeking Him alone with the heart's whole love.[3]

Bruno is here giving forth his reflections on the great Psalm 118

---

[1] Migne, *Patres Latini* CLII, 12.
[2] Cf. A. Landgraf, *Collectanea Franciscana* VIII, 1938, p. 542. The author adds that this Commentary entitles Bruno to be called the Father of Scholasticism.
[3] P.L. CLII, 1259.

Beati Immaculati in via, which, in the view of so many of the early commentators, maps out the course of the spiritual life. In his interpretation, Bruno constantly applies the principle laid down in his preface, of the Patristic three senses of Holy Scripture, the literal, the moral and the mystical or spiritual. The literal sense is to be explained consistently in reference to the spiritual; for this latter is the sense which the Holy Ghost particularly has in view in the Psalms, and which alone gives true understanding of them. Hence we must proceed from the literal to the mystical via the moral, from the moral life to the contemplative life, from earthly things to heavenly. Bruno is at one with all the spiritual writers of his time in insisting that though one may save one's soul by Christian moral living, there can be no perfect living without contemplation:

> Thou art my God and my King, Lord Jesus, my Creator and my Guide, effecting and ruling all the good that is in me. I shall exalt Thee ceaselessly in this life by my activity . . . and I shall praise Thee with an everlasting praise: that is, I shall glorify Thee with the glory of the contemplative life—here and in the life to come, according to the Gospel: "Mary hath chosen the best part, which shall not be taken away from her."[1]

In Bruno's age, the problem of relating the active part of Martha and the contemplative part of Mary was, for everyone but the monk, a personal problem of preserving sufficient freedom for contemplation in surroundings not organised for it. For the monk, no such problem existed. The active life, in our restricted sense of the exterior apostolate of preaching, teaching and the press, had not entered into, was foreign to, the monastic ideal. Monks were always active—*ora et labora*; but, at the most, their activity was that which they exercised in the words and works of fraternal charity within their community. A monk belonged not only to, but inside his own monastery—heart and mind. This is the context of such comments as: "and lest contemplatives should deem it harmful to descend from the summit of contemplation to the level of their neighbours' needs, Paul says you are to know that in every one of these you are serving the Lord." Bruno here is not encouraging the monk to go forth from his monastery, and engage in the "active" life. Each must serve the Lord in his own sphere—the cleric and

[1] P.L. CLII. 1396—Psalm 144.

layman in the exterior ministry, the monk, normally speaking, exclusively in his monastery. But we must notice also that in texts such as these, Bruno is not treating *ex professo* of contemplation and the contemplative life. Typical of his period he wrote no technical treatise of spirituality. The spirituals of his day were still what they were in the sixth century—eminent practitioners of the interior life, creators rather than exponents of the tradition from which the spiritual literature of the following century was to flow. The spiritual outlook is to be gathered from the historical background, occasional references, but especially from letters. It is epistolary literature which gives us a real insight into the monastic environment.

Bruno, who was born in 1030 and died in 1101, flourished towards the end of the "monastic age of spirituality," when monks were the more eminent and numerous of the spirituals. At this period the only form of religious life in the West, Celtic monasticism apart, was Benedictine, which had come to colour the whole outlook and activity of the Church in the West. But the new spiritual search, in which Bruno shared, was to lead either to a new realisation of the Rule, as at Cîteaux, to a return to the more contemplative past, as at Chartreuse, or to the birth of an entirely new religious form of life, one which by definition was to fulfil part of its vocation as an apostolate in the outside world, the Canons Regular of Premontré. Just as Cîteaux stands for more than mere discontent with a Cluny become wealthy and relaxed, so Chartreuse represents something other than disappointment with relaxation in general. It is rather a deliberate divergence from Molesme-Cîteaux; yet one which remains within the framework of the cenobitic Rule. Besides, these new founders were men of the superior culture which they had helped to create, Bruno and Stephen Harding, for instance, can compare favourably with Anselm and his contemporaries, masters of that intellectual revival which kept pace with the spiritual rebirth within the Church.

Entries on his bede-roll praise Bruno the master, the defender of the Church; but the majority praise his eremitical vocation: "Bruno the chief hermit," "the model of all those who lead the solitary life." He had sacrificed riches and a promising ecclesiastical career, faithful to a vow he had made to become a monk. He saw but did not accept Benedictine Molesme at the height of its fervour. And he found at last, in the alpine fastness of Chartreuse, the environment fit for that life of penance and prayer which he and his few followers longed for. Here they arrived in 1084, and here they remained faithful to their eremitical calling. They kept the solitude for which they had given up so much; and the only legacy they bequeathed to mankind was the example of their life of prayer without compromise. They wrote nothing about it.

But Guy I, "the Venerable," Bruno's fourth successor as head of the hermits of Chartreuse, who had lived with some of the Master's first companions, embodied his spirit in the *Customs*—the first official Carthusian document. Guy was prevailed upon by Hugh, bishop of Grenoble, to set the Customs down in writing for other local groups of hermits. He had been a solitary for twenty years when he did so, in 1127. Regretfully, only out of obedience, conscious of the anomaly of breaking the silence to speak about the silent life, he says:

> We have put off this task for a long time for motives which seemed reasonable to us; that is, because almost everything of a religious nature we are in the habit of doing here we believed to be contained either in the letters of blessed Jerome, or in the rule of blessed Benedict, or in the other authoritative writings. Furthermore, we considered ourselves in no way fitted to undertake or attempt any such thing. For we held it to be a part of our hidden way of life to be taught instead of to teach, to be a wiser thing rather to proclaim the blessings others enjoy than our own: for Scripture says, "Let another praise thee, and not thy own mouth: a stranger and not thy own lips." Our Lord in the Gospel also bids us: "Take heed that you do not your justice before men, to be seen by them." But since we are bound not to oppose the wishes, the authority, the affection of persons so important, let us recount, with His help what the Lord has granted us.[1]

Bruno and his followers saw the solitary life reflected in the lives of those "Holy Fathers on earth before us"—the great patriarchs and prophets, John the Precursor and the Desert Fathers; but most of all in the life of Our Lord Himself. So Guy writes in a note appended to his *Customs*:

> About the solitary life we need say very little, for we know how highly it is commended by so many holy and learned men whose

[1] P.L. CLIII, 631.

authority is such that we are not worthy to be called their followers. . . . And Jesus Himself, God and Lord, whose virtue is not increased by His Hidden life nor diminished by His public life was yet tried, in a manner, by temptations and fasting in solitude. Holy Scripture tells us that He left the throng of His disciples and went up alone into the mountain to pray. And when the time of His Passion was at hand, He left His apostles in order to pray by Himself. By His example He emphasised strongly how very favourable is solitude to prayer; for He was unwilling to pray together with His followers, even with the apostles.[1]

Bruno was remarkable for his friendship. Guy says of him that he was the very likeness of integrity, sincerity, and maturity: of a love that was fathomless. He had made his vow to become a monk with friends, he came to Molesme with friends, and he arrived at Chartreuse with yet other friends; and after his release from the service of Urban III, we find him in Calabria, leading the solitary life with other friends still. It is important to notice that in practice, if not in theory, a certain association of solitaries can often bring an added perfection to the solitary life. The anti-social individual could not stand the society of other solitaries. In an eremitical monastery, where the deliberate control, effected by religious obedience, safeguards the supernatural orientation of the whole personality, he would fail in stability. It was mainly for mutual moral support, in the lonely life of faith which true solitude of necessity implies, that Bruno introduced into the solitary life that cenobitic element borrowed from St. Benedict and earlier models. It is this element which supplies the necessary minimum of juridical dependence for the attainment of Christian perfection: the watchful eye of the master who loves his disciples, the holy rivalry and solicitude of the brethren.

In every new development of Western monasticism, there has been renewed contact with the authentic tradition of the East. Dom Jean Leclerq goes so far as to say that this tradition is to Western monasticism what the apostolic tradition is to the faith of the Church.[2] In Bruno's time, of the twenty-six Fathers regarded as the institutors of the monastic life, only four were Latins; and one of these was St. Jerome, at that time often considered as an oriental.

[1] P.L. CLIII, 769–70.
[2] L'amour des lettres et le désir de Dieu, p. 88.

St. Bruno belonged to this eremitical current which drew its inspiration from the tradition of the Fathers of the Desert. And if he did not equal their ascetical performance, he was their peer in zeal for loving contemplation, contemplation in love. The solitary life was never more flourishing in the West than in his time, when the ideal *de contemptu mundi* was driving religious men all over Europe into solitude. Later, William of St. Thierry, in his *Golden Epistle*, addressed to Bruno's sons of the Charter-house of Mont Dieu, summed up their Father's spiritual legacy, and outlined their vocation in the light of this same eremitical tradition of the desert. He hoped to see them, he says, "implanting in the darkness of the West and the cold of Gaul the light of the East and the ancient religious fervour of the monasteries of Egypt."[1]

At the same time Bruno was a European, not an oriental, and this fact marks the spirit of his reform. The particular accents in which he proclaimed to his sons the eastern teaching is echoed for us in two letters, the only writings attributed to him whose authenticity remains undisputed. He wrote them from his hermitage in Calabria, towards the end of his life. They reveal the old man's exquisite feeling, his heart and soul refined by years of contemplative prayer. Above all, they reveal his qualities as friend and mentor, delicate and guileless, and a love founded entirely in God.

The first of them is written to Raoul le Verd, Provost of the Church of Rheims:

> Your loyalty to an old and tried friendship is all the more noble and praiseworthy for being a thing so rare amongst men. Although a great distance and a greater span of time keep us apart in body, yet nothing can separate your soul from that of your friend.

Bruno goes on to describe the wilderness of his Calabria— its gentle climate, the natural charm of the mountains, valleys, trees, fields, rivers and springs. But he had not chosen Calabria for its radiant beauty any more than he had Chartreuse for its cold, bold majesty, but both precisely for the solitude they assured:

> Why should I dwell on all this? The things which delight a wise man, the things of heaven, are more agreeable and worthwhile by

[1] P.L. CLXXXIV, 309.

H

far. Still, these others often refresh the more delicate soul extended by a rather severe discipline and spiritual exercises, and bring it relief. The bow continuously strung tends to become slack and unfit for service. The advantage and delight that solitude brings to its lovers, they alone know who have experience of it.

A solitary is never less lonely that when alone, for he has God the more. Bruno, true to the eremitical tradition, associates silence with contemplation, solitude with the contemplative life, to the point of identifying them. Solitude and silence are not merely negative. They stand for what this self-denial alone can obtain: the complete self-dedication and love which seems possible only in solitude.

Here one learns to look with that serene gaze which wounds the Bridegroom with love: the spotless, undefiled beholding. Here is busy leisure and restful activity. Here God rewards his athletes with the longed-for prize, that peace which the world knows not, and joy in the Holy Spirit.

It is this consuming love of God, this overwhelming desire to possess the Divine Goodness, which is the root of Bruno's vocation, and of every Carthusian vocation; a love, a desire which imposes a sacred obligation:

Recall the day, my friend, when you and I and Fulk·. . . afire with divine love promised and vowed to the Holy Spirit to abandon without delay the fleeting things of the world and to strive after things eternal, and to assume the monastic habit. . . . But what is so fair, so beneficial, what so inborn, so becoming human nature as to love the good? And what else is as good as God? Rather, what else is good besides God? Wherefore the chosen soul, perceiving in some measure the matchless grace, splendour and beauty of this good, aflame with the fire of love, declares: "My soul hath thirsted after the strong and living God: when shall I come and appear before the face of God?" O, that you would not scorn a friend's advice nor lend a deaf ear to the voice of the Spirit of God.[1]

In his second letter, to his own brethren of Chartreuse, Bruno elaborates on the high grace of the eremitical vocation, "your blessed lot and God's bountiful grace in you." It is the divine deliverance from the dangers of the world, the heavenly port after raging storm, the longed-for home of the exile and the traveller. In a special message to the laybrothers of the community,

[1] P.L. CLII, 420.

the man of letters shows himself aware of the dangers of the new learning. His praise of the *docta ignorantia* would have stigmatised him, had he lived a century later, as an anti-intellectual.

Of you, my dearly beloved laybrothers, I say this: My soul doth magnify the Lord, for I see the greatness of his mercy towards you . . . for although you are unlettered, yet God the mighty has, with his finger, written in your hearts both love and understanding of his sacred songs. For in your deeds you declare what you love and what you know. Since your practice of true obedience is both careful and keen, it is clear that you have plucked the very sweetest and most wholesome fruit of divine Scripture. Obedience is the fulfilment of God's decrees, the key and the seal of all spiritual discipline. It cannot exist without great humility and an uncommon patience. Chaste love of the Lord and true charity go with it always. Therefore, my brethren, hold the ground you have gained, avoid like the pest that sickly herd of those worthless ones who hawk the world with their writings, and who hum and haw about things they neither understand nor esteem, to which their speech and behaviour give the lie. . . .[1]

A note added to his bede-roll (the obituary letter circulated at his death) says of him: "Bruno deserved praise on many counts, but on one above the rest: his equanimity, the even temper of his ways. At all times his look was cheerful, his speech moderate. Paternal strength and maternal tenderness were joined in him."[2] When the bede-roll reached the Monastery of Our Lady at York, the monks wrote on it: "His fame informed us, even before your letter did, not indeed of the man's death, but of his goodness."[3] Prayer tends to simplify the soul, and the thought of the man of prayer gradually resolves itself into one steady gaze towards God. Its expressions which once were protracted became short and aspiratory. The eastern "Prayer of Jesus" and Richard Whitford's "Jesus Psalter" are examples of this regular respiration of the soul. For St. Hugh of Lincoln it was the repetition, even in sleep, of the mystic word so often on Our Lord's lips, "Amen . . . slowly, silently, pausing, most quietly, at intervals, now more often, now less."[4] For Hugh's father and master, Bruno, it was *O Bonitas*: our exclamation "Goodness." But for him the word was a definition of God,

[1] P.L. CLII, 49122.   [2] *Ibid.*, 554 C.   [3] *Ibid.*, 591 C.
[4] *Vita Magna S. Hugonis*, p. 82.

and the meaning of the goodness he saw everywhere and in everyone: the measure of his own.

The vocation of St. Bruno was to a life of pure prayer, one for which he renounced the active apostolic life of preaching and teaching. Pius XI, in his frequently-quoted apostolic Letter *Umbratilem*, declares that Bruno was divinely chosen to reform the contemplative life as such, to restore it to its pristine vigour, and thereby to assert its superiority in the hierarchy of divine vocations. "For no more perfect state and rule of life than this [the eremitical] can be proposed for men to adopt and embrace, if the Lord calls them to it."[1] The importance of St. Bruno in the history of the Church's spirituality is that his life emphasises the degree of inward holiness demanded from those who lead the solitary life, and the effect of their intimate union with God on the body of Christ, the Church.

To-day, it is fashionable to seek out the faults of the saints, to seek to see in them something of our own failings. Modern hagiographers tend to look askance at the hyperbole of Gaubert of St. Quentin of Beauvais who declares: "Bruno was the only man of his time who had renounced the world."[2] Bruno is an obscure figure on other counts as well. It is not certain whether he ever became a priest; and there is no record of what part he played in the Roman Curia, when called thither by Urban. But all this is of minor importance when compared with his providential mission to restore to its first vigour the more perfect form of Christian perfection, the contemplative life.

Bruno, like every authentic solitary, went into solitude for the one end, to grow in greater awareness of, and nearness to God, to God Incarnate, Jesus Christ, and in necessary consequence, in Him, to be more aware of and near to every other Christian, to mankind, on the spiritual plane, in terms of the eternal values of truth and love. The perfection to which all without discrimination are called, "Be you therefore perfect, as your heavenly Father is perfect," is absolute only in Jesus Christ, our Head. For us, His members, His perfection is diversified in the several ways and states of the Christian life, that it may be realised not only by each individual, but by us all as a whole, the Church. Our age of specialisation easily appreciates this.

No one of us, no one special way, claims to be more than a

[1] *Acta Apostolicae Sedis*, 1924, p. 385.   [2] P.L. CLII, 578 A.

part in, an aspect of the perfection of the others. God our Father certainly hears the melody of each one's song, the prayer which is the individual Christian life. But He listens to the beauty, truth and love of the harmony, of the symphony He intends, human-divine, of prayer and activity. The lives of Martha and Mary amount to more than a sum of notes, more than a mere juxtaposition of parts. And if Holy Mother Church, in singling out Bruno's spiritual mission, makes the point of reiterating the hierarchy of vocations, the scale of the ways of perfection, it is also true that the most perfect are not necessarily nor always those called to the more perfect state of life. God, and He alone, if He so wills, can do a better work with a blunt or broken tool, can model better in a poorer clay, and to His greater glory He often does so. No truth is more fundamental in the solitary life than this.

The solitary life, painful to begin with, grows easy as one advances and becomes heavenly in the end. In adversity steadfast, in uncertainty trustworthy, it is unassuming in success. Sober in victuals, simple in attire, circumspect in speech, chaste in its ways, it is greatly to be ambitioned for being unpretentious itself. . . . It is given to study, particularly of the Scriptures and spiritual writings, where the marrow of meaning engages it more than the froth of words. And what will surprise you and what you will praise the more, is that it is a constant contemplative leisure because it is never a lazy one. Indeed, it so increases its service that more often it lacks time than a choice of things to do . . .[1]

About St. Bruno we know very little. In his age "many were the men in search of contemplation, but never has it been so little written about." In our day, the silence is frequently broken, that more may hear about the silent life. Yet in spite of all the wonderful and profound things said about it, its essence, supernatural silence, is not definable by talk. Master Bruno said all that can be said of it, in the lapidary statement, repeated by all contemplatives: "they only know it who have had experience of it." The only possible, profitable, breaking or penetration of this silence, this mystery of solitude, is when the soul itself breaks through its barrier, by grace and courage plunging into a deeper interior silence still, a purer and more powerful and universally efficacious prayer of faith.

[1] Cf. The letter of Guy, Prior of Chartreuse, 1109-27, in *Révue d'Ascetique et de Mystique*, 14, p. 337.

9. ST. BERNARD OF CLAIRVAUX[1]

William Yeomans

"I HAVE FOUND by experience that the English are more inclined to be dreamers than the French," wrote Pierre de Celle, a contemporary of St. Bernard. Be that as it may, one Englishman at least, St. Stephen Harding, was wide awake enough to recognise in the young Bernard of Fontaines-Lès-Dijon the makings of a saint. In all justice to Pierre de Celle, it must be admitted that St. Stephen would have been a very unobservant dreamer had he not detected something out of the ordinary in this novice whose force of character and fervour were the inspiration of the thirty companions he brought with him to Cîteaux. But St. Stephen also had the courage of his convictions when in 1115, only three years after Bernard's entry into the young Cistercian Order, he sent him out to make a new foundation. The *seniores* of Cîteaux were surprised (one might even say nettled) for Bernard was only twenty-five years old and not yet ordained, and they may have felt that on this occasion their holy Abbot had nodded. However, those who survived to see the rapid growth of the new foundation of Clairvaux, and the immense prestige and influence of its Abbot, would have had ample matter for meditation on those words —"A seniority there is that claims reverence, owing nothing to time, not measured by the lapse of years; count a man grey-haired when he is wise, ripe of age when he is without stain."[2] But they were Cistercians and would have asked for nothing better than such an object-lesson of the truth of that book which was their staple diet—the Bible.

[1] St. Bernard's works are in Migne, P.L., vol. 182 (letters and treatises), vol. 183 (sermons). The critical edition in nine volumes, of which two have already appeared, is being prepared by Dom Jean Leclercq, O.S.B.
[2] Wisdom 4: 8–9.

It is no exaggeration to say that the surest way of understanding Bernard is to approach him through the Bible.[1] Any single page of Bernard reveals his constant use of the Bible. But he does not regard the Scriptures merely as a source of apt quotation; if he pores over the sacred text it is because "it is the source of life and my soul knows no other."[2] Bernard drew the inspiration of his spiritual doctrine from the Bible, and he elaborated it by reflecting on the Bible with the aid of the great commentators, especially Origen, Jerome, Ambrose, Augustine, and Gregory the Great. It is the traditional method of exegesis by means of the four senses of Scripture which furnishes him with a method of reflection and a means of expression. Finally it is to the Bible that we must look for the meaning he attaches to the vocabulary of the spiritual life. He may, for example, use the language of the Stoics to speak of the virtues and the affections of the soul, he may borrow a definition from the philosophers, but the content of that vocabulary is biblical. Bernard's way of thinking is not that of the Scholastics, and he is "the last of the Fathers" primarily because of his attitude to the Bible.

When Bernard uses the phrase—the word of God—that term often includes the two meanings of the Incarnate Word and the written word of God. Just as the Word made flesh resumes in Himself the fullness of the Godhead, so in the written word of the Bible is contained the unique revelation of the divine mystery. The Bible contains no other mystery than that of Christ, for it is He who gives to the Scriptures their unity and their meaning. It is Christ who is the principle of that unity for He is everywhere present, pre-figured in the Old Testament and revealed in the New, hence "His coming was not that of someone who was absent, but the manifestation of someone who was hidden."[3] The shadows of the Old Testament disappear before the light of Christ. He is revealed in the great figures of the Patriarchs and Prophets, and even long before them, for He is also the new Adam. This unifying presence of Christ makes the Bible as a whole the heritage of the Christian. It is the Church's history because it is the history of Christ. Hence only the Christian can

[1] Cf. P. Dumontier, *St. Bernard et la Bible* (Paris 1953), and especially Père de Lubac's incomparable *Exégèse Médièvale* (Paris 1959).
[2] P.L. 183, 849 A, In Cant. 16: 1.
[3] *Ibid.* 43 D, In Adv. Dni. 3: 1.

read the Bible and attain its true meaning—*pars mea haec qui in Christum credo.*[1]

Speaking of the life of Christ, Bernard can say, "Whatsoever works He performed before men, all that He spoke and endured, He so accomplished that there was not the least moment, not even one iota which did not have its place in the hidden plan of God, not one that escaped the divine mystery."[2] The same expression comes naturally to Bernard when he refers to the Spirit who speaks in Scripture—"when he speaks it is not possible for one iota not to have meaning."[3] There is then nothing unimportant in the Bible "nor is it permitted without sacrilege to treat any of his (the Spirit's) words, no matter how small, as if superfluous or inept."[4] This principle of exegesis becomes a principle of the theology of the spiritual life: "what happened historically in the Head must, we believe, be brought about later on in the life of his Body."[5] The Christian life is the entry into the mystery of Christ in all its dimensions, and in His mysteries the whole history of the Old Testament finds a meaning for the Christian. This assimilation to Christ is effected through the Bible, in the framework of the liturgical seasons of the Church. Bernard can thus speak of the mystery of Advent and the mystery of Lent because he sees that each moment of the liturgical life of the Church, pregnant with the mystery of Christ, binds the members of the Church progressively closer to their unique Mediator.

Bernard's reverence for the Bible and his deep conviction of its unity have their source in his belief that the living God has made it His dwelling-place. But to find the inspiration for his ardent study of the Bible (it was said that he knew it by heart) we must go a step further. God does not simply speak everywhere in the Scriptures, He addresses His words *to us*, He reveals Himself for our sakes. The *propter nos homines* of the Incarnation is the *raison d'être* also of the Bible. The history related in Scripture shows clearly "how full of solicitude the divine majesty has been lest it should lose us for all eternity."[6] Hence it would be the grossest effrontery to neglect the divine word, to turn a deaf ear to the words which God speaks expressly for our comfort and instruction. The three divine Persons have poured their infinite

[1] P.L. 1134 D, In Cant. 73: 2.   [2] *Ibid.* 260 A, In Dom. Palm. 3: 1.
[3] *Ibid.* 716 B, De Div. 93: 1.   [4] *Ibid.* 982 B, In Cant. 40: 1.
[5] *Ibid.* 682 C, De Div. 58: 2.   [6] *Ibid.* 326 D–327 A, In Fest. Pentec. 2: 2.

power and wisdom and love into the work of salvation, and to spurn the Scriptures would be to make light of their labours. It is the realisation that God has chosen the Scriptures for His meeting-place with man which makes Bernard scrutinise their every letter. The infinite Creator of the universe puts Himself at the disposal of man in the pages of the sacred text, speaking to him in words and gestures which he can understand; such divine courtesy can in Bernard's estimation provoke only one response— let us approach with joy the fountains of the Saviour. But the Bible is more than a meeting-place between God and man, it is a tryst, for God is love. The divine majesty yields before His infinite love, so that He does not summon man to His presence, He does not impose Himself from on high, rather, becoming man He exchanges the transcendence of the "I am who am" for the loving companionship of the "I am with you all days." Bernard reads this supreme revelation in every line of the *Canticle of Canticles* which finds its true meaning in terms of Christ and the Church, the Word and the soul and "sings the praises of Christ and His Church, the grace of sacred love, and the mysteries of that eternal marriage."[1]

This enables us to see why Bernard attaches importance to the reading of Scripture, the *lectio divina* of St. Benedict, that reverent, prayerful search for the Word in the word. Reading the Scriptures is not merely an exercise of the memory and intellect, though it implies a careful study of the text and of the patristic commentaries on it. It is a work which engages the whole man, all his faculties and all his affective powers. The Scriptures are known only when they are lived, when they are translated into terms of one's own experience.[2] "The word of God is the bread of life and the food of the soul. . . . Therefore let it descend into the very entrails of your soul; let it pass on into your affections and actions."[3] The capacity of the soul to understand the mysteries of Scripture is in Bernard's mind strictly equivalent to the closeness of its union with Christ. For this reason he introduces his sermons on the Canticle with the words: "The things I have to say to you, brethren, are not those I would say to people in

[1] P.L. 788 B, In Cant. 1: 8.
[2] Cf. P. Claude Bodard, *La Bible—expression d'une expérience religieuse chez St. Bernard*, in *St. Bernard Théologien, Analecta Sacri Ordinis Cisterciensis*, July– December 1953.
[3] *Ibid.* 51 B, In Adv. Dni. 5: 2.

the world, or rather I shall say them in a different way."[1] The assimilation of Scripture is a becoming like unto Christ and therefore a grace of the Spirit; and hence the *Canticle of Canticles* is to be proposed only to those who are prepared to give themselves entirely to Christ.

To describe this prayerful search, under the guidance of the Spirit, for a living contact with Christ in the Scriptures, Bernard turns naturally to metaphors drawn from the refectory. Indeed the whole digestive process, and especially those audible expressions of satisfaction and repletion which eastern courtesy demands and western good manners abhor, are used as an analogy of the assimilation of the Scripture and the consequent showing forth of Christ in deed and word. He sees the monastic audience as rows of hungry mouths (which in all probability they were) eagerly agape to receive the good bread which he, the *fidelis coquus*, will serve them smoking hot from the oven of his meditation. To these gourmets of the word of God he gives cakes of the finest flour. Or he encourages them to champ the honeycomb of the letter and extract the sweetness of the Spirit, or it may be the marrow from the bone or the nut from the shell.[2] The word of God is to be ground up by these *ruminantes*, to be relished and savoured, digested and assimilated. Then at last comes the magnificent regurgitation, the *ructus*—which are the Sermons which have earned for Bernard the title of *Doctor Mellifluus*. He was so called not primarily on account of the rhetorical elegance of his discourses but because his words are redolent of the rich aroma of the Spirit, every line full of the sweetness of the Lord. *Doctor Mellifluus* is a tribute to Bernard as an exegete not as a latinist.

Scripture is given to the Church for the building up of the Body of Christ, and for this reason Bernard has a supreme confidence that the Spirit, who inspired the Scriptures, and who is ever present in the Church, will not fail to lead the children of God into the light of Truth. Bernard accepts the understanding of Scripture which he has received in prayer as a manifestation of the Spirit. Consequently it is the common patrimony of all, not Bernard's private property. The gifts of God to the individual members of His Church are at the same time gifts to the whole Church, and Bernard is convinced that whatever help he may

---

[1] P.L. 785 A, In Cant. 1: 1.   [2] *Ibid.* 1134 D, cf. In Cant. 73: 2.

receive from God is not the reward of his own merits, but given to him because of the needs of those who depend on him—"I never consciously omit what in my opinion would be useful to you. How dare I do such a thing? Especially in those matters upon which I have been given light for your sakes."[1]

As has been suggested, Bernard's attitude to the Bible was nothing new. He had the solid tradition of the Fathers of the Church and indeed of St. Paul to support him, and his heritage was that theology which flourished in the Benedictine monasteries. His use of Scripture is solidly rooted in the dogmatic, sacramental, and liturgical use of the Bible by the Church. In all this he is faithful to the great principle of exegesis, that Scripture can be read truly only in the Church and by the Church. Because his spirituality is biblical it is founded on faith in Christ, and pours its riches into the common fount of the Church.

The central core of Bernard's message is contained in the words "God is love" and "He has first loved us." The theme of love so developed by the Cistercians, and nowhere more sublimely than in Bernard's own De Diligendo Deo and the sermons on the Canticle, has its raison d'être in these phrases from St. John's first Epistle. The whole history of creation and of the fall of man; of the patient fidelity of God to His promise of a redeemer; of the working out of salvation in the incarnation, death, and resurrection of Christ; of the ultimate assumption of man into glory; all this falls into a pattern in the brilliant light of the revelation that God is love for man. He is the "ambitious lover,"[2] "who can nowhere and never not love because he is love,"[3] in whom man is "from eternity because he is eternally loved."[4] God does not treat man as a slave, or even as a hired servant, but as a lover. This is the vision which enthralls Bernard and enables him to write, "You wish to hear from me why and how God is to be loved? My answer is: the reason for loving God is God Himself, and the measure in which we should love Him is to love Him without measure."[5]

But Bernard could not have been so overwhelmed by that revelation had he not first of all learned with Moses that no man can see God and live. Bernard's notion of the God of love must

---

[1] P.L. 1117 A, In Cant. 82: 1.   [2] Ibid. 1110 A, In Cant. 68: 4.
[3] Ibid. 1117 A, In Cant. 70: 2.   [4] Ibid. 1126 B, In Cant. 71: 10.
[5] Ibid. 182, 974 A, De Dil. Deo 1: 1.

be understood against the background of his reverent adoration of the divine majesty, and in the light of the phrase he uses so constantly, "he that is a searcher of majesty, shall be overwhelmed by glory."[1] For God is the immutable Creator of the universe; He is infinite power and eternal wisdom who has no need of man. His majesty is incomprehensible and ineffable, far beyond the grasp of a finite mind whose choicest words are but the senseless mouthings of a baby—a, a, a—compared with the reality they seek to describe. The fundamental religious attitude of man before God must be that of awe and adoration. Without it Bernard's notion of the God of love loses its essential strength. His whole spiritual attitude is based upon this solid foundation and for that reason he can speak of love without ever becoming sentimental. His understanding of the transcendence of God makes him ready to accept the exigencies which the love of God imposes, to take up his cross daily and follow the lover of the human race.

It is because God takes such a loving interest in man that Bernard is led to follow Him, and to formulate the second principle of his spirituality, complementary to his notion of the God of love. To-day it would be called a Christian anthropology, but in Bernard's time it usually went under the title of a treatise *de Anima*. Bernard's own contribution is entitled *de Gratia et Libero Arbitrio*. Bernard learnt the principle of self-knowledge not from the philosophers but from the Bible—"Lord, what is man that thou carest for him?"[2] Hence his enquiry into the nature of man is essentially theological. He tries to see man through the eyes of God—to see the image and likeness of God in man. This traditionally Christian theme is developed first in terms of the liberty of man, in the *de Gratia et Libero Arbitrio*; in the Sermons on the Canticle (Sermons 80–83), he treats of it in relation to the *magnitudo* and *rectitudo* of the soul, its capacity for God and the directness with which it seeks Him; and finally, in the *Sermo 45 de Diversis*, he takes up St. Augustine's doctrine of the *vestigia Trinitatis* in the three faculties of the soul.[3] Bernard sees in the vital activity of the soul, in its very essence, and in the gift of liberty which distinguishes men from the beasts, the mark of the

---

[1] Proverbs 25: 27.   [2] Ps. 143: 3.
[3] On the intricacies of Bernard's doctrine, cf. M. Standaert, O.C.R., *La doctrine de l'image chez St. Bernard*. Ephemerides Theologicae Lovanienses, January–June 1947.

divinity and the possibility of attaining to union with God. The spiritual life is a progressive liberation and expansion of the soul, a development of all the capacities which God has given man. Hence "knowledge of yourself is a step to the knowledge of God; and from His image which will be renewed in you He Himself will be seen."[1]

It is undeniable that this first consciousness of self is an awareness of sin, but it goes far beyond a mere examination of conscience, a listing of vices and virtues. It is rather a consciousness of sin and of the awful destiny which awaits sin seen in the light of what man should and can be and of the glory to which God will surely lead him. It is the experience of the bitter contradiction which man finds in himself between the sublimity of his aspirations and the bestiality of conduct—"seeing himself in the clear light of truth man finds himself in the regions of unlikeness."[2] The essential point of this experience is not man's discovery of sin in himself, but the realisation that sin need not triumph. It is present but not victorious. The very acknowledgment of the inner warfare between good and evil is a movement of liberty which provokes the cry, "Lord, who is like unto thee?"[3] This primary religious act which is the admission of the uniqueness of God is a free act, the first step towards the rejection of sin, that ill-starred attempt to be like unto God by means other than those He has chosen.

Bernard's most violent denunciations of sin are invariably marked by the Christian optimism of the Epistle to the Romans. It is possible to condemn sin, to unmask it in all its hideous reality because Christ has conquered sin and it has now no hold over man. Bernard can say at the end of a vivid passage on the sinfulness of man: "Without doubt man has become like unto mere emptiness, man is reduced to nothing, he is nothing." But he does not leave man in this awful nothingness of sin. "Let us however breathe again, my brothers, since if we are nothing in our own hearts perhaps there is another opinion of ourselves hidden in the heart of God. O Father of mercies. O Father of the wretched. Why does your heart go out to them? I know why, yes I know; where your treasure is there is your heart. How then can we be nothing if we are your treasure?"[4] The testimony of

[1] P.L. 183, 970 C, In Cant. 36: 6.   [2] Ibid. 969 D, In Cant. 36: 4.
[3] Ibid. 1180 C–1181 C, In Cant. 82: 7–8.   [4] Ibid. 531 C, In Dedic. Eccl. 5: 3–5.

this opinion of God is written in the blood of the one mediator Christ. It is indelible. No accumulation of sin, no matter how monstrous, is ever a reason for despair. The true knowledge of self is not the scrupulous dissection of one's actions but the possession of self in God. Sin dislocates and dismembers the soul in the same way as death, the penalty of sin, brings about the disintegration of the body. When man enters into his own soul he enters into God who is "the soul of the soul"[1] and finds that divine life which alone can restore him to his integrity, uniting and developing all that is good within him.

This starting point of self-knowledge is the beginning of the road back to the Father. That road is Christ, who said "I am the way." Together Father, Son, and Spirit are at work helping man to walk with a firm and unwavering step. The Father draws man eternally to Himself in love, that is to say in the Spirit, who cries out "Abba! Father!" in the heart of man, assuring him of his adopted sonship in Christ. This is the mystery of salvation made known in Christ, the revelation of the Trinity of love who call man to share eternally in their love. Christ holds the central place in Bernard's spirituality because He holds the central place in the Scriptures. But Christ came on earth to bear witness to the Father and ascended into heaven to send the Spirit into His Church. Bernard is led through Christ to the Trinity. His devotion to the Saviour fructifies into consciousness of the presence of the three divine Persons in his soul and in the whole of creation. In the memory, which is man's awareness not only of the past but equally of the present and future, there is the power of the Father which fructifies in the theological virtue of hope, grounding all man's efforts solidly in the unconquerable might of God. The presence of the Son manifests itself in the intellect in the virtue of faith, which enables man to penetrate the surface appearance of reality and act in the light of the wisdom of God. In the will the Spirit of love pours forth that divine charity which will never pass away. Here Bernard unites the theology of the appropriations to the divine Persons with that of the virtues to emphasise the unity which should reign in the life of man. He may give priority to the will but he never divorces the will from the intellect and memory, any more than he separates the Father and the Son from the Spirit, or faith and hope from charity. The

[1] P.L. 569 B, De Div. 10: 4.

life of charity must be grounded in faith and spurred on by hope. This is only another way of saying that it is only from Christ that we receive the Spirit who leads us back to the Father. The same dogma can be expressed in the exegetical terms familiar to Bernard. For it is the tropological or moral sense of Scripture which intensifies the Christian life of charity. This tropology is simply the translation into experience of the allegorical sense which is the understanding and penetration of the mysteries of faith. Both these senses of Scripture lead to the anagogical sense, the contemplation of the realities of heaven already perceptible to the eyes of faith, and contained in germ in the life of charity. Thus Bernard welds into a unity the diverse disciplines into which theology is divided to-day—dogmatic and moral, ascetical and mystical and all the rest.

God is a spirit, and he who adheres to God becomes one spirit with Him,[1] but for Bernard the perfect union with God is reserved for the life to come. Meanwhile, man is a pilgrim far from his Father's house, and the corruption of his body hampers the *élan* of the soul. Bernard felt keenly the crushing burden which the necessities of the body impose on the soul. Indeed, one of his favourite texts is, "the soul is weighed down by the weight of the body."[2] Dom Jean Leclercq has said that the ill-health of St. Gregory the Great is one of the great events in the history of spirituality.[3] One might say the same about Bernard. He too was tortured by chronic ailments of the stomach which eventually prevented him from sharing the community life he loved so well. He too was a contemplative forced into an active life. In addition Bernard had the extreme sensitivity of a great artist. All this gave him a vivid perception of the paradox of man's being, that of an immortal soul in a mortal body, of an eternal destiny to be worked out in time. When Bernard inveighs against the body there is no trace of dualism in his thought; he is neither Platonic nor Manichean but Christian. He is simply stating the fact that man's earthly condition is marked by the penalty of sin, he must earn his bread by the sweat of his brow. No matter how ardently the soul desires to be united to God in this life, it must normally be content to wait for the perfection of union in heaven. It may happen that on earth the soul is rapt into the ecstasy of becoming

---

[1] 1 Cor. 6: 17.   [2] Wisdom 9: 17.
[3] *L'amour des lettres et le désir de Dieu* (Paris 1953), p. 33.

one spirit with God; but this is the rare experience of a brief moment. Such an instant of mystical union sharpens man's awareness of the innumerable cares imposed upon him by his earthly life, and increases his thirst for God. But such is not its main result. The soul returns from this embrace filled with divine love; and it is that very love which makes inevitable its return to the labour and misery of human existence. The more the soul is filled with the divine charity, the more is it capable and desirous of sharing in the work of redemption, to be done in the body and on earth.

The soul and body are bound together by a common love and together they must go towards God. So profoundly was Bernard convinced of this unity of soul and body that he was led to take up the doctrine of the waiting of the soul in heaven for the resurrection of the body. However unorthodox his teaching on this point may have been one cannot but admire the conviction which inspired it.[1] For it is not only his desire to preserve the unity of the individual soul and body which is behind his doctrine, but also his preoccupation with the great eschatological vision of the completion of the mystical Body of Christ and the theology of the Communion of Saints.

The body hampers the soul not because it is material but because it is corrupted by sin. The soul, liberated from the domination of sin by the victory of Christ, must work to free the body. This means going against the selfish instincts of the body which make man shrink from what is difficult and lead him to judge everything in terms of his own profit and comfort. The asceticism of Bernard is not a matter of doing what is unpleasant merely because it goes against the grain. Christian mortification is not an aimless cult of pain but a means of sharing more fully in the death of Christ in order that the fruits of His resurrection may be given to the world. The cross of Christ is not a symbol of death merely, but a symbol of a death which brings life. Sin shuts man in upon himself, separating him from God and from his fellow-men. The Christian asceticism of Bernard is designed to unite soul and body in divine charity, to enable the whole man to share in the work of redemption. The

---

[1] Every year the Jesuits pay at least lip-service to Bernard's opinion when they read second nocturn lessons for the feast of All Saints in the Society of Jesus. The lessons are taken from Bernard's third sermon for the feast of All Saints.

true Christian is ready to seek out and make his own "the needs of the poor, the anguish of the oppressed, the worries of those who are sad, the faults of sinners, in short all the tribulations of men even those of our enemies."[1]

It is true that Bernard seems to have gone to excess in the harsh, almost savage, treatment he gave his own body, but it is not for us to judge him. Bernard was prepared to lose all for the sake of gaining Christ and his inspiration was the generosity of the Cross. As Père Louis Bouyer remarks, "L'ascèse si farouche qu'elle soit chez lui, n'a rien émoussé mais bien tout intensifié de sa capacité prodigieuse de sentir et de vouloir."[2] Bernard's affective spirituality, as it has been justly termed, rests upon the rigorous life of the Cistercians. His affectivity has nothing in common with the mawkish sentimentality which has brought the term affectively into disrepute. Rather it consists in the development in divine love of all man's emotional capacity. Bernard sees man as a creature of feeling and emotion, his fears and joys, loves and sorrows are the mark of his humanity, they are all values which have to be preserved and transformed by grace so that man loves and rejoices, fears and sorrows in Christ.

For more than half of his life as a Cistercian, Bernard was caught up into an intense activity which led him far from the monastery and seems to be in contradiction to his vocation. But Bernard's active life depended upon his life of prayer and is a manifestation of his fidelity to his vocation. He is a man of action because he is a mystic. It is perhaps not mere fancy to see in the external activity of Bernard a symbol of the deep hidden spiritual activity which emanated from the Cistercian Order. The message of selfless charity was transmitted by Bernard and his followers to the whole Middle Ages. The doctrine of Bernard is to be seen at work in the Victorines, the Franciscans, and the Devotio Moderna, whilst through the *Imitation of Christ* and Ludolph the Carthusian's *Vita Christi* Ignatius of Loyola was in contact with the same influence. The monastic life may be a flight from the world but it is not a refuge from reality. The world from which Bernard withdrew was the world understood in the Johannine sense—a deadly complex of sin inimical to the Christian life, which stifles the love of God in the hearts of men. In the cloister he

---

[1] P.L. 183, 828, A–B, In Cant. 12: 1.
[2] *La Spiritualité de Cîteaux* (Paris 1955), p. 40.

I

sought above all the *socialis vitae gratia* which enables man to live as a true human being.

Bernard's message is essentially one of love and joy. It has the authentic note of Christian spirituality. If we ask him to teach us about God his answer will always be the same—God is love. If we seek in his writings an answer to the enigma of man we shall eventually come back to the statement that man is the chosen one of God, His beloved. Hence the relationship between man and God can only be fully developed in terms of love. It is only selfless charity which enables man to go towards God in the spirit of true liberty and not bowed down under the yoke of fear. The commandment of charity contains the whole law and the prophets, and the true lover of God is enabled to see in those commands of God not an intolerable burden but an expression of the exigencies of love. To arrive at such serenity and liberty there is only one road—Christ.

It is this doctrine which makes Bernard the enemy of any sort of individualism no matter how pious it may be. He writes to a nun who had desires of becoming a hermit—"You are either one of the foolish virgins (if indeed you are a virgin) or one of the prudent. If you are among the foolish the community is a necessity for you, if you belong with the wise you are necessary for the community."[1] No true Christian can live for himself, and an authentic spiritual life leads inevitably to a deeper integration of oneself through Christ into the life of His Church. This is as much the conclusion of Bernard's life as it is of his doctrine.

[1] Epist. 115, P.L. 182, 262 A.

10. WILLIAM OF ST. THIERRY

Odo Brooke

THE MYSTERY of the Blessed Trinity is at the very centre not only of Christian Doctrine but also of Christian Spirituality.[1] This statement cannot be contested, yet it asks a challenging question. Do we think of God above all as the Trinitarian revelation, and is our life and especially our life of prayer formed after the pattern of that dogma? Surely the tendency is to think rather of "God" and of His Providence, than of the Father as the origin of the whole Trinitarian plan of salvation, expressed so forcefully at the beginning of the Epistle to the Ephesians: "Blessed be that God, that Father of our Lord Jesus Christ . . . who has chosen us out, in Christ, before the foundation of the world, to be saints . . . marking us out before hand (so his will decreed) to be his adopted children through Jesus Christ. . . . In him you learned to believe, and had the seal set on your faith by the promised gift of the Holy Spirit."[2] Then from "God," our mind moves spontaneously to the Incarnation and Redemption. But are we always aware that through Christ, and as is so often forgotten, in the Holy Spirit, we are drawn into a Trinitarian relationship?

If asked why we are not more alive to the place of the Trinity in our lives and in our prayer, the reason may be that we think of the Trinity too exclusively in terms of the Processions within themselves and of the speculative theological problems arising from the mystery of three persons in one identical nature. However important this is for theology, if the Trinity is viewed almost entirely from this angle, it will inevitably appear remote from the lives of the faithful. The perspective is changed once it is realised that Revelation presents the Trinity first of all as the intervention of the Persons for our salvation, according to the relationship "From the Father, through the Son, in the Spirit

[1] Cf. Philipon, M-M., *La Trinité clé de route des mystères Chrétiens*, *Revue Thomiste* 58 (1958), pp. 5-19.   [2] Eph. I, 3-14.

to the Father," with the life of the Trinity in itself as the ultimate foundation of this plan. Through this pattern, the Church lives her faith in the official prayer of the Liturgy.[1] In Scripture and in the Liturgy, the Trinity is presented not only with an emphasis on the intervention in the history of salvation, but also on the Persons in their distinct relationship rather than on their unity of nature.[2] A further question arises. How is the dogma of the Trinity lived in the spirituality of the individual Christian, and especially how is it lived by the Mystics? The doctrine of William of St. Thierry is an important contribution towards an answer. His approach, though not to be identified simply with that of Scripture and the Liturgy, is a further testimony to the relevance of the Trinity for Christian life. The intervention of the Persons in the history of Salvation is now concentrated on Their intervention in the history of the individual soul. The spiritual life at its deepest level is seen as an experience of the Trinitarian life of the Holy Spirit. Mysticism is here shown to us not primarily as an advance in states of prayer to be analysed and charted. It is shown as the ultimate meaning of man, and that meaning is to be found in the Trinity.

Nothing is known of William's early life, except that he was born at Liége of noble parentage, in the second half of the eleventh century. It is very probable that he made his studies in the famous school of Laon, under its master Anselm, and in the company of Peter Abelard. We do not know, either, how long he spent in the academic world; only that he was there long enough to acquire a vast fund of intellectual learning which enabled him later on to argue with confidence against the errors of Peter Abelard and William de Conchis. He first took the monastic habit in the Benedictine Abbey of Saint Nicoise at Rheims; and in 1119–20 he became abbot of Saint Thierry just outside Rheims. Here he was intensely occupied for more than fifteen years with a temporal administration which involved all the complex relations inherent in a feudal régime with the nobility, the bourgeoisie and the villeins. He had at the same

[1] Cf. Vagaggini, C., *Theological Dimensions of the Liturgy*, translated by Doyle, L. J., Collegeville 1959, pp. 106–39, and Davis, C., *Liturgy and Doctrine*, London 1960, pp. 20–35.

[2] Cf. the testimony of the more general teaching of the Greek Fathers, and also of the Latin Fathers before Nicaea: De Régnon, *Etudes de théologie positive sur la Sainte Trinité* (Paris 1892), Vol. 4, p. 532.

time the direction of his monks, and was playing a prominent part in the monastic revival which was animating all the abbeys of his part of France. During this period he was wrestling with two personal problems, wretched health and a burning desire for the eremitical life. He found himself constantly drawn, as his own interior life developed through prayer and study, to the Cistercian ideal as he encountered it in Bernard himself. And yet, during these years as Abbot, he wrote his two great treatises on the love of God, *De Contemplando Deo*, and *De Natura et Dignitate Amoris;* his treatise on man, *De Natura Corporis et Animae*, on the Blessed Sacrament, *De Sacramento Altaris*, and a commentary on the Epistle to the Romans.

Finally in 1135 he retired from St. Thierry and joined the Cistercian community at Signy in the Ardennes. There he remained until his death in 1148. It was there that he wrote his treatises on the faith against Abelard, *Speculum Fidei* and *Aenigma Fidei*, his great commentary on the Canticle of Canticles and his Life of St. Bernard.

We know of only one absence from Signy during those thirteen years: a visit to the Carthusian Monastery of Mont-Dieu. It produced the famous treatise on the eremitical life, the *Epistola ad Fratres de Monte Dei*, which has come to be known as the Golden Epistle.

Within the various trends of monastic theology,[1] the Cistercian theological movement, represented principally by St. Bernard and William of St. Thierry, is of particular interest for the question of the relationship of dogma to the spiritual life. In contrast to those theologians among the black monks, as for instance Rupert of Deutz,[2] who tended to view the mysteries of Christianity more in the broad outlines of the history of salvation, the Cistercians dwelt principally on the reflection of this history as experienced within the individual soul. Their theology is dominated by the theme of the journey of the soul to God. This trend is

---

[1] Cf. Leclercq, J., *L'amour des lettres et le désir de Dieu*, Paris 1957. (English translation, *The Love of Letters and the Desire for God*, 1961), *S. Bernard et la théologie monastique du XIIᵉ siècle*, in *S. Bernard Théologien (Analecta sacri Ordinis Cisterciensis* 9, 1953 fasc. 3-4), pp. 7-23, and *The Monastic Tradition of Culture and Studies*, in *American Benedictine Review* 11 (1960), pp. 99-131.

[2] Cf. for example, the Prologue to his *De Trinitate* (P.L. 167, 199), which aims to show how the Trinity acts through the "book" of Creation and Redemption and divides history into three main phases, attributed respectively to the Father, the Son, and the Holy Ghost.

admirably illustrated in the trinitarian theology of William of St. Thierry, always related in some way, either directly or indirectly, to this ascent of the soul, and moving ultimately towards a mystical experience of the Trinity. Despite a more technical treatment of the subject in the *Aenigma Fidei* and in the polemical works against Abelard and de Conchis, he views the Trinity more as a principle of life than as a problem to be scrutinised. His deepest convictions can be found in the words of his friend Bernard: "To subject this mystery to profane scrutiny is rashness, to believe in it, true piety; to know it is life, and eternal life."[1]

Though William uses the Augustinian "created trinity" of memory, intellect and will as a metaphorical illustration of the Trinity and the order of the Processions,[2] he is not really interested in the discovery of created analogies of the Trinity. His aim was not to give a metaphysical explanation of how the Son proceeds from the Father and the Holy Spirit from the Father and Son. Nor was it even to give that kind of insight described by St. Augustine in his *De Trinitate*, when the mind is led, pedagogically, to a contemplative perception of the uncreated Trinity through the medium of created images.[3] For William, the image of God in man is the basis of the ascent of the soul to God. It is an imprint of the Trinity[4] which gives to the soul its initial capacity to achieve its final state of perfect likeness, *similitudo*. The *similitudo* is therefore the perfection of the *imago*.[5] As a mystical theologian, William was more interested in this likeness than in the image. For the likeness, as we shall see, implies his whole doctrine on the experience of the Trinity. But even where he gives a more complete analysis of the image as such, the whole trend of his thought is to portray the image as a dynamic force impelling the soul towards its perfection in the likeness.[6] The analysis of trinities in the soul is seen as less

---

[1] *De Consideratione*, P.L. 182, 799C. The tendency of William and St. Bernard to minimise the value of human reason and philosophy should be seen in the light of the rationalism of Abelard and his disciples.

[2] Cf. *De Natura et Dignitate Amoris*, P.L. 184, 382 C–D; *De Natura Corporis et Animae*, P.L. 180, 721 B–C.

[3] P.L. 42, 1035, 1088. But note that William's approach is also to be found in Augustine. Cf. *Ibid.*, 1051 and 1055.

[4] *De Natura Corporis et Animae*, P.L. 180, 721 CD.

[5] *Epistola ad Fratres de Monte Dei*, P.L. 184, 348C; 341D.

[6] Cf. *De Natura et Dignitate Amoris*, P.L. 184, 382A–383A; *De Natura Corporis et Animae*, 721B–723A; *Speculum Fidei*, P.L. 180, 365B–368C.

important than the movement of the soul towards the Trinity. The aim is not so much to illustrate the Trinity by metaphor as to reach out towards union with the Trinity.

In the *Aenigma Fidei* William speaks of the ascent to God by three theological stages, the way of faith, of the reasoning of faith (ratio fidei), and finally of "experience."[1] A great point of interest in this important text is its close parallel with a text in the *Golden Epistle* describing the spiritual ascent through the three states, *"animalis," "rationalis," "spiritualis,"*[2] rooted ultimately in a psychological trichotomy, *anima, animus, spiritus*.[3] There is no indication that William intended this trichotomy as a metaphorical illustration of the three Persons of the Trinity. Nor should the trichotomy be interpreted as a psychological division of the soul into three parts. It is a question more of three aspects of the life of the soul in the spiritual ascent. This relationship of theology to spirituality and to psychology offers an interesting example of theological method. For it is a theology developing in successive stages, each of which is proportioned in turn to the life of the senses, of the reason and of the spirit. Thus grounded in the spiritual life of the soul, William's theology shares in the movement of what Père Bouyer has rightly called *Une dynamique de l'âme*.[4] This movement is directed towards that state of likeness (*similitudo*), the experience of the Trinity which foreshadows the final vision of God in eternity.

The first theological stage, that of faith, is related to the *status animalis*, when man is under the dominion of the senses and needs the guidance of an external authority to rule his life.[5] This stage is closely connected with the Incarnation and the whole temporal economy as a pedagogic preparation leading man by degrees through what is perceptible to the senses towards the eternal, immutable life of the Trinity.[6] The Incarnation is seen as a *Sacramentum*, not as we use the term for the Sacraments strictly so called, but in the patristic sense of the word, implying the whole range of signs whereby what is eternal, spiritual and invisible should be manifested through the medium of what is

---

[1] *Aenigma Fidei*, 414B–415D.   [2] *Epistola ad Fratres de Monte Dei*, 315C–316B.
[3] *Ibid.*, 340C, 348CD–349A.
[4] Bouyer, L., *La Spiritualitè de Cîteaux*, p. 121 (English translation, *The Cistercian Heritage*, London 1958).
[5] *Epistola ad Fratres de Monte Dei*, 316C–317D.
[6] *Aenigma Fidei*, 402A–D, 403C–404A.

temporal, material and visible: "This is to be seen most clearly in the person of the Mediator, who, though he is God eternal, became man in time; in order that through him who is eternal and subject to time, we may pass from the temporal to the eternal."[1]

The second stage, that of the reasoning power of faith, brings us to the more technical and speculative development of William's thought in the polemical works, particularly the *Aenigma Fidei*. His writings against Abelard and de Conchis are directed against what appeared to him as a rationalism destructive of the mystery of the Trinity.[2] The *Aenigma Fidei* is a further development, to give an example of a more positive, constructive trinitarian theology as a counteraction to Abelard. Here William comes forward as the Irenaeus of the twelfth century, the champion of Orthodoxy and tradition, opposing the sources of the Faith in Scripture and the authority of the Fathers to the dangerous rationalistic speculations of some of his contemporaries.[3] But as Père Déchanet has shown, his return not only to St. Augustine, but also to the "Light from the East" of the Greek Fathers, held in suspicion by the conservative theologians of that time, reveals considerable originality in the choice of these sources.[4] In opposition to Abelard, William's *ratio fidei* places reason wholly under the dominion of faith, and from this angle he approaches the metaphysical problems of the Trinity. The central and more speculative section of the *Aenigma Fidei* shows both the weakness and the strength of this reaction. In the attempt to push further the analysis of such problems as that of the meaning of Person in the Trinity, it can hardly be said that on the metaphysical plane he equals the best achievements of the contemporary scholastic movement. His contribution lies rather in the fine dialectic with which he leads us at every turn towards the ultimate mystery of the Trinity. After approaching the Trinity from

[1] *Speculum Fidei*, 382D–383A.
[2] A persuasive defence of the orthodoxy of Abelard on trinitarian theology has been given by Cottiaux, J., *La conception de la théologie chez Abélard, Revue d'histoire ecclésiastique*, 28 (1932), pp. 247–95, 533–51, 787–828. But even if this is admitted, the expressions of Abelard were ambiguous, and there was the further danger from his disciples.
[3] *Non de fontibus nostris, sed de fontibus Salvatoris, ex Scripturis Sanctis, et certissimis auctoritatibus sanctorum Patrum. Aenigma Fidei*, 432C.
[4] Cf. Déchanet, *Aux Sources de la spiritualité de Guillaume de Saint-Thierry* (Bruges 1940).

almost every viewpoint, the emphasis of the Latin Fathers on the unity of nature alternating with that of the Greek Fathers on the distinction of Persons, *ratio fidei* confronts us at each conclusion with the impenetrable mystery. We are told that the human mind never understands the Trinity so well as when it is understood to be incomprehensible.[1] The initial mystery of the God who is both three and one is never lessened, yet William's speculations always explain more exactly just where the mystery lies in every aspect of the problem.

From speculative problems William passes to the final stage, mystical experience. Thinking about the Trinity gives way to experiencing the Trinity. For *ratio fidei*, even though so energised by faith that it becomes a unique power (*ratio sui generis*),[2] is still human reason, whereas in the final phase we pass beyond reason to the sphere of the Spirit. Here man's knowledge of the Trinity is not his own; it is that which the Trinity has of itself: "Those to whom the Father and the Son reveal each other know exactly as the Father and the Son know each other."[3] This knowledge is from the Holy Spirit; more, it is a share in the very life of the Spirit. It comes wholly from within the Spirit; and it is a stage of transition from faith to sight. It is an anticipation, however remote, of the final vision of God. *Ratio fidei* led to the incomparable mystery. This new knowledge, or rather the *amor-intellectus*, "love-which-is-understanding," gives a kind of insight. The mind is no longer perplexed by the antithesis of three and one.[4] This does not mean that there is no longer a mystery, that the antithesis is now reconciled by reason, so as to see how three and one are compatible. It means that the mind has passed out of the realm of conceptual knowledge, where the question whether reason can in any way explain the mystery no longer arises.

What is meant by the statement that this kind of knowledge is from within the Trinity and that it is the very life of the Holy Spirit? The explanation lies in the nature of knowledge, and the strict equation between knowledge and likeness to the thing known. From an analysis of sense knowledge, William describes how the eye cannot see unless it is somehow trans-

---

[1] *Aenigma Fidei*, 426C.   [2] *Ibid.*, 417B.
[3] *Speculum Fidei*, 393 A. Cf. *Aenigma Fidei*, 415A.
[4] *Meditativae Orationes*, P.L. 180, 214CD.

formed into what is seen, nor can the ear hear unless it is in some way transformed into what is heard.[1] So on an incomparably higher plane we cannot know God in the way in which he knows himself, unless we have been transformed into his likeness. This relationship between knowledge and likeness acts in reciprocal causality. Not only do we become like God in so far as we know him, but, reversing the text of St. John, it is equally true that we know him only in so far as we become like him: "To be like God there [namely, in the final vision] will be to see God, to know him. We shall see him, know him in the same proportion as we are like him. We shall be like him to the precise extent that we see him, know him. For to see God, to know him, is to be like him; and to be like him is to see him, to know him."[2] We become like him when the image of the Trinity in the soul has been perfected and brought back to a perfect likeness, the *similitudo*, the most perfect union between the soul and God compatible with the distinction between Creature and Creator.[3] It is achieved when the soul is raised to a created participation in the life of the Holy Spirit, who is the uncreated mutual union of the Father and the Son.

The *raison d'être* of this experience is the life of the Holy Spirit, as can be seen from the sequence of the argument. The foundation of the experience is likeness, and the foundation of the likeness is the Holy Spirit as the mutual union of the Father and the Son. William goes so far as to say that the experience *is* the Holy Spirit, though he guards carefully against any pantheistic interpretation:

We may say that the life of the Spirit is this union, not merely because the Holy Spirit effects it or that he brings man's spirit to it, but because he, the Holy Spirit, God, Love, is this union (*ipsa ipse est Spiritus Sanctus*). For he is the love, the union, the sweetness and the goodness of the Father and Son; he is their kiss, their embrace and whatever is common to them both in that transcendent union which is truth, in that truth which is union. Through him, then, all that belongs to the Son by substantial union in his relationship to the Father, or to the Father in his relationship to the Son—all this is given in due proportion to man in his relation-

[1] *Meditativae Orationes*, 213 AB; *Speculum Fidei*, 390D–391A; cf. James Walsh, S.J., *Guillaume de Saint-Thierry et les Sens Spirituels*, in *Révue d'Ascétique et de Mystique*, 137 (1959).
[2] *Speculum Fidei*, 393C. Cf. *Aenigma Fidei*, 399AB.   [3] *Ibid.*, 393B.

ship to God; and man, in the possession of this blessed experience, when Father and Son kiss and embrace, finds himself in some way in their midst. Through the Holy Spirit, the man of God becomes in some ineffable, incredible way—not God exactly; but what God is by nature, man becomes by grace.[1]

Nor does he hesitate to say that the Holy Spirit is himself the love by which we love God—*ipse enim est amor noster*.[2] Love and knowledge are so closely united in this experience that he describes it as a knowledge-in-love (*cognito amoris*); by which he means, not a formal identification of the faculties of intellect and will, but their interpenetration and union, in this knowledge of God which is *sui generis*. And the root of it is the trinitarian life. William's mysticism is essentially trinitarian in the sense that its whole meaning is to be found in this theme. Through the Holy Spirit we share in that mutual knowledge by which Father and Son know each other: "Those to whom Father and Son reveal Each Other know exactly as Father and Son know Each Other; that is, they have written in them the mutual knowledge that Father and Son have of Each other; they have Their unity, Their will and Their love; and all this is the Holy Spirit."[3] This is an experimental knowledge which foreshadows the final vision: "The sweet awareness (*sensus*) and experience of this infinite good, this indeed is life, the truly blessed life—even though in this wretched life it cannot be complete. But in the future life, life and its happiness will be brimming over, all the time, for ever."[4] Does this imply a direct intuition that the Holy Spirit is the mutual love and union of the Father and the Son? Such a possibility cannot be excluded, but it is not the most likely explanation. A more probable interpretation can be given on the lines of Henri Bremond's illuminating analysis of the experience of the Venerable Mary of the Incarnation.[5] He argues convincingly that mystical experience as such is on a different plane from conceptual, scientific, theological knowledge. According to his interpretation, Mary of the Incarnation, in reflecting on her experience would have attempted to express it in terms of the

---

[1] *Epistola ad Fratres de Monte Dei*, 349AB.
[2] *De Contemplando Deo*, P.L. 184, 376B.
[3] *Speculum Fidei*, 393AB.   [4] *Ibid.*, 394BC.
[5] Bremond, H., *Histoire littéraire du sentiment religieux en France* (Paris 1926), vol. VI, pp. 30–48. Cf. Mary Denis Mahoney, O.S.U., *The Venerable Mary of the Incarnation*, pp. 277–92 below.

current theological concepts. These concepts would evoke psychologically the memory of the intuition. As a result, she would pass imperceptibly from its description to its expression in theological concepts. So in the case of William of St. Thierry, first of all there would be the initial experience of union with the Persons of the Trinity. This would be followed by its theological expression in terms of the Augustinian Theory of the Holy Spirit. There is the clearest indication that William is talking of insight on the mystical plane, yet the explanation of this insight is given in terms of a theological theory. These two planes are so closely interwoven that in his writings they are inseparable.

Despite allusions to an experimental knowledge of the Trinity in the writings of the Fathers, there was no fully developed theology of this experience. The great contribution of William of St. Thierry is to have evolved a theology of the Trinity which is essentially mystical, and a mystical theology which is essentially trinitarian. He is therefore the initiator of the tradition of trinitarian mysticism, which is to be found especially in the writings of Ruysbroeck, Eckhart, Tauler and Suso.[1]

The structure of this theology is persuasive in its unified sequence of thought. But how far does its ultimate value depend on the initial premiss of the theory of the Holy Spirit as the mutual love and union of the Father and the Son, a theological opinion dating principally from St. Augustine?[2] Could it for instance be applied to the trinitarian economy, *Ex Patre, per Filium, in Spiritu*, to be found throughout the New Testament and the Liturgy, or to the theological explanations of the Greek Fathers based on this economy? The force of William's trinitarian spirituality lies precisely in the Holy Spirit as the bond of union, in whom we are united to the Father and the Son. The "similitudo," the "likeness," with its divine mode of knowledge received in proportion to this likeness, follow strictly from this basis. But in the Scriptural or "Greek" trinitarian economy no less than in the Augustinian theory, the Holy Spirit is the bond of union, whereby we are linked with the other Persons. The only difference lies in why this is so. According to the theology of the Greek Fathers, the Holy Spirit is the last Person in the sequence of the descending

[1] Cf. L. Reypens, art. *Dieu (Connaissance mystique)* in *Dictionnaire de Spiritualité* III (Paris 1957), 883-929.   [2] Cf. *De Trinitate*, P.L. 42, 1079, 1087.

movement from the Father through the Son in the Holy Spirit, and is therefore the first Person with whom we make contact and in whom we are drawn in the sequence of the ascending movement through the Son to the Father. As this initial point of contact with the other Persons, the Holy Spirit is the link, the bond of union, in whom we participate in the Trinitarian relations. William's mystical theology, despite its basis in the Augustinian theory of the Holy Spirit, can throw light also on the whole Scriptural and "Greek" Trinitarian tradition.

In conclusion, William teaches us that to discover our true selves is to discover the life of the Trinity. Created with the imprint of the trinitarian image, the soul is impelled towards the recovery of the perfect likeness to its archetype. In so far as the soul achieves this likeness, it is given an insight which passes beyond all that can be known by the senses or by human reason. In a finely developed sequence of thought, he shows how this experience of the Trinity is grounded in the Holy Spirit as the bond of union, giving us a share in the mutual communion and knowledge of the Father and the Son. This is to realise the promise of Christ to send the Holy Spirit to his apostles. "In that day you shall know that I am in my Father: and you in me, and I in you."[1]

[1] Jn. 14, 20.

11. GUIGO THE ANGELIC

Humphrey Pawsey

THE TWELFTH CENTURY was a golden age of contemplation, the trends of which were closely intertwined; the Benedictine, rooted in and rising from the Rule, the more speculative Victorine, and the eremitical, "drawing inspiration from the Fathers of the Desert, and rejoining them, if not in their ascetical performances, at least in their zeal for the 'theoria,' *contemplation in love*." In this connection, Guigo's brethren are reminded that if it is for all to seek God, it is for them to seek to see His face;[1] which means that in their greater solitude and silence, they are expected to aim at and attain to the more rare and pure degrees of that prayer of contemplation to which all Christians are called by the grace of God.

Carthusian contemplative life in this twelfth century, its first, is made known to us by a series of contemporary witnesses. Some of these saw it from without, its external framework of observances: Guibert de Nogent, Richard of St. Victor, John of Salisbury. Others knew it more intimately: St. Bernard, William of St. Thierry, Peter the Venerable. Alone they knew it truly who lived it; but self-revelation is hardly to be looked for from those who "according to their rule lead a secluded life remote from the din and follies of the world."[2]

However, a few of the early Carthusians did write about their contemplation, and some of their writings have come down to us. But the multiplication amongst them of the name of Guigo has given rise to confusion in the attribution of these works to their rightful authors. Research in recent times has done much to dispel this confusion; so that those writings of the twelfth century associated, by tradition or conjecture, with the name Guigo, and now known to belong to one or other Carthusian bearer of that name, may be enumerated and qualified with greater certainty. To Guigo the First, fifth prior of Chartreuse,

[1] Cf. *Dictionnaire de Spiritualité*, II, 1984, 1959.
[2] *Acta Apostolicae Sedis*, 1924, p. 385.

is attributed *Meditations*, which are a series of moral maxims and acute psychological insights into man and his misery and his need of God; and the *Customs*, passages of which are of marked spiritual import, in particular the epilogue, the *Recommendation of the Solitary Life*. Guigo the Second, the "Angelic," ninth prior of Chartreuse, is the author of the *Ladder of Four Rungs*, a short treatise describing the religious soul's climb to contemplation; and *Meditations*, which are meditations properly speaking. These works are dated *c*. 1145 and 1160–70.

If to these treatises are added *Eden's Fourfold River*, composed about 1190 by Adam of Dryburgh, a monk of Witham Charterhouse, Somerset, and the *Golden Epistle*, written about 1145 by William of St. Thierry in praise of Carthusian life, a fair idea may be gained of that life, and its inner meaning during the earliest years of the Order. However, the purpose of this list is merely to identify Guigo the Second, the "Angelic," and the two works attributed to him.[1]

Guigo was the Procurator of Chartreuse before he became Prior, in 1174.[2] After a few years in office he asked for his release, a thing all priors are now bound to ask for at each General Chapter. His request was granted in 1180, and he returned to his life of solitude, over which of necessity silence reigns. However, it is known that he arrived at a rare purity of contemplative prayer, which accounts for his being distinguished from his namesakes by the addition of the title "the Angelic." After his death, in 1188, many sick began to arrive at Chartreuse, wanting to be laid on his grave, hoping thereby for a cure. But Prior Jancelin, fearing this encroachment on the solitude, solemnly ordered Guigo to work his miracles elsewhere.[3]

The two striking aspects of Christian life in the Middle Ages were, virtuous activity dominated by neighbourly love, and *contemplative prayer*: the relationship between action and contemplation elaborated in the works of Pope St. Gregory the Great. In the spiritual literature of that time we find two types of aid for the contemplative life, the inner life of the spirit: the *Septenaires*, fixing for each day of the week the truth or mystery

[1] *I.e.*, the second Guigo to be Prior of the Grand Chartreuse.
[2] His successor as Procurator was Dom Hugh, known to us as St. Hugh of Lincoln, who became Bishop of Lincoln in the reign of Henry II.
[3] *Annales Ordinis Cartusiensis*, III, p. 44.

to be considered, early forerunners of the *Spiritual Exercises*, and the *Scalae*, "Ladders," fixing nothing more than the simplest framework, that could fit any subject for meditation for any time.

Guigo's *Ladder of Four Rungs* or *Scala Claustralium, Scala Paradisi*, as it was variously known, is a small work on the four spiritual degrees, or four stages of spiritual exercise. The Latin text is included in Migne's Patrology among the works of St. Augustine and of St. Bernard, to each of whom in the past it has been ascribed.[1] A middle English version is extant in three fifteenth-century manuscripts—*A Ladder of foure ronges by the whiche men mowe wele clyme to heven*—but these contain several interpolations that lengthen the text by at least a third.[2]

No other spiritual work of its kind and period seems to have been more read, nor to have received greater praise for its frank and devout mysticism—"a corner-stone of medieval spiritual writing." In its original form a prologue and epilogue make it clear that in substance it was a letter written by Guigo to a friend, a brother monk, a certain Gervaise, a man older than himself and to whom he owed a debt of gratitude. Guigo wishes to submit to the judgment of his friend what he has written about the spiritual exercise of cloistered monks. For Gervaise knows it all by experience and can amend where necessary. The letter concludes: "And now, brother Gervaise, when you receive the grace of reaching the top of this ladder, remember me."

Within the space of a few folios, in a bold perspective, the treatise embraces the whole of the interior life as envisaged in the young Order to which Guigo himself belonged. *The Ladder* is rightly called "a treatise on how to pray."[3] "Though it has," says Guigo, "few rungs, it is long and reaches to an unbelievable height; one end stands on the earth, the other pierces the clouds and reveals secrets of heaven." Its four rungs are Reading, Meditation, Prayer, and Contemplation.[4] By reading Guigo means before all else a careful scrutiny of Holy Writ; Meditation describes the activity of reason, *studiosa mentis actio*, a studious

---

[1] P.L. 40, 997–1004; P.L. 184, 475–84.

[2] University Library, Cambridge MS. Ff. vi. 33; Bodleian Library, MS. Douce 322; British Museum, Harley MS. 1706. Cf. Phyllis Hodgson, *Deonise Hid Divinite* (Early English Text Society, London, 1955). Appendix B, pp. 100–17, for a critical edition, based on these three MSS. A modernised version by Dom Justin McCann (now out of print) was published at Stanbrook Abbey in 1953. A new version is being prefaced by Eric Colledge and James Walsh, S.J.   [3] P.L. 184, 475.   [4] *Ibid.*, 476B.

investigation of the hidden meaning of the inspired word of God, what we would now call its mystical or spiritual sense. The example which Guigo uses to illustrate the development of his thought is a text of the Sermon on the Mount: *Beati mundo corde: quoniam ipsi Deum videbunt.* "Blessed are the clean of heart; for they shall see God." These few words are seen to be full of a rich meaning which is to nourish the soul, as the grape nourishes the body. The soul searches its heart, to see if it can understand and even come to possess this precious purity. It bites into the grape, begins to crush it in the wine-press of meditation; for meditation is not content with outward appearances, but searches deep beneath the surface. After pondering this way and that it comes to consider the reward for the possession of this purity; namely, to see the desired face of the Lord. "See, now," says Guigo, "how much juice there is that can be squeezed from the tiniest grape, how great a fire kindled from so small a spark, how that little piece of reading is hammered out on the anvil of meditation." As he continues, he does not hesitate to change the metaphor: "Now the alabaster-box is broken, the soul begins to inhale the sweetness of the escaping ointment; not its taste, yet, but its perfume; and from this the soul surmises how sweet it must be to experience this purity itself,[1] if even the meditation of it is so delightful."[2] "But we cannot achieve the experience of this sweetness through reading and meditation alone. The soul must continue to thirst after the true wisdom until it is bestowed by God, who gives it as and when He pleases. But He is more than ready to be moved by the soul's humble and persevering prayer." He does not even wait until the soul has finished praying; He invades it and inundates it with heavenly dew and fragrance. Here Guigo is not afraid to compare and contrast the delights of heavenly and earthly love. Just as in earthly love all use of the reason is obliterated and a man becomes as it were all body; so, in this supernal contemplation, all bodily delight is so destroyed that a man becomes, as it were, all spirit.[3]

Half way through his treatise, Guigo summarises his teaching on these four exercises:

Reading comes first, as the basis; it provides the matter, and leads to meditation. Meditation seeks most carefully what is to be

[1] *Huius munditiae sentire experientiam,* "to have experimental knowledge of it."
[2] P.L. 184, 477D.   [3] *Ibid.,* 479B.

K

wished for, and by its digging discovers and lays bare the treasure. But of itself is unable to grasp it, so it turns to prayer. Prayer, raised on high with all its might to God, gets what it wants, the sweetness, gladness, joy, of contemplation. Contemplation, when it comes, rewards the work of the other three, while it quenches the parched soul with the dew of heaven. Reading, therefore, is an outward exercise, meditation an inward understanding; prayer has to do with desire, but contemplation is above and beyond all the senses (*super omnem sensum*).[1]

These degrees are tightly bound together, so that each depends as much on the one that follows, as on the one that goes before it:

Reading without meditation is arid, meditation without reading will go astray, prayer without meditation is lukewarm; meditation without prayer is fruitless; prayer with devotion wins contemplation; to attain to contemplation without prayer is rare or miraculous. . . . There are four things that prevent us from mounting this ladder; unavoidable necessity, useful and virtuous activity, human weakness, and worldly vanity. The first is understandable, the second permissible, the third is deplorable, the fourth culpable.[2]

This quotation alone shows the author's maturity and moderation, and is a guarantee of the value of the expressions he uses to describe the contemplative experience itself. He says that this high contemplation implies the coming of the Lord to the soul and that the soul's tears of joy are the witness of His presence. They are, at the same time, tears of compunction, which purify the soul, as the spiritual interpretation of the beatitude testifies: "Blessed are you who mourn, for you shall laugh."[3] But, he asks, why should he reveal such secrets in public, or try to speak of the ineffable. He repeats what St. Bruno had said before him, what all the mystics say: "The uninitiated do not understand these things, until they read them in the book of experience."[4]

This grace of contemplation with its attendant consolations, is never a permanent possession in this life. It is a gift, not a portion which is our due; if it were never wanting, we might begin to believe that we were already home; and besides "over-familiarity breeds contempt."[5]

If the contemplative is faithful to the Divine spouse, the soul

[1] P.L. 184, 481C.   [2] *Ibid.*, 482D, 483D.
[3] The author conflates the two versions of this beatitude in Matthew (5, 5) and Luke (6, 21).   [4] P.L. 184, 479D.
[5] *Ibid.*, 480C. The Middle English text has its own version of the proverb: "Overmuch fellowship sometimes maketh men to be despised."

will be raised above itself, in the highest rung of the ladder, to experience the Lord's grace (*sentire gratiam Domini*), to contemplate the Divine glory as did Peter and John on the Mount of the Transfiguration. But this will be for a brief time only: the mind's eye is not strong enough to bear for long the brightness of the true light; the soul must descend gently into one of those other three degrees, dwelling now in one, now in another.[1]

It is not possible, here below, to have absolute certitude, based on rational proof, that God dwells within the soul. But the soul can have something as sure and far more profitable: the humble assurance that comes from growth in virtue and in the holy desire for God; and above all, the certainty that comes with *experience*, the experimental knowledge of God's presence. In speaking of this spiritual domain of divine experience, in an effort to describe the ineffable, Guigo has recourse to an analogy already traditional in his day: as the body has senses which give it a direct contact with the object of its desire, so the soul has its spiritual senses which enable it to reach God directly.[2] St. Augustine, in an endeavour to convey his personal experience, had used the same analogy:

> I love a kind of light, a kind of voice, a kind of odour, a kind of food, and a kind of embracing, when I love my God, who is the light, the voice, the odour, the food, the embracing of my inward man; where that light shineth into my soul which is not circumscribed by any place, when that voice soundeth which is not snatched away by time, when that odour pours forth which is not scattered by the air, when that food savours the taste which is unconsumed by eating, when that embracement is enjoyed which is not divorced by satiety.[3]

So Guigo describes the contemplative experience in terms of the sense of taste: "Contemplation is a certain raising up of the soul into God, where it is held rapt, whilst it tastes the sweetness of eternal joy." *Contemplatio est mentis in Deum suspensae quaedam supra se elevatio, aeterna dulcedinis gaudia degustans.*[4]

---

[1] P.L. 184, 481A.

[2] Cf. K. Rahner, S.J., *Les débuts d'une doctrine des cinq sens spirituels*, R.A.M. 1932, vol. 13, pp. 113 ff.; 1933, vol. 14, pp. 263 ff.; and J. Walsh, S.J., *Guillaume de Saint-Thierry et les sens spirituels*, R.A.M. 1959, vol. 35, pp. 27 ff.

[3] *Confessions*, X, 6.

[4] P.L. 184, 476B. Migne's text has been emended from the Manuscripts. Cf. Dom A. Wilmart, *Les Ecrits Spirituels des deux Guigues*, R.A.M., 1924, vol. 5, p. 142, note 1.

Sweetness: the word or its like appears on every rung of the ladder. It is difficult for us, whose physical craving for sweet things has constantly been satisfied (and often sated) from childhood to understand the thrill that the taste, say, of honey can bring to a delicate and unspoilt palate. It is only to the over-civilised taste that *sweetness* sounds lifeless and insipid (tasteless—vocabulary itself becomes perverted), and no longer has the overtones of the medieval *dulcedo*. And in any case, no word can express the consolation inseparable from contemplative experience, as the hymn *Jesu dulcis memoria* reminds us:

> *Nec lingua valet dicere*
> *Nec littera exprimere...*

Dulcedinis gaudia degustans: the ineffable sweetness of mutual love when lovers meet. But in this case, one of the lovers is God. It is therefore a fruit and a proof of the Divine presence, of union in love. But it is not the union itself and must never be taken as such. If it is, there is no longer the authentic contemplation, but the cult of self, self-love.

Guigo, in speaking of the contemplative experience, has recourse not only to the sense of taste, but also to the sense of sight. The aim of every contemplative is to see God's face. If the experience is a foretaste of the eternal sweetness, it is also a preview of the vision of the blessed. There is an unbroken continuity between the experience and the vision "face to face": the one is a real anticipation of the other.

Guigo is not concerned to theorise about the relationship between the beatific vision and contemplative experience, or about the various degrees of that experience. But another Carthusian of the same name, Guigo du Pont, writing more than a century later, in a treatise entitled *De Contemplatione*,[1] develops the main theme of the *Scala Claustralium*. After distinguishing between a form of contemplation which he calls *speculatio scholastica*, which may be taken to embrace the first three rungs of the ladder,[2] and contemplation in the strict sense, Guigo goes on to say that, at the summit of contemplation proper, there is

---

[1] Cf. J.-P. Grausem, S.J., "*De Contemplatione du chartreux Guigo du Pont*," R.A.M. 10, 1929, pp. 259–89.

[2] Intellectual, antecedent, active, or "acquired" contemplation, as distinct from infused, passive contemplation, which consists especially in an intuition of love.

a totally different experience, one granted only rarely, the *excessus mentis*, ecstatic contemplation. This, in turn, has two modes, the imperfect and the perfect. In the imperfect mode the soul truly sees God, uncreated Light. It sees him directly and not through a veil, just as one sees the sun when the cloud which hides it from view is suddenly rent. But just as the eyes are instantly blinded by the brightness of the sun, so the soul's gaze is unable to bear the brightness of the divine light. One sees, but what one sees most of all is that one cannot see. It is a furtive and passing vision, rapid and inconstant, like a streak of lightning, still so far from the clear and lasting vision of heaven that it should be called rather "through a glass in a dark manner," than "face to face."

The perfect mode, higher and still more rare, is the one such as St. Paul was favoured with. Whereas in the former case the soul, powerless to fix its gaze on the divine light, sees God rather by what is about than by what is in Him, it now contemplates Him in His very essence, *per essentiam*. It is in this way that the highest hierarchies of angels see Him. It is manifest that Guigo du Pont here speaks of immediate vision, and it seems that he claims the same for the imperfect mode; but he is aware that not all would agree with him, and concludes with the remark that the safest thing is to hold to the recommendation of Holy Writ: "Seek not the things that are too high for thee."

By comparison with his *Ladder of Four Rungs*, the *Meditations* of Guigo the Angelic are hardly known at all.[1] Eleven in number, their style is often lyrical, and they abound in extended metaphor and the allegory and symbolism of the medieval scriptural exegete. Their common theme is union with God in Christ, by imitation of Him. Like so much of the spiritual thought of the Middle Ages, the *Meditations* owe much to St. Augustine, and some of them are reminiscent of the devotional writing of St. Bernard, to whom they were wrongly ascribed for some time. They have been compared to the *Imitation of Christ* of à Kempis; but the likeness is mainly due to their belonging to a period prior to and free from the over-subtle

---

[1] They are extant in several MSS., two of which are in the British Museum, Harley 47, ff., 1r.–12r. (latter half of the thirteenth century) and Royal 8 F 1, ff. 101v.–110r. (c. 1200). The Latin text with a French translation was published in *La Vie Spirituelle*, Suppl., 1932–34.

speculations of the later medieval theologians, to which the author of the *Imitation* was striving to return.

Guigo's method in these meditations is to take a text of Holy Writ, meditate on it, converse familiarly with Our Lord, and then return to the same source for further meditation and contemplation. From the first he insists that the life of union with God calls for purification, moral and ascetical. This means solitude:

O bone Jesu—O good Jesus, may I have no one by me, so that I may be more intimately with You. *Woe to him that is alone*, with whom You are not the only one. How many there are in a multitude who are yet alone, because they are not with You. Though no man be with me, yet I am not alone: I am a crowd to myself.

It means humility of mind and heart:

Lord, You say: *Learn of me, because I am meek, and humble of heart*. Indeed, it is good to become humble, it makes for quiet; he who does not keep quiet is unable to hear him who speaks. Let the earth that I am, Lord, stop talking in your presence, so that I hear what You are saying within me, my God. Your whispered words are only heard where silence is deep; those wonderful words that raise a soul solitary and silent above itself: *for he that humbleth himself shall be exalted*. He who will remain in silence alone will rise above himself. But where is this high place? In his heart? But how can his heart rise above him? What is above him is the sovereign good, his God, seeing whom and loving whom, he is in a better way to see and love himself.

It means fidelity to God, especially in times of trial and affliction:

Speak, Lord, to the heart of your servant, because my heart speaks to You. Speak to the abandoned orphan: *To thee is the poor man left: thou wilt be a helper to the orphan*.

The hindrances that are in the way of union with God are a cloud, and the soul has to pass through it to reach the perfection of charity in contemplation. This cloud, which hides our prayer from God, is like the cloud through which Moses passed for six days; which means the practice of the virtues, particularly the contemplative virtues, the gifts of the Holy Spirit: fear, piety, knowledge, fortitude, counsel, and understanding. Charity, the love of God, unites all these, and from their unity comes profound peace of soul.

There is the cross of the body to bear, but also the cross of the
soul. The cross of the body is the mortification of its members.
The cross of the soul is the fear of God, for it fixes the soul in such
a way that it cannot turn aside, neither to the right nor to the left.
There is also another cross of the spirit; it is love: *With Christ I am
nailed to the cross.* This cross is a love that makes the heart to be
gentle, tender, a heart of flesh. This is why Christ was immolated,
as it were like a lamb. He who with such a love has passed through
the cloud pours out his prayer in the presence of God. Moses was
for six days in the cloud on Mount Sinai, but on the seventh day
the Lord called him out from the midst of the cloud. *And the sight,*
he said, *of the glory of the Lord was like a burning fire.* The six days
signify those six virtues by which we attain to wisdom. Wisdom
is at the summit, alone; there the fire of the most ardent love
manifests the face of divine glory. All the degrees below wisdom
are darkness and cloud.[1]

The purification and the regeneration of the soul are God's
work, and in this work of re-creation we discover anew the
image of God in ourselves. Almost instinctively the Carthusian
turns to meditate on the marvels of grace in Our Lady. She is
Virgin of virgins, "My Lady, whose beauty the very angels
covet." He presents her as the helper and protectress of our
spiritual rebirth. By her we go to her Son; being the Mother of
Christ she becomes the mother of the co-heirs of Christ.

God the Father prepared you for his Son, that you might prepare
us for Him. When we languish with a spiritual hunger that Christ
alone can assuage with the "Bread of Angels," Our Lady is the
mistress of that holy repast, a marriage feast. Through the Body
of Christ we gain the spirit of Christ: *He that eateth my flesh and
drinketh my blood hath everlasting life. The food of the soul is Christ,
living bread come down from heaven*; in this life He nourishes us
spiritually by faith, in the future life by the vision "face to face."
For, by faith, Christ dwells in us, and faith in Christ is Christ in
our hearts: *fides Christi est Christus in corde tuo.* The soul is nourished
by this faith, the mysteries of which the mind masticates in meditation, and the heart assimilates in contemplation. For wisdom,
though it begins in understanding, is perfect only in love. You
have understood in vain, unless you love what you have understood; for wisdom is in love, *in amore sapientia.* Understanding
does flow from wisdom, but only takes a taste; it is love that

[1] Meditation 4.

tastes the flavour, *intellectus quidem quasi in transitu gustat, amor autem solidum sapit*: the soul's whole strength is in love. Love is life, it commands the virtues; it goads us on to the imitation of Christ, above all in his Passion. For we not only eat the Body of Christ, but we drink the chalice of his Blood, a chalice of suffering; but we thirst to drink it; that is, we ardently desire to share in his sufferings, to suffer: *only he who has shared in the sufferings of Christ may share in the glory of Christ*.[1]

To suffer, to share in the sufferings of Christ. This facet of suffering is far different from the suffering of purification, the passing through the cloud by the practice of the six virtues in preparation for the seventh, wisdom, which is the presence and the vision of God. To share in the sufferings of Christ presupposes both purification and presence; for the sufferings of Christ were those of One who had no need of the one and who always enjoyed the other. The suffering of Christ was pure compassion with ours. Compassion: to suffer with, to suffer with another just because he suffers; but this can be only out of love; compassion is a form of love.

The authentic contemplative, like Our Lord, loves the sinner, for there is no suffering like sin. That is why the suffering, and the compassion, of Our Lord were so great. He who never sinned took on Himself the suffering of our sins. But the true contemplative is drawn to the sinner for another reason too, out of humility. There are two truths of which the true contemplative is keenly conscious. First, that nothing can help the sinner more than the high prayer to which he has come, by the grace of God. Secondly, that he owes his high prayer in some real degree to the lowly prayers of the sinner, for whom and with whom he prays.

There has never been what could be called strictly a "school" of Carthusian thought about spirituality. However, it is characterised by certain traits: "wise discretion, constant care not to lose sight of, even in the heights of the contemplative life, the lowly struggles of the purgative way, and a tender love for Our Lord."[2] The writings of Guigo the Angelic seem to fully endorse this remark. Moreover, for him, though contemplation is more affective than intellectual, it is still intellectual. There is no vision without love, no love without light. The emphasis is on love,

[1] Meditations 9–11.   [2] J.-P. Grausem, S.J., R.A.M., 1929, p. 289.

but not out of fear for being mistaken about the light in which he sees God. The mounting rungs of the "ladder," he says, are closely concatenated, and reading and meditating his doctrine of the ascent to divine contemplation remind you of the rings of colour in the rainbow, each merging imperceptibly into the one above, as he strives to tell us of this preview of Invisible Light, Truth eternal, which is also a foretaste, because that Truth is Love.

In amore sapientia, "Wisdom lies in love." The phrase is the key to the understanding of Guigo's aim and purpose. The gift of Wisdom is the gift of Contemplation, which comes when the soul is lovingly disposed to receive God and to recognise Him, in love, by His loving presence. Guigo in his writing wished to help his reader to arrive at the goal where Love itself is knowledge.

We cannot appreciate to the full his teaching on contemplation unless we bear in mind the conditions of his own religious contemplative life. Contemplation always depends on certain conditions, on a "way of life." Its characteristic feature, wherever it is found, is detachment from all that truly distracts the soul from God. This implies, at least in practice, some degree of separation from the world. Contemplation thus implies a spirit of asceticism (rather than any particular austerity); it implies periods set aside for habitual and continued prayer. It implies fidelity to the way of life decided upon (usually in consultation with a spiritual director). It implies reading, meditation and prayer, as Guigo describes these exercises.

Every Christian should strive to model his life on this ideal, in the simple Christian family, as well as in the Priesthood and the more active Religious life. Very many do so. They are in the world but not of it. They unite their contemplative life, which keeps them unfettered by the world, to their active life and its obligations. But the perfection of this ideal is much more surely realised in the monastic life, for this is expressly instituted for it. It stands for far greater separation from the world, for more exclusive consecration to penance and prayer, and for work, manual and intellectual, of a kind that will not hinder but favour it. The absolute of such a way in the Church is the ordered eremitical life.

12. ST. CLARE OF ASSISI

Gabriel Reidy

ST. FRANCIS and St. Clare were fellow-citizens, though drawn from different social classes. Francis, son of the well-to-do cloth-merchant, Peter Bernardone, was already a boy of eleven or twelve when the noble lady Clare was born on 16 July 1193 (or 1194), heralded, it is said, by a prophetic dream of her mother, Ortolana, which foretold the birth of "a certain light which will make the true Light shine forth all the more clearly." The naming of Clare is attributed to the prophecy, and the heavenly example of punning on this theme was not neglected, as witness the *clara re, Clara nomine* of the Breviary.[1] During the twelve years of Clare's childhood, Francis, because of his naturally gay temperament, his love for bright and coloured clothes, and his delight in music and lively companionship, was putting himself in a fair way to earn the reputation of being the chief "playboy" of the town. I had almost said "teddy-boy," for if we take away from that concept the sense of uprootedness, the blind anger and criminal proclivities, much is left in the guitar-playing, unconventionally but colourfully garbed modern youth which would have appealed to the saint of Assisi.[2] Consequently, the period of his conversion to God corresponds with the years of Clare's dawning young womanhood, and it is quite clear that the young convert's behaviour, whatever effect it may have had on others, made a lasting impression on the young girl, strong enough to make her his faithful disciple for ever after. Francis, for his part, was to find in her a God-given ally—*adjutorium simile sibi* (*Gen.* II, 18)—who would prove a source of comfort when so many others whom he had trusted let him down.

[1] Cf. *Legenda Sanctae Clarae virginis*, edited by Francesco Pennacchi, Assisi, 1910, p. 5. This life is usually attributed to Thomas of Celano, who also produced two biographies of St. Francis.

[2] One should read and make what one can of the initial three chapters of Celano's first Life. Cf. A. G. Ferrers Howell's edition (London 1908), pp. 2 ff.

The spiritual union between them transcends any attempt to explain it in purely natural terms, especially those of romantic sentimentality. It was a bond productive of enduring effects, especially the persistence through the ups and downs of seven centuries of two religious families still recognisably their sons and daughters. As religious founders their roles are precisely those of father and daughter, master and disciple, founder and co-foundress; the originality coming from his side, the fidelity from hers. St. Francis, as Coulton rightly observed, "was one of the most original characters in history: we cannot expect that two such should be born in one little town within a single decade or so."[1] The recorded facts lend themselves to an interpretation which asserts that the characters of Francis and Clare were complementary, each answering a deep need in the other, and so enabling them to fulfil specific roles in the total accomplishment of that new way of realising the Christian vocation which God had shown to Francis through reading the gospel. Others might prefer to say that each was the other's indispensable auxiliary in launching the "Franciscan movement," or in delivering the "Franciscan message to the world." Romantics, no doubt, would like to affirm that they "were made for each other," and either leave it at that, hanging ambiguously, or else be tempted to embroider upon the theme after the manner of their kind. The brute facts of history are against them. Francis and Clare were not made for each other; they were made for God, and they knew this, and it was a help to both of them in coming to their full stature as baptised members of the church of God. Francis, once converted, was too much enamoured, too deeply committed to the "Lady Poverty," ever to "fall for" any of the great ladies, who were, among so many others, attracted by the inescapable charm of his holiness, even for Clare, who unquestionably was the nearest and dearest of them all.

Clare, on her side, had given early signs of her resolve to be a spouse of Christ the Bridegroom. From the age of about five till she was ten Clare lived in exile with her family at Perugia. Her markedly devout life was known there, and still more when, on their return to Assisi, there was question of the usual sort of suitably arranged marriage for her. One feels that she would

[1] *Five Centuries of Religion*, Vol. 2 (Cambridge 1927), pp. 157-8.

have become a nun in any case, and possibly a remarkable one.
But it was the coming of Francis to preach the Lent in the
church of San Giorgio at Assisi in February 1212, which placed
the vision of Christ in His earthly image before her eyes. Thus
did Francis woo her for Christ, appealing at once to her senses,
her head and her heart, and thus did he determine her vocation.
Early that Holy Week she left home and went to him, filled
with the desire to lead the perfect evangelical life, in as close
accord with the model of Francis and his friars as was possible
for a woman in that age. Her cousin Ruffino was already among
the earliest companions of Francis, and soon, to the great dis-
pleasure and scandal of the family, her sister Agnes was to
follow her. The flight to San Damiano eventually included her
mother Ortolana, two aunts, and other cousins and relatives.

Henceforward Clare was one with Francis, though one with
him only in and through Christ, whom they both contemplated
by choice in His sufferings and death, in the Blessed Eucharist,
and in the lowly simplicity and poverty of His earthly life. In
all this their mutual responsiveness was such that there might
have ensued the sort of friendship which, while not detracting
essentially from their sanctity, might have seemed to dull it
somewhat, and prevent it from shining quite so brightly. They
form together an eloquent testimony that this need not happen:
each of them, in fact, added to the force and the lustre of the
other's holiness. Popular legends survive to show that contemporaries were quite capable of misunderstanding and traducing
their relationship. They were aware of it and reacted in the
classic manner of Christian ascetics. Their own and subsequent
ages have "justified their memory." The story of the saints'
discussion of this matter is a good deal more than a mere
"example" of chastity, self-control, the avoidance of scandal, and
so on. Clare's reactions, their parting, the miracle of the roses,
form a little idyll which recalls, but also transcends the episode
of Scholastica and Benedict. "It is time for us to part . . . when
shall we meet again? . . . when summer returns and the roses
bloom again . . . and so the saints parted no more . . ." This,
together with the tale cited by Karrer[1] of the moon in the well,
shows that Clare was to Francis what Beatrice became for
Dante—the real living symbol of everything dearest, best and

[1] Cf. Otto Karrer, *St. Francis of Assisi* (London 1947), pp. 62–3.

holiest in his life; she is identified with "our Sister Moon 'casta e
preziosa'," and also with Lady Poverty, and with Perfect Joy.

In attempting to analyse the spirituality of St. Clare, it is
well, I think, to underline in the first place, and as the very root
of it, her unwavering, even sometimes obstinate devotion to
Francis himself, or rather to the vivid and exact likeness of
Christ which he, more than any other, put before her. This
feature of her spiritual life shapes and colours everything she
thought and did. She has succeeded, also, in handing it down to
her daughters in every age. If you question modern Poor Clares
about the origins of their vocation, it is remarkable how many
of them are prepared to admit that they knew little or nothing
about Clare herself before joining her Order. St. Francis had
been the main force of attraction to them as to her. Familiarity
with Clare—and I mean the term in its most literal application
of an intimate *family feeling*—comes later; not so much by reading
about her, for the available sources are scanty enough, but by
the daily living of her Rule, which is, as far as she could make
it so, not so much hers as that of Francis.[1]

From the early part of Holy Week 1212 until the death of
St. Francis fourteen years later, there was a fruitful co-operation
between the two saints, notwithstanding the frequent absences of
Francis in other parts of Italy or abroad, and in spite of the
self-denying ordinances which he imposed on himself and his
brethren regarding actual visits to the convent of San Damiano,
of which Clare was now the abbess. It is not easy to "document"
the ways in which two such saints communicate with one
another and influence one another's work. We know enough,
however, to be sure that Clare received the necessary "formation"
and support from Francis and his early brethren, requisite to
make them truly Franciscan in spirit and outlook, whatever
mitigations of the primitive ideals may have been either then
or afterwards forced upon them. In fact, one of the few, if not
the only occasion where Francis is made to refer explicitly to
that very elusive thing the "spirit" of the Franciscan Order,
occurs in a chapter of Celano entitled "How he would have the
brethren behave themselves towards them" [the Poor Clares]:

[1] Poor Clares in England refer to "Mother St. Clare," as though she were
their contemporary. As there usually is a real Clare in the offing, this custom
can lead to a certain amount of confusion for the uninitiated!

He promised ever steadfastly to bestow the help and counsel of himself and his brethren on them . . . and, when nigh to death, commanded ever more to be performed, and that not negligently, declaring that it was one and the same spirit that had led the brethren and these Poor Ladies forth from the world.[1]

As much can be inferred from Clare's womanly reactions when some of this support was withdrawn.[2]

After the death of St. Francis, St. Clare had to bear a solitary witness to the pure Franciscan truth for twenty-seven years more until her own death on 11 August 1253. This period of "spiritual widowhood"—fully half her active life—must have been a bitter and lonely trial in many ways, for Franciscan ideals were being misunderstood and much travestied outside the faithful little enclosure of San Damiano. Yet it was a time of fidelity too, and therefore precious, during which the "plantuncula" of St. Francis, as she liked to call herself, made growth and bore fruit.[3]

In 1228, two years after the death of St. Francis, Pope Gregory IX, friend of both saints, came to the little Umbrian city in order to canonise the Seraphic Patriarch. One line of tradition places during this visit of the pope, the famous *privilegium paupertatis* which Clare's obstinate devotion to the dead saint and her importunity succeeded in wresting from Gregory against his better judgment.[4] Without here entering into the historical controversies on this subject, or into those on the interpretation of this paradoxical "privilege" granted to the nuns of San Damiano, "not to have any possessions whatsoever,"[5] we may at least affirm that the coupling together of these two events in the biography, whether intentional or not, whether chronologically accurate or not, is still of the greatest symbolic value and interest. It is like asking which of the two events is of the greater ultimate importance—an exercise of the infallibility of the Church to give a new saint officially to all as patron and model, as a means to the very many who will desire to follow him in a general way

[1] Celano, *op. cit.*, II, CLV. The two following chapters deal with the restrictions Francis himself imposed on these spiritual ministrations. Cf. Howell, *op. cit.*, pp. 332–5.

[2] Cf. *Legenda* (Pannacchi), p. 52, where Clare refuses to benefit by the temporal ministrations of the friars if their spiritual ministrations are to be curtailed.

[3] "Clare, unworthy handmaid of Christ, and *the little plant* of the most blessed Father Francis . . ." Cf. *The Rule of St. Clare and the Constitutions . . . St. Colette* (Dublin 1932), pp. 6, 36, 44.   [4] Cf. English text of the Privilege, *ibid.*, pp. 30–1.

[5] *Ibid.*, p. 30. Cf. also Coulton, *op. cit.*, pp. 158–9.

without either ability or desire to penetrate very deeply into his finest insights about poverty or other points of evangelical observance; or an equally authoritative act, however restricted, however exceptional, destined to preserve the wellnigh impossible ideal of Francis in at least one inviolable shrine, even if it should come to be mitigated or abandoned everywhere else.

On the subject of evangelical poverty, as in other points regarded as essential to the concept of Franciscanism, all the authorities are at one in holding up St. Clare as "the most authentic Franciscan" of all. She was the one who understood St. Francis best, and was able to appreciate his aims with the greatest purity and devotion, outstripping here even those great saints who brought the fruits of learning as well as of their own real sanctity, and the manifest successes of a wide-spread, up-to-date apostolate to their interpretation of his Rule and ideals. "Her soul," writes one of these authorities, "entirely permeated by the Franciscan spirit, ardently loved the Seraphic Patriarch, knew his mind and made it her own, better perhaps than anyone else."[1]

Such a chorus of agreement does not, of course, signify any such exaggeration as that Clare was the female counterpart of Francis, or even that she and her daughters were able to give *the* woman's reaction to the Franciscan message taken *as a whole*. It does mean that their part in it was a very important one, and that Clare was able, not only to enter more deeply than others into his ideals, but also to convey them to others, if not always in the more ordinary and orthodox ways, then in other ways not so easy to formulate. She still is, even in our day, an ever active and potent symbol of certain absolute and essential elements in the Franciscan life, understood in its highest and purest form. This is an arresting phenomenon, even if one does not care to use the term miraculous. For Clare is not the foundress of her own Order in any conventional sense of that term, nor can she rank as an outstanding spiritual teacher outside the walls of her own convent of San Damiano. She left no impressive corpus of spiritual writings behind her,[2] nor, though an ecstatic,

[1] Vitus a Bussum, O.F.M.Cap., De spiritualitate franciscana (Rome 1949), p. 33. Cf. also Mark Stier, Franciscan Life in Christ (New Jersey 1953), p. 135, and Gemelli, Francescanesimo (Milan 1932), pp. 78–9.

[2] Her writings consist of Rule, Testament and Blessing, all inspired by the cognate writings of Francis and in parts clearly modelled upon those sources. In addition there are five letters, mostly to Blessed Agnes of Bohemia, dealing

did she greatly excel as prophetess or seer of visions. Whatever
fresh impulse was given to the growth of her Order by the
reform of St. Colette in the fourteenth century, that is all very
much past history. now, and the Clares have had no recent
impulse at all comparable to that given by St. Teresa of Lisieux
to the Carmelites. The inference must be that Clare herself, as
symbolic of the Franciscan spirit, and as somehow mysteriously
a carrier of it even to the women of our own times, is still a
powerful factor in the life of the Church, and, indeed, even
beyond its visible limits. There were never more than five
houses of "Minoresses" in Pre-Reformation England; many of
the present-day Poor Clare communities of Great Britain descend
from the early seventeenth-century restoration of Fr. John
Gennings, who came here as refugees from the French Revolu-
tion.[1] But the power of Clare to inspire indigenous vocations
is testified amongst other things by the Colettine families associated with the convert Miss Imrie, and by the influence on a
number of Anglican communities recorded by Peter Anson in
his *Call of the Cloister*.

It follows from what has been said that the spirituality of
St. Clare, like that of St. Francis, must have centred entirely
around Christ, and in the manner and forms most according to
the bent of the Poverello: that is, a life-long contemplation of
the great work of the Incarnation and Redemption, as it has been
characteristically developed in Franciscan theology, mysticism,
preaching, literature, art and devotion. All this is a good deal
more than the gentle kindness and courtesy of Francis, his
striking outward resemblances to Our Lord, or even that thorough-
going interpretation of the gospel which turned the Italian
countryside of his time into a replica, in the eyes of so many,
of the Holy Land in the time of Christ. It was rather his complete
grasp of the mystery of Christ as a whole, and his power to
convey it to others, even though his expression of it may have
been lacking in certain respects. It lacked, for instance, complete-
ness and precision of theological statement; it was, as he himself
would have put it, a "simple," "unlearned," "unlettered"

with poverty and other points of observance. They are published in full in
English in *St. Clare of Assisi* by Leopold de Chérancé, O.S.F.C., translated by
R. F. O'Connor (London 1910), pp. 138–157.
   [1] Hermans, *The Franciscans in England* (London 1898), pp. 30 ff.

Christianity. It was preached with strong emphasis on certain aspects of Christ, preferring to stress, for example, the "human" side of the mystery, and even there selecting mainly the features more expressive of the weakness, vulnerability and condescension of the Word, His infancy, His cross and passion.

For these reasons, it is notoriously easy to give a biased picture of Francis, notwithstanding his admitted likeness to Our Lord. One can have a weakened picture of Francis just as one can have a weakened version of Christ—the "gentle Jesus" line of thought. There is, too, the widely diffused, but emasculated picture of Francis the sentimental nature-lover, which is not really Christian at all. Most dangerous of all is the more erudite but also more passionate presentation of Francis as the unique religious genius of all time, victimised and robbed of his most creative works by a legalistic, self-interested medieval Church, by Ugolino, Elias, the Ministers. The real Francis was a man entirely conformed to the whole revealed mystery of Christ. He had indeed a special attraction towards the infancy of Jesus, which was expressed by his lowly and simple way of life, and culminates in the story of the Greccio crib.[1] His preference for contemplating the sufferings of Our Lord was expressed by his life-long penance and culminates in his own stigmatisation. But it is equally necessary to underline his great devotion to and realisation of Christ in the Church, expressed in devoted obedience towards the Holy See, in veneration for the sacraments, particularly the Blessed Eucharist, and for the ministrations of priests. It is inconceivable that he should have wished to do anything himself or found anything for the sake of others which was not totally in conformity with Christian doctrine and Catholic practice as he knew and met with it in fact. That is why the "spirit" of Franciscanism, which sometimes seems so elusive a quality to the learned who write about it, and so varied according to each man's personal prejudices or pet theories, is best and most exactly stated in the liturgy—Francis was before all else *vir catholicus*, a Catholic man.

We shall naturally expect, since St. Clare was the most authentic follower of St. Francis, that her spirituality will turn out to be cut of the same cloth. This is precisely what we do find. Her devotion to him demands it; his policy about the formation

[1] Celano, *op. cit.*, II, CLI.

L

of the Ladies of San Damiano, and the rather fragmentary documentation of the way he put this into practice is sufficient proof of it. Naturally we shall not look in Clare and her sisters for that more evolved, reflexive Christology of a Bonaventure or a Duns Scotus. But we shall find in them what was one necessary ingredient of such things, namely, a devoted woman's immediate, direct and intuitional grasp of the marrow of the gospel, according to Francis. This comes out even in a legislative document like her Rule, which, as we have said, is, generally speaking, a mere adaptation for women of the Franciscan Rule. Yet there are interpolations in it which are not so accounted for, and may well be an echo of some conference or spiritual direction that he gave her verbally. One such passage concerns poor clothing and speaks with the characteristic accents of Francis:

> And for the love of the most holy and most sweet child Jesus, wrapped in poor little swaddling clothes and laid in a manger, and of His most holy mother, I admonish, beseech and entreat my sisters that they be always clothed in poor garments.[1]

As for the Passion, it is almost always precisely this point if no other which is brought forward to show the unique dependence of Clare upon Francis. She had, we are told, a very great personal devotion to the Passion and the Wounds of Christ, which she associated daily with the time between Sext and None. She used, and taught her novices to use, the special Office of the Passion which Francis had compiled. And her mystical life would seem to have reached its peak in a lengthy ecstasy lasting practically all through a certain Thursday and Friday of Holy Week.[2] She practised, and exhorted others to practise, a penitence which tended to excess, and seriously affected her health, so that even the penitential Francis had to intervene to moderate it.[3]

The devotion of Francis to Christ was rooted in orthodox sacramental theology, and this too he transmitted to Clare. His eye was so pure and so widely-ranging that we are apt to declare

---

[1] *Rule, op. cit.*, ch. II, p. 9. This line of devotion to the Infancy continues amongst Franciscans. St. Antony of Padua is one of the saints conventionally represented with the Infant Jesus in his arms, Bonaventure will write a *De Quinque Festivitatibus Pueri Jesu*, which is one of the most attractive developments of the theme since the *De Puero Jesu Duodenni* of St. Aelred of Rievaulx in the twelfth century.

[2] Vitus a Bussum, *op. cit.* 35-36; Stier, *op. cit.* 135-136.

[3] Vitus a Bussum, *ibid*.

that it saw God in everything, yet his own explicit declaration is to the contrary:

> I see nothing bodily in this world of the most high Son of God Himself, except His most holy body and blood, which they (priests) receive and they alone administer to others. These most holy mysteries I wish to be held in highest honour and to be kept in precious places.[1]

It was this Eucharistic devotion which made him so humbly reverent towards all priests, even the unworthy, and it partly accounts for his regard for France which he thought of as "the land of Christ's body."[2] We may be sure that the Eucharistic devotion at San Damiano goes far beyond the prescriptions in St. Clare's Rule that the novices must be examined on their knowledge of the sacraments, that the nuns should confess twelve times and communicate seven times each year, frequent for those days if not for ours, or such disciplinary details as the arrangements for receiving communion through the grille without their being seen. The sureness of touch with which Francis had managed to hand on to St. Clare and her companions this central and life-giving Eucharistic cultus is, perhaps, more easily gauged from Celano's account of an event of 1241, when the abbess's fortitude and devotion to the body of Our Saviour miraculously delivered the convent from an onslaught of Frederick II's "Saracen" mercenaries. She appeared before the enemy, undaunted, preceded by the silver pyx within an ebony case in which the Blessed Sacrament was reserved. After a few prayerful exchanges between the Abbess and her Lord, whose voice was heard "like that of a boy," the Saracens were affrighted, clambered back over the convent walls and scattered. This event is represented in a well-known statue of the saint holding a somewhat anachronistic monstrance in her hands.[3] Her biographer also illustrates her great personal devotion to the Eucharist, by referring to her humble and tearful demeanour in reception, and her truly Franciscan and practical devotion towards the decency of the altar and its furniture. Thus, even when confined to bed very ill, she sat, propped up with cushions, to sew "more than

---

[1] So St. Francis in his *Testament*. Cf. *The Rule of St. Francis* . . ., (Dominic Devas O.F.M.), London, 1927, pp. 49–51.

[2] Celano, *op. cit.*, II, p. 329.

[3] Cf. Celano . . . Pennacchi, pp. 30–31.

fifty pair of corporals," which she enclosed in purple silk cases and sent around to various churches of the diocese.[1]

The Mendicant Friars developed a new theory of an *apostolic* form of the religious state, with a new statement of spirituality to accompany it. After one has read St. Thomas Aquinas and St. Bonaventure, and their vindication of it, there is some risk of taking it for granted, and supposing it to have been inherent in the original religious movement which gave rise to the friars. Yet it was in fact, at least as far as the Franciscans are concerned, something of an unexpected phenomenon. Francis himself began as a hermit, moved by the very same gospel texts which, according to St. Athanasius' celebrated *Vita Antonii*, first drew Antony into the desert, the father of all monks, but an anchorite. Francis falls naturally into that ever-recurring series of western monastic reformers like Bruno, Romuald, Peter Damiani, etc., who reacted against the normal European trend away from the eremitical towards a more organised cenobitical monasticism. Francis, like the nineteenth-century Curé of Ars, retained a yearning for this side of monasticism, a preference for silence and solitude and the recollected contemplative prayer which it favours, even to the end of life. He and his companions preferred either no fixed habitations at all or the small informal "little places" in mountains or wastes, to the typical monastic establishments of the other Orders, or the urban friaries which were so soon to become typical of their own. A deliberate return, at least in theory, to these basically eremitical origins has characterised the beginnings of most of the Franciscan reform movements in the course of history, and there are still traces of a "desert spirituality" tradition in some branches of the order.

This tendency towards eremitism in the early days of the Franciscans may be connected with Francis's marked preference for manual as distinct from intellectual work, even despite his call to preaching, and with a number of other features of Franciscan life. Here again, it is evident that Francis handed on to St. Clare and her sisters some of his dearest predilections. On a superficial level, and adopting the "division of labour" scheme which was so popular in the Middle Ages, though far less so nowadays—it is the function of the knight to fight, the peasant to till the soil, the monk and the nun to pray for others,

[1] Celano, pp. 39-40.

within a fairly static "Christendom"—then it is obvious that the Poor Clares still preserve within the Franciscan Order that original eremitical side of the life, with an asceticism based on lowly manual labour, and aiming at an apostolate concentrated in contemplative prayer. But on a much deeper and more fundamental level, it is interesting to note that the Clares are not merely the conservators of this side of Franciscanism, however essential it may be, but also contributed to the shaping of the *vita apostolica* of the friars themselves.

Although, admittedly, St. Clare was not the "original" but dependent on the direction of Francis, there were occasions when the roles were reversed and she directed him. It was so in reference to the Franciscan apostolate for souls. Francis, torn between love of souls and love of solitude, submitted the case to two independent judges. Or were they *independent* in the usual sense, and not biased in favour of eremitism? One was the cloistered St. Clare the other the priest Silvester who lived apart as a hermit. Both agreed, however, that the special vocation of Francis was more for the sake of others than merely for his own salvation. Francis accepted this adjudication humbly, as an obedience, and joyfully set about carrying it out.[1] In fact, as his infirmities increased, and as the government of the Order slipped more and more from his grasp, there were many opportunities as well as need to interrupt his preaching for periods of solitary retirement. The incident of Clare's judgment, or the text recording it, may be taken as one of the chief Franciscan contributions to the subsequent full working out in theory of the *vita mixta*, the apostolic version of the religious state which we now associate with the medieval friars, and which St. Thomas and St. Bonaventure so valiantly defended against its traducers. So important is this for the whole development of Christian spirituality that it would be a distortion of history not to record the part played in its formulation by the almost hidden figure of Clare. The intuition of this cloistered contemplative may not have been the decisive influence in shaping the apostolate of the friars, but at least it furnished a text and a precedent without which the theoretical justification of their apostolate might have proved much more difficult.

Should it be argued that altogether too much is here attributed

[1] Cf. S. Bonaventurae Opera omnia, Quaracchi, *Legenda S. Francisci*, nn. 1-2; *Fioretti* Cap. XV.

to a small, passing incident, one reply might be that we are apt to be defeated by the sheer wealth of documentation concerning Francis, to say nothing of the difficulty of its interpretation. One is left with the impression that his stature is so great that anyone coming within radius of his shining personality is thereby unduly dwarfed in significance. We must not grumble at our sources for succeeding in what they tried to do, and for "failing" to do what they did not even attempt. There is still enough in them to show that St. Clare had an *essential* role in receiving and interpreting Franciscan spirituality *as a whole*. Without irreverence we may perhaps follow the line of comparison inaugurated by Bartholomew of Pisa's famous book *De Conformitatibus*, and liken the position of Clare in the Franciscan sources to that of Our Blessed Lady in the gospels. The documents, in both cases, are not *about her*, but about someone and something else ineffably greater, yet if her part is small, it is an important one which *must be played*, and not simply an added beauty. St. Clare and the Poor Clares are an essential, though not of course a complete vehicle for the transmission of Franciscan spiritual teaching. Neither they alone, nor the First nor the Third Order alone, nor the many admirers of Francis both within and without the Catholic Church alone, nor, in my judgment, all of them taken together, have, so far, succeeded in delivering wholly and definitively the Franciscan message to the world. Like Christianity itself, in Chesterton's phrase, Franciscanism has not failed, for the very simple reason that it has not yet been fully tried.

If St. Clare is so significant, and if her Order has so important a statement to make as has been asserted, why then is it not done? The answer lies partly in the fact that Poor Clares do not seek for publicity and are not greatly familiar with its means, and that, at least as an exception, is no bad thing in these days. But a better and fuller answer is that their sort of influence is independent of such means, and all the more powerful for being hidden, and unrecognised even by those who need it most, and in fact, owe to it the greatest debt. It is the proper lot of the true contemplative apostle to be ever in our midst, but unseen, unheard and unfelt, like our own souls.

Yet even when such a reply has been made, numberless minor puzzles remain to plague the mind, or possibly to keep it awake. Why is it, for instance, that the great summaries which catch

and distil and render to us the very quintessence of the Ages of
Faith, have so little to tell us of Clare, and of this "woman's
aspect" of the Franciscan life? Implicitly, of course, they do. The
great *Summa* of St. Thomas, the small gem-like mystical *Summa*
of St. Bonaventure (his *De Triplici Via*) speak eloquently of the
paramount claims of the purely contemplative life, and of the
need for contemplative prayer even outside the visible framework
of that life. The great stone *summas*, the Gothic temples, with
their soaring columns and spires, they too speak of these same
things in their own dialect. But why is it that the greatest literary
and poetic *summa* of all, the *Commedia* of Dante, is so reticent on
the subject of St. Clare?

She is there, naturally, ·though not so prominently as we
should have liked or expected. Only a bold critic would dare
to take the great Christian poet to task upon his omissions,
or his right to place whom he will in what receptacle he will of
his other world. It might seem particularly ungrateful for a
Franciscan to make objections considering the wonderful eulogy
he gives of the Seraphic Patriarch himself. All the same, it seems
odd that Dante the theologian, Dante the Franciscan soul, above
all, Dante the enthusiast for the contemplative life, and Dante
who so much appreciated the part played by the Christian woman
in the making of a sane and godly world, should have omitted
to make more of the virgin of Assisi. From one point of view
his whole poem may be viewed as being organised on the theme
of Mary's intervention in the salvation of a man's soul, largely
through auxiliaries of her own sex, Lucy, Matilda, Lia and
Rachel and, above all, Beatrice. Why not Clare? As everybody
knows the poet does indeed encounter a Poor Clare, his own
wife's relative, Piccarda Donati, in Paradise: he meets her shade
in the third heaven of the still earth-shadowed, inconstant moon.
She figures there as an example of a dedicated soul who through
no personal fault has been unable to live up to the strict letter
of her vows, unable to run the shuttle right through to the end
of the weft.[1] But she is also there to tell us in a typically oblique
Dantean fashion, that Clare is in heaven too, and very much
higher up! Her name is not actually pronounced, either there,
or with that of Francis in the Mystic Rose,[2] nor where it would
fit in most naturally among his early companions and imitators

[1] *Par.*, III, 97 ff.   [2] *Par.*, XXXII, 35.

in holy poverty, but we may be sure that she is there, with her Rule and her programme for the perfect life, and her merits, and the Order she has left behind her in the Church and the world. Every Poor Clare to-day, and many another woman too, may learn with a kindling warmth at her heart that,

> "Perfetta vita ed alto merto inciela
> donna più su," mi disse, "alla cui norma
> nel vostro mondo giù si veste e vela,
>
> perchè fino al morir si vegghi e dorma
> con quello sposo ch'ogni voto accetta
> che caritate a suo piacer conforma".[1]

[1] " 'Perfect life and high desert,' she said to me, 'place in a higher heaven a lady by whose rule in your world they take the robe and veil, so that till death they wake and sleep with that Bridegroom who accepts every vow that charity conforms to his pleasure.' " Cf. *The Divine Comedy of Dante Alighieri* . . . John D. Sinclair, *III Paradiso*. London (revised edition), 1949, p. 55.

13. MECHTILD OF MAGDEBURG

Edmund Colledge

WHAT LITTLE WE KNOW about Mechtild's exterior life we learn from scattered and oblique references in her book, *The Flowing Light of the Godhead*; and although they still give rise to conjecture and controversy, enough is agreed to help us to relate her writings to their times. She was born about the year 1210 in the Low German-speaking areas about Magdeburg, on the great plain of the Elbe in central Germany. Her literary tastes, her language and knowledge all indicate that she was probably of aristocratic birth; and there is no doubt that she herself wrote the original drafts out of which her work is made. Of one experience she says "I cannot describe it in German, and I do not know Latin"—although her writings show that she had memorised many Latin phrases from the liturgy—and when, elsewhere, she says that she is ignorant of *schrift*, she obviously means, not "writing" but *scriptura*, the Latin text of the Bible and the Fathers. At the age of twelve, she tells us, she received her first powerful intimations of God's presence and nature, and these continued daily for more than thirty years. When still young she left her family and went to Magdeburg, to seek solitude and freedom from all her ties, and there, it would seem, she joined a community of Beguines, one of the many households of pious women living in poverty and chastity and devoting themselves under religious direction to a life of prayer and good works, although not permitted by the Church to organise themselves into any regular Order or to take solemn vows. Towards middle age, the life of ecstasies and consolation which she had for long experienced underwent a change, and she entered upon a long period of bitter desolation and affliction. We do not know whether in her earlier life she had written anything, but during the time in which she felt herself to be abandoned by God she at first endured a numbed silence, from which she was suddenly released, and felt herself commanded by Him to record her experiences. This she began to do, and it is evident that her writings only added to her afflictions, since they earned her the reproaches of many detractors, "my Pharisees," as she wryly calls them later, some of whom accused her of indiscreet enthusiasm or hypocrisy, others of doctrinal error tantamount to heresy. The burden of all this appears at one point to have broken her bodily, if not in spirit, and she hints that for a time she returned to her family home and was there nursed back to health. But she left them again, and lived in Magdeburg under Dominican direction if not according to St. Dominic's Rule, until, in advanced age, she entered the Cistercian house of Helfde, famous already for its ecstatic visionaries. She seems to have lived into her eighties, and dictates the last Book of her revelations as a blind, ailing old woman, weighed down once again with office, still singing of the love of God and longing for death that she may be with Him.

What we can discern of how she wrote will remind us greatly of St. Bridget of Sweden. In her case we still have one relic, a loose leaf on which she herself had written in Swedish one of her "Revelations"; and we know that during the second half of her life she was surrounded by a group of clerics, diligently collecting her jottings, arranging them, translating them into Latin, and, on some occasions, taking considerable editorial liberties with them. Although none of Mechtild's autographs have survived to us, nor has anything been preserved in her own native Low German, the *Flowing Light* as it survives shows all the traces of a similar editorial process. She herself sometimes wrote, sometimes dictated, short, isolated chapters; some are in prose, some in rhyming metre, very many are of the nature of prose poems. During her middle years these were collected, more or less in chronological order, and the person chiefly responsible for this would appear to have been her Dominican spiritual director in Magdeburg, Henry of Halle. This collection, "the diary of a soul," as Professor Hans Neumann, the leading Mechtild scholar today, aptly calls it, was copied and would seem to have been widely circulated, still in Low German, in her lifetime. Of the seven books into which it is divided, the first six were translated into Latin at a Dominican house in Halle, before her death, probably in the 1280's; and although this Latin version contains many errors of incomprehension and much drastic watering down of her doctrine and language, and departs completely from Henry's ordering of the chapters, still it offers indispensable information about the original text. This has entirely disappeared; and our chief source today is the manuscript at Einsiedeln of the High German translation made, 1343-45, by the Basel "Friends of God," under the direction of Henry of Nördlingen, from what was obviously a good Low German copy, which contained Book VII, composed in Mechtild's last years, and after the death of Henry of Halle. Many fragments survive: but here we can only mention MS. Additional 11430 in the British Museum, a collection made during two centuries by German Dominican nuns of material relating chiefly to Margaret Ebner, Henry of Nördlingen's spiritual daughter, which contains Mechtild's Book V, chapter 35, in a version obviously derived from an exceptionally pure medieval examplar. This has never been printed, but it is hoped that Neumann will give us the full critical edition which we so badly require. Till then, we have to make do with Gall Morel's edition of the Middle High German and the Solesmes Benedictines' Latin text, neither of them adequate; and English readers have available to them Lucy Menzies' translation, careful and readable but often wrong in detail.

In the first two books as we have them, there is much which manifestly was composed during a brief period of great release after long silence, the accumulation of many years' experience suddenly ripening into a whole succession of brief, ecstatic outpourings. Her lyrical gifts are here most evident, and she is most influenced by the ideas and language of *minne*, the poetry of carnal, courtly love. The opening of Book I is an incomparable dialogue between two ladies, Love and the Soul. Gravely, courteously, ceremonially they salute each other, each praising the other's excellence. So Iseult and Guinevere might have met and deferred and extolled one another's prowess in the lists of earthly love; and so the Soul says:

> My lady, many years you strove
> With the great Trinity above
> Till you had conquered God, and did compel
> Him within Mary's humble maidenhood to dwell.

This is the love for God of which His bride sang in the Old Law, strong as death, the unquenchable fire, the treasure which no man's riches can buy, which St. Paul praises as invincible, supreme and everlasting: it is a Christianised *minne*, a love practised and sung in the courts not of princes but of Heaven, yet still a love which is also a struggle to the death. "You have robbed me of every earthly treasure I possessed"—"You have not been cheated, you have a fair exchange." "You have destroyed all the days of my youth"—"I have made you free of heaven." "Love, you are a merciless thief: how can you ever restore me what you owe?"—"Soul, take me as your payment."

In the poems of this early period, Love will often appear as the relentless adversary and huntress, strong in her power over God Himself:

> To hunt you pleased me,
> To seize you eased me,
> To bind you appeased me:
> I wounded you, and so we two were one,
> Victim and slayer, conqueror and slave.
> I drove Almighty God down off His throne,
> I robbed Him of His mortal life,
> Back to His Father gloriously I Him gave;
> How could you hope your wretchedness to save?

The next chapter is a passage of prose which tells of the soul's rapture in God. In this rapture it is given comprehension of Trinity: "she sees a God, One in three Persons, she recognises the three Persons in an undivided God." But God greets the soul in the language of His court, which is not spoken in this earthly kitchen, and He and the soul are alone, playing the game of love. (Mechtild here is certainly echoing Hugh of St. Victor's dialogue between Man and his Soul, in *De Arrha Animae*, where it is said of the *ludus amoris:* "He comes that He may touch you, not to be seen by you; He comes to give you a glimpse of Himself, not to be understood by you; He comes not to satisfy you but to make you long for Him. . . .") None of the saints, not Our Lady herself, has any part in this, and the body knows no more about it than the peasant at his plough or the jousting knight. When the soul must return to earth, it experiences bitter woes, St. Paul's longing for dissolution and reunion with God; but still the chapter ends, "Ah, sweet Lord, all fire within, all radiance without, could I but know again that life which is Your gift to Your great ones, and which You have shown to me who am the least, I would gladly go on suffering here. No one can or should know Your embrace until he has risen above himself and has become annihilated."

Although the German text and the Latin version (in which it is IV 12) show certain disparities here, the last phrase in both is quite unambiguous—"und ze nihte worden," "et ad nihilum redigatur." This is a theme which will frequently recur in the mystical literature of Western Europe, in Hadewijch and *The Mirror of Simple Souls*, it is the untranslatable "noughting" of Julian and *The Cloud of Unknowing* (to which the inventive, restless, fanciful mind of *The Cloud's* author added a complementary "alling").

Those who teach of the soul's annihilation are in the first instance instructed by St. Paul, yet in later medieval times few such teachings escaped the censures of those who feared that all such doctrine was tainted with Manichaean dualism. A generation later than Mechtild, Margaret Porette was condemned and burned for what she taught; and there can be no doubt that one proposition to which she steadfastly adhered was: "That the soul annihilated takes leave of virtues, is no longer in their service and uses them no more, but they are obedient to the bidding of the soul." Whether or not Margaret was justly condemned (and that is a question recently reopened by the suggestion that *The Mirror of Simple Souls* is in fact her work), it seems plain that the chronicler William of Nangis is attributing to her words and thoughts not her own when he expands this proposition to: "That the soul annihilated in the love of its Maker can and should yield to nature whatever it desires, without any remorse or reproach of conscience"; but this very attribution shows us what follies were being taught by the simple, such as the heretics of Swabia whose doctrines St. Albert examined, or the perverted, like the notorious and mysterious "Bloemardinne" against whom Ruysbroek was to preach. To such persons, "annihilation" and "deification" were catchwords to justify monstrous perversions of the truth, and it is not surprising that the very words, in any context, became signals for alarm. Mechtild's "Pharisees," we can clearly see, took fright at her teachings, yet we can also see that her doctrine is wholly devoid of any such heretical taints.

The lover of God, she tells us, must leave the world, in soul as well as in body, must seek for a cessation of all activities. Yet we can read in her poem in Book I, "The Desert Has Twelve Qualities," that there is in her mind no question of a false passivity or Quietism:

"No-thing" your love must be,
And from "Thing" you must flee.
You must stand alone,
With no man make your home.
From striving cease,
From all beings find release.
Loose what you captive find,
And what is free, fast bind.
Bring comfort to the sick,
For yourself nothing seek.
You must drink the water of affliction
And kindle the fire of love with the wood of virtues,
And so you will truly dwell in the desert.

The Latin has a much-diluted prose version of this, beginning "Love abjection, flee admiration . . ."; but the translators need not have been frightened. Mechtild is here teaching, as William of St. Thierry had done a century before, that the soul has a likeness with God "which is above virtues," but in this same poem she insists, as in many other places (see, for example, III 6, the "six things" which the soul which will truly follow God must have) upon what Ruysbroek was finally to expound with utmost clarity, that though the essence of the soul may find essential union with God above virtues, above created activity, above even likeness to Him, still the soul in the body must go on practising virtues and exercising likeness to God.

There are many places in her book which also show us that although she never felt called to a fundamental exposition of heretical errors such as Ruysbroek undertook, still she is well aware of the dangers of false mysticism, and, in particular, of how easily it can be mistaken for sublime truth. Here is a prose-poem from Book II:

Lady Knowledge, it is written for us all
How St. Paul was led aloft to the third heaven.
This had never happened to him, had he still been Saul,
And had he found the truth

In the first heaven and in the second,
To the third he never would have climbed.
There is a heaven which the devil has made,
Fair as his skilful cunning can contrive.
Our thoughts roam sorrowfully here about,
Our soul can find no comfort here,
Where no love is but love of nature.
So the soul is inconsolate
And the foolish senses are deceived,
And in this heaven the devil shows himself
Sometimes transfigured like a shining angel,
Sometimes like God and with His Sacred Wounds.
Oh, simple soul, be on your guard!

Yet for her there seem to be no difficulties or bewilderment.
"One cannot understand divine gifts with human faculties. That
is why men go astray . . ."; and in IV. 2 she tells us that when
one of her evil angels presented himself to her at Mass as a
pseudo-Christ, showing her his stigmata, she put him to silence
with the brusque common sense of a Catherine of Siena or a
Teresa, asking him, if he be Christ, to say "who this can be Who
here and now, Son of the living God, is in the hands of the true
priest?" She displays the clear and exact theological knowledge
which medieval laymen could enjoy, if they had ears to hear.
Those who still put about the legend of a Church which educated
its higher ranks at the expense of the laity, left in the darkness
of ignorance and superstition, are themselves ignorant of the
evidence which simple people such as Mechtild have bequeathed
to us of how well taught they were. In the allegory, IV. 3, of
the maiden with the chalice and the sword who expounds to
her the three gifts of wisdom which God bestows, there is precisely the sequence of thought and exposition which we find a
century later in the dialogue between the lady and the poet in
Piers Plowman. Either character declares herself to be Holy
Church, giving baptism and conveying "priestly wisdom" to all
whom she receives; but either then reminds us that we are also
endowed with natural understanding, the faculties and capacity
for recognising truth which we shall use well or ill according
to the measure with which we seek and receive the third wisdom,
God's grace.

When we come to examine Mechtild's teachings upon that
other most suspect topic, "deification," we find again perfect

lucidity and orthodoxy in her thought. As with all her visions, she insists upon the purely supernatural character of what she has known and believes in: ". . . that was no earthly thing but spiritual, a thing of the spirit which the soul alone saw and rejoiced in. But the body had no part in it. . . ." What she has revealed in her writings has brought her much detraction and abuse, but there is nothing for her but to write: if she does, she fears ignorant men, but she fears God more should she keep silence, for He has commanded her to speak, and He assures her that He alone is her teacher.

> Then I was warned about this book,
> And men spoke threats against me.
> They did not want it kept:
> They wished to burn it. And I wept,
> And did as since my childhood I have done:
> In trouble, in my prayers to God I've run.
> So I fell down before my Love, and said:
> Alas, Lord, how You grieve me!
> You leave me for Your glory in my night.
> This is how You deceive me,
> For it was You who said that I must write.
> And in that moment God Himself did stand
> Before my sorrowing soul, my book in His right hand,
> And said: My love, take comfort now.
> No man can burn up truth.

In her earliest poems she had recorded that she had become one with God, and she had employed hyperbole which had given scandal to her contemporaries, as it still could today to partial or inattentive readers: in I. 44 we find,

> I had to go from all created things into God
> Who is my Father by nature,
> My Brother in humanity,
> My Bridegroom in love,
> And I am His without end.

Her Latin translators jibbed at this, and substituted:" How shall I not hasten into my God, Who is to me a Father to be venerated, a Brother to be longed for, a Bridegroom to be loved?" But those who had read her own German had been perturbed by it, as she shows in one of her later commentaries. "In one place in this book I said that the Godhead is my Father by nature, but you did not understand this, that everything which God has done with us is all of grace and not by nature . . .," and, characteristically, she continues, "You are right; and I too am right." They are right to insist that we must never believe other than that we, who are God's mortal creatures, only become His sons through the adoption of His grace; she is right to tell that through that adoption she has known a union with Him in which she could no longer perceive any difference between herself and God. This is the vision of divine union which gives her book its title, the knowledge of how the Godhead flows into the soul and the soul into It which Ruysbroek was to develop so powerfully; and it is of this that she makes God say to the soul, in words almost untranslatable, "My Lady Soul, your nature has entered so much into Me (ir sint so sere genaturt in mich) that between you and Me nothing can interpose" (I. 44); and it is not inapposite to point out Neumann's recent observation that these words, versified but with uncontaminated sense, are found in the next century in the pious anthology, Der Minne Spiegel, which was widely copied and read in German religious houses.

Yet Mechtild is remarkable, in her teaching upon deification, because although she has many of the ideas which Eckhart and Ruysbroek were to develop, such as the soul's likeness to God "above virtues" and the impossibility to the deified soul of sin, she also perceives that such union brings with it great responsibility and heavy cares. In V. 16 she says that there are learned people who say that it is human to sin; but she says that to sin is devilish. Christ was true man, and He did not sin; and if we wish to be like Him we must live like Him, or else be saved through our repentance of sin. The soul's own insufficiency, its need for union with God, is the theme of the next chapter, the poem called "The greeting and praises and prayer of a sinner" :

> . . . Remember, Lord, You can command
> A soul made pure to be Your bride.
> Perfect Your work, stretch out Your hand
> And set me, all unworthy, at Your side.
> Bid me come up, Lord, to Your feast:
> Then will my soul be clean and bright.
> But till I am from my own self released
> I shall remain in sorrow and in night.

M

She finds deep consolation in her contemplation of Christ's glorified humanity.

> Whenever I think that now His divine nature has bone and flesh, body and soul, I am lifted up with great joy, far above my merits. The angels are formed in their own fashion like to the Holy Trinity, and so they are pure spirit; but only the soul will dwell in her flesh in the Kingdom of Heaven, and sit there, a guest beside her everlasting Host, most like of all to Him. Their eyes will meet, their spirits intermingle, their hands will touch, their lips converse, and His Heart will speak to her heart.[1]

Yet these joys, unmixed with sorrow, are still to come. At times she can say that she is in hell upon earth in her longing for God; and it is impossible to read unmoved her accounts of what her soul's torments were like.

There is nothing in III. 10, "the Passion of the loving soul which it has from God," which need offend any pious reader if it be read aright. The allegory of the soul bearing her cross, being nailed and lifted up on it, thirsting, dying, rising again, is all achieved with the deepest reverence and devotion. On one level of meaning Mechtild is saying that she does as she is bidden, that she has taken up her cross and is following after Christ; but there is a further, deeper meaning. Her afflictions are manifold; the contempt of the world, her knowledge of her own sinfulness, her earthly cares and distractions all contribute to them, but they are rooted in the pain and torment which Christ's very love and her longing for His love bring to her. She was in "great darkness" for many years, she says; and she adds that no soul can be verily pierced by God's love without such sufferings, yet she avers that she would not be spared an instant of them, for they are to her more precious than any consolations which He might send. For precise description of the states of this affliction, we must wait for Walter Hilton and St. John of the Cross; but Mechtild is among the mystics perhaps unique in the love which she shows for her sorrows, because they are Christ's, and because she has learned that He will do as He has promised to us all. He did not say that He would take them away and put something different in their place, but "I will turn your sorrows into joy." Mechtild

---

[1] IV, 14.

is the poet of a sanctified, transfigured, glorified sorrow, most acceptable offering to the divine heart of Jesus.

In IV, 12 she writes of knowing the consolations of God's love for a period of eight years, and of how He then offered her yet greater tokens of His love, which she refused, asking instead for affliction which might be of profit to the souls of sinners. Then she describes, more clearly than anywhere else, what such affliction was. Her former knowledge of God, her "light," disappeared, and she asked for fortitude. Unbelief surrounded her with darkness, and she prayed for faith. Then next came a sense of abandonment by God, and the soul cried out, "Welcome, blessed abandonment!" and asked God to take away even fortitude from her, so that she might bear abandonment unalleviated; and it was even better to her than her knowledge of God had been. Then, when she at last knew that she had reached the limits of suffering, she offered it up to God, and "Our Lord came out from the gate of the Kingdom to greet it, and said: 'Welcome, Lady Suffering. You are the garment I wore next to My flesh on earth, and over you I was robed in the world's contempt.'" Yet Christ says to Suffering that she cannot enter heaven: she can sanctify many, but she herself is not holy, and she was born in Lucifer's heart. The imagery and the language of this is charged and vital, the thought lucid, precise, and beyond all question Catholic, devoid of the faintest taint of heresy. At the end of her life she could write: "It is the nature of love to be first filled to overflowing with sweetness, then to be rich in understanding, and then at last to be all desolation," and, again: "A miserable old woman lamented her wrongs to our Lord, and God replied: 'In childhood, you were the friend of My Holy Spirit, in youth you were the bride of My humanity, but now that you are old you keep house for My divinity.'"

To keep house, to be useful, to work—this is a wish always in Mechtild's heart. Even in her terrible, Dantesque visions of Hell and Purgatory, there is none of the repellent *schadenfreude* found in such writers as Richard Rolle, but, instead, only deep sorrow and a great zeal to win the souls of departed sinners by her prayers, to win them from Lucifer, to win them, in her favourite paradox, by constraining God Himself. "Then the soul was greatly oppressed, and prostrated itself at the feet of our most precious Lord, and longed to labour in love (for the Holy

Souls), and said: 'My dearest one, You know what I desire.'
Then our Lord said: 'You did right to bring Me here, I shall
not leave them here forgotten.'"[1]

The nun of the sixteenth century who copied into the British
Museum codex her extract from the *Book* did well in choosing
one of Mechtild's greatest and most characteristic prayers; and
let this account, partial and inadequate as it is, end in her own
words:

> Ah, Father of all goodness, I thank You, poor sinful woman that
> I am, for all the faith that You have held with my afflicted body
> and my miserable soul, with my sinful heart and my oppressed
> senses and my life so contemptible to the world. Lord, Father, this
> is my lot, and nothing else. And I thank You for Your dear Son
> Jesus Christ, and for my community with all Your creatures, whom
> You once made in that innocency to which they shall be restored,
> as the most glorious state for which they can long.
>
> Ah, sweet Father, I praise You today for all these things: and for
> the faithful shelter which You have ever given to my poor body
> and my miserable soul. Through these very things, great God, I
> thank You, Lord, for all the merciful gifts which You have ever
> given to my body and my soul. Together with all Your creatures,
> I long, here and now, for Your glory in all things and through all
> things, as they flowed spotless from Your loving heart. But I pray
> You, Love above all loves, to glorify Yourself, Lord, with all these
> things, so that poor sinners who today lie in mortal sin may be
> truly transformed and wholly converted. And I entreat You, my
> true Love, for a holy growth of all virtues and Christian religion
> in those blessed ones who live here free from mortal sin.
>
> Yet still I pray You, my very dear one, for all tormented souls
> who are in purgatory because of our sins, whom we should have
> protected by our good example. I pray You, Lord, for holy healing,
> for faithful protection, for the inpouring of Your Holy Spirit in
> all those especially who have helped me here, miserable wretch that
> I am, in body and in soul, for love of You. I pray You, Lord so
> rich, through Your Son Jesus Who was so poor, that You will turn
> the torment of my impoverished soul and the gall of my bitterness
> into honey for my soul to taste.

[1] III, 15.

14. ST. BONAVENTURE

Anselma Brennell [1]

ST. BONAVENTURE, called by Pope Leo XIII "the Prince of Mystics," may be described as a contemplative in action: a mystic, indeed, but one whose feet were firmly planted upon the ground: one who, favoured with the highest contemplative graces, was able to govern a great religious Order, defend it against enemies within and without, see it through a crisis which threatened to destroy it, and go down to history as its second founder and greatest glory after Francis himself.

It is tantalising that no contemporary biography exists and modern research has rejected much of what was once accepted, whilst considerable discrepancy in important dates adds further difficulties for the biographer.

He was born at Bagnorea, near Viterbo, the son of John of Fidanza and Maria Ritella, and although baptised "John" and also known as "of Fidanza," seems from an early age to have been called "Bonaventure;" why, we do not know. There are grounds for thinking that his father was a physician, and, however that may be, we are told that both parents were of good family, well to do, and devoutly religious.

In the Prologue to his Life of St. Francis, Bonaventure tells us how when a child he fell dangerously ill, so that parents and doctors despaired of him, whereupon his mother dedicated him to the *Poverello*, imploring the latter to cure him. To the general astonishment, the child recovered to remain thenceforward strong and healthy. "In childhood," he writes, "through his (Francis's) intercession and merits, I was rescued from the jaws of death. . . and did I fail to proclaim his praise I should fear to be reproached for the sin of ingratitude."

The knowledge of his mother's vow begot in the boy an intense devotion to Francis which strengthened with the years. Francis is his ideal, in whom he sees the highest state of prayer fully realised, and one of his leading works, the *Itinerarium mentis in*

[1] The writer is a Benedictine of Stanbrook Abbey.

Deum—the Way whereby the soul returns to God from whom it has departed through original sin, was composed when Bonaventure was in retreat at Mount Alverno.

In either 1238 or 1243, he entered the Friars Minor and, apart from gratitude to St. Francis, he tells us that the Order attracted him because its form of life seemed to resemble that of the early Christians. "It was not invented by human prudence but by Christ. In it, the learned and the simple lived as brethren."

He was sent to the University of Paris, and having completed the Arts course, a necessary preliminary to further study, began his theology under some of the leading masters of the period, chief among them "our Master and father of happy memory," Alexander, native of Hailes in Gloucester, and the first Franciscan to profess theology at Paris. In 1248 Bonaventure, as a Bachelor, was lecturing on Holy Scripture, and in 1253, after commenting on the *Sentences* of Peter Lombard, the famous textbook so long the standby of medieval theologians, he was granted his doctorate by John of Parma, Minister-General of the Order. However, owing to the uproar raised by William de Saint Amour and the secular doctors of Paris, both he and Thomas Aquinas were refused admittance to their degrees. The two mendicant Orders appealed to Rome and the two future saints were ordered to defend the cause. For that occasion Bonaventure wrote his treatise *De Paupertate Christi*. In 1257, after the condemnation of the secular Doctor, both Bonaventure and Thomas received the doctorate by order of Pope Alexander IV.

The former's teaching days, however, were over, for in the same year, still under thirty-six, he was unanimously elected Minister-General of the Friars Minor. The Order was passing through a difficult time owing to the controversy between the "Spirituals" and the Observants. The former stood out for such small friaries as still delight the pilgrim to Grecchio and the *Carcere* of Assisi, and inveighed against large houses and churches, whilst also opposing the brethren going in for higher studies and living upon any material resources excepting alms. The other side protested that the personnel of the Order had altered. If Francis had once written: "the brother who comes to our Order not learned, let him not seek to become so," now many recruits were priests and clerics, and such must be taught. After all, the learned Anthony of Padua, formerly an Augustinian of Lisbon, had taught theology in the Founder's lifetime. The little band which had once gathered around Francis in the Portiuncula had developed into a great religious family, called to preach and instruct the faithful, and those large "preaching churches" were needed.

Patiently the General dealt with the crisis that threatened to become a schism. In a long letter to a friar, he answers the latter's difficulties point by point, agreeing with his correspondent whenever he can, and the only words remotely suggestive of reproach are: "I ask you, beloved, not to abound too much in your own sense." In a General Chapter held at Narbonne, the Franciscan legislation was codified and revised, and until 1273 the General occupied himself in visiting the provinces of the Order, making useful changes, writing his great ascetic and mystical works, and preaching far and near. And, as we are told, his subjects were astounded at the amount of work he managed to accomplish whilst remaining before all else a man of prayer.

In 1265, Clement IV wished to make him Archbishop of York, but Bonaventure managed to decline the appointment. However, in 1273 he was compelled by Gregory X to accept the see of Albano and the cardinalate. In the following year, once more with Thomas Aquinas, destined to die on the way, Bonaventure was ordered to attend the Council of Lyons, where a short-lived reunion was achieved between the Church and the Greek schismatics. There he did good service, but on 14 July 1274, he died.

He was buried in the Franciscan church at Lyons, in the presence of the Pope and a great and distinguished throng, the Dominican, Peter of Tarantaise, himself also to be raised to the altars as Blessed Pope Innocent V, preaching the panegyric.

We may cite a few details as to his personality and person. He was, we are told, well made, good looking and healthy; "grave of countenance, angelic of aspect," so that men were struck with admiration. Impressed with his innocence, humility and gentleness, Alexander of Hailes used to say that "Adam did not seem to have sinned in Bonaventure." Always cheerful, he lived up to his own dictum that "a spiritual joy is the greatest sign of divine grace dwelling in a soul." He enjoyed taking his share in community tasks and was a devoted infirmarian.

In considering him as a spiritual theologian, we may remark

that though hailed as the greatest light of his Order after its Founder, strictly speaking he is not "the Franciscan Doctor," which title belongs rather to John Duns Scotus. For example, asked whether the Incarnation would have taken place had man not sinned, Bonaventure replies in the negative. Along with the Dominicans and some of his own brethren, he rejects the doctrine of the Immaculate Conception as then understood; although with St. Bernard he holds Our Lady's absolute sinlessness, remarking that he has never heard of any saint who had not a special devotion to her.

His spirituality is outstandingly Christocentric, and in him there shines out that devotion to the Sacred Humanity for which the Mendicants were noted, albeit St. Bernard had been their forerunner. A great traditionalist whose works are "saturated" with the Scriptures, learned in the Fathers, no mean classical scholar, we can yet hear him singing a new song. Two of his works, *Vitis mystica* and *Lignum Vitae*, have supplied the first Nocturn lessons for the Office of the Sacred Heart, and passages from the same source are scattered through the Office, especially in the hymns. Centuries before the feast would appear, he loves the expression "Christ the King." With him, the Passion and humiliation of the Son of God are never separated from His essential glory. The "grievous joy" of the Franciscan always marks the saint's profound devotion to Christ crucified, and he is one of those who have loved to dwell upon the majesty of God.

He treats of the spiritual life according to the classical "Three ways" but these compenetrate and the soul must live in all three, although at different stages of its development the exercises of one or other will predominate. There is nothing shadowy or merely poetic about his mysticism. It is raised upon a solid foundation of dogmatic and moral theology. The theological virtues, the virtues and gifts of the Holy Ghost, the divine indwelling of God in the soul by grace are his great subjects. Christ crucified is the way to the Blessed Trinity, and all the practices of the Christian life, above all prayer, careful avoidance of sin, examination of conscience, mortification, frequent Confession and Communion, devotion to the Blessed Sacrament and to Our Lady, must find their due place in the rule of life of anyone sincerely striving after holiness.

St. John of the Cross particularly prescribes the works of

St. Bonaventure for study in the Reformed Carmelite noviciate, and we can see why. Both saints teach that contemplative prayer, even of a high order, is not an extraordinary grace, or a thing to be feared, that it is something quite apart from the extraordinary concomitants which may or may not accompany it, and which must not be desired, far less prayed for. All should aim at the highest union with God and pray for it, provided they are willing to pay the price and do what is in their power. Holiness is not the preserve of the few. If there are few real contemplatives, it is merely because few souls are sufficiently generous to make the efforts and sacrifices. As for the "extraordinary" occurrences, like every other master of the spiritual life, Bonaventure warns his readers that visions and revelations should rather be distrusted and feared.

"Rectitude of mind consists radically in love," he says, "but love cannot be rightly ordered if a soul love anything more than God, or as much as God, or if it loves anything for its (the soul's) own self. Man's spirit is not perfectly submissive to God unless it loves Him above all and for Himself." It is the same old teaching, from Benedict and Bernard, down through the ages to Ignatius, John of the Cross, Teresa and the rest. "By Christ, through Christ, we reach Christ," he says again.

The practice of virtue must correspond with the prayer in its progress, if any case is genuine, and here, again like all masters of his craft, Bonaventure insists that humility must be thoroughly cultivated before there can be any question of contemplative union. "There is not a page, not a line in Holy Scripture that does not preach humility." "Believe me that if a man be truly anxious to humble himself, he can acquire more grace in a month than another in forty years." Yet the saint does not favour artificial or exaggerated humiliations, though he says they may help sometimes, but he reminds us that "temperance," in other words right ordering of the spiritual life, must have its place here as elsewhere.

He treats of the gifts of the Holy Ghost in several of his works. In language suggested by St. Gregory's *Moralia*, he tells us that each Gift "holds a feast in its day," and each day has its morning, its noon and its eventide. The morning corresponds to the Purgative Way, and he treats first of the Gift of Fear, since it is the beginning of wisdom which is the highest of the contemplative Gifts. But that does not mean that the soul is ever deprived of any of the Gifts, any more than it means that because, in the early stage of its life its chief work is to repent of its sins, and work at its faults, it is entirely deprived of any kind of prayer excepting beginners' meditation. Only, as the soul progresses, other Gifts will come increasingly into play, so to speak, just as meditation will be replaced by other forms of prayer and, as Bonaventure says himself, will simply drop out at the higher stages, having done its work.

At first Fear is more or less servile, but if the soul is faithful it develops into that loving, filial fear which, he says, is very valuable for *advanced* souls, because it inspires reverence, and Bonaventure is one of those who dislike anything savouring of casual behaviour—*la sans-gêne*—in our attitude towards God. But that Gift, as the whole Purgative Way, leads to peace, and when the evening of life is drawing nearer there is only the fear which is the result of a great love, and shrinks from the slightest offence offered to that God whom the soul loves intensely. When all wilful sins and wilful imperfections have disappeared, "The whole soul is aflame with the fire of compunction." There remains, when the soul "rests in the Sabbath" of the prayer of Union, only that peaceful, abiding—but how deep only saints can teach us!—sorrow for every shadow of offence towards God, which is never depressing since it but increases the soul's realisation of His unspeakable love. He who proclaimed himself the chief of sinners could also say that in him divine grace had not been in vain.

Through Piety, we acquire that simple, childlike demeanour with respect to God, and learn to direct all our works towards Him, whilst our love of our neighbour becomes purer and more generous. There is, however, nothing childish, no posing in our religion, for this Gift banishes hypocrisy. It leads to wisdom, for as it has more play so the soul comes to see God more perfectly in its neighbour, and to become more humble. The same Gift also leads to an increasing love for divine worship, for the Church and all for which she stands, whilst enabling the soul to grasp the real meaning of obedience and obey "manfully."

With the Gift of Knowledge, the soul seeks for and learns all truth, gaining a right and sure judgment as regards what must be believed and done. It now especially reads and ponders upon the Holy Scriptures, and here Bonaventure quotes Augustine's saying that, for example, once the Passion of our Redeemer is really understood, nothing is too hard and we can bear it bravely; for we count as little what we may have to endure if we compare it to His Passion. In view of the controversy in the Franciscan Order in his day, it is interesting to note that although the saint teaches constantly the fundamental doctrine that sanctity is within the reach of the most unlearned, provided such have the necessary spiritual dispositions, nevertheless, he insists upon the importance of the Gift of Knowledge and its right use. It is natural for us to long to know, and whereas the ancients fell into error because they lacked the key to right knowledge, which is God-made-Man, we have that precious condition of all wisdom. This same Gift also enables us to rise from creation to the Creator, but the soul must see nature *in* God, and try to realise something of Absolute Beauty; so that it is fain to break forth into praise or, alternatively, just remain silent in adoration. Such is the spirit of Francis's *Canticle of the Sun*, and the *Benedicite* of the Liturgy.

Fortitude prepares the soul for the perfect following of Christ by crucifixion of self and that, says the saint, is the great work to be done in the Illuminative Way. He warns his readers that it will not be easy. From A to Z, the spiritual life is ascetico-mystical, and here we find him speaking not only of the difficulties of old imperfect habits, and of those trials which God may send, but of *acedia*—that weariness in well-doing, the sheer spiritual fatigue of just "going on," which will have to be faced as the wearing down and discipline of what spiritual theologians know as the Nights of the Soul shut in. By Fortitude the soul is helped to go forward despite all, whilst this Gift rectifies the concupiscences, safeguards the memory, understanding and will and, finally, subjects all the powers to the Blessed Trinity, the goal to which Our Lord is the way.

With the Gift of Counsel, we enter upon the Illuminative Way. The soul rouses itself to be conformed to the divine will, as it is inspired by the Holy Spirit; it strives to avoid all wilful sin, to obey all the divine precepts, and inclines to follow the Counsels of Perfection. Once it has thus resolved upon perfect living, all its powers are purified: it is saved from making wrong decisions and is continually inspired and instructed by the Holy Spirit. Its understanding is continually more enlightened, whilst its love becomes ever purer and more fervent. Here Bonaventure dwells at length upon the abiding presence within it of the Blessed Trinity, so that its life becomes continually more informed thereby.

Intellect and Wisdom belong to the Unitive Way, and are the Contemplative Gifts par excellence, so that we must see something of Bonaventure's teaching upon prayer. He never defines "contemplation," though he says much about it. Prayer is the secret of holiness and the only way thereto, and he confesses that he is amazed that so few people seem to be recollected and to enter into themselves. Mental prayer is the higher form and vocal prayer is ordained to it, though vocal prayer said in common, and above all the Divine Office, must always be carried out as perfectly as possible, and that whether recited in choir or privately, as when travelling, since it is the official prayer of the Church. We catch a glimpse into the spirit of the ages of faith when he reminds his readers that the simple faithful love to come into church and listen to the Office, and that it behoves religious in choir to see that such are not disedified. Always we find the practical side in his guidance. For instance, acts of charity must not be refused on the ground of giving more time to prayer, nor must a superior be so intent upon guarding his own peace and recollection as to shirk the correction and training of his subjects. Another thoughtful reminder is to be found when, treating of religious, he remarks that they must not be content to "live like baptised children"; that is practising a negative sort of piety, blameless in a sense but satisfied with pious routine. A soul must be instant in prayer, take its spiritual obligations as seriously as possible, and strive for familiar friendship with Christ.

In the Illuminative Way the soul practises what later authorities call variously, Prayer of simplicity, " 'beginners' contemplation," "acquired contemplation," etc. This may be expected to follow on from earlier Meditation, above all on the life and Passion of Our Lord, which develops and simplifies into Affective Prayer. Such contemplation is not strictly speaking mystical; though there is an actuation of the Gifts of the Holy Spirit, albeit such is not sensibly experienced by the one who prays. Real mystical contemplation cannot be produced, even for a moment, by the soul's own efforts, nor can it be prolonged once God ceases to give it. But in the Unitive Way Bonaventure says we meet with "mystical contemplation," and this is what is normally known as

Quietude. Thenceforth all progress is an intensifying of that. "The soul dies to the world and sees God," but there are not normally any extraordinary phenomena even then. The saint gives it as his opinion that one in whose prayer the element of adoration is tending to predominate increasingly is not far from the state of union.

In conclusion, something must be mentioned of his treatment of ecstasy which is exceptional. He calls the unitive life, in which the soul attains to the "Transforming Union," the "Ecstatic life," and those he terms "ecstatics" have reached the culminating point to which union with God can be reached in this world. He owns that such are rare, and that he knows personally of only St. Francis himself, whose last days after the vision of Mount Alverno were spent in that state, and probably Blessed Giles of Assisi. Yet we know from contemporary evidence that Bonaventure experienced ecstasies himself, and was seen in such at Paris. Possibly the explanation is that theologically he was an Augustinian, and St. Augustine had written: "It seems to me that all the saints have been in ecstasy." For those of this way of thinking there is nothing abnormal in the fact that people serving God very faithfully, whose wills have become identified with His so that, as St. John of the Cross says, "There are no longer two wills, but one, namely God's," should sometimes be drawn "out of themselves." For them ecstasy is prayer of mystical or infused contemplation which has completely dominated both intellect and will; an actuation of the Gift of Wisdom more or less prolonged, wherein the soul enjoys an experimental union with God of great intensity, through the love that unites it to Him. Bonaventure speaks also of ecstasy which is an actuation of the Gift of Understanding, but it is not easy to see much, if any, practical difference. There need not be any extraordinary grace, such as a vision or revelation, and usually the ecstasy is not very long, though cases vary. Bonaventure does distinguish between ecstasy and rapture, which latter he does consider an extraordinary grace and characterised by pure passivity. However that may be, it is clear that he is considering ecstasy here as occurring so often that it seems more or less continuous and has become a state. Also, at this stage, it certainly weakens the body, which is not necessarily the case if it happens rarely. A simpler case to study is that of St. Thomas Aquinas, about whom we have more detail. On the feast of St. Nicholas, when saying Mass in the church of San Domenico at Naples, he had a long ecstasy the after-effects of which never left him. He refused to complete the *Summa*, declaring that such things had been revealed to him that all he had ever written "seemed but so much straw." Thenceforth he was constantly falling into ecstasy whilst the body was obviously failing. Three months later he died in transports of love and joy. Surely, before such divine masterpieces, distinctions and analyses must fail, and we find ourselves synthesising!

But if to live one's last days in ecstasy is granted to the very few, as the saint admits, Bonaventure's summing-up of a saintly life is within the reach of all who are willing to take the means: "The perfection of a religious man is to do common things in a perfect manner, and a constant fidelity in small matters is great and heroic virtue!"

15. ANGELA OF FOLIGNO

Ann Stafford

IN THE YEAR 1285, Angela, the beautiful, proud and pampered wife of a wealthy nobleman living in Foligno, near Assisi, a woman who scoffed at piety, who had given herself over to every extravagance of pleasure, underwent a dramatic conversion. After the death of her husband a few years later, she entered the Third Order of St. Francis, lived entirely on alms and devoted herself to prayer. She became a great mystic and a teacher whose writings received the Church's approval even during her lifetime. On her death, in 1309, she was popularly acclaimed as a saint and her cult was approved by Pope Innocent XII in 1693.

The story of Angela's spiritual odyssey between 1285 and 1296 is told in the *Memoriale*,[1] written by Brother Arnold, a Franciscan friar, one time chaplain to the Bishop of Foligno and her confessor. For although Angela could read Latin sufficiently well to follow the Breviary and the Missal, she could not write herself, even in the vernacular. Yet her intelligence was acute; she had a flair for analysing her own mental processes and she became extraordinarily sensitive to the light and shade of spiritual experience. Brother Arnold was a most conscientious scribe, who added nothing, embellished nothing, nearly always read his record over to her and tells us when he did not.[2] His testimony is the more valuable because for some years he viewed her with the greatest suspicion.

An understanding of the *Memoriale* is essential to any apprecia-

---

[1] As there is no reliable English text of Blessed Angela's works, this article is based on Fr. Paul Doncoeur's edition of the *Memoriale*, and other documents appended to it, published in Latin, and in a French translation, entitled *Le Livre de la Bienheureuse Soeur Angèle de Foligno du Tiers Ordre de S. François* (Paris, 1926). In translating the passages quoted, both the French and Latin texts have been consulted, but the references throughout are to the French edition as being the more readily accessible.

[2] *Le Livre de la Bienheureuse Soeur Angèle de Foligno*, edited by Fr. Paul Doncoeur, pp. 33, 48–9, 55 and 121.

tion of Angela's teaching, for she taught out of her own experience; all her advice to her followers is but an elaboration of what she herself had learned, first, after her conversion, from her sorrowful consideration of her sharp and sinful contact with the world's delights, then from penance, then from the Holy Spirit Himself, at work in her soul. It is this blend of hard-bitten shrewdness and supreme insight into the things of God that makes her so invaluable a teacher, specially for those who seek to pray and yet must live and work against the background of an almost pagan society. For though few of us will ever come to the heights of mystical prayer, most of us will recognise, mirrored in her great experiences, our own lesser ones, our moments of insight, strange apprehensions of truth and love, our so often grudging response to the touch of God's grace. Over and over again, we meet ourselves as we read Angela's pithy comments on herself and those others whom she advised. But she also gives us a picture of ourselves as we could be, of human nature sanctified and healed, of soul and body, heart and head brought into harmony because the will is at last one with God's will and so the whole personality is set free to fulfil itself in joyful love.

Angela expresses herself in the highly-coloured idiom of her times, so that many of the locutions and the visions, particularly the early ones of the Passion, shock our sophisticated susceptibilities. It is only too tempting to write them off as the imaginings of a neurotic woman who would to-day be given psychiatric treatment; or at best, as the pseudo-religious fantasies of a hypersensitive artistic temperament. But they have to be seen in the context of Angela's spiritual development, as manifestations of grace working in a soul, and serving to bring her not only to a life of heroic virtue and an extraordinary grasp of theological truths but to a direct experience of union with God.

Brother Arnold only gives a summary of the first stage of Angela's pilgrimage, for he did not begin to write until 1291, though he first came into contact with her in 1285, when her conscience was burdened with a sin so grievous that she had been unable to make a full confession of it. At last, tormented and hesitant, she prayed to St. Francis, and the next day she heard Brother Arnold preach and knew him at once for the confessor she sought.[1] Immediately her confession was made her attitude

---

[1] *Le Livre de la Bienheureuse Soeur Angèle de Foligno*, 32.

to life changed completely; she shunned the pleasures she had once loved; no penance was too hard for her, no humiliation too great. So began the slow and painful process by which Angela was detached from the world and became the penitent friend of God. Brother Arnold and Angela, using the traditional manner of describing spiritual experiences, divide this phase into various steps. "And you must understand," she says, "that at every step one hangs back; and it is with great sorrow and great heartbreak that with so slow and heavy a tread and with such pain the soul drags itself towards God. . . ."[1]

Throughout this period, she was dominated on the one hand by an ever more acute knowledge of herself, a deeper and deeper consciousness of her sins, and on the other, by an ever more vivid realisation of the merciful love of God as revealed in the redeeming Passion of our Lord. In her loving contemplation of our Lord dying upon the Cross, she was made to understand in what pain He had died until she could say: "I felt that I—I myself—had crucified Him."[2] Then, standing before her crucifix, in a spontaneous gesture of love reminiscent of St. Francis himself, she stripped off her finery and offered herself to Christ without any reservation, vowing herself to chastity and penance, though she knew how difficult a penitential way of life would be in that household, where her feeble efforts at austerity made her the jest of her family and her friends.

Soon after this, possibly in some pestilence, her entire family died. She says herself that she sorrowed bitterly; and yet, since she realised that God required a complete surrender of all she held most dear, she rejoiced.[3] For Angela was an all-or-nothing person, and her readiness to sacrifice every family tie, every friendship, every penny for love of God expressed her acceptance of, and readiness to co-operate with, His grace. She may well seem to us an extremist: and, unlike her, we tend to shun extremes lest we should be labelled neurotic. We cling to our idea of what is safe and normal, even at the risk of being mediocre. Angela's spirituality challenges our mediocrity: it is a salutary reminder that the recitation of conventional prayers before romanticised pictures of the Way of the Cross is a poor substitute for the hard,

---

[1] *Le Livre de la Bienheureuse Soeur Angèle de Foligno*, 33.
[2] *Ibid.*, 35.   [3] *Ibid.*, 36. cf. p. 64.

N

clear thinking about the grim reality of the Passion by which
Angela was brought to so great a love of God.

Yet even in an age which had no use for half-measures, she
seemed to be going too far; for against the advice of her relatives
and her spiritual advisers—including Brother Arnold who still
had very little use for her—she began to sell all her possessions,
until at last she had only one small estate left, a little place she
loved so much that she could hardly bring herself to part with it.
But at last, she sold even that, not merely as a just penance, but as
the expression of her love of God. "Lord," she cried, "even if I be
damned, yet will I do penance and give up my possessions and
serve You."[1]

Then indeed she began to find comfort; prayer was no effort;
she would often forget to eat, so absorbed was she in her thought
of God. She began to cry out whenever she heard the name of
God, and her tears at the sight of a picture of the Passion seemed
literally to scald her flesh. She was the talk of Foligno—but
Brother Arnold was still suspicious.

When at last the business of disposing of her property was done,
she set out with some companions on a pilgrimage to Assisi. On
the way, at the junction of the road to Spello, she was suddenly
inundated with God's love for her; she seemed to hear the Holy
Spirit speak to her: "My daughter, my spouse, who art sweet to
me, I love you more than any other woman in the valley. . . ."[2]
Instinctively, she recoiled—as indeed do we. But there is a sense
in which every soul is dear to God as is no other, just as there is a
sense in which the mother of many children may say to each
with perfect truth: "Darling, I love you best"—that is, my love
for you is unique. At this first assurance of God's unique love for
her, Angela's reaction was a most wholesome mistrust of her
imagination. But she was made to understand that the Holy
Trinity had indeed come to her soul, and that the sense of God's
loving presence would remain with her that day until she had
visited the church at Assisi a second time. In fact, when she did
re-enter the church after the midday meal, the presence left her,
whereupon she cried out: "Oh unknown love, why, oh why, do
you leave me? Why?"[3]

This outburst brought the friars running from the cloister—

---

[1] Le Livre de la Bienheureuse Soeur Angèle de Foligno, 41.
[2] Ibid., 60.   [3] Ibid., 63.

among them Brother Arnold. He was shocked and embarrassed,
furious with his penitent for making herself so conspicuous.
With the utmost reluctance, he decided that on his next visit to
Foligno, he must see her and enquire into her experiences, to see
whether they were of God, or, as he then thought, of the devil.
As much to her surprise as to his, he became convinced that God
required him to take down every word she said.

The experience on the road to Assisi marked a turning-point
for Angela, for now, she was not merely a suppliant penitent;
she was the penitent friend of God. Her soul no longer "dragged
itself" towards Him, for as the Gifts of the Spirit came into flower
in her soul, Angela lost the initiative and the Holy Ghost Himself
took charge.

Yet at first, she sought more than anything else the assurance
that she was loved and that her experiences of God's amazing
love for her were valid. It seemed to her that with the eyes of the
soul, she saw His eyes on her. But she longed for some sign, some
physical sign, which would show that she was not deceived. And
the voice said: "Behold the sign I will leave with your soul . . .
I will leave you so great a love of Me that your soul will always
burn with it." After this "anointing of the soul," she says: "He
left me this sign which is always with me so that I know this is the
straight way of salvation, to love and to wish to suffer for one's
love."[1]

Now, as she meditated upon the great doctrines of the faith, her
mind was illuminated by the gift of understanding. She came
more and more to penetrate behind the dry husk of dogma and
to know these doctrines as a living truth. What the theologian
expresses in carefully balanced and accurate phrases, she learned
to express in terms of a personal experience. So she was brought
to an ever clearer understanding of the Blessed Trinity and of the
Incarnation and the hypostatic union. Once, after meditating on
the Passion, she had a vision of Christ, of which she says: "I understood that this extreme beauty sprang from His divinity and that
through the medium of His beauty I saw His divinity."

At this time, Brother Arnold pursued Angela with questions,
sometimes about her experiences, sometimes about doctrine,
sometimes about matters concerning his Order. So did others.
All these things she referred to God in prayer; and it happened

[1] *Le Livre de la Bienheureuse Soeur Angèle de Foligno*, 74–6.

that on one occasion, when she felt it was mere pride and folly to ask for enlightenment on certain questions, her soul was lifted up and she saw the Divine Wisdom "as it were a table without beginning or end." The word table, she says, was left in her mind, for of the feast, the abundance of Divine Wisdom itself, she could tell nothing. Yet from that time, she could judge all spiritual people and all spiritual matters with understanding. "I no longer judge erroneously as I used to do, but with quite another and true judgment which I understand. . . ."[1]

But before this phase was over, she entered upon a period of trial which Brother Arnold calls a revelation of her own unworthiness and her re-fashioning at the hands of God. Darkness and light alternated, so that at one moment she saw the Divine Power with the eyes of the soul and cried out: "The world is great with God."[2] Then for several weeks she could not feel the presence of God at all; she was black with a sense of sin and all her fears of being deluded returned. In her desolation, she meditated continually upon the Passion until at last she could say: "All my joy now is in the God Man who suffers."[3]

Shortly after this, when Brother Arnold spoke to her of the mystery of evil, Angela said that she had been considering this very matter, and had been drawn up to a height of prayer "which is quite beyond our natural powers." She saw the Power and the Will of God as if she had been brought through darkness into light.[4] At this point, probably in the autumn of 1293, Brother Arnold was forbidden by his superiors to have anything to do with Angela, for the hours he spent in the church, writing at her side in full view of the public, were giving scandal. So he sent a little boy to take down what she said in the vernacular, and later he translated into Latin the record of the revelations made to her when she was meditating upon the Passion. She seemed, she says, to enter into the mind of Christ and to feel His sufferings with an intensity of which she had never before been capable; she speaks of herself as being transformed into very great suffering and adds: "And then the Sovereign Good gave me this great grace that of two things He made one, for I cannot any more will otherwise than as He wills."[5]

---

[1] Le Livre de la Bienheureuse Soeur Angèle de Foligno, 102–3.
[2] Ibid., 106.   [3] Ibid., 116.
[4] Ibid., 118–9.   [5] Ibid., 124.

This marked another turning point; Angela was no longer concerned with being loved; her whole personality was concentrated upon that perfect act of charity which is to love. Her visions, too, change; they seem to by-pass her imagination and to be entirely in her intellect. She saw nothing that she could describe, but as she looked upon God, she was entirely absorbed in that looking; and in the great light in which she understood the -infinite abundance of the divine Goodness, her soul knew neither joy nor tears.[1] But in 1294, acute suffering was interwoven with her joy. Brother Arnold, now permitted to work with her again, says briskly that he did not trouble to take down all she told him about her trials, but she seems not only to have endured extreme physical pain, but also to have been on fire with temptation, to have known within herself the flare up of all her old vices and many others which were new. In her own simile, her soul felt like a man hanging by the neck from a gallows with his hands tied and his eyes bound, who, so hanging, yet lives, knowing no comfort, no support, no help. She herself said later that she recognised these trials as a necessary purification, a final cutting out of pride.[2]

Indeed, before this period of desolation was over, Angela was drawn up into that darkness in which she saw the Godhead. She speaks, in the paradox of the mystic, of the abyss of this height.[3] Brother Arnold would have nothing of this dark seeing, it was beyond him. But Angela was now completely sure of herself.

"These things cannot be told [she says], but they bring great joy. But when God is seen in this way, in the darkness, no smile comes to to the lips, nor any feeling of devotion to the heart, nor fervour, nor burning of love. The soul sees nothing, yet sees All. And the body sleeps and the tongue is silenced. And all the endearments He used to me and all the words He spoke to me and all you have written . . . is so much less than the Sovereign Good I see with so much darkness that I do not set my hope in them . . . for it is most surely set in this Sovereign Good which I see in such great darkness."[4]

In this dark seeing of the Blessed Trinity, she did not think upon anything corporeal, not even of God made Man. But when she was withdrawn from the darkness and set apart from it, then she saw

---

[1] *Le Livre de la Bienheureuse Soeur Angèle de Foligno*, 131, 137–8.
[2] *Ibid.*, 148.   [3] *Ibid.*, 171–3.   [4] *Ibid.*, 159.

God made Man, "through Whose eyes and through Whose countenance shines forth that which I saw in the darkness . . ."[1]

Brother Arnold's account ends here, in 1296; with Angela's permission he showed the book to two other friars minor, and in the course of time it was approved by a commission of scholars.

But Angela lived and taught for another thirteen years, and other scribes took down her words.[2] She was no longer much concerned with her own visions; the few which are recorded seem to have been given her less for her own consolation than for that of her growing family of spiritual children. She longed that they too might receive the assurance of God's unique love for which she had once hungered.

She made no attempt to organise her family. Many of her children were Franciscans, whether regulars or tertiaries. But we get glimpses in her letters of men and women much involved in worldly affairs, of others who lived a life of poverty like her own. She tried to give them, not any one method of prayer, or rule of life, but a certain basic formation which would bring them to so great a love of God that they might, if God willed, be led to the same height of supernatural prayer.

Though the style of the thirty-five letters, instructions and odd notes appended to the *Memoriale* varies almost from document to document, the essence of her teaching does not. One theme constantly recurs: If a man would seek God, he must know God and himself. Angela is almost classically Thomist in her insistence that the will follows the intellect. "As we see, so we love."[3] "The more excellently we see, the more excellently we love."[4]

> So the first step which the soul must take if she would come to God is that she should truly know God. ". . For the soul, knowing God truly, knows Him to be good—and not merely to be good, but to be the Sovereign and Perfect Good. And finding Him good, she loves Him for His goodness and loving Him, desires Him and desiring Him, gives all she has in order to possess Him."[5]

"What is the use of contemplation," she says, "if a man has not this right and true understanding of God and himself?"[6] "Understanding must come first and then love will follow."[7]

[1] *Le Livre de la Bienheureuse Soeur Angèle de Foligno*, 161.
[2] These are the documents given in Parts II and III of Fr. Doncoeur's edition.
[3] *Le Livre de la Bienheureuse Soeur Angèle de Foligno*, 203.
[4] *Ibid.*, 196.   [5] *Ibid.*, 271.   [6] *Ibid.*, 245.   [7] *Ibid.*, 273.

In another letter, she says: "To know God presupposes a knowledge of self, in this way: a man must consider well against Whom he sins and then consider well and understand who he is who thus sins. . ."[1] This is the true self-noughting, to know oneself incapable of any good. This clear-sighted view of self enables a man to realise the supreme goodness of God Who humbled Himself and stooped over man's nothingness. So,

> with the help of grace a man begins to come to a knowledge of God. And the more he knows, the more he loves. And the more he loves, the more ardently he desires to possess that which he loves and the more ardently he desires to possess what he loves, the more ardently does he strive after it and this striving is the sign and measure of his love. For by this one may know if love is pure and true and upright, if a man loves and strives after that which his Beloved loved and does those things which his Beloved did.[2]

If a man would learn to do this, he must study in the Book of Life, which is Christ, Whose life was all poverty, humility, suffering, lowliness and true obedience.

The supreme purpose of all Angela's teaching was to show her children the merciful love of God, so that they might learn to love God, through Christ, and to love all creation because it is His. "Our Creator, God Incarnate, Sovereign and Perfect Good, is all love. . . ."[3] "Oh Lord, make me worthy to understand the depth of the most high charity which You showed in this Your most holy incarnation."[4] "Oh little children of God, look with all your might upon this martyred God Man and do not turn your backs upon Him Who has so greatly loved you."[5]

Angela must have known intimately every grade of love from the most profane to the most sacred. She is able not only to dissect the workings of the human heart as it plunges about in its desperate attempts to love, but to give us a most exquisite picture of Divine Charity in the soul. She is never sentimental about love: she knows precisely what she means by it; it is that stretching forth of the will towards the Beloved in an ardent desire to be in some measure identified with the Beloved. Over and over again, she speaks of this identification of the lover and the beloved, this transformation of the lover into the will of his beloved. As the

---

[1] *Le Livre de la Bienheureuse Soeur Angèle de Foligno*, 226.
[2] *Ibid.*, 226.   [3] *Ibid.*, 270.   [4] *Ibid.*, 341.   [5] *Ibid.*, 306.

human lover and his beloved are rightly of one heart and one mind, so the soul in love with God longs to be identified with the will of God, to be of one heart and mind with Him.[1]

It is with this transformation of the whole personality by the love of God that Angela is concerned, whether she is writing about poverty and humility, about love or about prayer. And though she writes about them all in the context of her own experience of contemplative prayer, she never contrasts the active and the contemplative life, or commends the one at the expense of the other, nor does she ever suggest that they are incompatible. The whole personality is to be transfigured into the personality of Christ; she herself offered herself to Him without reserve, not only head and heart, but hands and feet. Writing of Christ as the Way, she says: "By this Way must go hand and arm and shoulder, foot and leg and every part of the body."[2] It is a total self-giving.

Her own absolute surrender is expressed in the many passages in which she speaks of being taken out of herself, lifted up, identified with the suffering of Christ. But it is equally clearly expressed in the account she gives of how she and her companion set out one Maundy Thursday to seek Christ in His poor and found Him there indeed. With a gesture that echoes the kiss of St. Francis for the leper, she, so little time before a fastidious and spoiled woman, drank the filthy water in which she had washed the lepers' feet and felt that she had received Christ.[3]

Angela herself never sought a completely solitary life, nor was she ever inaccessible. She was not of the world, but she lived right down in the mess and muddle of it. She went about the countryside, she did the household chores. Once indeed, when she was washing lettuces, a voice, which she judged to be of the devil, asked her if such a task was worthy of her—implying no doubt that she should have been set apart for better things; she immediately replied that she was only fit to cart dung—and went on washing lettuces.[4] "Speaking or eating or doing any other kind of thing never prevented her from being lifted up in soul and spirit,"[5] remarks Brother Arnold, though he adds that she was often very absent-minded.

"It is good," she wrote to one of her followers, "that with all the fervour given you by grace, you should pray and keep vigil

[1] *Le Livre de la Bienheureuse Soeur Angèle de Foligno*, 299, 207.
[2] *Ibid.*, 282.   [3] *Ibid.*, 94–6.   [4] *Ibid.*, 110.   [5] *Ibid.*, 163.

and do all other good works. . . . But if this grace of fervour be withdrawn, strive still to pray, still to keep vigil, still to expend yourself on all good works."[1] But works should never separate the soul from God, for the soul should never be given over to them: ". . . never give yourselves or even lend yourselves to any creature, but give yourselves to Him Who is," she wrote. "And when one of you preaches or hears confessions or gives advice, let his spirit not be set upon these things, but let it be with the Creator."[2] Speaking of herself to Brother Arnold, she says:

"Though I feel joy and sorrow, somewhat, outwardly, yet I feel them but little within, for in my soul there is a cell into which neither joy nor sorrow may enter, nor any delight in any virtue, nor delight in anything which can be named, for there is the Sovereign Good than which there is no other good."[3]

She kept this solitude of heart most jealously and was concerned that her children should keep it also, whether they lived in the world, or in the cloister. For, she points out, "Our Lord did not say: Learn of Me to despise the world and live in poverty . . . but only this: Learn of Me for I am gentle and lowly of heart."[4]

Humility, she insists, is the matrix of all the virtues. "One of the signs by which a man may know that he is in a state of grace is this—that he is never puffed up."[5] And poverty, she teaches, is the root of humility. For absolute poverty, material and spiritual, means so absolute a dependence upon God that all self-confidence is taken away.[6] But though she herself clung to the ideals of St. Francis and believed that absolute material poverty was the ideal way of life, she also knew that it was not possible for all. So she did not insist that her disciples should follow her example and sell up their possessions—but she did insist that they must learn not to have the slightest concern over wealth or worldly honours. In any case, strict material poverty is but the first stage of the three-fold poverty she commended. Merely to be poor in this world's goods is not enough: our Lord made Himself "poor in friends." So the soul which gives itself totally to Him will strip itself of all human relationships which may hinder its progress in the love of God. And finally, just as our Lord "emptied Himself "of all His

[1] Le Livre de la Bienheureuse Soeur Angèle de Foligno, 252.
[2] Ibid., 300. [3] Ibid., 175. [4] Ibid., 284.
[5] Ibid., 195. [6] Ibid., 146.

power, His glory and His wisdom, so the soul must strip itself of all confidence in its own gifts, of all self-reliance, of all spiritual consolations.[1] But just as knowledge leads the heart to love—and has no value unless love accompanies it—so this three-fold poverty, this complete detachment, not only prepares the heart for love but is an expression of love. It was not for nothing that Angela saw in a vision Divine Love "as it were a scythe,"[2] or that she speaks of human love cutting deeply into the heart. For human love, however legitimate, however noble, even when it is directed towards God, is so easily warped; and once warped, it is dangerous for it works the soul's destruction more surely than anything else.[3] And Divine Love, "as it were a scythe" is dangerous to the self, for it threatens the sovereignty of the self in its self-regarding loves.

As Angela saw it, the whole purpose of the spiritual disciplines is not to adorn the soul with virtues but to lay the self open to the scythe of Divine Love, so that through the operation of this love, the little loving human soul may be severed from all lesser affections and so set free to be transformed into the Divine Love which is its Beloved; and being so transformed, may love all creation because God Himself has taught it how to love.

But when we first come to the point at which we say we long for God, we may not be entirely sincere, for we are not yet able truly to want God: body and soul may not be completely at one with each other, and so the will is divided.[4] Angela speaks in one letter of the many who say they love our Lord, but flinch from the poverty and pain which would bring them nearer to Him, indeed, spend their time praying that they may be delivered from such things, are racked with anxiety lest they should not escape them.[5] This is one of the many passages in which we meet ourselves. For few of us ever know that absolute integrity which Angela describes when she says:

> "But when all the members of the body are in unison with the soul and the soul is so much at one with the heart and the whole body that she can answer for them, then the soul is truly able to desire God. But this will to desire God is given by grace."[6]

Angela considers that this transformation or divinisation of the

---

[1] *Le Livre de la Bienheureuse Soeur Angèle de Foligno,* 277.
[2] *Ibid.,* 126.   [3] *Ibid.,* 311 sq.   [4] *Ibid.,* 136 and 142.
[5] *Ibid.,* 279.   [6] *Ibid.,* 136.

soul comes about in three stages which correspond to the three main phases of her own experience. In the first, the soul is inspired by grace to strive to love what Christ loved and to do as He did, as Angela herself was inspired after her conversion. Next, the will is united with the will of God, as Angela's was after the great vision of the Passion; and the soul receives a wonderful insight into the ways of God and is given great consolations; and these things can be expressed after a fashion. But in the third stage, the soul is transformed by a yet more perfect union, the soul in God, God in the soul; and what she then perceives cannot be expressed at all.[1] Angela says with beautiful accuracy that when the soul is thus transformed, "her own substance is not changed, but her life is changed into God by love and by love becomes as it were divine."[2]

In the first phase, the attempt to imitate Christ is not sufficient to safeguard the human heart; for we have not yet been given that complete integration of body and soul, heart and mind, in which we can truly desire God alone. And so our natural affections may still lead us astray; we may even go astray in spiritual matters, for we may desire virtue for the wrong reasons and our very love of God may have an element of self-seeking in it.[3] But in the second stage, the will is so intimately united with God's will that the heart cannot stray. And in the third stage, grace infuses into the soul a certain wisdom, so that the soul knows how to love God and how to love His creatures.

> "That most excellent and pure love is that in which the soul is drawn out and led to the vision of God . . . and she sees that every creature has its being from Him who is Being . . . and from this sight she draws an ineffable wisdom, an unshakable wisdom, a mature wisdom. . . . For in truth this Sovereign Being teaches us to love all which has being from His Being . . . and He teaches us to love rational creatures . . . specially those who are loved and cherished by this Sovereign Being. . . . And [the soul] learns and knows how to love creatures fittingly, either more or less, according to the dispositions of this Sovereign Being and in nothing does she exceed the due measure."[4]

It was with this love which is the perfect act of charity that Angela loved God and her children. She wrote tenderly to them;

[1] *Le Livre de la Bienheureuse Soeur Angèle de Foligno*, 299, 312–3.
[2] *Ibid.*, 272.   [3] *Ibid.*, 313.   [4] *Ibid.*, 322–3.

she made their sorrows hers, their joys hers. She was free to love them so spontaneously, so joyously, so warm-heartedly, precisely because of her complete detachment, her single-minded, single-hearted love of God. Writing to one of her children with the utmost affection, she could yet say: "My heart is His and His heart mine."[1] For she had been given that vision of the Godhead "which leaves in the soul that uncreated Love and the soul can do nothing ... but that Love does all ... Love Himself does all the works of Love."[2]

If her followers would be brought to this vision of the naked Godhead, then they must be fervent and constant in prayer. "If you would make progress, pray. ... But if you can come to the summit of perfection and would be enlightened yet more so that you may be established there, pray. ..."[3] Prayer, she says, is where God is found. Though she distinguishes three schools of prayer, bodily, mental and supernatural, she sees all of them in the context of her own all-embracing contemplative prayer. Bodily prayer is the prayer of words and gestures disposing the whole personality, body and soul, mind and heart, to the worship of God. It is a fundamental discipline and one she never abandoned, for there is no short cut to the higher states of prayer. In fact, she laid great stress upon the saying of the Divine Office at the appropriate times and she begged her followers not to scurry through their prayers to get a certain number said, "like little women bustling about doing tasks on piece-rates." They were to attend to what they said, to consider well; for from such consideration, they would come to mental prayer, in which the mind is so entirely occupied with God and in God (*circa Deum et in Deo*) that it cannot attend to anything else. This prayer "stills the tongue for it is not possible to speak." Yet what the soul learns in this state of attention to God can be expressed, is not totally beyond its understanding. It seems clear from her description that the soul is actively occupied, either in keeping the mind fixed on God, or at least in denying entrance to all extraneous thoughts. But, as Angela suggests, the content of the prayer is divinely given—the mind is "full of God" Who stoops to "occupy" the soul. This is the state of perfect mental prayer, from which the soul is raised up (*elevatur*) or drawn up (*trahitur*) into supernatural

---

[1] *Le Livre de la Bienheureuse Soeur Angèle de Foligno*, 253.
[2] *Ibid.*, 324.   [3] *Ibid.*, 191.

prayer, in which the natural powers of the soul are not sustained, but entirely suspended; the soul begins to experience super-naturally.[1]

Angela repeatedly and most emphatically insists that super-natural prayer is not mental prayer raised to a higher degree. It is totally different. It is not something we can do or even begin to do. Angela says that she could not will it, desire it or ask for it.[2] She speaks of being led by God, dominated by God, seized by God. For this is not something the soul does, it is something God does to the soul. "The soul is drawn up above what is natural to it, and by the supernatural light of understanding, the soul understands more of God than is proper to human nature . . . and the soul knows that she can never fully understand; and what she does understand, she cannot express, for all that she perceives and apprehends is beyond her nature."[3] "The soul is rejoiced in this Sovereign Good; and she sees nothing that can afterwards be expressed in words or even savoured in the heart."[4]

These three main stages of the same contemplative prayer seem to correspond to the three main stages of Angela's own develop-ment, to the three-fold poverties, and to the three stages of the soul's transformation or divinisation. The first goes with the twenty-one steps which Brother Arnold summarises in the *Memoriale*, with contrition, penance, self-knowledge, with the active attempt to imitate Christ, to love what He loved, to do as He did. The second seems to correspond to the next period, after Angela's experience of God's unique love for her on the way to Assisi; in this period of friendship with God, she would be "occupied" with the thought of God not just for hours, but for days at a time. It is the period of the locutions and some of the great imaginative visions; it is a period when in fact she was "poor in friendships," and the climax is reached when her will is united with God's will, and "of two things He made one."

The highest degree of supernatural prayer seems to correspond with what Brother Arnold called the seventh step, in which Angela was made to experience the great darkness—that darkness in which the soul is so completely dazzled by the light of the Godhead that it cannot see at all. "You will come then," she says

---

[1] *Le Livre de la Bienheureuse Soeur Angèle de Foligno*, 221–2.
[2] *Ibid.*, 177.   [3] *Ibid.*, 222.   [4] *Ibid.*, 158.

to a follower, "to the fullness of light—for you will understand that you cannot understand."[1]

In each main stage, there are many degrees and variations, though Angela makes no methodical attempt to analyse or grade them. A higher state of prayer seems often to have been anticipated, glimpsed, as it were, though but briefly, in what she reckoned a lower stage of development. In fact, the stages really only stress the fact that a point has been reached in which the soul is now more habitually in one sort of prayer than in another. For instance, very early on, she tells how in saying the *Pater noster* her mind was illuminated, and she began to taste somewhat of the divine sweetness.[2] And even before the union of her will with God's will, she had the "sight" of the Divine Wisdom, which marked the beginning of those intellectual visions, although these were not habitual till much later.

She herself says that when the soul is first united with the will of God, this union is not perfect and not continuous, and therefore the soul is always striving towards a more complete conformity with Christ, so that it may be more pleasing to God and more apt to be perfectly united with Him.[3] She speaks of a supreme experience of God which—at any rate up to about 1296—she had known only three times.[4] Yet later, she speaks of an experience of God, supreme and inexpressible, which she had known not once, not a hundred, but more than a thousand thousand times, and that not just for the space of a flutter of an eyelid, but in a less marvellous way, almost continuously.[5]

Yet to those who consulted her about prayer and were perhaps dejected because they did not receive any extraordinary graces, Angela said, quite simply: "Be content to do your part: God will do His."[6] And she adds:

"Let the soul know that this good Saviour of ours is better pleased with the services of a poor man who serves faithfully, without benefit or reward, than He is with the services of a rich man, who receives great rewards every day. . . . So the soul which God enriches with great consolations and which runs to Him in love, is not to be commended so much as that soul which runs to God and serves God

[1] *Le Livre de la Bienheureuse Soeur Angèle de Foligno*, 196.
[2] *Ibid.*, 41.   [3] *Ibid.*, 222.   [4] *Ibid.*, 159.
[5] *Ibid.*, 177–8.   [6] *Ibid.*, 253.

with a like great love, without any reward or comfort but in continual suffering. It seems to me that it is the divine light which comes from the life of Christ which shows me this, for He is the Way by which we must go through love, to God and in God."[1]

[1] *Le Livre de la Bienheureuse Soeur Angèle de Foligno*, 282.

Edmund Colledge

RUYSBROEK "the admirable, the astonishing, the marvellous"; what gained for him this appellation, and the veneration, instant and widespread in his own lifetime, which has endured until now? Apart from his personality, and of that we must presently speak, the reason is surely that he was a perfect child of his own times, standing before his contemporaries, as he stands to-day for us, the embodiment, in his life and in his works, of those highest aspirations of the human spirit to which late medieval Catholic Europe gave inimitable expression.

He was born in 1293, the son of simple village folk, it would seem, in Brabant. Thus he saw the close of the century which had produced the Franciscans and Dominicans, the Beguines, the Umiliati and the Beghards, the waves of popular, lay religious enthusiasm and the Church's campaigns lest these should lead altogether to disorder, heresy and schism: the century which, as none before it, produced so many women visionaries and teachers of divine love, giving to the Low Countries alone such great names as Marie of Oignies, Beatrice of Nazareth and Hadewijch of Antwerp: the century which was not to close before the German Dominican Eckhart was well launched upon that spectacular career as an exponent of mystical theology which was to end in disasters which shadowed the lives and the works of his followers in the succeeding age. We can see all these influences at work upon Ruysbroek. Himself a son of the people, he studied, not, it is thought, at any university, and he was ordained, about the year 1317, to the secular priesthood. Then he ministered for almost a quarter of a century in the collegiate church of St. Gudule in Brussels. Not a member of any religious order with a powerful international organisation for promoting the higher studies of its younger men and securing advancement and celebrity for them in academic life, manifestly not interested in gaining any of the other rich prizes which the medieval world

could offer to able and ambitious churchmen, he might well have
spent all his priesthood in humble retirement, and be to-day
forgotten and unknown. But we can glean something about how
he passed the years of obscurity. In the first place, plainly they
were used for devoted study of the Scriptures, the Fathers and
the classics of mystical theology: that shines out from every page
which he was later to write. Some of his devotees, it is true, were
to write of him afterwards as "a simple and unlettered man," but
this is rhetoric, not to be taken literally, as one of his sharpest
critics in the fifteenth century, John Gerson, himself Chancellor
of the University of Paris and a powerful figure in international
scholarship, was to discern. An *idiota* Ruysbroek was to remain
until the last of his many days, but it was a simplicity of the
heart, not of the intellect; and, as to his lack of "letters" (by
which, as usually in such medieval contexts, we are to understand Latin literature) it was and it remains one of the chief
elements in Ruysbroek's incomparable achievement that he was
able to make a balance and harmony, not only between popular
mystical enthusiasm and the Church's classical teaching upon
mystical theology, but also between the Latin vocabulary of the
masters whom he knew so well—from Augustine and the Western
versions of pseudo-Dionysius to the *Summa*—and the Dutch
vernacular language of divine love, as he found it in such works
of lay devotion and speculation as the letters of Hadewijch,
Gerard Appelman's *Gloss upon the Our Father*, and the *Gaesdonck
Tracts*. Those who come to Ruysbroek's Dutch from the German
of Eckhart and Tauler, and are struck by their many similarities
of terminology as well as thought, may be tempted to suppose
that Ruysbroek's language in some way echoes theirs; but we
now have several conclusive demonstrations, notably from the
two distinguished Belgian scholars, J. van Mierlo, S.J., and
S. Axters, O.P., that when Ruysbroek spoke of the mysteries of
divine union he used language which he had learned from his
countrymen, though none of them had spoken it with the
impeccable accuracy and inspired lucidity which he was to
employ.

Nor should we take too seriously the claim that he was a self-
taught rustic. When the Church beatified him, she left us no
room for doubt that his inspiration was of the Holy Spirit; but
there is not one of his writings which does not brilliantly exem-

O

plify for us his perfect mastery of didactic method, a mastery which points to the good teaching which he must have received in the schools, as well as to his many patient years of self-improvement as preacher and catechist. He was a man of superabounding intellectual vitality and curiosity: his passing remarks upon natural history and on the scientific theories of his day are still fascinating; and as we read such a magisterial exercise as the exposition, at the beginning of *The Kingdom of Lovers*, of his text, "The Lord has led the righteous man by straight ways, and has shown him the kingdom of God," or consider the austere beauty of structure of the three great books of *The Spiritual Espousals*, we feel ourselves in the presence, we seem to hear the voice of another Seraphic Doctor. Very different though their lives and works were, St. Francis and Blessed John Ruysbroek have one rare quality in common, a strange power to compel, down the centuries, the love of those who learn from them.

Throughout his lifetime, he seems to have exercised a compelling fascination for those who knew him. In 1343 he had taken the step traditional among those who long for a more perfect way of life, renouncing his cure of souls in Brussels and retiring with two companions to the nearest "desert," the forest of Zonienbosch outside the city; but, as so often, his spiritual flight was impeded by the many who sought out his cell to gain counsel and consolation. So this little family of hermits embraced a more regular and secluded rule, Ruysbroek being professed in 1351 as an Augustinian canon: until his death thirty years later he ruled the house, which he filled with brothers who loved him truly and sons who served him faithfully.

It is usually of these later years, and of the many close spiritual ties which he then made, that his own writings and his biographers tell us. Yet we know that there must have been many who in his early life recognised this humble young priest for what he was. A fragment of conversation at a Brussels street corner as he went by has come down through the centuries to us. "Look at him! I'd like to be in his shoes—he's a saint"—"Not for me: I couldn't enjoy myself then!" The story is preserved for us because in later life he used to tell it to his brothers in religion, and to add that he then thought to himself, "Poor, unhappy man, not to know how sweet the Lord is to those who taste His Holy Spirit!" Yet, by a paradox, the world first came to know of him, not as we remember him to-day, as an apostle of the essence of God's love, but as a stern opponent and denunciator of false doctrine. Again, we are recalled to the world into which he had been born, we remember Innocent IV's bull of 1252 in which he says that he is convinced that the duties which he has imposed on the Dominicans of supervising nunneries are interfering with their proper work, "and especially preaching against heretics": we see that among the proposals submitted for the agenda of the Council of Lyons in 1274, the Dominicans were concerned for the abuses of religious poverty, the Franciscans for the dangers of vernacular theological exposition by amateurs and for the spreading heretical tendencies among the Beguines, and a representative diocesan bishop, characteristically, for growing rebellion against ecclesiastical authority. So we need not be surprised at what little we learn of "Bloemardinne," the woman who had led the heretics in Brussels against whom Ruysbroek preached. Perhaps the first thing to be said of her is that her identification with Hadewijch of Antwerp is purely mythical, as van Mierlo has proved, and a gross injustice to Hadewijch, whose genuine works are of irreproachable orthodoxy, whereas Bloemardinne seems to have taught (her works have not survived) some at least of the tenets of the "Brethren of the Free Spirit."

There is no need here to enquire into the beliefs, often varying, and the practices, doubtless grossly distorted and exaggerated in contemporary accounts, of this sect; but the present writer has tried elsewhere to show that there is an essential connection between their perversions of divine truth and Ruysbroek's perceptions of it. What little we are told of Bloemardinne by Pomerius, the early fifteenth-century biographer of Ruysbroek, shows plainly enough that she had preached, in "the liberty of the spirit" and "the seraphic nature of free love," a Manichaean dualism which taught that those who in this life attain to a region of grace can no longer sin, that they are "free in spirit" from the flesh, which may be left to do as it pleases, and from the law, which binds only the imperfect. So it is that we find in Ruysbroek's writings, as in perhaps no other Christian teacher since Augustine, by whom he was deeply influenced, a constant regard for man's true nature, a repeated referring-back of all his other demonstrations to their basis, his knowledge and beliefs concerning human psychology. This has been well demonstrated again

for us in recent years by Albin Ampe, S.J., in his four masterly
volumes on the mystic's doctrine (it is only to be regretted that
his work is in Dutch, and so inaccessible, apart from each volume's
concluding Latin *compendium*, to all but a few outside the Low
Countries: those who do know his work will recognise at once
how much this present essay owes to it), and especially in the
last book. The whole of Ruysbroek's mystical doctrine is rooted
in and grows from his wonderful perception of the mysteries
implicit in our Christian knowledge that God made man in His
own image and likeness. So he writes, in one of his later, shorter
treatises, *A Mirror of Eternal Blessedness*:

> Holy Scripture teaches that God, the heavenly Father, created all
> men in His image and in His likeness. His image is His Son, His own
> eternal Wisdom, and St. John says that in this all things have life.
> And the life is nothing else than the image of God, in which God has
> everlastingly begotten all things, and which is the cause (*orsake—
> causa* in its scholastic sense) of all creatures. And so this image, which
> is the Son of God, is eternal, before all creation; and we are all
> made in this eternal image, for in the noblest part of our souls, that
> is, in the properties of our highest powers, we are made as a living,
> eternal mirror of God, in which God has impressed His eternal
> image, and into which no other image can ever enter.

The terminology used here will be easy and familiar to those
who read medieval philosophy, and the ideas may at first seem
to be general and received: but the implications are vast, stretching far beyond the usual "theology of the image," carrying with
them a trinitarianism which pervades all Ruysbroek's teaching
about man and about God. He, like so many men of the Middle
Ages, was haunted by the Pauline simile of the "mirror," but as
we can see here, the mirror for him is not only man's dim,
earthly vision of God, but also God's bright perception of man,
as He first begot him and made him to be like Him and to be
one with Him, in a unity which was and is the end of creation.

"Deification," then, is one of the great themes of his teaching:
but we must look, not as Gerson did, at a few isolated passages,
but at the whole of his works if we are to understand how perfectly in harmony with the mind of the Church his doctrine of
deification was, how carefully contrasted with the false and
blasphemous tenets of the many foolish and misguided enthu-
siasts who flourished in his times. Again in the *Mirror*, he says:

Where I write that we are one with God, by that is to be understood one in love, not in being or in nature. For God's being is uncreated, and our being is created, and God and the creature are immeasurably unlike; and therefore, though they may be united, they cannot become one. If our being were to become nothing, we should know nothing, love nothing, have no blessedness. But our created being is to be regarded as a wild and barren desert, where God lives, Who governs us. . . .

(This figure of human existence as a desert in which God lives will recall to English readers Julian of Norwich's famous allegory of God as a lord seated in a place "simple, on the earth, barren and deserted, alone in a wilderness.") Here is Christian commonsense, seeing clearly that any "image-theology," in its very recognition of man's likeness to God, implies his difference from Him. "We are all one life in God, in our eternal image. . . . Yet therefore we are different from God, and cannot become one (identical) with Him, but must remain in our difference, persisting in ourselves, each man in his own person."[1] It is significant that in this book, which at least in part (it seems to be a composite, made by his disciples out of the works in progress when at last extreme old age forced him to stop writing) describes and directs the devotional life of the Beguines, we should have this plain allusion to the false doctrines imputed to some of their number: and there is an even clearer refutation and rejection of such heresies in the conclusion of another later work, *The Little Book of Enlightenment*, written to help the Carthusians of Herne to understand passages which they had found difficult in *The Kingdom of Lovers*, his first book, written as a secular priest in Brussels, and not later approved by him as altogether suitable for general publication:

As I have said to you before, you should hold yourselves aloof from those men who in their empty ignorance are so deceived that crassly and foolishly they believe that out of their own natures they have found within themselves the indwelling of God, and who wish to be one with God without His grace and without the exercise of virtue. . . .

"To be one with God without His grace and without the exercise of virtue." Here Ruysbroek points to the Pelagianism

[1] *The Twelve Beguines.*

and the quietism which, as St. Albert the Great in the generation before him had recognised, were the hall-marks of the heresies then fashionable. Since Ruysbroek's teaching that man in "essential union" with God is "above grace and beyond reason" caused his critics, quite baselessly, to accuse him of precisely these errors, his complete freedom from them must be stressed; and we can do this best by reverting to his essentially trinitarian conception of man in his relation to the universe and to God, though one can here give only a bare and fragmentary account of his teaching.

To him, as Ampe has remarked, "the similitude and image of the Holy Trinity is seen in the whole universe, and in particular in man." In the mirror in which man darkly sees God, he perceives a trinity: there is the Godhead, the divine essence, there is the divine nature, and there are the Persons. The divine essence is "simple," it is "idle," it is "without manner": the most and the best that we can say of it is its *isticheit*, its "beingness" (the concept is Augustine's, the term was common to German and Dutch mystics before Ruysbroek), that "it is." (This is the idea somewhat clumsily expounded by the author of *The Cloud of Unknowing* as "naked being": and he is very close to Ruysbroek and their common sources when in Chapter VII of *The Cloud* he treats of our recollection of God's attributes, as of the Passion and life of Our Lord, as inimical to our perception of His "naked being.") So too in man, the "created trinity," a threefold nature and a threefold life is seen. There is his *anima*, his spirit, forming and "in-forming" his personality with all its attributes and properties, and fulfilled in and guiding his active life. There is his *animus*, his reason, controlling his inward life, in which he lives more highly, beyond the active life, achieving and being given by God an active unity with Him, attained by God and by man through means and recognisable by manners, modes; and the greatest of all these means and modes is the Incarnation of the Word, the Second Person of the Trinity in Whom the divine nature is manifested to man, by Whose life and death man's redemption was created. And yet (and here we have that aspect of theocentric mysticism, cardinal to Ruysbroek's whole theological scheme, which can often puzzle and distress the devout) man has still another nature, the essence of his soul, through which he leads the contemplative life of essential union with God and suffers God's transforming effect upon the soul, a suffered or passive union in which there are neither manners nor means. It is of this state of the soul, truly mysterious in that it defies reason and is only to be comprehended through faith, that Ruysbroek wrote with a fervour and a knowledge not to be paralleled even in the works of the master of all the mystics, "Dionysius": here is one such passage, the triumphal conclusion to *The Spiritual Espousals*:

God's impenetrable lack of manner is so dark and so without manner that in itself it comprehends all the divine manners, and the work and the attributes of the Persons, in the rich embrace of Their essential unity; and in the abyss of God's namelessness it makes a divine delight. And in this there is a delectable passing-over and a flowing-away and a sinking-down into the essential nakedness, with all the divine names and all manners and all living reason which has its image in the mirror of divine truth: all these fall away into this simple nakedness, wanting manner and without reason. For in this unfathomable joy of simplicity, all things are embraced in a delectable blessedness, and the depths themselves remain uncomprehended, except it be in our essential unity with God. Before this, all created personality must fail, and all that lives in God, for here there is nothing but an eternal resting in a delectable embrace of the flowing-out of love.[1]

If we are to understand aright what he is trying to say in such a passage as this, we must read it with close attention, and we must read it in its whole context. As it stands, it tells us not only how man can come closest and become most like to God, but that we must remain eternally unlike to Him, Who is uncreated and Who made us. And if we read the *Espousals* in its entirety we shall see that even the least of its merits, that it is a work of consummate literary art, derives from its author's persuasion that the active life (the subject of the first book), the "life of yearning for God" (which occupies the second book), and the life of essential union in which God is contemplated are an indivisible three. To each is its own appropriate way, and each complements the others. It is by *regiratio*, "the return in the cycle", that man will mount out of "the region of unlikeness" into that likeness to God which is essential unity with Him (and one need here hardly stress the soundness of all these conceptions, nor their acceptance

[1] I am grateful to Messrs. Faber and Faber, publishers of my edition of *The Spiritual Espousals* (18s), for permission to use my translation of this work here.

by the Church long before Ruysbroek expounded them): but the "return to the image of God" is made by a reversion to Him of man's free will, and it is through the power of the redeeming grace of Christ Crucified. Only through such grace can man come to contemplate God "above grace": only by God's means, and above all in Christ, making free to us that grace which has in Him its fullest measure, can we with Christ be like God, exercising in Him our active unity with God, and then, if by grace we can transcend our created activity, following Him, simply and in faith, towards that divine enlightenment which is "essential union". But this is begun in the active life, and is continued, to the end of our life on earth, in the life of yearning and seeking for God: it is a *vita Christiformis*, a life made like to that of Christ, made like by the means which God has created for us, and above everything else by our life with Christ in the faith and in the sacraments, most of all in the Eucharist.

If we to-day still seek for a defence of Ruysbroek against charges of quietism and pantheism, if, better, we look to him for an answer to those heresies, we find what we need in his devotion to the humanity and the Passion of our Saviour, and to the Mass.

> At supper at the high feast of the Passover, when Christ wished to pass from this exile to His Father, when He had eaten the paschal lamb with His disciples, and all the old law was fulfilled. . . . He took bread in His honourable and venerable hands, and consecrated His holy body and thereafter His holy blood, and gave them in common to His disciples, and bequeathed them in common to all good men to their everlasting profit. This gift and this dish gladdens and adorns our every high feast and every banquet, in heaven and in earth. In this gift, God gives Christ to us in three manners. He gives to us His flesh and His blood and His bodily life, glorified, full of joys and sweetnesses. And He gives to us His spirit, with the highest powers, full of glories and gifts, truths and righteousness. And He gives to us His personality, with divine clarity, which exalts His spirit and all enlightened spirits into the exalted and delectable unity.[1]

If we read such passages as this in the light of Ruysbroek's whole doctrine, we cannot mistake its meaning: however exalted in the search for union with God man's spirit may, by God's grace, become, even if by the exercise of his reason and the inpouring of grace the essence of his soul be brought to where it sees God

[1] *The Spiritual Espousals*, Book II.

and is like Him "above grace and beyond reason," still he remains
God's creature, sanctified and made like to Him only as he is like
to Christ. The continuation of the passage just quoted from the
Espousals could not be more explicit: in the active life man may
come to such devotion to the Passion that he may feel that he
suffers with Christ, yet in the contemplative life we may, by
means of Christ, come beyond means and beyond manners, we
may "pass beyond ourselves and beyond the humanity of Christ,
and have rest in our heritage, which is the divine nature in
eternity." It is Christ's will that this should be; "and He wills
that we should receive Him, sacramentally and spiritually, as
often as it is fitting and proper or advisable."

This threefold life of man, then, is to be lived simultaneously,
and man upon earth will never be free of his need of grace and of
its means, will never escape from the exile of unlikeness to God.
There is nothing here of pantheism, nor, in what he teaches us of
the soul's most exalted moments of communion with its God, is
there any taint of quietism. In a famous sequence in *The Treatise
of Perfection of the Sons of God*, in which he might at first seem to
be teaching, much in the manner of Eckhart and Tauler, of an
ascending order of ways of life, he shows how far from perfected he regards the highest forms of contemplation to be achieved
in this life, where he speaks of the soul's thirst for God as

> an impatient hunger, ever striving for what it lacks, ever swim-
> ming against the stream. One cannot leave it, one cannot have it:
> one cannot lack it, one cannot gain it: one cannot tell it, one cannot
> conceal it, for it is above reason and understanding . . . but if we
> look deep within ourselves, there we shall feel God's Spirit driving
> and urging us on in the impatience of love; and if we look high
> above ourselves, there we shall feel God's Spirit drawing us out of
> ourselves and bringing us to nothing in the essence of God, that is,
> in the essential love in which we are one with Him, the love which
> we possess deeper and wider than every other thing.

Again we have the idea of simultaneity, and with it the complete
rejection of any kind of earthly perfection or deification which
will make man free of his own nature or of his need for divine
grace. We should observe, too, here how very careful Ruysbroek
is to avoid the language of *Brautmystik*, not to use any term which
might suggest analogies between divine and carnal love. Ruysbroek at all times shows himself a consummate artist, alike in his

most abstract arguments and demonstrations and in the touching, simple verses with which he adorns *The Twelve Beguines*; and on occasion he shows how deeply he was moved by the divine poems of others—one thinks especially of the place in *The Seven Steps* ("The Holy Spirit works in us, and with Him we work all our good deeds; and He calls from within us, with a loud voice, saying always 'Love Love, Who loves you everlastingly. . . .' ") where he makes a clear allusion to one of the *Letters* of Hadewijch. But always for him art served his vision of truth, and language must be strictly governed: never could he be called, as Eckhart has not unjustly been described, "the victim of his own style."

Still less could it be claimed for Ruysbroek that he is equally comprehensible to East and West, to pagan and Christian. It was no merely formal profession of faith when he wrote, at the end of *The Little Book*, "In all things which I understand or feel or have written, I submit myself to the judgment of the saints and of Holy Church: for I will live and die as the servant of Jesus Christ, in the Christian Faith; and I long to be by the grace of God a living branch of Holy Church." How richly this humble prayer has been answered, six centuries have shown.

17. JOHANN TAULER

James M. Clark

MEDIEVAL GERMANY produced many great scholars and
eloquent preachers, but no more lovable figure than the
humble friar whose sixth centenary was celebrated on
15 June, 1961. Both in good and evil times, in years of prosperity
and years of persecution, Johann Tauler continued by precept
and example to show forth the beauty of the Christian life.[1]
About the year 1300 he was born in Strasbourg, a city which
had a very active religious life and which was one of the greatest
centres of preaching in Europe. He came of a wealthy local
family, and although documentary evidence is lacking, it is
almost certain that he entered the Strasbourg Dominican friary
and proceeded later to the *studium generale* at Cologne, where
St. Thomas and Albertus Magnus had once taught. Tauler is
never described as "Magister," and it is only in the spurious
Vita and in later manuscripts that he is given the title of "Doctor,"
from which we conclude that he did not complete his theological
studies in Paris, though he may have visited that city for a short
time. His attitude to the learning of the schools shows antipathy
rather than enthusiasm. Nor is this surprising: the victory of
Nominalism over Realism had shaken the belief in the unaided
power of human reason. The will took the place of the intellect
in the scale of values and speculation was discredited in the eyes
of many religious-minded men.

There can be no doubt of Tauler's sense of vocation. In later
life he related how strongly he had been attracted by the seemly
discipline of the "saintly brethren," and how he desired to share
the austerities they practised. The Order of Preachers was still

[1] The best edition is that of Ferdinand Vetter, *Deutsche Texte des Mittelalters*,
xi, Berlin, 1906. English translations by Sister M. Imelda, O.P., in *The Life of
the Spirit*, Blackfriars, Oxford, 1948-50, iii, iv (7 sermons); Elizabeth Strakosch,
Blackfriars Publications, 1958 (17 sermons). A translation of selected sermons
with introduction by Sister M. Jane, O.P., and Eric Colledge was published
in 1962.

at the height of its fame. Many young men of noble or patrician birth thronged to join its ranks, renouncing their patrimony in favour of voluntary poverty. Tauler was intensely proud of his Order and its founder. "Truly, children," he once said in a sermon to Dominican nuns, "the holy Order to which we belong, you with me, and I with you, is a very sublime and worthy institution. Hence we should all be grateful to Our Lord because He has invited us out of this troubled world in order that we might wait upon Him alone and live for Him alone."[1]

It was indeed a troubled world in the third decade of the century. The tragic conflict between the papacy and the empire had reached its culminating point. The Emperor Lewis the Bavarian had defied Pope John XXII and had actually caused himself to be crowned in Rome by an anti-pope of his own choosing. In 1325 John XXII excommunicated the Emperor and laid his possessions under an interdict. Strasbourg was one of the towns that supported Lewis. The local Dominicans remained loyal to the Pope, and Tauler preferred exile to submission to the temporal power. In 1328 he left for Basel, where he was free to say Mass without let or hindrance.

Nor was this all. In 1327 the trial of Eckhart had opened at Cologne. Eckhart had lectured at Strasbourg in 1314[2] and later he taught in Cologne. It may well be that Tauler was his pupil at one or the other of these two schools. The connection between them, as evidenced in their writings, is so close that personal contact is the only possible inference. The condemnation of their beloved master in 1329 must have been a terrible blow for Tauler and his friend Suso. In addition to this private sorrow there were public catastrophes. After years of famine alternating with destructive floods there came devastating catastrophes: the Black Death in 1347-8 and the earthquake of 1356. It is small wonder that the end of the world was widely expected.

It was against this sombre background that Tauler once preached to nuns on the tenth Sunday after Pentecost, on the benefits to be derived from receiving Holy Communion. He told them of the time when the world was so wicked that the wrath of God was kindled against mankind and "He would

[1] Vetter, p. 269, 17-20.
[2] Cf., however, Josef Koch, "Kritische Studien zum Leben Meister Eckharts," *Archivum Fratrum Praedicatorum*, xxix (1959), 40-1.

have destroyed the world if it were not for the intercession of St. Dominic." Once more the world was in the same precarious state and no one knew what the future held in store for them all. There was no better way than "to give up everything and cast it away and be gloriously united with God in the holy Body of our Lord."[1]

Thus, in the midst of almost universal gloom we hear a note of calm confidence and unfaltering faith. It was in this spirit that Tauler worked in Basel, where he profoundly influenced the religious life of the time. Here he met a secular priest named Heinrich von Nördlingen, with whom he formed a firm friendship. Together they became the leaders of a movement known as the Friends of God (Gottesfreunde). It was not a religious order, but a group of like-minded persons, friars and nuns, laymen and laywomen, united by common aims and ideals. After Tauler returned to Strasbourg in 1347-8 the good work did not cease. His fame as a preacher spread far and wide. Speaking of him and Heinrich von Nördlingen, Christina Ebner, a Dominican nun of Engeltal, near Nürnberg, wrote about 1350: "They have set the world ablaze with their fiery tongues," that is, with their inspired eloquence. There are strong reasons for believing that Tauler spent a year or two in Cologne, and he may well have stayed there on more than one occasion. He also made frequent journeys to other friaries and nunneries in the course of his pastoral work, but his headquarters were at Strasbourg until his death in 1361. For a time he was the confessor of the Strasbourg merchant Rulman Merswin, the founder of the house of Knights Hospitallers at Grüneworth. According to an ancient tradition, Tauler died in the garden of the Dominican convent of St. Nicholas de Undis, where his sister was a nun.

Tauler's sermons must have made a profound impact on his hearers. He evidently adapted the tone and treatment of his discourse to those whom he addressed, bearing in mind the stage of education and of spiritual growth they had attained. But his influence was by no means limited to the spoken word. The sermons were written down, not by the friar himself, but by the nuns or layfolk who heard them. In this way other religious houses and later generations benefited from them. Excerpts were made from the sermons and were used to form short treatises.

[1] Vetter, p. 268, 33- p. 269, 6.

The demand for edifying reading was great in the friaries, convents, monasteries and Beguine houses in the populous valley of the Rhine and in other parts of the Empire.

The existing material, though incomplete and sometimes imperfectly recorded, is nevertheless adequate to give us a picture of the man behind the words, the personality of the preacher. Contemporary references to Tauler, though not frequent, supplement the impression. He was not a man of great erudition, although he was well grounded in scholastic thought, as it was then taught and interpreted. He did not attempt to extend the range of human knowledge, but he faithfully transmitted to others the knowledge which he had acquired, laying on it the stamp of his own kindly, gentle personality. He was not a systematic theologian, nor were his sermons composed for theologians; they were all in the vernacular and were, in the main, intended for simple, pious folk. Although very few of Tauler's sermons were built up round a central theme, he was quite able, on occasion, to construct a sermon on scholastic lines, dividing the text in the customary manner. A specimen of this technique is a sermon preached on Eph. 4, 1–6.[1] The theme is God's call to mankind. This is divided into four questions: (1) Who calls? (2) To what does He call? (3) How does He call? (4) How should we respond to the call? In the second section is asked: Who is called? The three kinds of persons who are called are described in the traditional manner as beginners, proficients and perfect.

Most of Tauler's sermons are familiar, informal talks. They have every appearance of being hastily prepared or even improvised, the work of a busy priest who had little time for study and reflection, and whose subject-matter lay ready to hand. He was one of the greatest exponents of medieval German prose, and dealt skilfully with the most varied topics in his own homely Alsatian dialect, increasing in a marked degree its flexibility and its abstract vocabulary. He could on occasion rise to great heights of eloquence, when he is carried aloft by his soaring thoughts. But what he has to say is in general expressed simply, in a practical, direct style. There is little use of imagery; there are few *exempla*, or moral tales, such as formed so large a part of the repertory of Franciscan friars.

[1] Vetter, p. 240.

It is characteristic of the practical trend of Tauler's thought that we come across the word *werc* (work, activity) on almost every page of his sermons.[1] They are, in the main, trumpet calls to action, to service. Thus, when preaching on the tenth Sunday after Pentecost, on the words from the Epistle, *Divisiones operationum sunt, idem autem Dominus est*,[2] he deals with the diversities of gifts with which men are endowed, although the same spirit works in them all. Men should exercise their particular gifts in action. Hard work never hurt anyone. To those who complain that daily drudgery afflicts their conscience and prevents them from attending Mass, he says: "It is not the work itself that causes this restlessness which you feel, but disorderliness." All work is noble, even the meanest and humblest. It is a human duty to work. "If I were not a priest," says Tauler, "and a member of an Order, I should think it a great thing if I could make boots and shoes, and I would gladly earn my bread with my own hands."[3] This humility and modesty is typical of the man.

The work should, however, have a meaning, an aim, if it is to be effective: "You should hold in your hands a burning lantern, that is, loving activity. Children, the activity of true, ardent love within and without should never go out of your hands as far as you are able to hold it, and especially in all devotion towards each other according to your capacity."[4] He sees the danger of quietism, of passively allowing God to act for us and of doing nothing ourselves. He had himself come across this tendency in his pastoral work:

> In some places people are to be found who cultivate a false passivity and divest themselves of all activity, and internally they even suppress good thoughts, and then they say they have attained peace and they will not even practise good works, saying that they have got beyond that. They have a devil sitting beside them who forbids anything that might disturb them in their inward or outward peace, in their thoughts, or their behaviour.[5]

Work that is done merely for the praise of men, for one's own interest and profit, is not to be encouraged. There are also questions of the relative merit of our actions. Should one stay away from the office or from Mass in order to help one's

---

[1] See F. W. Wentzlaff-Eggebert, "Studien zur Lebenslehre Taulers," *Abhandlungen der Preussischen Akademie der Wissenschaften*, 1939, Phil.-hist. Kl., No. 12, pp. 20-6.   [2] 1 Cor. 12, 6.
[3] Vetter, p. 177, 14-27.   [4] *Ibid.*, p. 216, 11-14.   [5] *Ibid.*, p. 218, 11-16.

neighbour? Which is the prior duty? Tauler answers that we should give the priority to religious duties unless the neighbour needs our help urgently and action cannot safely be postponed. It is God's will that everyone should do the duty which God has imposed upon him, however inconspicuous it may be; even if it is work that anyone else could do as well. No matter how mean the task, how poor the skill required to perform it, it comes from God and is a special grace. We must render to God an account of our skill and of the work we do for the benefit of our neighbour.

Which is the more valuable, the active or the contemplative life? Are we to follow Martha or Mary? Tauler replies: "Our Lord rebuked Martha, but not for her works, because they were holy and good. He rebuked her for her anxious care, for worrying about her work."[1] He then proceeds to tell us of "One of the greatest Friends of God, who has been a ploughman more than forty years and still is one. And he once asked Our Lord if it was His will that he should give it up and go to sit in the church. But He said 'No.' He was not to do so, he was to earn his bread in the sweat of his brow in honour of His noble and precious Blood."[2] While condemning "false passivity" as leading to quietism and to hypocrisy, he acknowledges the need for silence and contemplation in the religious life. He postulates a sane balance between receptivity and activity. Although someone may, apparently, be doing nothing but meditating on action, God may be, unknown to him, performing a hidden work in his soul.[3] Everyone should find out for himself what kind of attitude best promotes the approach to God.

It is not enough to act, we must act wisely. Our actions must be well directed. We must see the end in the beginning, foresee the consequences of our acts before performing them. One whole sermon is preached on this theme.[4] The rubric tells us: "This sermon from St. Matthew's Gospel, from the Vigil of the Epiphany, concerning Joseph's fear and the death of Archelaus, teaches us to perceive prudently the end in the beginning of every action and it warns us of the three enemies which assail our souls. The enemies are the world, the flesh and the devil."

Nor should our actions be too vehement. Tauler strives to

[1] Vetter, p. 178, 23–4.   [2] *Ibid.*, p. 179, 20–4.
[3] *Ibid.*, p. 189, 20–5.   [4] *Ibid.*, 12–16.

restrain those over-eager souls who rush to carry out their plans without considering whether they have the strength to complete them. They take their own enthusiasm for a guarantee of success. We must not regard our allotted task as our own, but as God's work, done in or by us, and should accordingly be humble. The impulsive souls are only too apt to be irresolute; when the first difficulties arise they are at once plunged into depression.

Unlike Eckhart, who laid the chief stress on the *via unitiva*, the final phase of the threefold way, Tauler says much more about the first stage, the *via purgativa*, or way of purification. It is fatal to try to rush the pace, to run before we can walk. Until the soul has been purified of its grosser elements it cannot proceed to the higher stages of the way. With deep knowledge and experience of the human heart gained by hearing confessions, Tauler recognised temptation in its most subtle forms and exposed it relentlessly. He appeals to the authority of St. Bernard, urging his hearers not to yield to self-deception. He detects hypocrisy and dishonesty both in the active and the contemplative life. They may be present even in good works, such as almsgiving, charitable donations, gifts to the Church, prayer and fasting.

It should be added that Tauler did not in any sense condemn the good works prescribed or approved by the Church. He did not oppose, as Luther later wrongly assumed, pilgrimages, fasting or other bodily austerities. All that he said was that outer works are of no avail if they are not done in the proper spirit, if the doer is not well disposed. They may be useless, even dangerous, if they are allowed to lead to hypocrisy and pharisaism. There is no reason why those who are physically frail should go to extremes in ascetic practices. To console those who are distressed on this account he tells his hearers on more than one occasion of his own sorrow that his delicate health prevented him from observing the Rule of his Order in all its severity. His detractors even accused him of being less strict than they were and boasted of their own austerities. We should be merciful and refrain from judging others. Uncharitableness is a grievous sin and one which destroys the effectiveness of good works. "Children, however many good works you may perform, however good your intentions are, the devil will make you his laughing stock if you are guilty of this sin."[1]

[1] Vetter, p. 148, 18–20.

P

The serious student of Tauler may be puzzled by a seeming inconsistency in the good friar's writings, and this observation also applies, *mutatis mutandis*, to Suso. On the one hand we hear the homely, practical teacher and preacher, who avoids what is too abstract, too speculative, and keeps to the great truths about the moral life, exhorting, admonishing, encouraging or comforting, and at times boldly denouncing evil in all its forms, sparing neither clergy nor laity. But on the other hand, we find passages and even whole sermons in which the speculative element looms largely. The glories of mystical union are painted with glowing colours, the splendours of supernatural experiences are described in the language of Eckhart or Pseudo-Dionysius. We must not exaggerate: these sermons only constitute a fraction of the whole, and few of them contain passages which, properly understood in their context, really verge on pantheism.

These passages are certainly authentic. The very sermons in which the mystical element is most strongly in evidence always contain a phrase or a word that belongs to the specific vocabulary of Tauler. Tauler identified the Pseudo-Dionysius, as did his contemporaries generally, with the Greek convert of St. Paul, and regarded him as a saint of the Church. Indeed, he refers to him as "St. Dionysius." If there was any conflict between his doctrines and those of St. Thomas Aquinas (whom Tauler highly revered), Tauler would be inclined to think that this was the kind of problem which he was not competent to solve. He would leave it to the "great theologians."

Of Tauler's orthodoxy there can be no doubt. "By the grace of God and from Holy Church," he says:

> I have received my Order, this habit and my priestly office, with authority to teach and to hear confessions. If it were to come about that the Pope and Holy Church wished to deprive me of these things, I would give them back wholly to them, and would don a grey coat, if I could get one, and I would never again join the friars in my convent. I would go away and never again be a priest or hear confessions, or preach again, all for God's sake. For those who gave me these things can also take them away. It is not for me to inquire the reason, for I would not wish to be a heretic, or to be excommunicated.[1]

We come across many of Eckhart's most famous sayings, either

[1] Vetter, p. 255, 11-22.

paraphrased or unaltered, in Tauler's sermons, for instance:
"Better one master of life than a thousand masters of arts," or
the remark that the soul has two eyes, one internal and the other
external. Tauler's attitude to scriptural exegesis is the same as that
of Eckhart. He maintains that, in addition to the traditional
interpretation of a biblical passage, many new meanings can be
discovered: "If one reads Holy Writ and preaches about it and
meditates on it, one will find more and more truths never as yet
discovered by man."

Like Eckhart and Pseudo-Dionysius, Tauler uses the word
Nothing of God and speaks of Him as the "Divine wilderness."
He explains the meaning of "Nothing" thus: "This is the Nothing
of which St. Dionysius said that God was not anything that one
can name or understand or grasp."[1] But these phrases and other
similar ones, in spite of their pantheistic sound, were in common
use in religious circles in fourteenth-century Germany. They
belonged to the vocabulary of the Friends of God and were
understood in a Christian and not in a pagan sense.

If we examine carefully the mystical passages in Tauler, we
find again and again a note of caution. We feel a sense of hesitation, which indicates that this is to be regarded as exceptional,
that it is not entirely in keeping with the usual trend and tenor
of Tauler's thought. Rarely does he speak of the "spark of the
soul," which phrase was first used in German by Eckhart, who
found the Latin equivalent *scintilla animae* in Richard of St. Victor
and, in a restricted sense, in St. Thomas. Instead Tauler speaks
of the "Gemüt" (higher reason, spirit) or of the "ground of the
soul," and "ground" was one of his favourite words, as it was
with the Friends of God. He uses the word "abyss" of God,
signifying that He is unfathomable in His nature, and he also
speaks of the abyss of man, but hastens to add that the latter is
a "created abyss." Tauler is fond of speaking of "sinking into
the Divine abyss." This might suggest absorption into the Divine,
which would be pantheistic, but the context shows that Tauler
meant "contemplation of the Divine."

The use of the words *gotvar, vergotet* (godlike, deified) might
easily lead to misunderstanding. But here again we must consider the prevalent meaning of such terms. Although Neoplatonic
in origin, they are Christian in significance. Tauler uses them to

[1] Vetter, p. 201, 8-9.

describe the moral transformation of man by grace to the image (*ad imaginem*) of God.[1]

The doctrine of the birth of the Word in the sanctified soul by grace may be described as the cardinal teaching of Meister Eckhart. Fr. Hugo Rahner, S.J.,[2] has traced the long development of this doctrine in its various forms and ramifications from Origen and Gregory of Nyssa through Peter Lombard and Richard of St. Victor. It is not surprising that we find echoes and reminiscences of this conception in Tauler's sermons, though the formulation is more guarded than it was apt to be in Eckhart's writings. Instead of saying that the Word, the Son of God, is born eternally in the human soul, and that by grace man can become the son of God by adoption, as Eckhart does, Tauler usually speaks of the "transformation" or "overforming" (Überformung) of man in the Divine image. The meaning of Eckhart's phrase is the complete moral regeneration of man as part of the *corpus mysticum Christi*, as Fr. Kertz has convincingly demonstrated. Why does Tauler tend to avoid Eckhart's phraseology? One can only assume that the cause of this cautious approach was the condemnation of Eckhart. No less than four of the condemned propositions concerned the just man as the son of God. One cannot but think that Tauler, like his friend Suso, believed that Eckhart was innocent, but he did not wish to rebel, or even to seem to rebel, against constituted authority in the Church. It is generally assumed that Eckhart was Tauler's source, but Fr. Rahner suggests that in one case Tauler's doctrine was derived from St. Augustine's *De Virginitate*.

In the most difficult sermon of all, in which we find the most conflicting opinions about the Holy Trinity, we come across the following, very cautious and truly Taulerian conclusion:

> One could pile up an endless mass of words about this, without saying or understanding anything about the manner in which the super-essential Unity exists in Trinity. On this topic it is better to feel than to speak. . . . It is above the understanding of angels. We commend this theme to the great theologians, for it is their task to find words to express it for the defence of the Faith, and they have good books on the subject, but we should simply believe.[3]

[1] See Fr. Karl G. Kertz, S.J., "Meister Eckhart's Teaching on the Birth of the Divine Word in the Soul," *Traditio* (1959), p. 363.

[2] "Die Gottesgeburt aus dem Herzen der Gläubigen," *Zeitschrift für katholische Theologie*, Vol. 59 (1935), p. 410.   [3] Vetter, p. 299, 15–24.

Tauler was a harmonious personality: there was no conflict between the moralist and the mystic. These were but two aspects of the same rich personality. Like other great religious leaders, he could find the right words for practical men and women absorbed in the problems of their daily round, but he could also inspire the heroes and heroines of the spiritual life in their strenuous efforts. He had to deal with many different types of persons. Most of his sermons were, it is true, preached to nuns. Nowhere in Western Christendom were the nunneries so numerous as in Upper Germany; they far outnumbered the friaries. In Strasbourg alone the Dominican sisters had seven houses. At this time not merely individuals, but whole communities were affected by a mystical movement which had no parallel elsewhere. Ecstasies, visions, trances, stigmata were the order of the day. It was not Tauler's task to stimulate mysticism, but rather to restrain it, and to guide it into safe channels. What he had to say about the union of the Divine and the human fell on willing ears, but it had to be carefully defined. Tauler was wise enough to know when to warn and when to encourage others. The keynote of his life was struck by the words: "Dear Lord, Thou knowest I seek nothing but Thee."[1]

[1] Vetter, p. 265, 23.

18. DENYS THE CARTHUSIAN

Anselm Stoelen

ENYS THE CARTHUSIAN was born in 1402 or 1403 in the village of Rijkel, in the Flemish north-east of Belgium. After attending the nearby abbey-school of Sint Truiden (St. Trond), he completed his studies at Zwolle, *c.* 1416–21, where the daily spiritual influence of the practical *devotio moderna* did not quench but rather encouraged an already growing desire for recollection and interior prayer. In 1421 we find him, still too young for the Carthusian life, studying *in via Thomae* at the university of Cologne, taking a Master's degree in 1424, and, even more important, finally conquering a violent moral crisis which echoes in his writings in many expressions of unaffected humility. In 1424 or 1425 he became a Carthusian at Roermond, where he died on 12 March 1471.

During all these forty-six years he lived the quiet, regular life of a Carthusian, enjoying the solitude of his cell and leaving it, as a rule, only three times a day, for matins, mass and vespers. His early biographers tell us that "according to the rigour of the old rule" he did not take any sleep or rest after matins, but saved that time for study and prayer. This could be misunderstood. Following the introduction, at the end of the twelfth century, of the daily conventual mass, and, towards the end of the thirteenth century, of the daily individual low masses, Carthusian life at the beginning of the fifteenth century differed from both the old and modern observances in one important point. In order to ease the strain of the long uninterrupted series of offices, an hour's rest after lauds and before prime and conventual mass was permitted. Since, at this time, the "midnight" office had not yet been adopted by the Carthusians, the period of sleep before matins was still by far the longer. Denys, therefore, did not, as has too readily been assumed, regularly give up half of his sleep; he merely did not avail himself of the recent permission with which his robust constitution could dispense. "My head is of iron, and my stomach of brass," he used to say when his friends expressed concern about his diet. And they had good reason to do so: he liked his game very high—but that game, of course, was fish—and as to his vegetables, he was not put off his food by conditions, dwelt upon with some relish by his biographers, which would have ruined the appetite of others.

Denys had to sacrifice the quiet regularity of his Carthusian life only during three relatively short periods. First, when, as procurator, he had charge of the temporal administration of the house and of the spiritual direction of the lay brothers. This happened, not about 1458, as has generally been supposed, but while Denys, as a young priest, was writing one of his books on the praises of Our Lady, about 1433. We are not told how things and people fared under his providence; we can only make a good guess from the reputation he made as a great despiser of money, *maximus pecuniae aspernator*, and from the exuberant hymn of thanksgiving with which he celebrated his release. Some eighteen years later, from September 1451 to March 1452, the Cardinal Nicholas of Cusa insisted on taking Denys with him on his reform visitation, as a papal legate, through the Rhineland and the Low Countries. Finally, in 1465, Denys was chosen as one of the little band sent out to start the foundation of 's Hertogenbosch (Bois-le-Duc), which he governed from 1466 to 1469, when failing health forced him to resign. In 1458 he played an important part in the reconciliation of the Duke of Guelders with his son. But nothing in the documents supports the assumption that Denys was the procurator of Roermond who, on that occasion, went to see the Duke and made him agree to an interview with his son. The role of Denys was purely spiritual. He prayed and received through an angel a message from God which he transmitted to the two parties. Henceforth he was known as "the man who speaks with the angels."

His literary activity began about 1430, with a treatise on recollection during office in choir. His last work, on meditation, was written in 1469 after his return to Roermond. Leaving aside the three interruptions mentioned above, during which his literary output would have lessened considerably, we can say that he had at least thirty-two years for quiet and regular work. If we take into account the very simple nature of many of his writings there seems, therefore, to be little need to speak with some of his biographers of a great miracle, *ingens miraculum*. At the same time, the catalogue of his writings is most impressive;[1] and as he became more widely known as a man of learning and a spiritual director of repute, his correspondence, often with very important personages, ecclesiastical and lay, steadily increased to alarming proportions. Hence the question arises: how could such activity fit within the framework of a purely contemplative life?

On this subject Denys has expressed his mind repeatedly and clearly:

> Considering how divine, salutary and meritorious it is to teach, exhort, redress, convert and save others by one's preaching, and because by the kind of religious life I have professed I cannot leave the enclosure and do not possess the privileges required for preaching, the less I can do these things by word of mouth, the more I wish to do them by writing, correcting and dictating. . . . It is true that the purely contemplative life has greater dignity and stability than the purely active one. But a way of life which includes both contemplation and action is the highest of all, provided that the activities we choose are such as presuppose the perfection of the contemplative life and are the fruit of the plenitude of contemplation. . . . Even our own Carthusian statutes make this perfectly clear.

Denys was right when he appealed to the statutes. Whereas St. Benedict underlines only one aspect of work in the life of the monk, namely, its ascetical importance—idleness is the enemy of the soul—Guigo I, author of the fundamental Statutes or *Consuetudines* of the Carthusians, c. 1116–20 (?), impresses upon his religious the duty of working in a spirit of devotion to the Church: "*Dei verbum manibus praedicemus*, Let us preach the word of God by our hands. With every book we write, we produce in our place a preacher of the truth." Pius XII, as recently as 1956, in a letter to the Prior of the Charterhouse of Vedana, gave the same directives. Apostolic prayer, penance and contemplation, undoubtedly. But that is not all. The old monastic maxim, *Ora et labora*, and the motto of St. Thomas, *Contemplata tradere*, apply just as well to the Carthusian. By the example of his virtues, but also by his literary productivity, *studiorum vestrorum commentationes*, he must contribute his share to help his fellowmen.

[1] The works of Denys in the modern edition (Montrieux-Tournai-Parkminster, 1896–1935) extend to forty-two large volumes, with two volumes of *Indexes*.

The literary contribution of Denys was exegetical and theological, as well as ascetical and mystical. The catalogue of his works includes more than a hundred items. We find first a full Commentary on Sacred Scripture, written between 1434 and 1440 and between 1452 and 1457.[1]

Next in importance we have, c. 1459–64, a *Collectarium* (usually called *Commentarium*) of extracts from the medieval commentators on the "Books of Sentences" of Peter Lombard. The personal remarks added by Denys show his intellectual independence. Yet he seldom abandons the *Doctor Sanctus*, as he calls St. Thomas, on a point of real importance, and it is only by misreading the facts that it has been possible to describe him as a Thomist converted to Albertinism. Further, among the longer works, we meet a complete set of sermons for seculars and religious, c. 1452; commentaries on the works of the Areopagite, c. 1465–67, on the *Scala Paradisi*, c. 1453, and on the *De consolatione philosophiae* of Boethius, c. 1465; a revision of the *Instituta* and the *Collationes* of Cassian, c. 1450; and a *Summa fidei orthodoxae*, c. 1468, which is nothing more than a summary of the *Summa theologica* of St. Thomas.

Amongst his most important *opuscula* is his treatise, written c. 1430, on the gifts of the Holy Ghost (the gift of wisdom plays a prominent part in the mystical doctrine of Denys) and two works on Our Lady, which both comprise several chapters on the special graces of contemplation of Mary, but fall short of a clear acknowledgment of her Immaculate Conception.[2] We may also mention two works on the Carthusian life, c. 1435–40 and c. 1455–1460, the first of which was unjustifiably quoted by Fénelon in defence of his Explanation of the Maxims of the Saints; three books on the authority of the Roman Pontiff, c. 1440–47 and c. 1465, which were quoted as a vindication of Bossuet's Defence of Gallicanism, but wherein Denys professes the subordination

---

[1] In 1440 or 1441 Denys wrote his *Protestatio*, explaining to his Superiors the spirit in which he had undertaken his work on Sacred Scripture, and asking to be permitted to finish the work. The long interruption in this work may have been due to the fact that Denys was under a cloud at this time. The general chapter of 1446 refers to some unspecified abuses and transgressions committed by Denys and another monk.

[2] On this issue, Denys was not prepared to abandon the fundamental positions of many of the great scholastics until, in his work on the Sentences, he finally bowed to the authority of a decree passed some twenty years before, in 1439, by the pseudo-council of Basel.

of the Pope to the general council only in very extraordinary circumstances, at the same time, however, attributing the privilege of infallibility not to the Pope personally but to the Church. Like Bridget of Sweden and Catherine of Siena, Denys was favoured with visions referring to the imminent punishment of the Church. These are recorded in an appendix to his letter to Catholic princes, 1454. Some twenty other writings of his deal with the reformation of the Church on all its various levels, ecclesiastical and social. One of these writings was addressed, in 1467, to Isabella of Portugal, widow of Philip the Good. Denys's treatise on the last things (c. 1455-60) was a favourite book of Leo XIII—a work viewed with suspicion in the sixteenth and seventeenth centuries by the inquisition in Spain and Italy. Denys had not been satisfied merely to repeat with approval the famous vision of Purgatory by the Monk of Eynsham; he had extended to the souls of all those who were responsible for the sins of others the punishment of remaining uncertain in Purgatory about their eternal salvation, a psychological torture which theologians are not prepared to admit in more than a very few exceptional cases.

The treatise on Contemplation, c. 1440-45, deserves a special mention. It was not one of his popular works, but its substance passed into one of the most widely read of his minor writings the De Fonte lucis, c. 1455. The De contemplatione was first published in 1534, and never had a second edition until it was reprinted by the Order, together with several other of the spiritual writings, in 1894. This treatise gives the most comprehensive outline of Denys's views on the mystical experience.

Denys has been called the Ecstatic Doctor, Doctor Ecstaticus. His early biographers tell us that he had many ecstatic experiences which not infrequently lasted several hours. He himself has described some of his visions and ecstasies: one series of three, during the office of matins on 23 December in the successive years 1441-3, referring to the state of the soul of a deceased priest buried in the choir of the Roermond charterhouse; another series of three, during conventual mass on the feast of the Purification, 2 February 1454, on Passion Sunday, 22 March 1461, and on the third Sunday after the octave of Easter, 3 May of the same year, referring to the fall of Constantinople and the evils of the

Church; finally, during the night before Epiphany, 1458, the vision of an angel which has been mentioned above.

The first two experiences of the first series were visions which Denys saw, fully awake, with his bodily eyes, but which remained invisible to his neighbour; the third was of a purely intellectual nature, with such complete alienation of senses as he had seldom experienced before: "I could not open my eyes, I could not say the psalms, I could not stand upon my feet." We are not told how long this ecstasy lasted. The second series of ecstasies seems to mark a progress upon the first: all three were purely intellectual experiences in the way now usual to him, *more sibi solito*. The first two consisted of a mental dialogue which took place between God and the soul. Denys says that they lasted the whole length of the conventual mass. He adds that regaining consciousness was a very painful process, and that the whole experience of the expression of the divine wrath against the corruption of the Church left him so depressed and weak that he could not take his meal before the evening.

Denys's earliest biographer, Peter Dorlandus, a Carthusian monk of Diest, who died in 1507, quoting from what seems to have been a written account of revelations, tells us that Denys, like Eliseus, had frequent musical ecstasies. Some special occasions are mentioned: one in 1469 in the church of 's Hertogenbosch, provoked by the playing of the organ; two more, without date, one induced by the singing of the Carthusian *Veni sancte Spiritus* at the ceremony of a novice being conducted to his cell; the other by the anthem *Suscepimus Deus misericordiam tuam*, which must have been the Introit or the Gradual of the feast of Candlemas. From the same source, and from an answer of Denys to his closest assistant, Dom Charles of Herck, we learn also that Denys had many visions of deceased souls and many a tussle with the devils.

Denys knew that the revelations he received and the ecstatic phenomena which accompanied them were not necessarily connected with sanctifying grace. They were *gratiae gratis datae*, intended directly for the spiritual benefit of others. But he attached great value, both religious and apologetic, to those ecstatic experiences which, according to the rules laid down in his treatise on the discernment of spirits,[1] were to be considered

---

[1] *De discretione spirituum, c.* 1458.

as the natural condition of the essential mystical state; natural, that is, as a result of the weakness caused by the original fall of mankind. If human nature had not been affected by sin, it would have been able to stand up to the stresses caused by the mystical experience. This was the case with the Blessed Mother of Christ. In her, unitive experience did not upset the balance of natural activities, and she enjoyed it without any suspension of the normal operations of her physical and psychological faculties. With one notable exception, however. The beatific vision, the direct vision of the mystery of the Blessed Trinity, which, according to Denys, was frequently granted to Our Lady during her life on earth, and also, at least once, to Moses and St. Paul, perhaps to St. John, and possibly to some other saints, necessarily required the suspension of the normal conditions of the natural life. Denys does not explain how that suspension manifested itself outwardly. But for Denys the meaning of the word *ecstasy* was not restricted to the effect of certain modes of mystical experience on the senses and other natural faculties. For him, ecstasy meant above all the final stage in the invisible and ineffable meeting and union of the soul with God. The call to contemplation had come very precociously to Denys. In a Dialogue on the Passion, the Saviour reminds him of the early days of his vocation:

How often, when you were still a little boy and hardly capable of distinguishing between right and left, did I send you graces of internal visitation, of heavenly illumination, of loving fervour, of contemplative admiration, of hidden consolation, as you now recognise with wonder, more than in the past. Moreover, when you were hardly ten years old, I inspired you with that desire to enter the Order in which you now live. If it had been in your power, you would at once have fulfilled that aspiration. And for that I praise you. Indeed you cannot forget how often in the meantime, when you had been rebuked, you looked back with tears and sighs at the church of the convent as long as you could catch a glimpse of its tower. Yet, during that period of delay you committed serious sins, and you would have sinned much more grievously if I had not filled your heart with at least a servile fear, so strong that you came to regret that you could not sin without great apprehension and remorse. And now for so many years I have thus acted and still act with you, and I show myself to you, as you well know.

Unlike other great mystics, Denys has not left us a direct description of the privileged moments of his most intimate dealings with God. But if we approach the study of his doctrine on contemplation in a disposition less of theoretical curiosity than of religious sympathy, we soon realise that here we have the faithful echo of a deep personal conviction and the authentic resonance of an enthralling spiritual venture. The gradual development of the views of Denys on contemplation has been analysed elsewhere. Here we must limit ourselves to a general and synthetic description of the essential mystical experience as understood and lived by one of the most fervent admirers of the Pseudo-Areopagite. This disciple of Plotinus who, at the beginning of the sixth century, wrote under the name of the Athenian convert of St. Paul, thereby securing in mystical matters an unrivalled authority throughout the Middle Ages, had completely carried away the fifteenth-century Carthusian. Denys was convinced that the teaching of the Pseudo-Areopagite was a direct reflection of the experience of the Apostle when he was caught up to the third heaven. He gave to the doctrine of the Pseudo-Dionysius a more systematic, or perhaps we ought to say a more technical expression. It is, however, certain that in so doing, the Carthusian laid bare his own soul and its most intimate aspirations. Traditional teaching and personal experience are here fused into one harmonious and convincing unity of introspective theology at its best. For Denys, contemplation in the highest sense of the word (which, after his patron, he always calls mystical theology) is the exercise of the negative knowledge of God. by which a soul, in the heroic degree of love of God, with the help of the gift of wisdom, and stimulated by a special grace of illumination, is brought into unitive ecstasy.

The concepts of positive and negative theology—positive and negative knowledge of God—are in themselves, says Denys, purely philosophical. They have no necessary connection with the supernatural elevation of man, and may therefore be verified in the heathen or in the sinner, as well as in the saint. Negative theology supposes the positive which considers God as the infinitely perfect cause of all created perfection. It applies to him, in an absolutely exalted and pure degree, all the concepts which we borrow from our knowledge of creatures, either by our natural power of intelligence, or under the illuminating guidance of faith; the only condition being that these concepts should not contain in themselves anything unworthy of God. At this stage we cannot yet speak of contemplation, except in a loose and analogous sense. Simple knowledge of God can very well exist without sanctifying grace. A theologian who lives a sinful life may possess such knowledge in an eminent degree. Still more, he may have received his knowledge, for the benefit of others, as a special gift from God. But even if we possess sanctifying grace with the virtues and the gifts of the Holy Ghost, our knowledge of God will remain cold and purely speculative until it belongs to us in an intimate, living, experimental way, as the children of God.

To transform and to sublimate in this way our knowledge of God is, in Denys's view, precisely the function of the gift of wisdom. When we are born anew of the Spirit, we receive in our soul a kind of superior, Christian instinct which allows us to appreciate and to savour,[1] in the things of the faith, the con-naturality established by sanctifying grace between the soul and the supernatural world of God. It is the role of the gift of wisdom, or sapience, to develop the subtlety and the promptness of this new sensitiveness. When a soul who has acquired a certain proficiency in the ways of God, and is already on intimate loving terms with her creator, is visited by a special, actual grace of illumination, the soul, helped by the gift of wisdom, at once reacts with love and joy. The knowledge of God in that soul may be very imperfect from a purely scientific and abstract theological point of view, but the illuminative grace and the gift of wisdom impart to this knowledge a warmth and vitality of meaning which make it no longer merely speculative and theological, but truly religious. It is thus that this positive knowledge really becomes contemplation.

But it sometimes happens that a soul who has once tasted God finds that there is no lasting peace in this first adoration of her creator and saviour. No matter how much she mentally purifies the perfections of creatures in applying them to her Maker, she is uncomfortably aware of how far short they fall of the excellence and simplicity of the divine being. She is full of fear that, in spite of all her endeavours, anything created might defile the idea of God. She doubtless knows that the Cause, God, must in some way or other contain the effect, the created perfection. But the purity

[1] In Latin: *sapere;* hence: *sapientia,* better rendered by *sapience* than by *wisdom.*

of the divine truth compels her to turn aside from the contemplation of the divine perfection through the mirror of the
created world. Stimulated yet again by illuminative graces,
she turns to the "negative way." Whilst her reason says: "God *is*
almighty, God *is* wise, God *is* good," the contemplative soul,
with the help of the gift of wisdom, stammers out: "God is not
almighty, God is not wise, God is not good. All these qualities
have been borrowed from creatures, and then purified; but I
shall never be able to purify them thoroughly enough to be
applied to the infinitely perfect object of my love. God is . . ." And
here the loving soul cannot go further. She remains buried as in a
thick "cloud of unknowing." She is happy to rest thus impotent
and silent, knowing very well that this impotence itself is the
deepest and purest surrender of the creature to its God. Then the
ineffable experience takes place. It is love that has brought the
soul so far. And now if her love is sufficiently purified, from the
bedrock of humility, love, not knowledge, shoots upwards,
through the cloud, towards the perfect union with the infinite
Being of the Beloved: "Love enters and penetrates where knowledge remains outside." But here all attempts at description must
cease, because, as Denys insists, he alone can understand these
things who has received them.

Denys knew that illusions are easy in this matter, and that it is
only in exceptional cases that the authenticity of mystical
experience can be recognised with certainty. He believed that it
was not possible to say anything about the duration of mystical
union, except that it is usually very short. He knew that, in this
state itself, there are different degrees of perfection; but that none
of these, not even the highest one, can bear any comparison with
the immediate vision of God. He frequently emphasised that no
degree of human holiness on earth could lay claim to the graces of
contemplation; and that the soul may have reached the most
eminent degree of perfection without receiving from God that
special grace of illumination which would lead it to the mystical
theology. He also says repeatedly that the grace of contemplation
does not depend upon the natural endowments of man. A soul
which, naturally speaking, might be described as ignorant and
coarse, could just as well be elevated by God to the highest state of
contemplation. Finally, he insists that usually the soul must prepare itself carefully for contemplative graces over a long period

of time. Yet, sometimes God does not wait, but takes a recently converted or still imperfect soul and helps it, or even as it were forces it to reach at once to the sublimest degree of mystical theology.

Denys's unqualified admiration for the Pseudo-Areopagite, and the experience of his own psychological temperament, have never allowed him to hesitate in expressing his preference for the negative contemplation, mystical theology, as compared with the positive contemplation, whose degrees, culminating in lofty consideration and loving adoration of the Blessed Trinity, are described in several of his works. At one time, in the period when he wrote the treatise on contemplation, he even went so far as to reserve the mystical theology exclusively to the superior, unitive way, assigning the positive contemplation to the relatively inferior, illuminative way. But in the end he dropped this forced and fallacious parallelism, realising no doubt that the pure, unitive love of God does not discriminate between the two ways of reaching the Beloved, as long as it finds its food and its inspiration in the essentially twofold approach of the human soul to the One Truth and Goodness.

Habent sua fata libelli. The first edition of the commentaries of Denys on the Gospels was dedicated, 14 March 1532, to Henry VIII. It has been suggested that this homage was inspired by the prior of the London Charterhouse, John Batmanson, whose letter to Denys's editor, Dirk Loer, vicar of the house of Cologne, was printed in the 1532 edition of the commentary on Acts. It is true that the prior and community of the London Charterhouse are recommended by name to Henry in the dedicatory letter of the Gospel commentary. But we must note that in the same year 1532 the *Opera minora* were dedicated to Clement VII and Charles V, and the *Contra perfidiam Mahometi* to Ferdinand of Austria. It was only natural that the "Defender of the Faith" should not be forgotten. We do not know whether the royal theologian ever cast his eye over the pages of the bulky volume. If he did, he may have been chagrined to discover that the unsuspecting Carthusian sought his patronage for an interpretation of Leviticus xx. 21 which knocked the bottom out of his claim against the validity of his marriage with his deceased brother's wife. The prohibition of Leviticus, says Denys, applies only as long as the brother lives, and becomes an order to marry the widow if the brother dies without issue.

Prior John Batmanson died in November 1531. The new prior, John Houghton, wrote to Dirk Loer on 13 July 1532, congratulating him on his edition of Denys and placing a substantial order for copies. Loer's grateful answer is dated 15 September 1532. More letters were exchanged, as we gather from the dedication to Thòmas Cromwell, with which Loer, apparently still unaware of the approaching tragedy, prefaced the edition of Denys's commentaries on the Sapiential books. The date was 24 June 1533, ten days before the excommunication of Henry VIII by Clement VII. Once more the vicar of Cologne made it a point to recommend the new prior of the London Charterhouse and his community to Cromwell's benevolent patronage. In one of his letters to Dirk Loer, John Houghton had highly praised the Lord Chancellor for his kindness, and this praise was duly quoted. We know that Cromwell did not wait very long to change his attitude towards the saintly prior, who was hanged, drawn and quartered on 4 May 1535.[1]

Neither in England nor on the continent were the works of Denys destined to play a direct role in the front line of the Reformation battle. New troops and new methods were needed for that purpose. But the providential part of Denys in that struggle was none the less an essential one. In an effort to stem the tide of moral deterioration and to prevent the disaster which he saw was threatening the whole of Christendom, he had, with true prophetic freedom, warned the princes, the clergy and the Pope, respectfully but unequivocally. He had instructed and advised the faithful, reprimanded and encouraged the religious, put his pen at the service of the missionaries in the field. When the storm finally broke over the Church, his place was on the home front, where his printed works prolonged his influence. God alone knows how much evil he was able to forestall, how much good to keep alive and bright. But we may recall that, before the end of the sixteenth century, his Gospel commentaries had seen nineteen editions, the epistles of St. Paul twenty, the rest of the New Testament seventeen, the Old Testament at least four, and the Psalms six. In the same period his Sermons were printed four times, and ten of his practical spiritual works from nine to thirteen times, with a record figure of twenty-seven editions for the treatise on the last

---

[1] Bl. John Houghton is one of the Forty Martyrs, whose cause for canonisation is now proceeding.

things. The life of the Church persists through the centuries without any break in continuity: the promises of her divine Founder pledge her immortality. But at decisive moments of her history the arteries carrying the vital flow of her apostolic tradition develop dangerous strains which threaten to become breaking points. Then God raises up the men whose vocation it is to strengthen the channels of the living truth, and to ensure that life continues to flow and to reach all the members of the Mystical Body.

19. BERNARDINO DE LAREDO

Kathleen Pond

A N OUTSTANDING FIGURE among the precursors of St. Teresa
and St. John of the Cross in the field of mystical writing
in Spain was Bernardino de Laredo,[1] who belonged to the
Franciscan school of spiritual writers of which St. Peter of
Alcántara and Osuna are the best-known examples in the
Peninsula. Himself influenced by the Victorines and later by
Hugh of Balma, the Carthusian, and Harphius, Laredo's own
influence through his writings extended to St. Teresa, Jerónimo
Gracián and Tomás de Jesús among the Carmelites, Juan de los
Ángeles, like himself a Franciscan, Juan Falconi, the Merce-
darian, and possibly to the Augustinian, Alonso de Orozco. The
evidence for his influence on St. John of the Cross is inconclusive.

Not very much is known about Laredo's life. Born of a distinguished family in Seville in 1482, he became a page in the
service of a Portuguese nobleman, the Conde de Gelves, but as
early as the age of twelve felt an attraction for the Franciscan
Order. The major-domo of the Gelves' household dissuaded him
from trying to enter the Capuchin province of Los Ángeles in
southern Spain and he then devoted himself to study. He followed first an Arts course and then studied medicine. Some
authorities have assumed that this took place in the university
of Seville, but there is no positive evidence to show that this
was so. Laredo seems, indeed, to have been largely self-taught.
He developed an enthusiasm for the study of theology and Holy
Scripture and his writings show a knowledge of ecclesiastical
Latin. Throughout his studies Laredo was assiduous in the
practice of virtue and when one of his companions, a doctor
in Laws, took the religious habit and became a Franciscan lay-
brother, Bernardino's original vocation returned to him with such

[1] It is possible that the surname, *de Laredo*, is an indication that the family
originally came from the small fishing port of that name in the province of
Santander.

intensity that he instantly sought and obtained admission to the Convento de San Francisco del Monte, a house of Franciscans of Regular Observance, in the humble capacity of lay-brother. His life there was exemplary and his vocation a genuine one. His austerity was such that on Mondays, Wednesdays and Fridays he took nothing but bread and water, while on the other days he ate the friars' leavings but in such small quantity that his continued existence seemed a miracle. He was appointed chief infirmarian in the Province and effected some remarkable cures. King John II of Portugal asked for Laredo to attend him and he restored the king, who was dangerously ill, to health. Authorities differ as to the date of Laredo's death, Aran de Varflora giving it as 1540 and Olmedilla as five years later.

Laredo left a number of writings—two treatises on medicine, written in Spanish despite their Latin names,[1] the work for which he is best known—the *Subida del Monte Sion*, which for convenience will be referred to in this article as the *Ascent*, the *Josefina*—a short treatise on devotion to St. Joseph,[2] usually printed with the *Ascent*, and some twelve or fourteen letters also usually so printed. His *Reglas de Oración y Meditación* may be identified with the *Ascent*. It is not possible within the scope of one article to deal adequately with all these writings and I shall therefore confine my study to Laredo's treatise on contemplation, the *Ascent*.

Of recent years this work has attracted some notice, both from the late Professor Allison Peers who translated the third part of it and who also discusses Laredo in his *Studies of the Spanish Mystics*, and from the Spanish Franciscan scholar Fidèle de Ros (who wrote in French), to whose masterly analysis of the book this article is indebted.[3] In Spain, too, it formed the subject of a study by P. Crisógono de Jesús Sacramentado, O.C.D., known for his well-documented life of St. John of the Cross.

The book was first published in 1535, a second edition, in which Laredo's teaching had undergone a considerable change, appearing in 1538. Professor Allison Peers translated the third part of the book (using the 1538 edition), on contemplation

---

[1] *Metaphora Medicinae* and *Modus faciendi: seu ordine medicandi*.

[2] It seems that it was from this work that St. Teresa took her idea that St. Joseph was not old at the time of his betrothal to Mary, but a youngish man of about forty—cf. *Autobiography*.

[3] Fidèle de Ros, O.F.M. Cap., *Le Frère Bernardin de Laredo*, Paris 1948.

proper, in 1952,[1] but appeared to be of the opinion, one cannot but think mistakenly, that the *Ascent* did not merit translation as a whole. A glance at the table of contents, however, shows that the work set for the Christian soul to achieve, described in some detail in books I and II, is the indispensable preparation for the contemplation which forms the subject of book III. The work should be read in its entirety, though admittedly its lack of ordered arrangement and its repetitions make it difficult for a modern reader. Its homely and conversational style, however, is pleasing, as are the picturesque images and comparisons, though on occasion the latter can be tedious.

In his introduction to the *Ascent of Mount Sion*, Laredo explains that book I is to deal with the crushing of self which he calls "annihilation," book II with meditation on Christ's Passion and Resurrection, and book III with contemplation proper. He stresses the absolute necessity of perseverance and discusses the difficulty of giving clear expression to the things of the spirit. A somewhat arbitrary division and sub-division into weeks and days of the week is inserted only for convenience and each reader must take as little or as much at a time as his soul needs.

To the process of "annihilation," he assigns three "weeks" or stages, the first to be spent in answering the questions:

Who am I?
Where do I come from?
Which way did I come?
Where am I?
Where am I going?
What do I carry with me?

The questions are assigned one to each day of the week, Sunday, however, being devoted to quiet repose. The second stage or "week" of this first division deals with virtues and vices, and the third with bodily penance.

The answers to the questions are intended to ground the soul in the virtue of humility. Laredo insists that the cross is the door that leads to contemplation and that self-knowledge and humility are indispensable conditions. Contemplative prayer, he says, is for all, not only for friars but for layfolk and married people, if they will only dig deep the foundations of humility and follow

[1] E. Allison Peers, *The Ascent of Mount Sion*, London 1952.

Christ. It is a mistake to aim too high at first. We should learn to
recognise God in His creatures, studying the habits of the ant, or
even such an ordinary thing as a brick, made up of mud and
water—as man is.[1]

For the second "week," Laredo uses to introduce his teaching
a complicated and unusual comparison, that of a horseman and
his mount. The rider needs a brake, a pair of reins and a saddle,
preferably of leather, and a housing—also in leather. Two
stirrup-leathers, two stirrups and two spurs are likewise necessary. The brake, we learn, is for the tongue, the two reins
signify the love of God and love of our neighbour, both fed at
the fire of uncreated Charity. The saddle is persistent prayer and
the housing the guard of our outward senses, the leather of
which both saddle and housing are made representing the soul's
interior recollection. The two stirrup-leathers represent obedience and charity and the stirrups patience and humility. The
spurs are reverential fear and filial love. It will be observed that
there is some confusion in this comparison, since charity is
represented both by the reins and by one of the stirrup-leathers.

Laredo is particularly insistent on the guard of the tongue.
The rules he gives are, never to say a word that is not true, or
pure, never to speak of anyone except to say something good of
him, to refrain completely from idle words and never to speak
without profit. One should know what to say and when to say
it. He further enjoins upon those who would attain to contemplation the guard, not only of the tongue, but of the whole man.
To achieve this, one must cut off occupations not required by
obedience or the duties of one's state of life, as also contacts with
others where this can be done without lack of charity. Keeping
one's nothingness in mind, one will seek out solitary places. One
must have singleness of purpose, keep one's conscience free from
sin and one's soul detached. The mind should be "captive in the
chains of faith," set on the following of Christ, and the will
determined never to be content with anything that is not God.
Self-knowledge and the struggle to crush self are necessary, as is
austerity in the following of Christ. In prayer the spirit must be
raised to God with careful attention and we should not seek too
comfortable a posture—or flit from one subject to another.

[1] "Mud are ye both and thou art the viler of the two, for the viler is thy corruption"—Peers: *The Ascent of Mount Sion*, p. 19.

As to bodily mortification, Laredo is insistent on the importance of fasting and vigils. He himself seems to have been a man of robust health, well able to undertake such austerities. In the refectory, he says, one should be content with bread and water, herb broth, a few vegetables and occasional fruit. Particularly, as far as strength allows, should one abstain from both meat and wine. Yet to avoid harmful exaggeration one should pray before undertaking such practices, and consult one's superiors. One must also beware of the temptation of vanity and see that one has a right intention. As a physician Laredo would, of course, realise the need for discretion.

If these things be observed, we may begin to mount the lowest rung of the ladder of contemplation. For this a two-fold movement is required of us—the entering our own hearts in quiet recollection and the rising above our hearts, seeking from our prayer only the glory of God. We must seek to know God to revere Him, and self in order to despise it. Just as when we touch the honeycomb with the tips of the fingers, they become coated with sweet honey, so with the fingers of desire we taste Christ's sweetness, Laredo tells us. The cross is the door by which we enter into love and we shall fulfil Christ's command to pray always if our will is set unswervingly on Him.

In book II, the first twelve chapters treat of the Incarnation and Nativity of the Word, chapters 13-32 of the Passion and chapters 33-53 of Christ's resurrection and glory. Laredo thus sees Incarnation, Passion and Resurrection as one essential moment of the work of man's redemption. He describes the eternal birth of the Word and shows that the three divine Persons co-operated in the formation of Christ's humanity at the moment of the hypostatic union.

Bernardino's comparisons are certainly original for he now introduces an elaborate metaphor in which he represents the cosmos as a metallurgical workshop, with God as the chief craftsman and engineer. The planets are secondary agents and the four elements are four contractors entrusted with the smelting of the less valuable vessels, namely the plants and animals created for man's service. God reserves to Himself the most delicate work, namely, the creation of the human soul made in His own image and likeness.

These chapters close with a sermon for Christmas eve and a

long meditation on the feast, in which Laredo insists that our affection for the Mother and the new-born Babe must not be too natural; rather, by faith we must fix our attention on Mary's virtues and always remember that the Child in her arms is divine.

When he comes to write of meditation on the Passion of Christ (chapters 13–32), Laredo suggests a somewhat novel method for contemplating Christ's sufferings, though its originator was not Laredo himself but Francisco de Osuna, author of the *Abecedario*.[1] It is no longer necessary or desirable to visit the Holy Places in imagination, he says; all takes place within one's own heart. In the scourging of Christ, for instance, it is our heart that is the column, on Calvary, our heart that is the stony ground in which the cross is fixed. This recollected consideration of Christ's humanity, it is suggested, will serve as a preparation for pure contemplation.

Laredo returns at this point to the conditions for prayer he laid down in the introduction, chiefly the consideration of our own wretchedness. To know this wretchedness we must seek the truth about ourselves from outside. Pure contemplation of the divinity is internal and comes about by a receptive act of the will. The consideration of Christ's humanity shares in both processes—we take the letter of the Gospel, thus approaching it from the outside, and then engrave it in our hearts. The usual division into reading, prayer, meditation and contemplation follows, with a note added on the pure and simple prayer which attains to incorporeal objects.

Here follows a series of scenes on which to meditate. A medical explanation, in accord with the scientific knowledge of the time, is given for Christ's sweat of blood in His agony. There is a long allegory of Joseph as the type of Christ our Redeemer and three chapters on the anguish of Mary. The best way of honouring the cross, Laredo says, is to fast on bread and water and to imitate the spirit of penance of Christ and St. Francis. The style of this part of the book is unduly elaborate, with many apostrophes and rhetorical questions.

The remainder of book II is concerned with the triumph and glory of Christ. Laredo presents us with a series of comparisons —some of them curious—the dejection of Mary is contrasted

[1] An English translation of part of the *Abecedario*, the *Third Spiritual Alphabet*, was made by a Benedictine of Stanbrook in 1931.

with the joy of St. Joseph, the compassion of St. John the Evangelist with the glory of the Baptist, and so on. Thus we shall have joy and resplendent light in the upper part of our soul, sadness and darkness in the lower. Then follow subtle allegories and mystical interpretations, particularly in regard to the heavenly Jerusalem, with its image of Christ as the paschal candle from which all other candles take their light, the description of which fills the last six chapters of this book.

In the 1538 edition a chapter on charity is here inserted. It is apparently misplaced and would seem to belong to book III, ch. 38, where it will be found in the earlier edition.

Book III of the *Ascent* presents a problem. In the first edition of the work, which appeared in 1535, the stress is on the intellectual nature of contemplation and Laredo's teaching follows closely that of Richard of St. Victor. Three years later, in the 1538 edition, he has changed his point of view. The part played by the mind in the act of contemplation now falls into the background and all the emphasis is placed on the affective prayer of aspirations.

We must first examine the contents of this third book. After the labours of the first two books, Laredo says, the third brings quiet and joy of spirit, though penance and meditation on Christ's sufferings must still continue. The first eleven chapters are introductory, the body of Bernardino's teaching occupies chapters 12-32; in the following chapter the conclusion is stated and four appendices and the letters bring the book to a close.

In the introduction, Laredo asks why there are so few contemplatives, and finds the great obstacle to be the instinct of "possession." He further considers that too many persons seek consolation or personal profit in prayer. In this life meditation on the mysteries of our Saviour is always necessary, even though to some extent it may prove an obstacle to the quietude of the will which seeks only God in His divinity. Let the soul, then, tend towards the Godhead by fervent desires, but the body take up the cross in honour of Christ's humanity. Thus while the Passion is always present with us through the body's participation in it, the soul is free to contemplate the Godhead.

Again basing himself on Richard of St. Victor and in particular on the *Benjamin Minor*, Laredo says:

1. The understanding seeks truth in order to know causes and effects.

2. The mind fixes its attention on the truth acquired.
3. The quiet will comes with great joy to associate itself with the mind.

In chapters 12–32, Laredo develops more in detail the two ways of seeking God, that is, for actives through discerning the divine attributes in creatures and for contemplatives in the direct contact with God through recollection in one's inmost self. There is emphasis on recollection and on the guard of the heart. The plan of the book is again repeated and reference made to the comparison of the elect to candles in book II. There is some reference to the "way of negation" of pseudo-Denys and a comparison of the Trinity with fire, the sun and the human soul which earned a note of caution from the censors. In chapter 20 Laredo returns to the theme of going to God through creatures. After twenty-six distyches on the effects of divine love and further remarks on charity, Laredo finally establishes that there are three degrees of contemplation:

1. To seek God in creatures.
2. To seek God in the depths of one's being.
3. To seek God in himself.

Laredo seems to have realised that his setting out of book III was somewhat illogical and disorderly and for that reason to have provided a synthesis in which he sets out the stages in contemplation as follows:

1. The soul recollects herself, occupying the understanding in meditation on God's attributes and the relations of the Three Persons of the Trinity.
2. The soul enters into herself, thrusting aside thought and discourse to fix her attention on the memory of God alone.
3. The soul rises above herself and all created things to rest in God.
4. To go further, the soul must move out of herself—the stage of ecstasy is then reached.

The first two stages depend on one's own initiative, whereas the two last are supernatural.

The additional chapters of book III consist of a censor's letter on the discernment of spirits and similar documents. The fourteen letters appended were for the most part written to religious who had asked Laredo's counsel. Space prevents us from examining them in detail.

The text of 1538 is very different. The influence of Richard of St. Victor has now been replaced by that of Hugh of Balma (sometimes erroneously referred to by Laredo as Henry of Balma), a Carthusian who wrote in the second half of the thirteenth century, Harphius and pseudo-Denys, the method of aspirations into which knowledge does not enter is now advocated for attaining union with God and the terminology of the book is different. There are now 31 chapters, divided as follows:

1. The stages of the spiritual life (ch. 1–6).
2. A detailed description of union with God (ch. 7–13).
3. New aspects of the prayer of quiet (ch. 14–31).

1. Beginners must work at self-knowledge, Laredo says, progressives meditate on Christ's mysteries and rise to God through creatures, the perfect directly unite themselves to the divine essence. Then, viewing his subject from another angle, he makes four divisions of spiritual men: *infans, puer, adolescens, juvenis*. The *infantes* concentrate on their own wretchedness, the *pueri* imitate Christ, *adolescentes* rise to God through the visible universe, the *juvenes* are united to God by affections of the will. This book is concerned with the two latter categories.

2. This "hidden wisdom" is a sudden upward surge of the soul which rises directly towards God on the wing of affections. Perfect contemplation is the union of uncreated love and created charity infused by God into our souls. Laredo then refers to the way of negation. The mystic way is greatly superior to speculative knowledge. He again brings up the question of meditation on the Sacred Humanity, for which he proposes his own special method to which reference has already been made, and says that such meditation may never be omitted.

3. After going to God by the way of negation, souls finally achieve a union with Him which for them is as natural as the operation of breathing, that is, without effort and almost uninterrupted. For this, perseverance and the incessant practice of ardent aspirations are necessary, with confidence in God.

Chapter 21 shows the influence of Harphius. It speaks of conformity with God's will, detachment from consolations, from all self-interest, etc. Scholastic meditation moves from creatures to the Creator, perfect contemplation, which requires the quietening of imagination, memory and understanding, possesses and dominates the created, in the love of God. Vocal prayer, however, must not be suppressed. Of ourselves, we can only *dispose* ourselves for contemplation, though if generous souls persevere they will arrive at the goal.

The appendices now consist of a treatise on the Blessed Sacrament inspired by Suso, twenty-four spiritual distyches on charity after the manner of Harphius and a review of certain points of the prayer of quiet. Instead of the original fourteen letters, there are now only twelve.

What has happened? It would seem that between 1535 and 1538 Laredo's attitude underwent a change, under the influence of Hugh of Balma and of Harphius with whose works Bernardino was previously unacquainted, and is now more in line with the spirit of his Order. With considerable courage, he does not hesitate to abandon the teaching of Richard of St. Victor whom he has hitherto followed in favour of the prayer of aspirations in which the mind has little or no part. In both editions the subject of book III is acquired and infused contemplation. In 1535 the emphasis was on the simple action of the mind gazing on Truth, in 1538 it is on a restful adhesion of the will to God.

The first edition of Laredo's book also owes something to Osuna's *Abecedario*, whence he derived the notion of the body "meditating" on the Sacred Humanity by devoting itself to penance. In the 1538 edition there is little trace of Osuna. The theory of aspirations and love without knowledge will be found worked out in Hugh the Carthusian's *Mystica Theologia*. From Harphius (*Directorium* and *Collationes*) Laredo takes his teaching on disinterested love, which in Harphius himself goes so far as hypothetical acceptance of eternal damnation. Laredo's teaching is both more reasonable and more human. The dialogue between wisdom and the soul in the 1538 edition is based on Suso.[1]

If we abstract from Laredo's arbitrary divisions into weeks and days and if we take into account the fact that his classifications are not intended to be watertight compartments, some of the difficulty of the *Ascent* disappears. He makes it clear that the spiritual activity which he assigns to one category of souls often

[1] Cf. Suso, *Little Book of Eternal Wisdom*, London 1953.

flows into that assigned to another and that there is not necessarily or, indeed, usually a consecutive progress from a lower
stage of contemplation to a higher one. There will rather be
advance and recession, like the ebb and flow of the tide.

All Laredo has to say about asceticism and self-discipline is
good and useful. His scheme (borrowed from Osuna) as to how
one may meditate on Christ's humanity without its being a
barrier to contemplation may not seem completely satisfactory,
yet it is an attempt to acquire at least a virtual attention to the
Passion of Christ. The real difficulty in Laredo's teaching concerns the nature of the act of contemplation. In 1535 we have
the rising to God by means of creatures which, so long as the act
remains discursive, Laredo calls *meditation*; the dwelling on
Truth in a single gaze—*imperfect contemplation*; and the stage
beyond, *ecstasy*, of which he admits he has no personal experience.
He then adopts Richard of St. Victor's distinction between *cogi-
tatio*, *meditatio* and *contemplatio*. The last comes from the mind
alone and belongs to the highest faculties. When the full light of
God shines on some truth, the mind remains fixed on it with
admiration and the will clings to it with joy.

In 1538, however, we must close the eye of the mind and open
that of the will (which had some place in contemplation in
Laredo's earlier scheme of things) and the ladder of ascent is now
as follows:

1. The soul seeks God in the mirror of creatures.
2. By faith the soul can move from Creator to creatures,
   know them and love them in and for him.
3. The will rises to God through the understanding which is
   changed unto pure intelligence (Laredo explains that when
   the understanding ceases to reason in order to enjoy the
   truth it is meditating on in peace, it takes the name of
   intelligence—pure intelligence if no created thing enters.
   This is not yet pure and perfect contemplation).
4. The will rises to quiet contemplation without any intermediary of thought, etc. It darts suddenly by way of
   burning love to unite itself to the source of love. This act
   is without antecedent or concomitant knowledge.[1]

[1] Cf. Bk. III, ch. 11 and 15. "Wisdom is a very exalted knowledge of God by
the mode of not-knowing in the union of the will. . . . This can be understood
in two ways. At first the soul, enclosed in her quietude, is occupied with nothing

It must be made clear that when Laredo speaks of love without knowledge, he is referring purely to the mystical contemplation of aspirations and maintains that the axiomatic principle that knowledge precedes love applies *until* this stage is reached even in supernatural, but imperfect, contemplation. Moreover, Laredo does teach in this later edition of his work that in the act of quiet contemplation God infuses knowledge into the soul, so that even in the act itself there is subsequent though not antecedent, knowledge. Scholastic teaching, of course, maintains that there can be no love without a known object.

Laredo's teaching on the gifts of the Holy Spirit is that God pours these gifts into the soul in the act of contemplation, particularly the gifts of Wisdom, Understanding and Knowledge.

Perhaps, as has been suggested by P. Fidèle de Ros, it is largely a question of terminology. Laredo was not a professional theologian, and was writing not a scientific treatise, but for the most part as a response to those who wanted to know more about contemplative prayer for the benefit of their own lives. He tried to describe his own experience and to stress the aspects of it that seemed to him most important.

The theory of love without knowledge was not without its popularity in Spain, being taken up, among others, by Juan de los Ángeles in his *Triunfor del Amor de Dios* and the *Lucha Espiritual*, and also by Jerónimo Gracián, the Carmelite.

This article is merely an attempt to draw attention to Bernardino de Laredo and some of the problems presented by his *Ascent of Mount Sion*. It does not seek to offer a solution for them—that is a matter for theologians. Space precludes a discussion of several interesting points, such as Laredo's influence on St. Teresa and other mystical writers, his teaching on consolations and, following pseudo-Denys, on the way of negation. Despite certain archaisms in the style and a lack of clarity in its arrangement, the book repays careful reading and has a freshness and sincerity not always to be found in more scientific treatises.

outside God. Afterwards, in the secret of this wisdom, the soul knows that it is united to God by the knot of love; it knows without knowing how it knows. It knows that it knows God, but since the one it knows is incomprehensible, it knows without understanding. Yet its satisfaction is perfect in this not-understanding, for it desires nothing else, but to love; moreover, while loving, it does not know how it loves. . . ." (III, ch. 11).

20. ST. IGNATIUS LOYOLA

Elmer O'Brien

SAINTS, for the most part, keep their secrets well. For every Augustine or Thérèse of Lisieux, whose words are windows through which anyone may gaze at will, there are dozens of others whose words are walls of a superlative opacity. Just such a one, splendidly secretive all these years behind walls of his own construction, is St. Ignatius Loyola.

Yet, as every schoolboy knows, there is really no staying the pens of biographers when their ink-pots are full and a market awaits. Ignorance, which perhaps should, appears rather to awaken ingenuity instead. A notably insomnious ingenuity presided at the slow creation over the centuries of the Ignatius most people know: the "soldier-saint," unlettered; slow and stiff of intellect; the exigent idealism of the impoverished nobility whence he sprang continually tilting with the windmill pragmatism of his peasant surroundings; Don Quixote de Loyola being ceaselessly nudged this way and that across the face of Europe by Providence until he founded the Company of Jesus, an ecclesiastical light-infantry of an Order military in its discipline and (innocuously) martial in its intent and ever at the ready to man each disputed barricade of the Church with the all-purpose weapon, the *Spiritual Exercises*, firmly in hand and the cry, *Ad majorem Dei gloriam*, frenziedly in mouth. A pity that except in the imagination of hard-pressed biographers and of their readers, this Ignatius never existed. He sounds such fun.

St. Ignatius's secret today as through all those yesterdays remains his own. But today there are biographers who have not been content to remain outside his wall of words kicking their heels and cursing their fate and making, *faute de mieux*, ingenious guesses about what manner of man he might be. And of late, armed with the scholar's tools, they have effected small, venturesome breaches here and there in the wall so that today one can at least catch glimpses of the man within. One does not, of course, see him whole. But what one does see makes it clear that St. Ignatius is quite other than ingenuity had led previous generations to believe.[1]

Something of that "otherness" I would attempt to describe and discuss here, limiting myself to two of the most fascinating and hitherto unsuspected aspects of the man behind the now slowly crumbling wall: the theologian of the spiritual life and the mystic.

To begin with, he was the first because he was the second; his discoursing on God and on all things else in their relation to God, which is theology's function, was initially caused and consistently formed and deepened thereafter by his experience of God. In other words, his was a deliberate transfer from personal experience to doctrinal utterance—truly an alarmingly perilous business for anyone to engage in. The danger, of course, is that one tends to make men, made in the image of God, in one's own image. It was a danger he succeeded somehow in avoiding. How he did so may be disputed, but there is no gainsaying that he did. Thus, although they trust they bear a family resemblance to their father Ignatius, Jesuits do differ somewhat markedly; they always have; precisely to the extent that they remain his sons, they always will. Again, one need only recall how diversely hundreds of laity, priests, and nuns were formed to sanctity by him during the days when he was practically the spiritual director of Europe. It would seem that he avoided the danger usually inherent in the method because his mystical experience and the theology based upon it went so very deep, moving in an area beneath individual differences and according solidity and meaning to them all. Such at least is the conviction which will pervade these pages.

The mystical experience of St. Ignatius was of a piece from the very beginning. His own relating of an initial instance (told, as was his custom, in the third person) will serve to situate discussion:

> One day, he went out of devotion to a church which stood just over a mile from Manresa. . . . The road to it runs alongside the river. On his way, occupied with his devotions, he sat down for a little while while facing the river, which ran below. As he sat

[1] I have in mind such worthy pioneers as James Brodrick, *Saint Ignatius Loyola* (London, 1956), and Hugo Rahner, *St. Ignatius Loyola: Letters to Women* (London, 1960).

there, the eyes of his understanding began to open and, without seeing any vision, he understood and knew many things, as well spiritual as those appertaining to the faith and to the realm of letters, and that with such clarity that they seemed to him things completely new. It is impossible to set out in detail all that he then understood, and the most he can say is that he received so great an enlightenment of mind that, taking together all the helps he has received from God and all the things he has learned or known during the whole course of his life, he does not think they amount to as much as he received from that one illumination. It left him with an understanding so greatly enlightened that he seemed to himself to be another man, with another mind than that which was his before.[1]

This signal experience would seem to have taken place in the autumn of 1522. Already the year had been one of exceptional graces. As he lay in the diminutive Castle of Loyola, convalescing from wounds sustained defending the fortress at Pamplona in July of the previous year, he had asked that books of romance and chivalry be brought him to help pass the time. None could be found, so they brought him the four fat tomes of Ludolph the Saxon's *Life of Christ* and a Castilian translation of *The Golden Legend*. Now a veritable library on the life of Our Lord and a collection of saintly lives generously laced throughout with the legendary would not, one would think, be precisely this man's cup of tea. For this man, at thirty, was in many ways still a boy of thirteen. The fairer of the opposite sex still peopled his imagination unduly. Daydreams of large feats of prowess in which he would signalise himself (particularly in feminine eyes) jostled for attention as much as ever. But to the dreams of the boy undergoing court training at Arévalo was now added a stain, dark and disturbing, relic of the subsequent sordid exploits of the man; that would seem to be the only difference. Yet boredom did its work uncommonly well. Ignatius, "much addicted to gambling and dissolute in his dealings with women, contentious and keen about using his sword,"[2] found himself in spite of himself browsing from time to time in the gentle books provided him. As weeks passed, a pattern of reading and reverie formed itself. And, increasingly, the reading would

[1] Quoted in Brodrick, *Saint Ignatius Loyola*, pp. 107–108.
[2] The description of Ignatius at this time is provided by Juan Polanco, his secretary and companion later in life. Quoted in Brodrick, *op. cit.*, p. 45.

R

provide the matter of the reverie. But not always. The thought of one woman in particular, he tells us, "carried him away to such an extent that he would be wrapt up in it for two, three or four hours, without being conscious of the passage of time."[1] Yet he did find himself musing, however briefly, about St. Dominic or St. Francis· and thinking that he should do such things as they. From this alternating of the sacred and the profane in his idly wandering thoughts there came, one significant day, a lesson. He enjoyed his profane thoughts, but when they passed he was left discontented and dry. He enjoyed his holy thoughts, but when they passed he continued to be filled with the joy and gaiety and lightsomeness of spirit they had induced. This rudimentary lesson in how to distinguish the workings of good and evil influences upon one would of course, nuanced and broadened and deepened, become a valued part of the *Spiritual Exercises* in later years. But its chief value, even if one has the eventual composing of the *Exercises* solely in mind, would seem to have been this: the frivolous extrovert, gross in his spiritual ignorance, who had never apparently been properly introduced to himself, learned the worth of introspection. It was a lesson he was never to forget. Operative in every line of the acute psychology of the *Exercises* is an informed awareness of the positive role of feelings in the life of the spirit. Now, in the months which followed, he applied his lesson to good purpose as he concluded to the authentic or counterfeit coinage of such things as successive visions of Our Lady and Child, of a "very beautiful object shining with the likeness of many eyes," of the Trinity under the form of three keys of a musical instrument. He was ready, when it came, for the mystical experience upon the bank of the Cardoner.

In recalling the event thirty years later he was careful to record that it was not a vision. "Without seeing any vision, he understood and knew many things. . . ." It was an instance of Ignatian mysticism in what might be called its pure state. All other instances of which we have record had a visionary accompaniment of one sort or another which can make the interpreter's task, difficult at best, more difficult still. For mystic experience is one thing. Visions are something else again. They must be always and everywhere distinguished one from the other. But where the one ends and the other begins it would

[1] Brodrick, *op. cit.*, p. 66.

often take a Daniel come to judgment to determine. Especially is this so with mystics who, as Ignatius, are also visionaries. Great, therefore, is the historical value of his account of this one vision-less occurrence, for in every other respect it is identical with every other mystic experience he is reported to have had in the years that followed. It is a description of Ignatian mysticism "in its pure state." It is, accordingly, given priority of treatment here.

What it describes as having happened that day on the bank of the River Cardoner was a direct experience of the Godhead which flooded the recipient with knowledge. It is to this "know-ledge" that one should chiefly attend. It was not knowledge delimited and defined and accorded in concepts: his inability then or later to express it in so many words is sufficient indication that it was question of a direct *experience* in the order of knowing quite as that of the majority of other mystics is a direct experience in the order of loving. It was, further, knowledge that was had in an act of judgment, in an affirmation of the true which was accorded him, by Truth, in the very substance of his being. The mind boggles, I know, at anything so difficult to grasp as what is being suggested here: the occurrence of a human affirmation which was yet a "received," a "passive" act. Yet the contrarieties involved are basically no different than those theology encounters in its efforts to explain the divine operation which is operative in every act of every man, and they need not detain us here. What must, however, be inquired into more closely is the level upon which this experience occurred, for to understand that is to understand both the role of the visionary in his other experiences and how those experiences could be so satisfactory a basis for his distinctive theology of the spiritual life.

The suggestion was made above that "an affirmation of the true . . . was accorded him . . . *in the very substance of his being.*" By "substance" was meant what Thomism conventionally means by the term: the abiding existential substratum of faculties, of habits, of acts in the human composite. One may call it, more descriptively, the *fundo del alma* with St. Teresa or the *Seelengrund* with Meister Eckhart; it matters little. Whatever expression is used, what one would indicate is that which is ontologically prior to, and normative of, *all* differentiations of the volitional or intel-lective order. Here, where (in Thomist theory) habitual grace is received, was apparently infused that knowing affirmation.

Ignatius's direct experience of the Godhead always seems to have had its effect in these psychic deeps and nowhere else. A being of volition and intellection he was transformed there where there is no intellection but only its generic matrix. Because knowing is an existing, it is a truism that one knows as one is. Ignatius ever after knew differently because he was different ("he seemed to himself to be another man") and the basis of this new being and new knowing was the affirmation of truth which was accorded him then and thereafter.

If there is a magisterial cohesion and depth in his theology combined with a fragmentary and often disconcertingly super-ficial mode of expression—and there is—the reason lies in the mode of his mystic experience. He came himself to refer to it, more often than not, as being like the entry into his depths of a "white light." Think, then, of this infused act of affirmation as a lucent whiteness which contains within it all colours of the spectrum, blended, their variety imperceptible, now only a luminous oneness. Of such all-containing light, received upon a level prior to all conceptualising, there could not be in his theo-logy anything more than scattered refractions. Yet each refrac-tion, each reflected ray, is in harmony with every other because of the common hidden source. Hidden, unexpressed because inexpressible, the source gives coherence to what is disparately visible and, more important still, affords a dimension in depth to what appears only on surfaces.

There is always among the mystics an all but unbridgeable chasm between experience and expression. In Ignatius it was absolutely unbridgeable. Most other mystics have experienced God with the totality of their spiritual being; not only the substance of the soul but its faculties as well were suffused with His felt presence; they have in consequence been able to build a bridge of sorts from experience to expression because the basic organs of expression, the faculties, had themselves partaken of the experience. With Ignatius this was not so. Only the substance of his being was affected.

There would seem to have been two chief results from this relatively limited nature of his mystic experience: it was of almost unbroken duration throughout the last years of his life, and it was—paradoxically enough—theologically more informa-tive than a less limited experience would have been.

It would seem to be the rare and exceptional mystic whose experience of God is practically constant. Venerable Mary of the Incarnation[1] perhaps was such a one. St. Ignatius certainly was. The ability he had of "finding God in all things" which was the admiration of his later contemporaries would seem to have been something much more than the practice he recommended to his Jesuit sons. That, however helpful and salutary, was largely based upon a theology of the *als ob*: one should accept things "as if" coming from the hands of God, one should attend the superior's will "as if" he were Christ, and so on. As is clear from the few pages of his spiritual diary that have come down to us (2 February, 1544, to 27 February, 1545), he could *experience* God's presence almost at will. All that was required was an explicit advertence which in the days recorded in the diary he could not always effect but which in subsequent years, according to the testimony of his companions, he found no difficulty in doing. What he did, it seems, was merely advert consciously and deliberately to what he was already experiencing, for to suggest that he or anyone else could have an authentic mystic experience at will is a particular nonsense we have no intention of indulging in here. And by this free advertence his awareness of what habitually he was experiencing came more sharply into focus— he "found" God. A homely example may serve to clarify the central point here. Take a young man; he is wonderfully in love; his step has a new resiliency; his eye a new brightness; all the world, which in accord with the adage loves him, is bright and gay. His happiness, so prolific in felicitous consequences whether ambulatory or oculatory or social, is habitual. He goes to sleep at night with a smile on his face; he awakes in the morning with it still there. Now and again (say, first thing in the morning) he asks himself, wonderingly, why he feels so happy. And, with his answer to himself and with the advertence it involves, his happiness comes more sharply into focus and he experiences it more fully—he "finds" it. Substitute "God" for "happiness" and one has not too inexact an idea of what Ignatius was able to do, and why he could do it.

He could do much else besides. Unlike the majority of mystics, who when they have their experience of God are so invaded that they can experience nothing else, Ignatius could carry out

[1] See pp. 277–92.

the most absorbing and distracting occupations. The reason he could do so was because the experience was limited to the substance of his being. There was no ligature of the faculties. Intellect and will were free to engage in any and all employments. Because they were left free in this experience of Himself, God could accord it to Ignatius uninterruptedly throughout whole years of his life. For it does not seem in the designs of Providence, this side of Paradise, that anyone for long should be only and totally absorbed in Him.

As theologian of the spiritual life, Ignatius again is a mystic with a difference. He provided no such enrichments of the Christian heritage as have Origen or Bernard or John of the Cross with their subtle analyses of the mystic encounter. It would perhaps be to engage in profitless speculation to wonder, at this late date, if ever he was tempted to try it. All the indications are that he never was. He might have been were there a progression and a variety in his experience. But there was none. Or had there been darkness in it or doubts about it. But, again, there was none. Most important, however, was the experience's leaving the faculties untouched for it is only with the data provided upon that level that traditionally one began one's analysis. There was no such data. There was only the magnificent datum of his conscious juncture, deep in his being, with the operative Godhead. There he knew, he tells us, how God created, how the divine Persons proceeded, how Christ is present in the Eucharist, etc. Thence he learned, experientially, before ever he sat in the theology classrooms of Paris, the doctrine of the instrument.

Today, the beneficiaries of successive revivals in Thomism and in liturgical studies, we are only beginning to explore to our profit the rich relevance of instrumental causality for an understanding of the Christian dispensation and the manner of God's acting within it. From the day by the Cardoner to his death decades later in Rome, St. Ignatius saw everything in terms of it. The hundreds of letters of spiritual counsel he wrote or had written for him, the Constitutions of his Order, the *Spiritual Exercises*, all are dominated by this one master intuition. To be apt and pliant instruments in the hands of God is the end of all being for all upon this earth—that is his constant theme and, theologically, it is impossible to think of one more basic or better. It is a doctrine that can be parodied, as it was in the *canard* that Jesuits taught the end justified the means. It can, if cut from its roots in the liturgy, end a stick much to the liking of activists with a particular apostolic drum to beat. It can easily be turned inside out and made an excuse for the lack of personal initiative. But, with a modicum of good sense and a mountainous patience in its application to oneself and to others, it introduces one infallibly if not to the luminous experience of Ignatius at least to the expression, equally luminous, of the will of Him whom Ignatius thus learned to serve.

Perhaps the paradox indulged in above will by now have been pardoned. The mysticism of St. Ignatius was theologically more informative than a less limited experience would have been because it conveyed an insight into reality which is valid for whatever time or place or condition, which undercuts all differences in schools of spirituality and diversities of possible apostolates and varieties of character or temperament while according an added firmness and meaning to them all. One could hardly wish it to have been otherwise.

21. ST. ALPHONSUS RODRIGUEZ

William Yeomans

WHEN ALPHONSUS RODRIGUEZ[1] first applied for admission into the Society of Jesus, the four prudent Fathers who examined him, in his native town of Segovia, rejected his application. Nor could anyone have reasonably accused them of faulty judgment. Alphonsus was then in his middle thirties. Though he knew some Latin, his education had been scanty, and he was now considered too old for further studies. Moreover his health was poor. Excessive penance, and probably too, the shattering blows dealt him by the failure of his business and by the deaths of his wife and two children, had left him frail and sickly. Such a man could be of little use to the Society, which is not a home for invalids, be they never so pious.[2]

However Alphonsus did not accept this first rebuff. Away he went from Segovia to Valencia, to continue his studies. The two years he spent there did little to improve his health. Finally, after an ill-starred attempt at being a hermit, he again applied for admission to the Society. The Fathers who examined him did not share the enthusiasm of his Jesuit spiritual director Fr. Santander, and again refused his application on the very same grounds as their brethren of Segovia. Fortunately Fr. Antonio Cordeses, the Provincial, was prepared to accept the responsibility of tempering their prudence with a little folly. Alphonsus was too ill-equipped to be a priest, too old and too weak to be a brother—"Very well, we will have him to be a saint." Whether or not Fr. Cordeses realised at the time how true a prophet he was, matters little. He certainly did discern more in Alphonsus than had eight other pairs of prudent Jesuit eyes, and he had the merit of giving to the Society of Jesus a great mystic, the patron saint of its Brother Coadjutors.

[1] Not to be confused with the author of *The Practice of Perfection and Christian Virtues*.
[2] Another Jesuit mystic had had to fight against similar difficulties; but he, of course, was Ignatius Loyola.

On 6 January 1571, Alphonsus began his noviceship in Valencia.[1] In the same year he was transferred to Palma de Majorca, where he arrived on 10 August, the feast of St. Lawrence. There, at the college of Montesion, he was to spend the rest of his long life; for this delicate, unpromising novice confounded his critics by living to the ripe age of eighty-four.[2] But even on Majorca there were some who did not share Fr. Cordeses' confidence in Alphonsus. When the time came for his first vows, he had to submit to a two months' postponement, since there were still doubts about his suitability.

After taking his vows, Alphonsus was engaged in general duties until, in 1579, he was given the work which to-day identifies him. He was made doorkeeper. That one word sums up the external events of the thirty-eight years of life which remained to him. Until the age of 61 he carried out the duties of first doorkeeper. Then, because of his infirmities, he was relegated to the post of second doorkeeper, and second doorkeeper he was for twenty-three years. Nowhere is Alphonsus' greatness of soul revealed so clearly as during the quarter of a century which he spent "on the shelf." Only a saint could have transcended the dull monotony of growing older, feebler, progressively more useless. Only a saint could have consistently overcome the temptation to succumb to the passage of time and to wait for death with querulous passivity. Only a saint knows how to bring the spirit to full fruition uncontaminated by the increasing sterility of the body. Everything on the beautiful island of Majorca, climate, scenery, geographical situation made a perfect setting for a life of quiet but undistinguished piety. Externally, Alphonsus' life merged into the somnolent, sunlit, landscape; but underneath it all, there raged a mighty battle which ended only with his death on 31 October 1617. His was a life hidden with Christ in God; with a Christ continually at grips with the adversary; a Christ who, in the lonely silence of the desert and the physical helplessness of the cross, overcame the enemy of mankind. In Alphonsus' lifelong struggle there is more at stake than the individual issue of personal salvation. He moves in a world of eternal values, where once again, through the medium of his own life, the universal battle between good and evil, between Christ and the devil, is being

[1] Or perhaps Gandia. The two chief authorities disagree.
[2] We accept the date 1533 for Alphonsus' birth, instead of 1531.

fought and won. But Alphonsus' spirituality and mysticism is not a refuge from the dullness of temporality. He found eternity in the very sameness of daily, routine detail. And in a life where every moment is shot through with the unchanging, eternal presence of God, no single moment is unimportant. One of the keys to the understanding of Alphonsus' spirituality is this blending of the intensity of eternity with the duration of time. He never allows us to forget the paradox that the daily food of the christian is the bread of eternal life.

Alphonsus himself uncovers for us the concentrated interior activity which seethed beneath the calm exterior of his daily life. His spiritual writings fill three volumes in the edition of Fr. Jaime Nonell.[1] Unfortunately Fr. Nonell not only published but also edited and collated Alphonsus' fragmentary writings. The result presents the obvious problem. The individual pieces belong to Alphonsus but the systematisation and arrangement belong to Fr. Nonell. Fortunately, however, amongst Alphonsus' writings are accounts of conscience which Alphonsus wrote down at the order of his Superiors. There are twenty-one of these covering the years from 1604 to 1617, and they are untouched by editorial hands.[2] In them we can trace the major ideas upon which Alphonsus based his spiritual life, written down for the most part not as theories but as experiences. They bring Alphonsus to life again in a way which no systematic presentation can ever hope to equal. Untidy, sometimes rambling a little, apparently without logical sequence, they are still a uniquely valuable spiritual document.

"To wage war beneath the standard of the cross" is the ideal of the society which Alphonsus joined, and it never had a greater-hearted fighter than he. It is to be expected that the words "battle," "struggle," "labour," come constantly from the pen of one who was quite convinced that "without a battle there is no gain, nor victory, nor crown, nor virtues, nor imitation of Christ."[3] The surest way to sanctity was the way the Father chose for His Son—labour, suffering, persecution. Therefore sanctity

[1] Barcelona 1885.
[2] These are in Vol. I of Nonell's edition of the *Obras Espirituales*. However, we shall quote from the re-edition made from the original manuscripts by Fr. V Segarra, S.J. and published under the title *Autobiografía. San Alonso Rodriguez, S.J.* (Editorial Borgiana, Barcelona. 1956). We shall refer to this book by the letter A, followed by the page number.   [3] A. p. 173.

must be won "at the cost of many great labours in the interior battle to uproot vices from the heart and implant there the virtues in which sanctity consists; and all this with the grace of God."[1] Union with God in prayer is an illusion unless it is tried against the touchstone of trouble and trials. Alphonsus constantly refused to set any store by the visions, the gift of prophecy and miracles with which he was credited. Instead of consoling him, they filled him with "fear and dread of being deceived," and he clung to this fear as a bulwark against illusion. Suffering was the surest way, for "in enduring labours for God there is no possibility of deception." In this spirit Alphonsus fought all his life. He mentions one period of six years when he fought against scruples, and the background of his life is a tapestry of temptations which at times amount to a descent into hell. Temptations against chastity, against faith, against charity. Even on his deathbed the battle continued. But he expected nothing else, for two years before his death he wrote that "death must be the greatest labour there is in this world."[2] In all this, God was weaning him away from every last desire for self-reliance, teaching him to turn only to Himself. The extent to which Alphonsus learnt the lesson is shown in his final magnificent reply to a temptation against faith—"It is enough for God to be God, as He is, that everything which He does be, like Himself, infinite goodness."[3] There is complete acceptance of the utter transcendence of the infinite God who has no need to justify Himself before man; the renunciation of that tiny grain of self-assertion from which temptation takes root.

Alphonsus' struggle was a battle for the heart, a conquering of himself in order to give himself entirely to God. Deprived as he was by humdrum routine of proving himself in great exterior works, his works were "vehement interior acts of the heart, doing gentle violence to oneself, in order to give one's soul completely to God, interiorly, so that He may have His will with it and with all that belongs to it, and be Lord over it, and the soul have us part of itself for itself."[4] In this struggle he uses the weapons of prayer and mortification. These he regards not as separate but as one single exercise. The prayer by which a man renounces himself is a putting of himself to death; the struggle to make that prayer, an integral part of this prayer of renunciation. One without the

[1] A. p. 175.   [2] A. p. 227.   [3] A. p. 197.   [4] A. p. 224.

other is of little avail. The struggle begins whenever nature
instinctively stirs in rebellion against trouble, sickness, unjustified
admonition, or when it is plagued by temptation. For Alphonsus
it was the surge of annoyance at people who rang impatiently
at his door. The victory does not consist in mere repression, nor
in any sort of passive, stoical acceptance. It comes only when
man sees that all these things come directly from the hand of
God. What he means by this is best explained in his own words.

The third exercise is higher and more divine. By means of it the
soul exercises itself and wins great victories over its enemies and over
all the different kinds of fearful experiences, labours, and adversities
which this life brings. It is easy to believe that God teaches the soul
this exercise on account of the great benefit and conquest of self
which, by the grace of God, it gains from it. For in the exercise of
the acts of this virtue of resignation the soul lifts itself up to its God
and sees itself in God. There, it does not use acts of faith that everything comes from the hand of God, nor does it use that great light
which goes beyond faith. It does not consider how God takes up
instruments, so that, with His permission, they may put the servants
of God to the test with labours. Indeed, the servants of God succeed
in loving such instruments all the more for the great favour they do
them by giving them labours in which they can suffer something
for the love of God.

When therefore the soul is in its God, there in its God it sees
how He gives it labours as gifts, not using any instrument for His
purpose, but Himself giving them, He the primary cause. The soul
does not look at second causes, but at the first who is God, and at
the love with which He exercises the soul. There the soul is looking
in mind and spirit at its God, joyfully accepting from Him all that
He does to it and gives it as He exercises it with labours. There
with its God, the soul is greatly delighted that its Lord does what
He likes with it. And all the time, the more He uses the lash and
chastises it, the more the soul loves Him. And when the devil sees
that the servant of God takes no notice of him but only of its God,
off he goes, proud creature that he is, and at once disappears.[1]

Here Alphonsus, beginning with resignation, goes far beyond
it into regions which the theologians of the permissive will of
God (a most difficult concept) do not envisage. Here the soul is
"in its God," united so intimately with Him that it shares in that
provident power which informs all things, bringing everything

[1] A. p. 100.

together into good. What is bitter becomes sweet because the loving hand of God is seen in it. The only evil is sin for only sin is outside love. The soul becomes conscious that God's personal operative presence is communicating itself in every trouble, sickness, temptation and trial. This intimate communion goes beyond sense and need not be accompanied by sensible consolation or any perceptible alleviation of suffering and labour. It is what Alphonsus understands by virtue, for "virtue is a grace and communication of God there in the superior part of the soul. In the inferior part of the soul this is, rather, consolation and not always virtue, but rather the gift of consolation."[1] The soul is given love and strength and in that loving experience, which takes place in the deep of the soul, it finds the longing to suffer even more, in order to be more united with God. The experience of suffering is something which the soul shares with its God in Christ crucified.

The result is that the actions of those who achieve this union will often be inexplicable and seem foolish to others. Those who have not penetrated this mystery of virtue are like men who watch others dancing but who cannot hear the music. They see only strange gyrations, movements without apparent sense or purpose. Only the dancer who hears the music can understand the beauty and rightness of the actions he performs. Alphonsus' apt little comparison was indeed true of his own life. There was the famous occasion when some of the brethren were leaving Majorca. Alphonsus was asked by the Rector whether the voyage would be a good one. (His prophetic gifts had already been proven.) His reply was that the voyage would be a golden one. Golden it was, but for one who thought that "labours are an abundant goldmine of virtues and sanctity."[2] The Fathers and scholastics struck it rich, for they were captured by pirates and sold into slavery in Algiers. The more unmusical of the community at Montesion made sure Alphonsus knew how stupid they thought he was. The fact that Alphonsus delighted in being taken for a fool probably did not improve matters. The saints are often infuriating, not because they are saints, but because their brethren are not.

Foolish indeed Alphonsus appeared to many, but never so frequently as on account of his obedience. Was there ever a saint

[1] *Obras* Vol. III p. 745. We have tried not to improve on the saint's style, but to translate him literally. [2] A. p. 197.

who took obedience so literally and apparently so unreasonably. Once when the Superior came into the Chapel Alphonsus made to give up his place to him. "Stay where you are," said the Superior. Hours later Alphonsus was still there. On another occasion he was told "Eat up your plate," and he made vigorous attempts to do so. Examples of this kind are numerous. His own contemporaries told him that his obedience was that of a donkey. The learned professors of theology and philosophy at the College argued with him time and again, trying to show that obedience should be intelligent. His superiors tried to make him understand that their orders were not to be taken quite so literally. All this was of no avail. Alphonsus was convinced that "there is no need of *epikeia*,[1] since it is sufficient that the command comes from God our Lord."[2] To ask oneself what interpretation should be put on the words of command was to argue with God and fail in blind obedience. Time and again he quotes the example of Abraham who did not try, in the name of charity or *epikeia*, to interpret God's command to sacrifice his son. Abraham obeyed blindly because "the highest charity is to obey God."[3] Alphonsus had supreme confidence that no harm could ever come to the Society through the practice of such blind obedience, "for the Lord takes into His care those who imitate Christ our Lord by obeying in this way."[4]

Alphonsus' over-literal obedience exasperates us because he refused to use his judgment where we would have used ours. It is here that we run the risk of becoming irrelevant. The point of any study of spirituality is not to lead us to make comparisons but to enable us to catch a glimpse of the wonderful workings of God in His saints. Alphonsus himself gives a wise warning that those who imitate the mere material actions of the saints are in grave danger of falling into illusion and sin.[5] God alone knows what is in the hearts of men and He leads each along a distinctive path. Before the results of His action our attitude must be one of admiration not of slavish imitation. Furthermore the object of that admiration can be nothing other than the mystery of God working out the salvation of the world. The apparent stupidity and folly of the actions of many of the saints remains incompre-

---

[1] The New English Dictionary defines *epiky* or *epikeia* as "reasonableness, equity, as opposed to rigid law."   [2] A. p. 183.   [3] A. p. 184.   [4] A. p. 215.
[5] It was the mistake Ignatius made, as he admits in his Autobiography.

hensible as long as it is divorced from its context of the work of salvation in a particular person in a particular set of circumstances. The cross only makes sense to those who believe Jesus is the Saviour, and even then its mystery is not fully understood. It would be arrogant presumption to imagine that our finite intelligence is never going to be surprised and baffled by eternal wisdom.

Never does Alphonsus separate obedience from what he calls the exercise of the presence of God or from charity. Indeed, when his Superior commanded him to desist from his constant exercise of the presence of God, lest he should tire himself, he tried in vain to obey. The more he tried to obey the more he found himself with God. Obedience was for him a "being with" God. More than that, it was a becoming like God, for through it man comes to love what God loves, to want only what He wants, and that is "the greatest likeness to God that can be achieved on this earth."[1] God asks man to obey because He desires the co-operation of His creatures in His work. This co-operation means that obedience is not so much a question of man's doing something which God orders, as of man's accomplishing with God a work which God desires. It is "Christ who will look through the eyes [of the obedient man], hear through his ears, speak through his mouth, and work through his hands in such a way that his soul and body will be nothing other than an instrument moved by the hand of God."[2]

So the perfection of obedience is a more intimate share in the divine nature which deifies and seals man with the seal of the divine will. That seal is "a great and most intense love which the soul has for its God, and with this love which illuminates it, it knows clearly that what the Superior commands, God commands clearly and plainly."[3] Just as Alphonsus saw that all his troubles and trials came directly from the loving hand of God, so also he saw that every command of his Superior came directly from God. He began by seeing his Superior in the place of God but he ended by seeing God in the place of his Superior. His obedience found its source directly in God and this was the bed-rock foundation of his deep peace of soul.

This mystical union with God which Alphonsus achieved in his obedience puts his apparent stupidity in a completely different

[1] A. p. 214.   [2] A. p. 215.   [3] A. p. 215.

light. The question we must ask is not how he could be so literal, but how could God require of him such literal obedience. From here on we must tread with wary reverence since we approach the mystery of God's dealings with a particular person. But perhaps we catch a glimpse of the truth when we consider the humdrum ordinariness of Alphonsus' life. Routine can be completely destructive of the spirit of obedience and his life was all routine. Humanly speaking he would never have had the chance of exercising the heroic obedience of Abraham or of Christ crucified. It seems that God made up for that in His own way.

Co-operation with God inevitably leads to a sharing in the divine will to save the world. Alphonsus was haunted by a yearning to see all men saved. His desire was so great that he can call it a torture. It was as if living on a small island only served to increase his apostolic desires. He writes of himself:

> This person has such a fervent desire for the salvation of souls that he had this experience. He found himself, in spirit, at one time and in one place, as if he were with all the people there are in the world, all in each particular one, and all in all together. He was dealing with each one in spirit and with all at one and the same time, speaking of the shortness of life, the pains of hell, glory, the infinite goodness of God and how much He deserves to be served for ever. He was setting every one on the right path so that they should serve God and be saved.[1]

Here God allowed Alphonsus to see that the effects of sanctity are not restricted by the limitations of time and space. Before God, the opening and shutting of a door can be a means of saving the world, when the doorkeeper is a saint.

This greatness of soul and universal ambition to save the world for Christ was the spirit which formed Peter Claver. Every day, during his three years on Majorca, he spent part of his recreation talking to Alphonsus. In the old brother, this nervy, undecided, young man came into living contact with the divine love which sacrifices itself to save the world. From Alphonsus, Claver learnt a hard doctrine of mortification, self-conquest, and sacrifice. But he also learnt that immense love without which he would never have survived the stinking slave marts of Cartagena, no more than Alphonsus would have survived the soul-destroying monotony of his daily routine. Alphonsus made Claver into a

[1] A. p. 147.

man because he himself was growing to his full manhood in
Christ.

Four years before his death, Alphonsus writes that his chief
prayer is to ask God insistently for these four loves: "love of God,
love of Jesus, love of the Virgin Mary our Lady, and love of his
neighbour."[1] Later he describes the love which consumed him as
"a great martyrdom." Love consumed him, but at the same time
it was only love which prevented him from breaking down under
the intensity of his interior life, and under the accumulation of
sickness which he suffered as the years went by. Alphonsus' way
of the cross terminated during his last years in a Calvary of
physical and spiritual suffering. Unable to move from his bed,
unable even to remember his prayers, all he could do was love.
All his life he had sought only God, at first from fear, then
gradually from the perfection of love which transformed servile
dread of punishment into filial reverence and fear which is the
constant companion of love. Nothing, neither exterior works, nor
interior acts were worth anything unless they came from "that
sea whence comes . . . all that is good in the soul, which is the love
of God and the great familiarity of the soul with God and the
value of exterior works."[2] There was obvious heroism and
obvious value in Claver's work for the slaves. In Alphonsus'
simple duties there was none of that. But it was the same divine
love which inspired both lives and gave to both their eternal
value in Christ. Claver looked for Christ in every one of his
slaves and lepers. Whenever Alphonsus opened the door he
expected to find Christ on the doorstep. Neither was ever
disappointed.

[1] A. p. 187.   [2] A. p. 37.

S

22. ST. FRANCIS DE SALES

Anthony Levi

THE CULTIVATED but unworldly prelate who succeeded Granier as Bishop of Geneva in 1602 was already by any standards a remarkable man. Just thirty-five years old, Francis had achieved real intellectual distinction, success in the Chablais mission, acclaim in the most famous pulpits of Paris and Savoy and the protection of the most powerful. Yet there is a sense in which his whole life up to this moment had been little more than a necessary and arduous preparation for the great work which lay ahead. This gentle, serious, almost taciturn priest who was to become one of the very great spiritual directors, and his doctrinal *via media* with its deeply humanist approach to the spiritual life, are both explicable only in terms of the diffidently intellectual, affectionate but reserved disposition of the young Francis. The conciliatory prelate who attained confident resolution comparatively late in life is the final flowering of the sensitive and timid young man, pliable even to excess, whose spiritual life was a constant quest for that peace of soul, that *debonnaireté*, which is the key to his later spiritual direction.

Francis's years of study at La Roche, Annecy and at the Collège de Clermont were characterised by a piety which was perhaps somewhat uneasy and by a slightly subservient attitude to the tutor who accompanied him to Paris, the not especially gentle M. Déage. This temperamental timidity, later to develop into a more engaging diffidence, certainly contributed to the one event of paramount significance which took place during the years at Paris, the critical six weeks during which Francis was convinced he was to be damned. The agony was finally resolved before the

[1] Apart from the works of St. Francis de Sales in the Migne edition and the critical Annecy edition which also contains the valuable comments of Dom Benedict Mackey and his associate editors, I have relied to some extent on Bremond's excellent treatment of the saint in the *Histoire littéraire du sentiment religieux en France* and on the Lives by M. Hamon and Mgr. Trochu. Fr. Liuima's *Aux sources du traité de l'amour de Dieu, I*, has also been of service.

statue of the Blessed Virgin at St. Etienne des Grès. Francis owes to the painful reminiscence of his anxiety on this occasion the first pregnant realisation of the primacy to be allotted to peace of soul in the spiritual life together with his later protagonism of the Molinist position in the disputes about grace and predestination.

After his studies in Paris Francis was sent for three years to Padua, still accompanied by Déage. In 1591 he gained a brilliant doctorate in jurisprudence and in the following year returned to Annecy. His father had always intended him to enter the magistracy, and there ensues one of those strange twilighted periods in his life when hesitancy inhibited all decisive action. Francis, now an official "avocat," had refused promotion to the senate of Chambéry, and had entrusted his cousin with the delicate task of informing his father about the firmness of his intention to become a priest. It was Granier whom the cousin finally approached and Francis, who had received the tonsure at Clermont, was nominated *prévôt* of the Cathedral chapter, the second rank in the diocese. His father, who had been understandably irritated by Francis's reserved deportment on two visits to the bride he had chosen for him, was informed only when the nomination had been ratified and now acquiesced. Francis was installed in May and ordained priest in December 1593.

The following years were spent in charge of the mission to the Calvinists of the Chablais and saw the preparation of Francis's first major work, usually called *Les Controverses*, an unfinished treatise defending the Catholic position from an ecclesiological point of view and drawn up in a series of leaflets for distribution to the Calvinists who were forbidden to attend his sermons. This treatise is already remarkable for two traits which were to characterise all the saint's writing. The style is penetrating and shows evidence of a trained legal mind, never unnecessarily complex but always acutely conscious of the strongest points in the argument, and, secondly, the treatise was written not as an abstract dissertation, but for a particular practical purpose in a quite concrete situation. Even much later his compendious treatise on the love of God was to be composed with definite people in mind, the sixth, seventh and eighth books for Mère Anne-Marie Rosset, the ninth for Jeanne de Chantal.[1] Meanwhile

[1] A. Liuima, *Aux sources du traité de l'amour de Dieu*, I, 311.

the controversial technique is sure, ardent, but never ill-humoured and always relevant to the immediate situation.

It would be easy to exaggerate the refinement of Parisian society in 1602 when Francis arrived on an important diplomatic journey, but Francis, although intellectually brilliant, was none the less clearly conscious of his provincial background. We find him apologising for his gaucheness and deliberately cultivating the art of classical allusion and the *tours d'esprit* he was to regret ten years later. With the leaders of the great spiritual renaissance in seventeenth-century France the young prelate was equally hesitant, preferring to observe in silence and visibly shrinking from directing the ecstatic Mme Acarie who was then negotiating for the foundation of the French Carmelites and to whom the young Bérulle had introduced him. But his fame was beginning to spread. A course of Lenten sermons, preached at short notice before the queen in the Louvre, met with such success that the king at Fontainebleau summoned him too, and his sermons became the talk of Paris. Henry IV, who was short of well-born prelates both learned and devout, pressed him, not for the last time, to stay in France and, when he would not, tried in vain to make him accept a pension.

This success in Paris and Francis's brief contact with the leading mystics of the reforming movement in the early seventeenth-century provided him with the final experience necessary to complete his formation and to bring him to maturity. On 29 September Francis learns of Granier's death on his way home from Paris. By the end of the year he had been consecrated Bishop of Geneva and had written his first letters of spiritual direction.

It is probably true that little more than the foundations of his personal sanctity had been laid. The style of the *Introduction à la vie dévote* was not yet natural to him, and he was certainly far from the spiritual maturity of the *Traité de l'amour de Dieu* with its mellow and sometimes lyrical style and its developed personal doctrine. Already, however, his own life was firmly rooted in vigorous habits of devotion and all the basic traits of Salesian spirituality can be observed. Francis's devotion to the Church had been shown in the magisterial exposition of *Les Contro-verses*, where his doctrine of a visible and infallible institution, united under the Vicar of Christ and faithful to Apostolic tradition, anticipated a great deal of what was to be defined by the Vatican Council. And with his veneration for the Church had gone an obvious concern to establish the scriptural basis of doctrinal positions. Francis, whose knowledge of Scripture was profound, quotes with a liberality and, indeed, an ingenuity which, if it does not always contribute much to proving the point at issue, shows at least a clear concern for the authority of Scripture whose integrity he so firmly defended against the Calvinist ministers. On occasion and to make a particular point he could refer to Hebrew or Greek texts in a more scholarly way, but generally it is the Vulgate which comes bubbling forth with spontaneous affection and which, for instance, he defends in the preface to the *Traité de l'amour de Dieu*.

In one Good Friday sermon Francis tells us that he could never read St. Paul's reference to the Crucifixion in the third chapter of the Epistle to the Galatians "without trembling and being seized with terror," and the most obvious fruit of his devotion to Scripture was his great love for the person of Christ. Indeed, when considering the love which inspired the death on the Cross, Francis in some ways anticipates the revelation of the Sacred Heart to St. Margaret Mary, and by the end of his life the "love of our crucified Saviour" came to exclude almost every other affection from his mind.

The chief source for Francis's spiritual doctrine is his letters of direction; and it is certainly not fortuitous that this doctrine should first have been elaborated in so intimate a form. There are many series of these letters, to Rose Bourgeois, abbess of Puits-d'Orbe, and her sister Mme Brûlart, to Mme de Charmoisy, Angélique Arnauld, Mme de la Fléchère, to Mère de Blonay, abbess of Sainte-Claire at Evian and above all to Mme de Chantal and the first members of the Visitation. There was in St. Francis de Sales a certain refinement and sensibility which made him peculiarly at ease in the direction of educated and often highly cultivated women. It is in these letters that he achieved freedom of expression and found the facility and grace which he frequently lacked in personal intercourse.

In himself Francis united the tenderness which could refer to the *mignardise* of Christ's love and to God's *infinie débonnaireté* with a spiritual strength which occasionally dismays. He could if necessary insist on absolute obedience from his clergy. And he once wrote to Mme de Chantal—I do not think he would have used these words to anyone else—"your heart must be flayed alive to be offered as a living holocaust to our God." Similarly if he was attracted to the direction of women St. Francis preferred them, as he said, to be endowed with vigorous spirits and independent minds. With such women as these he became chiefly successful, although the capricious temperament of Rose Bourgeois and Angélique Arnauld's taut nerves were, in the event, and for whatever cause, to prove too great an obstacle to his counsels. Most successful of all was naturally the direction of St. Jeanne-Françoise de Chantal whose influence on St. Francis was, however, probably as great as his on her.

By 1602 the youthful diffidence seems no longer to have inhibited Francis's resolution so much as to have informed it with sensitivity and delicacy. He once complained to the Bishop of Belley, "I do my best to hurry, but the more I hasten the less I move forward. I have difficulty in finding words, more still in speaking them," and to the end of his life his decisions were to cost him sustained intellectual and spiritual effort. It is precisely this groping of the mind which so strengthened his powers of practical judgment. Whereas in Paris Francis had not responded to Mme Acarie's quest for direction and had remained silent in the parlour of the reforming Abbess of Montmartre, Marie de Beauvilliers, Francis did commit himself to the task of directing Mme de Chantal when approached by her in March 1604. But this was only after hesitating for five months, because "I wanted to be sure about God's will, and that there should be nothing in this affair except what His hand directed."

The hesitation was the more remarkable because St. Jeanne-Françoise was tortured during this period to think that by confiding in St. Francis she had broken one of four vows by which she believed herself bound to her usual director. We do not know the name of this no doubt well-meaning, but also stupid and domineering man; he had, however insisted that Mme de Chantal should vow to obey him, not to change to another director, not to reveal what he said and not to discuss her interior life with anyone else. Two outside opinions which were sought agreed that these vows were invalid, but it is not until 25 August that Francis comes to Mme de Chantal, "very early." "Let us sit down. I have not slept. I have been considering your case all night. It is indeed true that it is God's will for me to charge myself with your spiritual direction and for you to follow my advice." After a short silence Francis continues, "Madame, shall I tell you? I must tell you since it is God's will. All your four vows can result only in destroying your peace of conscience."

Slow, measured prudence and the mortified insistence on complete purity of intention characterise all Francis's direction. There is often severity in his counsels, never harshness, always the absolute primacy of the soul's love of God. But to love God the soul must be free, liberated from its own scruples, inhibitions, constraints and free to respond in its own way to the divine initiative. Consequently Francis insists little on definite practices, although he is not afraid to suggest them, but he desires above all to establish a way of life based on the complete dedication of which only a mature and self-possessed person is capable. He writes a detailed letter to Mme de Chantal in October 1604, "Here is the general rule of our obedience in capital letters: *We must do everything out of love, nothing by force; we should love obedience more than we fear disobedience. I leave you the spirit of liberty.*" Unless there is inner tranquillity, self-possession, ardour will not suffice.

The message is often reiterated, as in the masterly letters to Angélique Arnauld who, in 1622, was hoping to resign as Abbess of Port Royal in order to enter the Visitation. "We must await word from Rome, and all the same remain at peace; and when word has come, remain at peace; and whatever the reply is, remain at peace, and always remain at peace with all our strength." The subsequent history of this intense and aristocratic personality makes a pointed commentary on St. Francis's shrewdness. "Would it not be better," he once said to her of her apostolic activity, "not to take such big fish, but to take more of them?"

Dom Benedict Mackey, writing of the saint's spiritual direction, points out that the great work of self-reform requires calm and patience rather than provocative ardour and violent combat. Hundreds of letters constantly insist on the necessity of avoiding agitation, tenseness, anxiety, of moderating all practices which disturb peace of soul. "In everything and through everything we must live in peace. If we are in interior or exterior pain, we must accept it peacefully. If joy comes to us, it must be received peacefully, without agitation. If we must flee evil, it must be peaceably, without disturbing ourselves. . . . Essentially therefore the life dedicated to God should be sweet, or in that typically Salesian word, *débonnaire*. One should not be too punctilious in the exercise of virtues,· but take them roundly, frankly, simply, in the old French way, with freedom and good faith, *grosso modo*. What I fear is the spirit of constraint and melancholy." Sadness, he tells us, is "almost always opposed to the love of God."

The love of God is sweet, but it is also exigent. The peace is interior, "it is not quietness which brings Our Lord near our hearts, it is the faithfulness of our love; it is not the sentiment of His sweetness which we have, but the consent we give to His holy will." Sometimes it is necessary to use "knife and scissors" to cut off attachments which prevent our complete dedication, and Francis has no illusions about what abnegation is required of the most favoured persons. The sacrifice can be very great indeed. Mme de Chantal's exclamation *"Que le rasoir a pénétré avant!"* was wrung from the heart in the ultimate steps of self-denial, at a time when the highest mystical graces were being showered on her. St. Francis, who had told her he would strip her of every-thing, replied, "Our Lord loves you, Mother, He wants you to be His alone; allow His arm alone to support you. . . Think no longer of the friendship and unity God has made between us, nor of your children, nor of your heart, nor of your soul."

St. Jeanne's is an extraordinary example, but it emphasises the way in which Francis's direction was always tempered to suit the capabilities of the penitent. He had been slow to allow his spiritual daughter to turn to the mystical states of prayer, but he was not unthorough in encouraging her to correspond absolutely to the exigencies of divine love. Yet on the other hand the dominating concept in the foundation of the Visitation was the need for an Order in which the least robust could dedicate themselves to God, while with Marie de Beauvilliers and the Filles-Dieu, Francis had insisted on the gentleness needed with the older members of convents to be reformed. And the mildness of the *Introduction à la vie dévote* was by no means invariably a mere prelude to the more rigorous treatise on the love of God; for, although he leaves the way open, St. Francis regards it as normal that his *Philothée* should only seldom graduate into *Théotime*.

The formal treatises grew in a very real sense out of the letters of direction. Like the letters, they are concrete and practical, a form of generalised spiritual direction rather than theoretical dissertations on the spiritual life. The *Introduction à la vie dévote* elaborates the advice already given to Mme de Charmoisy and was written with her in mind. Later additions deliberately universalise this advice, so that it shall be generally valid for persons living in the world—a reference to the reader's husband is, for instance, supplemented by the words "or wife." The book's startling originality lies in the complete seriousness with which it provides a practical spiritual guide for persons whose vocations are neither religious nor even lay contemplative. The chapter, for example, "*de l'honnêteté du lit nuptial,*" unfortunately omitted in many modern editions, treats of its subject with a grace, clarity and plain good sense which makes it still among the best available reading on the point. The devout life, practised according to "the strength, business and duties" of each, is within the capabilities of all, and St. Francis is at pains to show, in detail, how it can be pursued amidst all the exigencies of a developed social life.

The teaching itself is classical—mental prayer, frequent communion, the sacraments, patience, humility. There is an extended treatment of the social virtues and vices, the various forms of friendship, a consideration of different temptations and some recommended practices of devotion. None of this is strictly new; much can be traced to the *Spiritual Combat* and to the spirit, at least, of St. Teresa's *Way of Perfection*. What is new is the embodiment of these doctrines in a systematic guide for devout lay people and the emphasis on the interior virtues, the primacy given to mental prayer. Purification of the heart is the aim, and this can be effected without exaggerating the mortification of the body, "I have never been able to approve the method of those who, to reform the man, begin by the exterior, by the expression, the clothes, the hair."

It is a cardinal doctrine for St. Francis, as indeed for the whole French school of seventeenth-century spirituality, that all progress in the spiritual life comes through the practice of the interior virtues. The interior humility counselled by the *Introduction* is contrasted with the exterior virtue which approximates more closely to "*sagesse*" than to true humility. Interior virtue alone excludes the *vaine gloire* and *complaisance* which for St. Francis are two principal obstacles to true piety. And St. Francis insists not only on the rigorous exclusion of complacency in the acquisition of virtue, but he is sensitive also to the different interior virtues required of different persons: "Each should devote himself particularly to the virtues which are required by the sort of life to which he is called." It is necessary to distinguish between the virtues required of prelates, princes, soldiers, married women and widows. Since, therefore, virtue must be interior and since different states of life, different temperaments, call for different spiritual paths, St. Francis leaves a large freedom with regard to particular practices of devotion and piety. He lays down only the framework of prayer, Mass, the sacraments, and, in order to guard against illusions and the dissipation of all attention and effort, insists only, as a preliminary to beginning the exercise of the devout life, on the choice of a suitable spiritual director. It is through the director that the Holy Spirit leads and forms the individual soul and that the capabilities and duties of each are respected.

St. Francis insists that no one is incapable of mental prayer as taught in the *Introduction*. The *Traité de l'amour de Dieu* also avoids unnecessary difficulties, and was recommended by St. Francis to people living outside religious Orders. The widespread diffusion of the love for God was the principal aim of all Francis's activity and the foundation of the Visitation showed the primacy he attributed to it. "This congregation," he wrote in a memorable sentence, "has been instituted so that no great harshness should prevent the weak and the sick from entering it to cultivate there the perfection of the love of God." Difficulties enough are imposed by the ultimate aim, the perfection of the love of God, and no one must be turned away by further and therefore unnecessary demands. So the Visitation came into being, a halfway house between Carmel and lay devotion, and its spirit is embodied in the treatise on the love of God.

Perhaps the most striking feature of this work is its point of departure, "the natural and first inclination to love God" which makes it impossible to think of God without feeling "a certain sentiment of love which the secret inclination of our nature draws from the depths of the heart." These first green buds of love excite the will, wherein finally love comes to reside, in harmony with the higher part of the soul, ignoring the heaviness, the

agitation, the revolt of the senses. The union of our will with
that of God, revealing Himself to us in the highest point of the
soul, is the essence of the whole *Traité*. Setting out from the
natural inclination to love God, "which shows that God is God
of the human heart," we are led through the unity of wills to
the highest perfection of "loving God above all things." This is,
I think, one of the most encouraging books ever written about
the spiritual life, and yet the difficulties are not glossed over.
Perhaps the overriding characteristic is the joyful, expansive
optimism with which even the difficulties of establishing divine
love in the "highest region of the soul" are envisaged, an optimism which flows over into the delicate exuberance of the baroque
style, supple, sensitive and graceful while remaining always
strong and clear.

Not surprisingly St. Francis has been found to have affinities
with the preachers of natural virtue during the preceding decades,
for although he is at pains to go beyond them and to point out
their insufficiencies, he can praise Epictetus and be courteous, if
critical, on pagan virtue. He teaches prudence, as they had done,
but carefully distinguishes it from mere worldly wisdom—*la
prudence humaine*—and adopts much of their vocabulary. Dom
Benedict Mackey has pointed out how St. Francis emphasised
the role of the passive stoic virtues, their *"sustine et abstine,"* and,
if St. Francis penetrates much further into the workings of grace
than they had done, he shares their basic optimism about the
human condition.

His doctrine is in the finest sense humane. Starting from man's
natural inclination to love God, Francis forms and develops it,
requiring for spiritual growth exactly that self-possession and
peace of soul which are also the normal prerequisites for the true
flowering of the human personality. The freedom from constraint which St. Francis personally achieved and constantly
advocated is seen by him to be the condition for self-transcendence
in the all-dominating and all-demanding love of God. He goes
further than the Christian stoics, much further, but he does not
materially contradict them.

St. Francis often quotes from the stoics of antiquity; and if he
distrusted Seneca and Plutarch it was not so much because he
disagreed with their moral maxims as because true moral virtue
is the work of the Holy Spirit in us rather than our own unaided

achievement. Just as in the spiritual direction, so lenient on externals, rigorous internal mortification of all pride and complacency had been called for, so now not the doctrine but the accompanying sense of achievement is excluded. Self-knowledge led the Christian stoic to find and follow that nature whose laws lay hidden inside the human personality; for St. Francis the deepened humanity of the self-possessed leads to the discovery of the "God of the human heart." To possess oneself and in one's self-possession to find the natural inclination to love God, this is the essential aim of Christian humanism.

To the modern Catholic the word humanism has, perhaps inevitably, come to possess unfortunate associations. At the best it is suspected of meaning unsupernatural, at times it has been provocatively used as a synonym for paganism or worse. Perhaps one may rejoice that St. Francis lived in an age, the last, when a real synthesis of antique *sagesse* and Christian piety seemed possible, when a Doctor of the Church and an authority on the mystical life could so unequivocally extol the virtues of reason and of human nature. His Christmas Eve sermon at the Visitation of Annecy in 1620 answers the question *"Pourquoi l'Incarnation a-t-elle été faite?"* quite simply, *"pour nous enseigner à vivre non plus brutalement . . . mais avec et selon raison."* And at the start of his career he had written "Whether in nature or above nature, reason is always reason and truth is always truth . . . Truth above nature and in nature is always the same, there are only different lights which show it to our understanding; faith shows it to us above nature and understanding in nature."

When St. Francis talks with this supreme confidence in "the uprightness and probity of human reason" and in nature, the *"si sage ouvrière"* which leads us by its "holy inclination to love God above all things," he is referring to nature and reason aided by grace, as we experience them in our lives. He never uses the abstract and negative technical concept of "pure nature" from which theologians exclude the exigence of supernatural life. For him, as for ourselves, supernature is part of that which is experienced in nature, faith is part of what he refers to as reason, "the heavenly wisdom and holy reason" of redeemed man.

In the speculative first four books of the *Traité de l'amour de Dieu* St. Francis accepts the traditionally Platonist conceptual framework of mystical theology and leans heavily on St. Augustine. The vocabulary is intricate and St. Francis is not entirely at ease with it. The "lower" part of the rational soul reasons discursively on data derived from sense perception, while the "higher" part or *esprit* enjoys an intellectual knowledge quite independently of the senses. To this portion of the soul belong the humane sciences. The reason or soul (the words are used interchangeably) possesses an even higher faculty to which belongs the discursive knowledge of the objects of faith and finally the "certain eminence and supreme point of the reason and spiritual faculty" which is the seat of non-discursive knowledge infused directly by God. Here will and understanding are reduced to their simplest forms, and here is the "special residence and natural abode" of the infused virtues of faith, hope and charity, where God reveals Himself to us in the *obscure clarté* whose certitude satisfies the mind and entices the will.

This view of man's spiritual faculties underlies all St. Francis's teaching. It emphasises the harmony between reason and faith, nature and supernature. Unless the soul is disturbed by passion within itself or prevented by malice of will it naturally concords with the *raison divine* by virtue of its own discursive acts. The direct activity of God in the soul, in mystical gifts or the ordinary life of grace, is characterised by the manner in which the experience of God's infused gifts satisfies the soul, eliciting the simple assent of understanding and will.

> Faith is the great friend of our mind . . . making us love the beauty of its truth and believe the truth of its beauty by the sweetness which it imparts to the will and the certainty it gives to the understanding . . . The assurance of faith begins in a loving sentiment of complacency which the will receives from the beauty and sweetness of the truth proposed, so that faith includes a beginning of love which our heart feels for divine things.

It is perhaps true that for St. Francis the Fall injured our will more than our reason, but he himself, who liked and quoted Montaigne, who knew d'Urfé, author of the enormously long and best-selling love story, the *Astrée*, who encouraged and in a sense envied his gay and uninhibited admirer, the novel-writing Bishop of Belley, regarded sanctity as transcending, but also as perfecting and completing the life of highest human wisdom. When therefore Bremond describes Francis's doctrine as "the spirit of Christian humanism . . . but deliberately applied to the spiritual life and presented to every soul," a summary it would be difficult to better, he brings out that which, however suspect it may sound, is none the less the essence of the saint's doctrine, his true and personal originality.

As a bishop his life was simple, almost austerely so, and completely taken up by his unending pastoral activity. Yet his letters abound in personal affection and in the preface to the *Traité de l'amour de Dieu* his style is reminiscent of the self-revealing charm of Montaigne's late essays. As Montaigne's achievement was patiently to break through doctrines and parties in order to be simply himself, to establish that *"forme sienne,"* the *"forme maîtresse,"* so St. Francis gradually overcame his initial anxiety, his timidity and diffidence, finally achieving the mature and settled self-possession of his preface.

In his last years there was to be added to this maturity a more complete and obvious detachment from everything outside the love of God, which he himself notices almost with surprise. He writes to St. Jeanne, "What is not God is nothing for us. How can it be that I feel this, I who am the most affectionate person in the world, as you know, my very dear Mother? But I do feel it; and it is marvellous how I can reconcile all that in myself, for I seem to love nothing except God and all souls for God." With this attitude comes, of course, the supreme abandonment to God's will which Francis had preached as insistently as he was now able to practise.

The *Traité de l'amour de Dieu* carefully guides our steps from the initial experience to the complete rule of the love for God in the soul. It is a spirituality which builds on nature from the beginning, which co-operates with it and moulds it. Perhaps this simple advice to Mme de Chantal sums up Francis's approach to the spiritual life, if it says nothing of his doctrine, *"Avoir son coeur en un lieu et son devoir à l'autre, n'est pas à propos."*

23. VENERABLE MARY OF THE INCARNATION

Mary Denis Mahoney

IT WOULD NEED a flamboyant mystic indeed, so one would think, to stand out in the jostling crowd of *beati* that thronged the spiritual highways of the seventeenth century. For mysticism in the France of the Medici was very much *à la mode*. It was "the thing"—one might say the fashion, and what Frenchman wants to be out of fashion? Consequently mystics abounded, both false mystics and true. Mistress and servant, soldier and statesman, all alike experienced supernatural dreams, divine touches, interior locutions. Into such an environment was born Marie Guyart who was to become one of the greatest mystics of this extraordinary mystic age.[1]

And yet, although there is much that is unusual about the paths God destined for Marie, there is little that is flamboyant about her. The various manifestations verging on hysteria which characterised so many contemporaries are singularly lacking in Marie. The extraordinariness of her graces is matched only by the extraordinariness of her response—a response vital, faithful and, above all, remarkably controlled. Even in the face of an imminent ecstasy Marie maintains that poise and balance which is one of her most individual characteristics. If she stands out from her contemporaries, it is not because she is more colourful but rather because she is more tranquil, with that delicate poise of spirit which so aptly fits her for her mystic graces.

Wife, widow, cloistered religious, missionary—Marie passed through all these states in turn, states which in God's providence did not contradict each other but prepared and reinforced her vocation. God would have all; God would be all. And in

[1] Marie Guyart was born in Tours in 1599. At the age of seventeen, despite her longing for religious life, she became the wife of Claude Martin, a Tourangelle silk merchant. In 1619 a son, Claude, was born, and shortly thereafter Monsieur Martin died, leaving Marie free to follow her spiritual attractions.

establishing His absolute dominion over her soul, He led her in great zig-zag lines which only a soul made docile by faith would have followed.

Her conscious entrance into the mystic way occurred on the vigil of the feast of the Incarnation in the year 1620. Marie was at that time a widow of twenty, harassed by the demands of a failing business and the care of her child who was less than a year old. It was in order to settle some business matters that she walked eastward along the busy streets of Tours on that memorable morning. As she walked, suddenly, without warning or explanation, the visible world fell away from her eyes, and to the eyes of her soul there appeared a world of spirit, so true, so terrible, so utterly real that until the end of her life the impression was never effaced from her heart. There she stood, stock-still in that busy street, while her first great mystical experience swept over her. And as the women with their market baskets brushed past her and the workmen trudged by in their clumsy shoes, Marie saw her soul plunged in the Blood of the Son of God. Before her were the sins of her life—each one clear, distinct, unmitigated, and so horrible in its aspect that, as she writes, "I think I would have died of fright had not the goodness of God sustained me."

It was at once solace and new shame to see that it was for her, in the abjection of her nothingness and the wilfulness of her sin, that the Precious Blood had been shed. She was at once humbled and exalted, and fumbled, as she will do so often later, to explain this experience which to the end will defy human expression.

There is no human language to express it; but to see a God of infinite goodness and incomprehensible purity offended by a mere worm surpasses the very horror itself; more than that, to see a God made man dying to expiate sin, pouring out all His Precious Blood to appease His Father and so to reconcile sinners to Him— one cannot describe what the soul feels at this wonder. And beyond this, to see that one is personally responsible and if she were the only one who had sinned that the Son of God would have done for her what He had done for all—it is this which consumes and annihilates the soul.[1]

[1] All references are to the biography written by her son Claude: *Vie de la Venerable Mère Marie de l'Incarnation*, 1677. The translations are my own. I am also indebted throughout this article to the work of Dom Albert Jamet, O.S.B., *Marie de l'Incarnation: Ecrits Spirituels et Historiques*, 4 vols. (Paris, 1929–1939).

When she came to herself, she found a new creature, so strong
had the divine action been upon her. All that she had ever
thought herself to have done for God, all that had appeared to
her to be love for Him was ashes beneath her feet, while within
her burned a flame which left no portion of her body free from
the anguish of love. In her bewilderment she adds, "And what
is more incomprehensible, this mercilessness seems sweet."

We are singularly fortunate in possessing Marie's own account
of this initial grace and of the many others that follow it. Living
as she did in the age of memoirs and diaries, it is not surprising
to find that at least twice during her lifetime her confessors (Père
Raymond de St. Bernard, a Feuillant Father, and Père Jérôme
Lallemant, a Jesuit) ordered her to write accounts of her spiritual
life. These accounts, in addition to several hundred letters and
some miscellaneous spiritual notes, provide the source for the
extensive life of Marie completed by her Benedictine son, Dom
Claude, shortly after her death. Marie's prose, like everything
else about her, slips the bonds of artificial convention and frees
itself from the "ornamental flowerets," from the "emblems and
allegories" which decorated much of the religious prose of her
day. But, unfortunately, she leaves much unsaid; she wrote under
obedience, despite great repugnance, and with the sole purpose
of satisfying her directors concerning her spiritual life. Such a
purpose naturally excludes the details of daily life, and the
biographer who attempts to piece together Marie's exterior life
must often walk cautiously amid conjecture.

And yet in the realm of the spiritual, Marie's memoirs leave
little to be desired. Her limpid prose, at once free and strong,
is extraordinarily adequate for the task before her. She possesses
a singular gift for descriptive expression and analogy, and also
an ability for objective analysis which enables her not only to
describe what has happened to her but also to evaluate and
classify it. When, then, Marie labels this vision of the Precious
Blood as the day of her "conversion," we must concede its
importance even while hesitating over the meaning of the word
"conversion." That this was in any way a turning from sin to
virtue is manifestly false; Marie's life had always been one of
unswerving fidelity to God. Her son Claude himself explains it
as his mother no doubt meant it: "By this conversion we must
understand the firm resolution which she took to think no longer

T

of the world with its cares and hopes in order to give herself wholly to God and to live solely for His Love."[1]

This is precisely what she set out to do. Her eyes had been opened and her vanities torn from her; so that she conceived a great horror of acting solely for her own interests and pleasure. The empty ceremony of Tourangelle society became a distasteful burden, and more and more she withdrew into the solitude of her father's simple household. When at last her period of mourning for her deceased husband was over and she put away her widow's cape, it was only to assume clothes even more unattractive; her gowns became less full than fashion demanded; her bodices were less ornamented with the delicate lace and heavy ribbons so popular in her day. To all the entreaties and reproaches of her family and her friends she turned a deaf ear. She had no intention of marrying again, she assured them, without being able to explain that this choice was not hers but God's, that it was He who was demanding of her a life totally consecrated to His service—a life of prayer, a life of suffering, a life utterly sensitised to the Spirit of God who stirred and moved within her with increasing force.

This direct operation of the Spirit within her neither frightened nor puzzled her. She accepted it without question as she continued throughout her life to accept both the graces and privations which God lavished upon her. In an age which bristled with spiritual directors, Marie kept her own counsel. It was neither pride nor diffidence which caused her to act thus, but the clear-eyed candour of a child who saw no problem in carrying out with loving fidelity what God so obviously asked of her. Although she was overwhelmed with grace and enveloped in mystic prayer, no mention of any of this was made to her director. The Holy Spirit was her only guide. She felt no need for any other.

The manner of life which she had chosen to live at this time was entirely compatible with the direction in which God was leading her. She remained in her father's house, caring for her child, helping with the household tasks, visiting the poor, and spending long hours in that tranquil union with God which now formed her ordinary state. Doubtless she looked happily ahead to a whole life lived in this even tenor, a life which quite satisfied

[1] *Vie*, p. 29.

the cloistral aspirations of her heart. It must then have come with something of a shock that, when her sister asked her to move to her busy household to help with the management of the family, the Spirit within her impelled her to say yes. Imprudent, disagreeable, capricious as such an action must have seemed, Marie had no doubt that it was God's wish for her, and for God's wishes she had but a single answer. "It is He who gives the orders and we who must obey," she wrote later, summing up succinctly her whole code of action. To the Buisson household she went, without a single backward glance at the solitude, the silence, the hiddenness which but a short while before she had thought to be hers forever.

Thus began in circumstances singularly unsuitable the most extraordinary period of Marie's ascesis. Claude, Marie's sister, had felt sure that she could count on her generosity, her talent for work, her devotion to duty. What Claude had not counted on was the presence of a saint in her house, and this, apparently, despite Marie's extraordinary prayer and penance, was a secret that God kept from the worldly and self-seeking eyes of the Buisson family. Even in these infelicitous surroundings, her prayer and mortification never diminished. Beneath her plain dress were the hair shirt and chain for which her director had given his permission, within her cupboard was her well-used discipline, while the sweetness of God's presence was the air she breathed.

It is at this time that the distinctively Christo-centric nature of her spirituality begins to appear. When she had been living with the Buissons little over a year, she describes a "new gift of prayer," consisting in a "union with Our Lord Jesus Christ touching His Sacred Mysteries from His birth to His death. . . . I experienced in this gift of prayer that this Divine Saviour was the Way, the Truth, and the Life. . . . I entered into Him, and by Him and in Him were disclosed to me these divine mysteries by which I live, and my soul was fed."[1]

With the deepening of the union of her soul with the spirit of Christ comes an increased passivity before the Divine action which became more and more powerful. The initiative was entirely in God's hands now, and Marie became daily more aware that her part was only to consent. There were months of grace upon grace, as God revealed Himself to her one day as

[1] *Vie*, p. 37.

Incarnate Love, another as a great sea of purity, again as a suffering God enduring His Passion. She, abashed before such prodigality, sought in vain for a suitable response. How, she wondered, was she ever to give a total gift of herself to this God Who had given Himself so completely to her? As she probed for an answer, there came to her the thought of making privately into the hands of her director the vows of poverty, chastity, and obedience. But even this thought still left her restless and unsatisfied.

During these days she lived, as she says, "in expectation," without being able to explain the source or term of her desires. She suffered without being able to understand her suffering. Although God seemed to communicate Himself to.her with rare liberality, she could not be satisfied. Her soul tended constantly toward a more intense communication; but, even more, toward a communication that was in some way different from any that she had hitherto experienced. "I was filled and encompassed with a heavenly sweetness," she writes, "and although I felt so entirely surrendered to God, my heart yearned to be united to Him in a wholly different fashion." How long she remained in this restless anxiety we cannot say, but one day it ended as quickly as it had begun. As Marie prayed, clinging to a desire for she knew not what, begging for what she did not understand, she heard Our Lord speak to her interiorly. The words she heard were the words of the Prophet Osee: "I will espouse thee to Me in faith, I will espouse thee to Me forever." The mystery was ended and the vision was clear before her: that toward which her soul was tending with the persistent wilfulness of a compass was espousals with the Son of God.

With these words came an entire change in her interior dispositions; her occupation was no longer with the Humanity of Christ but with His Divinity. Whatever she had known of prayer before seemed nothing compared with what she now experienced. In trying to express this, she writes:

> I no longer felt the Spirit of God stealing through me with sweetness; for now as soon as I prepared for my actual prayer, I had to go to some hidden place and sit down or find a support, for otherwise I would have fallen in front of everyone. I felt myself drawn powerfully and instantaneously without having the time or ability to make any interior or exterior act. I seemed to be wholly lost in God, who withdrew all my power to act. It is a

suffering of love which we must bear as He pleases, for we cannot extricate ourselves. It seems to the soul that she has swooned before her Beloved, made so weak by love that she cannot speak. Thus I remained for an hour, or perhaps two. Toward the end I felt a great sweetness of spirit and I was amazed when I found myself once more in my usual state of intimacy with Our Lord which, however, had become stronger and more powerful.[1]

This state of prayer affected her body as well, and although she practised the most rigorous penances, she writes that none of these weakened her as much as this intense recollection. God no longer came to her sweetly, in a calm peace, but brusquely, almost with rudeness, vanquishing her liberty, seizing her soul as captive to His power. But through it all her exterior life was not diminished. Her penances continued with her director's approval; and her works of charity, now more works of love than ever before, were, if anything, increased. She found in them solace and relief from the flame which consumed her.

Her soul veered toward God with an action that never ceased, and love was her only passion. She walked always in God's presence, and yet, as she is so careful to say, in a way that was wholly spiritual—"in the understanding and the will," for the imagination played no part in this. At some times more than others, she was aware of Jesus very near her, at her side, accompanying her in her duties. This presence and company were so sweet, she writes, "that I cannot express it as it really was."[2]

Her house was in order; her world was at peace. With her days filled from end to end, with never a moment to herself, with silence an impossibility, her union with God was undisturbed. She had cried, "Take care of me then, Oh my Love, for you have given me care of so many things," and God had heard the cry. He had further promised that at a time that He willed their espousals would be completed, and meanwhile He had said, "Peace to this house." She had entered, so it seemed, into the land of promise, for so firmly was her soul established in Divine Love that she wondered if any power on earth were strong enough to move it. Suddenly, without warning, without reason, this dwelling which had seemed so invincible shook about her and above her, and Marie was swept into a whirlwind of temptation to which there seemed no ending.

[1] *Vie*, p. 50.   [2] *Ibid*, p. 52.

Everything which formerly had made her joyous now began to fill her with weariness and loathing. The thought of those austerities which but a week before had been for her a source of joy now made her writhe in rebellion. Each night she turned to the hard board which for so long a time had been her bed and revolt swept over her in waves; each night there was the same grim battle, but each night when finally she fell asleep it was without having permitted herself any alleviation.

In the morning she rose, unrested, unconsoled, to face another day. While the streets were still grey with the first dull light of dawn, she walked in a chill of body and heart toward the chapel where God had always awaited her. She looked ahead to the long hours of the day and found nothing to sustain her. "It seems to me," she writes, "that I was like those poor beggars who go trembling from door to door." Always before when she was not sure of her path, she had had recourse to Dom Raymond, and under the directions of obedience had found peace; but now the thought of such a solution filled her soul with repugnance. To confess all this—the weariness, the temptations, the near-despair! To find words to express it and then to drag this squalor out of the depths of her heart and spread it before the eyes of him who for a single fault would humble her to the ground! To be humiliated, scorned, despised: all that she had prayed for so ardently, she now turned from in sickness of soul.

As she struggled to force herself to go to Dom Raymond and open her heart to him, another temptation, more insidious than all the others, came upon her: was not all that she had revealed to her director in the past but a piece of deception? Graces in prayer, hunger for austerities, wishing always to be the least of all—were not these but the lies and subterfuges which she had used to appear holy in his eyes? What use of saying more when she could not trust her own thoughts. But the conviction that in obedience she would find God's will drove her forward, and on her knees before Dom Raymond, the inexorable, she told her miserable story. As he listened, he saw far beneath the surface of her words and discerned the heroic proportions of the trial which God had let fall upon her. For once there were no harsh words; he confirmed her in the path that she was travelling, explaining that all this was but the devil's way to make her give up all that was most precious. Despite his kindness, however, her soul remained in the hands of God where no human solace could reach it. She rose from her knees unconsoled, seemingly unstrengthened, and in sheer weariness of heart abandoned herself once more to God. But with this final act of hope came the grace of which she had almost despaired: God removed the darkness and sent peace once again.

Now God's sunshine was about her, and the old familiarity of love was resumed. The trial had done its work well, for she was saturated with the realisation of her own nothingness, and, despite the liberty which God permitted her, she was often crushed before His Infinite Majesty. In this new light she saw her own powerlessness more clearly than ever before, realising the profundity of those words, "We can do nothing of ourselves." She found pride skulking in unexpected quarters: in the way she appropriated credit to herself for those qualities both interior and exterior which were God's undeserved gifts to her; in her desire for esteem and the secret complacence which she took in herself. God in His own time willed to free her from these subtle temptations, for one day as she opened a book to the words of the psalm: *Nisi dominus aedificaverit domum, in vanum laboraverunt qui aedificant eam*, she was suddenly liberated from the blindness engendered by her pride.

In these months of preparation for her espousals our Lord became for her now more than ever "the Incarnate Word." Her devotion to the Incarnation was to the essential mystery itself: the indescribable fact of this Divine Utterance taking upon Himself human flesh and yet remaining in the bosom of the Father. It is this emphasis on Christ as the Divine Word of the Trinity which lends an aura of reverence to her spirituality. It is the majesty of God which is so impressed upon her spirit, and more and more she finds her soul borne by Christ, Incarnate Word, to the home of the Eternal Three.

It is this increasing tendency to find rest only in the Trinity which prepares her soul for the peak of mystic revelation in which she will see ("in a manner wholly spiritual") the very heart of the Divine activity proceeding without cessation in the bosom of the Trinity. Fortunately, she has left us a detailed account of that first vision of the Trinity which occurred on Pentecost Monday of 1625 in the Feuillant church where God had given her so many signal graces. As she knelt in her usual

place, her eyes travelled over the curiously carved angels which
formed the base of the massive candlesticks; suddenly she was
wrenched from this world of reality and borne into an indescribable realm of the spirit. Thirty years later in an attempt to
recapture for her son one of the most glorious moments of her
life, she writes:

> . . . in a moment my eyes were closed and my spirit was raised
> and absorbed in the sight of the most holy and august Trinity in
> a manner that I cannot express. In this moment all the powers of
> my soul were stayed, enduring the impression which was given
> to them of this Sacred Mystery. It was an impression without form
> but clearer and more intelligible than any light, which convinced
> me at first sight that my soul was in truth; there, in a moment,
> it made me see the Divine intercourse which the Three Divine
> Persons have together.[1]

So the woman of fifty-five begins to describe the incredible
experience of the girl of twenty-five. If she stumbles in her
narration, it is not because the vision has dimmed but because as
she herself so often maintained, "there is no human language to
express it." Nowhere does she draw the line more clearly
between the mystic and the theologian. She does not profess
to explain, only to describe, and with that terminology which
is not the studied language of the theologian but the analogous
expression of the mystic.

She must have wondered, surely, if this were not the promised
grace of espousals, but even as the thought rose within her a
divine wisdom warned her that her preparations were not yet
complete, that the work of purgation was not yet consummated.
There was more to come: more love, more glory, and more—
much more—of the cross.

It was within weeks of this first vision of the Trinity that Marie
again felt her soul descend into that mysterious and terrible abyss
from which only the arms of God could draw her. Once again
all human and divine consolation was deprived her and she
trembled at the thought of her own presumption in believing
that she had been the recipient of unusual graces. "I was abandoned and totally deprived of all the graces which I had received,"
she writes, adding "even the remembrance of them redoubled
my pains, for I was tempted and even persuaded to believe that

[1] *Vie*, p. 77.

they were not true graces but no more than a loss of time in which I had amused myself." For this grief there was no solace, and even the direction of Dom Raymond did no more than make her shrink into herself like some poor wounded creature who has suffered so much that even the gentlest touch has become an unendurable agony. Trembling with fear even for her salvation, she had no need to turn to God, for the thought of God had never left her. He was in the air she breathed, not for comfort but for further crucifixion. She writes: "What caused me the greatest pain was that it seemed to me that I did not love Him."[1]

Despite these trials which could not but have reacted on her physically, her exterior manner remained unchanged. That balanced control of her emotion, which was such a characteristic note of her spirituality, was never broken, and, apparently, no one in the Buisson household was aware of the interior storms which swept over her for months at a time. What the Buissons did become aware of, however, was Marie's remarkable business sense; and Paul Buisson, with his own talent for never losing a good bargain, "promoted" (ambiguous word!) Marie from her position as *châtelaine* to business manager for his transport company. It was, indeed, as they pointed out to her, an honour and an opportunity—an honour and opportunity from which Marie's whole being recoiled. She accepted only because of her vow of obedience which made it clear that this was God's will for her. God's will had now become the very warp and woof of her existence, as one by one all other natural and supernatural supports were removed from her. God's will was, in truth, all there was to cling to when the very promises of God seemed contradictory. Had He not promised her the deepest possible union with Himself? Had He not even given her hope when she had pleaded with Him to take her out of the world and let her become a religious? And yet with each divine promise, He pushed her deeper into the affairs of men, withdrew more inexorably the possibility of that silence and solitude in which alone, she felt, He could be found. And now, less alone but more lonely than ever, she took up her stand on the wharves of the Loire to do a man's business in the toughness of a man's world and relinquish, perhaps forever, the only aspiration of her heart.

The two years which followed, years worthless in Marie's

[1] *Vie*, p. 95.

sight with their increasing preoccupation with business matters, were in God's sight a precious period of preparation, disposing Marie as nothing else could for that complete abandonment to God so necessary for her final espousals. Two years, almost to the day since her first vision of the Trinity, God drew her once more into Himself and fulfilled His Promise: "I will espouse thee to Me forever." In the account of her spiritual life written for her director in 1633, we can catch the freshness and indescribable wonder of her soul in the face of this consummate grace which had been so long in preparation:

> Our Lord again raised me and in a most loving way to a knowledge of the Trinity, Whose grandeur was revealed to me in the unity of the Three Divine Persons, and altogether differently from what I had hitherto been taught of it with respect to knowledge and love. The first time it was more a question of admiration rather than of love or possession, but this time love predominated. I saw the internal communication of the Three Persons as I had previously, but I was more fully instructed concerning the generation of the Word. . . . I forgot the Father and the Holy Spirit and lost myself in the Divine Word who caressed my soul as though it belonged wholly to Him. He made me understand that He was all mine and I all His through a powerful union which held me captive. Even more, it seemed to me that He was given to me to be my own, to enjoy at my leisure and, if I dare say so, that all His goods were now our mutual possessions. . . . It was then that I knew experimentally that the Word is truly the Spouse of the soul.[1]

With the conclusion of this vision, Marie reached that peak of mystical union called by theologians spiritual marriage. The grace for which other great mystics have waited until the close of their lives was given to this young widow before she had reached her twenty-eighth birthday.[2] Forty-five years of life

---

[1] *Vie*, p. 107.

[2] Although Claude Martin uses the term "spiritual marriage," he attempts to water down the meaning of the term by suggesting two spiritual marriages: this grace, then, is a kind of initiation for the second marriage which will occur later on. Dom Jamet points out the uselessness of the term if it is to be given such a dual meaning; Jamet, following Sandreau, has no hesitation in employing the term in its full significance but warns against making it consonant with "full" or "transforming" union. Such fine distinction of terminology must be left to the theologians; it seems sufficient here to indicate that for Marie this second vision of the Trinity did constitute a state of union with the Incarnate Word as her spouse. Cf. *Vie*, p. 127; Jamet, *Ecrits* I, 251–2; A. Sandreau, *Les Degrés de la Vie Spirituelle* (1920), II, 237.

stretched before her, years to be lived in the heart of this mysterious and exalted union. Here, perhaps, we may find a subtle boundary between the essentially contemplative character of Marie's early years and the manifestly apostolic character of her later period. This is not to suggest, of course, that these terms are in any way mutually exclusive. And yet in following Marie's life we cannot but be struck by the chronological order of events and graces. First came those graces centred on the mysteries of the Redemption; then followed those concerning the Divine attributes; and ultimately occurred the two visions of the Trinity which led to her espousals. A few years following this last grace she entered the Ursuline monastery, the "paradise" which she had so long desired. Yet far from being paradisal years, her first years as a religious are among the most difficult of her life. In the midst of everything she felt sure would make her radiantly happy, she is desolate, lonely, restless, and almost despairing. Her director is taken from her; her superior who had hitherto been her guiding model becomes a further source of distress for her; above all, her twelve-year-old son is an unending source of anguish.

These are strange years; years which, it would seem, God used to test the strength of His own graces to her, and also years which prepare her for what is to come. How often, in those long bleak hours in which she could not pray, she must have wandered in her own past, admiring and envying a little that lively young widow, Madame Martin, overwhelmed by graces, longing for humiliations, and convinced that nothing could be difficult in the service of God. How often, too, she must have looked ahead, wondering what would come of it all, trying to believe in the sufficiency of God's grace, desperately trying to live one day at a time lest peering into the future she might be tempted to despair.

But out of these years emerged the religious whom God destined to be His first woman missionary in that strange land, "terrible yet pitiful," which men called Canada. Hers was indeed a unique vocation demanding unique graces. Having broken the bonds of convention by leaving her widowhood (and with it her small son) to enter an enclosed convent, she was called upon to break further bonds to prove to all the world that a cloistered nun might, in God's plan, become in actual fact a missionary.

Her definitive entrance into the missionary vocation seems to have taken place in December of 1633 with her mysterious dream vision in which she saw before her the valleys and mountains of a "vast and lonely" country. What the country was, or what her relationship to it was to be, she was not told; this was to be a secret for another three years until in 1636 God Himself revealed His designs: "It is Canada that I have shown you; you must go there and build a home for Jesus and Mary."[1]

Thus became more clearly defined the apostolic goal for which God destined her. She had long felt the stirrings of a spiritual apostolate in her soul. Such a spirit was already alive when she had turned from the purely contemplative life of the Carmelites and Feuillantines and begged entrance in the monastery in La Rue de Poitou. She had chosen the Ursulines because "the salvation of souls" was dear to her; and she saw in the Ursuline rule the opportunity to teach others the secrets with which God had already filled her. But with the dream of the unknown land, her apostolic spirit grew so strong that she could not restrain it, and she who had formerly wanted nothing but to bury herself in God now found that when she came to Him it was with children hidden in her arms, clinging to her habit, pulling at her veil—as though she had assumed the motherhood of the souls of all the world:

> My body was in our monastery, but my spirit, re-united to that of Jesus, could not remain shut up there. This apostolic spirit carried me in thought to the Indies, to Japan, to America, to the East and to the West, to the most inaccessible northern countries —in short, to every part of the inhabited world where there were rational souls who belong by right to Jesus Christ.[2]

Three more years were to pass before her dreams and aspirations became a reality. It was not until May of 1639 that Marie, accompanied by her two Ursuline companions, sailed from Dieppe for New France. In the months preceding her departure, her abandonment to the Divine Will was sorely tested. Not only did opposition and misunderstanding overwhelm her, but God tested her interiorly with spiritual trials which, as she wrote, she found far more painful than any suffering inflicted by human beings. Marie was to undertake her apostolic mission stripped of illusions; the sense of glamour, of romance, of adventure which might gild the experience for younger hearts was wrenched away, and instead she saw "crosses without end." It was God Himself who promised her that instead of spiritual consolations she would find only interior desolation; instead of respect and gratitude from those for whom she gave her life, her reward would be coldness and misunderstanding; instead of success she would be fed the bitter fruit of hidden and obscure labour.

And in actual fact such was her life during the thirty years that remained to her. Not indeed that such years were without their joys: her happiness at the first baptism she witnessed at the completion of their new monastery and at the zeal and courage of the religious whom she governed, was inexpressible. There was immense gratitude at the moment when she received word of her son's entrance into the Benedictine Order and his subsequent ordination. There was, as she heard news of the martyrdom of Fathers de Brébeuf and Lalemant, the wistful hope that some day, perhaps, such a grace might also be accorded her. But this grace, so ardently desired, was denied her, and she died in obscurity as God had promised—the simple, peaceful, "ordinary" death of a tired missionary who had become a little lame, a little blind in her work for the salvation of souls.

In speaking of Marie's "mystic evolution" properly so called, one might safely conclude, then, with the year 1627. For close to a decade God had overwhelmed her with extraordinary graces, graces which formed and purified her contemplative soul until it was the perfect instrument of the Divine Will. Yet the instrument is fashioned not for passivity but for action, and following the years of testing came the period when every portion of her delicately fashioned soul and body was employed for God's service. Perhaps nowhere do we find a clearer example of the training of an apostle as well as an illustration of the true apostolic spirit: a spirit which is simply the necessary overflow of the contemplative life. Should we feel that this point is too strongly made; that the suggested dichotomy between Marie's early contemplative life in France and the later apostolic life of Canada does not in actual fact exist, Our Lord's own words will suggest that this is not so. Before Marie's departure for New France, Our Lord spoke to her, warning her of what was before her and concluding with a command which is manifest proof of the point which has been suggested: "Go, and serve Me now at your own expense; go, and give Me proof of the fidelity which you owe Me in return for the great graces which I have already given you."[1]

Her cup had been filled very early in life, but the process of emptying it lasted for over forty years. In 1672 the cup was "empty" at last and as her religious gathered about her deathbed asking for a share in her prayers, she could only murmur, "I have nothing left; it has all been given away."

[1] *Vie*, p. 378.

24. JEAN-JOSEPH SURIN

Michel de Certeau

JEAN-JOSEPH SURIN was born at Bordeaux in 1600. He entered the Society of Jesus in 1616 and at the end of his period of training, he came under the influence of Père Lallemant, whose teaching he treasured. His health was poor. He was first sent to Marennes in the district of Saintonge, then in 1634 to Loudun as exorcist. Here in an atmosphere of nervous excitability he became so worn out by excessive strain that he contracted a mental illness which he attributed to the devil. This obsession with the devil and despondency lasted for nearly twenty years. When at last he was freed from this trial, which had already been marked by extraordinary graces, he began writing the works which made him one of the foremost French spiritual writers.

Surin's output was considerable, but for the most part still needs careful editing.[1] An incisive lucidity marks all his writings. It is not strictly speaking an insight of a psychological order, nor the fruit of a profound scholarship, but is essentially an understanding that comes of experience, an unerring recognition of what is true and what is false. The accuracy of Surin's diagnosis is accompanied by a clear, absolute and passionate choice of God, which enables him, in all the circumstances of daily life, to distinguish between the helps and hindrances to love, and to unravel what is from God and what is not. Heart and head are inspired by the same singleness of purpose. Surin's thought flashes and cuts like a diamond. His love is violent: that is the soul of his clarity.

Surin built no theological system, and he did not attempt any abstract description of interior states of soul. He kept to the realm

---

[1] Apart from the first two volumes of his *Lettres* (ed. 1926 and 1928) the *Fondements* (ed. 1930), the *Questions sur l'Amour* (ed. 1930) and the *Poésies* (ed. 1957) the following works are quoted either from older editions or from manuscript: *Guide Spirituelle, La Science Experimentale, Le Triomphe de l'Amour, Les Dialogues, Le Catéchisme Spirituel*, and the remaining letters.

of facts, and in this way tried to present an experimental science
of the spiritual life. His aim was to trace its logical structure in
the successive phenomena which the soul experiences and which
mark the development of a human life created by God. For the
mystery of the human personality is also the mystery of divine
action. The problem of man is therefore placed in the context of
man's own life, itself an infinite gift and source of a true love.
This teaching is not peculiar to Surin, but he adopted it with a
special emphasis, expressed it in illuminating language, and above
all lived it with an exceptional intensity. Here was a soul who had
visited the frontiers of human experience, and had experienced
the depths of madness and despair and the inaccessible heights
which are known to us only through the accounts written by
mystics. He was an eye-witness from unexplored regions, where
few have ventured, an explorer into the abyss both of his own
nothingness and the divine indwelling. His extraordinary
experience gave clarity to a truth that is a commonplace of the
Christian life; and he saw it with an intensity that can hardly
be imagined by those whose experience is ordinary. He had run
the risk of utter failure and had known the extreme of ecstasy
and despair; now he perceived in all its purity the internal
dialectic of the soul's meeting with God. There can be no doubt
that this is the ultimate reason for the clarity we find in Surin.
His message deals with the absolute, and he knows what he is
talking about. But before sketching his doctrine, it will be as
well, perhaps, to recall his life.

In 1656 Père Surin occupied a room in the infirmary in
an out-of-the-way corner of the thriving Jesuit College at
Bordeaux. His colleagues were esteemed and were responsible
for the education of the most brilliant and well-to-do pupils of
the town. Surin was confined to the house by the mental sickness
which had crippled him for nearly twenty years. On the evening
of 9 June, as he was standing beside his bed, he was (so he tells us)
again seized by the thought that haunted him, "Tu es damné."

> This thought began to cause me great distress, and I felt a strong
> stirring of the heart which made me resigned to this state, if it
> should be the will of God. I uttered these words, I desire it, if God
> desires it, and I buried my face in the bedclothes to mark my total
> submission to the divine will.

Though without hope he did not renounce his love. He wished

at least to acquiesce in the Almighty's inscrutable design, but his practice of abandonment united him to the God he thought he had lost. In his own words, "From then on I seemed to feel within me a second wave which submerged and engulfed me and brought peace to my soul."[1]

This episode marked the beginning of his cure. His behaviour is typical of the man. He was divided between the obsession haunting his mind, and the deeper spiritual movement which comes from the heart. In him, the "Thou" and the "I" confront each other. Although the prospect of damnation is presented as certain ("Thou art damned"), yet the voice condemning him is not his own, ("Thou"). When he reflects on damnation, the idea becomes a mere hypothesis (If God desires it)—the limiting case of a love which knows no limits. Such a dichotomy is a sign of sickness, but even in his sickness a deeper self comes to the surface ("I desire it"). Surin no longer tries to carry absurdity to the lengths of committing suicide. He faces up to the psychological fact of his misfortune and accepts it. This acceptance is not something purely passive, it is an offering of self and stems from something more radical than despair. His indomitable desire to remain united to God, whatever the cost, gives the lie to the apparent acceptance of his loss. It transforms the whole psychological situation and reduces what seemed a fixed decree to the status of hypothesis. The soul is open to the mystical "flood"; the divine presence within him takes possession of a soul that is thus intent on appointing no limits to the gift of himself. From now on the powerful wave welling up from the depths of the Godhead will gradually wear away the superficial split in his personality which is the outward sign of his madness.

This crisis marked the turning point in the malady whose origins Surin had analysed with great clarity and which he regarded as diabolic possession. He wrote in 1635:

It is as though I had two souls, one of which is evicted from my body and deprived of the use of its organs, and which stands on one side to watch an intruder at work. I am conscious of being damned, and dread it. I feel myself pierced with shafts of despair in an alien soul which seems to be mine, while my other soul is full of confidence, mocking the feelings of dread, and perfectly free to reprove their author.[2]

[1] *Lettres* 2, 66-7.   [2] *Lettres* 1, 127.

U

It is probably correct to diagnose this as a case of psychosis: dispossession of self, morbid hypersexuality, obsession, and hallucinations akin to persecution mania. But it is impossible to doubt that for nearly twenty years Surin suffered from a dual personality. Whatever the precise nature of his malady, and the circumstances attending his cure, it is certain that extraordinary graces and a great holiness of life existed along with his morbid condition. Surin's sincerity when he describes the graces he has received, cannot be called in question. The precise account he gives of them, as well as his behaviour as a religious, his apostolic charity and his spiritual teaching, put their authenticity beyond doubt.

After this long period of trial he felt the need to give expression to the truth he had experienced. His was not the desire to reach a wide public, for he did not foresee that his work might one day be published. But he felt an urge to describe a truth which had rescued him from his obsessions and opened his soul to the action of God's infinite presence. At first he was incapable of writing himself, so he dictated the first books of his *Spiritual Catechism* ("Like a trumpet" was his own phrase, and it was surely a hymn of victory). This was not a personal memoir but an enunciation of the Truth and the Way that leads to it. He adopted the dialogue form spontaneously, both because every catechism makes use of question and answer, and because this method served to prolong his interior experiences. The answers were also a witness to the victory which God had won over his anxiety of soul.

The blessings he had received were to benefit many others. In telling of the ways in which divine love works he had already helped to make these ways better known, for his books were soon widely circulated. Surin, an apostle by vocation and by temperament, was eager to set others on fire with his own zeal. He wanted to set all Christians on the path along which he had been led and enlist them all in the same crusade. From the first moment he was able to leave his house, until his death in 1665, this indomitable little man limped his way along the roads of France to preach in convents and country villages the theme of love.

No one consecrates himself to God without making a complete

break with his past. "Every good *habit* calls at first for violence."[1]
It is this "foundation of the spiritual life," which Père Lallemant
calls "second conversion" and Surin "the first step." It consists
of a *determined resolve* to refuse God nothing, to do *everything* in
one's power to meet all His wishes. However good a man may
be, anything he does before taking this resolve is strictly speaking
outside the scope of the spiritual life.[2] There is no spiritual life,
no life that is to say, animated by love and holiness, without a
"leap"[3] marking the transition from the relative to the absolute.
Where it is a case of all or nothing, the beginning must be of the
same nature as the end proposed—namely, universal and absolute.
A man must fix no limits to God's claims if he is to correspond
to His limitless essence.

Here a parallel may be drawn with philosophy. For Descartes,
the *point de départ* is universal doubt; for Hegel the resolve to
throw oneself headlong into philosophy. In the same way the
soul can set out on the search for God only in a spirit of complete
submission. He must place himself and his whole life entirely at
God's disposal The absolute character of the undertaking calls
for a correspondingly absolute disposability on the part of the
subject. Surin never tires of harping on this point; "I have but
one theme-song—empty the heart of everything."[4] "God does
not want half-hearted determination. He wants whole-heartedness with no back-sliding."[5] "Some things have got to be done
at one stroke. It is no use deliberating and putting them off; if
you start making conditions and compromises, you achieve
nothing.[6] Sticking to the maxims I mentioned—complete self-
renunciation—is a case in point."[7] Surin is well aware that any
reservation, however slight, on a question of principle does more
than set a limit to one's abandonment to God; it completely
alters one's whole spiritual attitude. "To win everything you
must lose everything: to keep back even a *little* is enough to
miss the *whole* prize."[8] The Christian who is ready to do everything, but with certain reservations, is not really ready to do
everything. He is a complete non-starter. "Throw aside this

---

[1] *Dialogues 1, 15.*   [2] *Fondements 5, 11.* (The italics throughout are mine).
[3] *Questions 1, 2.*   [4] *Letter,* late 1660 to Madame du Houx.
[5] *Letter* to Madame de la Chèze.
[6] Surin goes on to add: "People who make compromises only want to do
things by half."
[7] Letter to Anne Buignon, 1 July 1660.   [8] *Lettres 1, 264.*

half-service then, since the law demands everything. In other words, the perfection of the law demands that God should be *everything* to man, that Christ should be *everything* to the Christian.[1] The absolute character of this resolve shows itself in its immediacy. When once the soul has recognised God for what He is, no room is left for the many-sided claims of existence in time. Only a total and immediate renunciation can correspond to God's eternal omnipotence. Not that the self-renunciation is immediately effective, but the initial offer must be. "I mean that the desire must be formed all at once, though the carrying out of the desire is gradual."[2]

If this desire is lacking, spiritual writings are useless. For their whole purpose is to throw light on the stages of a spiritual progress that only begins with this firm resolution. Hence Surin frequently declares that he will keep in written touch only with those souls that are resolute. If they have taken the resolution he will spare no pains to help them; if not, his words go for nothing. It is unfortunately just this quality of decision which is so often lacking in souls who propose to give themselves to God, and who have not in fact weighed the seriousness of the choice they have made. "Most men are 'hesitating' and lack the firm resolve to do good. The enterprise calls for all men's energies, and they set to work with feeble hearts . . . Truly their salvation is in jeopardy. For when there is such a mixture of evil and good in their lives, when their allegiance is so divided, can one say that they have chosen God for their master?"[3] As a result they are incapable, not indeed of doing what is right, but of receiving all that God has in store for them and of fulfilling all that He wishes to achieve in and through them. Hence the vehemence with which Surin seeks for whole-heartedness, a vehemence which leads to his uncompromising attitude and tears off the mask from any "pusillanimity."[4]

Surin will never consent to "leave the field of battle."[5] Nor does he minimise the dangers of the rules of this "war." "The time is short, the task is great . . . You have only to give yourself to the love of Jesus Christ. Take this step with determination, make a generous effort, set your heart free, free from all attachment."[6]

---

[1] Letter to Anne Buignon, 1 July 1660.   [2] *Ibid.*   [3] *Dialogues* I, 11.
[4] *Lettres* I, 137.   [5] *Lettres* I, 170.   [6] *Lettres* I, 209.

It is a "hot-war" with many "knocks."[1] Surin is full of military metaphors—the need of courage in fighting the enemy, references to castles, victory, crusades. Death is a very real risk, for the scale of this war is measured by God's grandeur, and that says everything.

> Give yourself to Him and to His rule in your heart. Surrender all your rights . . . allow Him to strip you of everything . . . to separate you from everything . . . to tear you apart from yourself. His task is to destroy, to ravage, to strip and then to refashion, restore and replace. He is wonderfully terrible and wonderfully gentle. The more terrible He is the more desirable and attractive will He be. In the way He works, He is like a king at the head of His army, before whom everything must give way, yet His sweetness is so winning that it melts all hearts. He only desires subjects in order to share His kingdom with them. If He dares everything, it is to communicate Himself without limit. When He separates, His purpose is to unite to Himself those He has separated from the rest of the world. He asks everything and gives everything. Nothing can satisfy Him, and yet He is content with but a little, for He stands in need of nothing.[2]

"Hardiness" is the first requirement.[3] Then follow nakedness of heart and liberty of soul. After a soul has taken the first step, he must stand fast by the decision he has made. That decision may still stand with a great deal of hidden *amour-propre*. But from now on the man whose mind is made up hungers after lucidity. He wants to carve a way through the mixed motives which are found in all actions. Because he aims at truth, he recognises "the mixture of spirits within himself."[4] "The devil always mingles his own activity with that of God."[5] This is the period of discernment. It is at this stage that Surin places all his knowledge of spiritual things at the disposal of his readers and of souls under his direction. He helps them to unravel the secret contradictions in their deepest desire, to "unmask"[6] all their pretexts, and "oust the involuntary reluctance that disguises itself under high-flown sentiments."[7]

For a man truly to give up self-satisfaction, he must prefer God in everything. This is certainly the best way of showing his love. Everything must "tend towards God."[8] Hence it is the

[1] *Lettres* 1, 132.   [2] *Questions* 1, 7.   [3] *Lettres* 1, 201.   [4] *Lettres* 2, 127.
[5] *Lettres* 2, 120.   [6] *Lettres* 1, 190.   [7] *Lettres* 1, 191.   [8] *Questions* 1, 3.

intention rather than the nature of the action which Surin keeps constantly in view. After all is he not dealing with resolute souls; these do not have to be reminded of what the law forbids. But Surin also knows that selfish motives can inspire even the best of actions; while every action not in itself evil can be performed for love. From such a point of view spiritual formation becomes essentially a purification of motives.

"Which way does the heart tend?"[1] is now the fundamental question, and its purpose is not to bring the soul, now in ecstasy before the object of its love, down to earth again; it is rather to confront the object of desire with the ultimate goal of all desire, and so to bring about an interior *dépassement*. This is the road that leads gradually into the "realm of pure love."[2] Activity is now defined by its "purity," which consists in a rightly-directed love, an abandonment of self, and a desire to please God and share in His interests. It is characterised in "doing everything purely for God."[3] More explicitly, the motive of "God" is so pure that the soul is at pains to act solely because "His glory is at stake."[4]

The true scope of this doctrine comes out in its paradoxical nature. "I count all things as dung that I may gain Christ;" and yet this unique love does not exclude love for mankind. "We must so regulate our conduct towards our neighbour that we are ready to die for him and at the same time be prepared to look on him as our enemy."[5] Our neighbour is worth the sacrifice of life in so far as he is the object of divine love in which the Christian shares. He is our enemy to the extent that any attachment to him leads us away from our true destiny, namely, the Godhead who unites all men in Himself. Love of God and love of our neighbour do not conflict. The one embraces the other. The first is universal, the second particular. Divine love is the foundation of human love, which can have no other foundation. This intermingling of human and divine is the essence of the Gospel message.

However, it is possible for an opposition to exist at the level of a man's motives. God's primacy will then call for a painful separation from creatures. Contradiction besets the soul whose love is divided between two objectives and is unable to recognise their fundamental unity. For this reason unity features prominently in any pedagogy of the spiritual conscience, while it plays a very

---

[1] *Questions* 1, 7.   [2] *Questions* 2, 2.   [3] *Questions* 1, 5.   [4] *Ibid.*   [5] *Lettres* 1, 19.

minor role in the theology of love. Surin's whole aim is to eradicate this division from the soul, until it is able to concentrate entirely on God and seize upon all love in Him.

"Love is a powerful stream from God."[1] In man "purity" is the result of a union effected within a love that streams from God. In other words, it is an exact balance between the particular and the universal, the finite and the infinite. And so, after the necessary separation, Surin is all in favour of the soul abandoning itself to God's hands and practising the presence of God rather than making a frontal attack against particular attachments. Since everything that takes place ultimately manifests the will of God, nothing is fundamentally indifferent to a love that seeks Him alone. The important thing is not to leave everything, but to find God.

The same holds for the gifts which come to a faithful soul through its love of God. Is this love disinterested? If it is, should it go to the lengths of renouncing all reward and even the prospect of salvation? This question was to become one of the key problems of Quietism, and Surin dealt with it firmly. On the one hand, there are the favours which God showers on those who love Him: He is infinite fullness and plenty, and opens the "treasure-house of spiritual richness"[2] to those who are His own.

"Whatever you give up will soon be yours a hundred times over."[3] The benefits which Surin promises those who pray and seek for God are joy and happiness. "Blessed are they . . . ," this is the burden of his song. On the other hand, these favours depend on a single condition—the soul must love God for Himself. As soon as the soul in its love of God looks for anything beyond God, it can no longer claim to love Him above all else. It makes no difference if the desired gifts are those normally conferred on the faithful. There is of course no blame attached to hoping for these events, but it is an imperfection, a misunderstanding of the soul's true goal. "So, when the soul has reached the stage of looking only to God"—reached, that is, to pure love—"God *fills* her with His fullness, and the soul cries out 'My God and my all.' " This is true happiness. "But if the soul fixes her heart, however slightly, on any creature apart from God," by showing attachment to gifts which are not referred back to God—"then she cannot utter this cry quite sincerely."[4]

[1] *Questions* 1, 1.   [2] *Questions* 3, 1.   [3] *Questions* 3, 2.   [4] *Questions* 1, 5.

Pure love leads to a "dilation of soul," to a detachment from one's own interests, together with an interior expansion of the soul in God. To recognise the particular as a manifestation of the universal is not to deny existence to the particular, it is rather a refusal to look upon the particular as being everything, and is a corresponding acceptance of God through whatever particular medium He chooses to reveal Himself. Pure love is so true to this way of looking at things that it gives them all their true meaning; it never loses itself away from God. "God is enough for you. Be poor, and do not waste your time looking to see if all is going well."[1] To embroil oneself in petty considerations[2] is further self-love, and there is nothing worse than a heart whose horizon is bounded by trifles.[3] Nothing is to be gained by getting angry with oneself and concentrating on personal worries and interests; this only diverts from God the attention which He really deserves. It is His business to cure and to compensate; we have His word for it. "Be patient then and carry the cross of your natural impurity"[4] and you will be free to give all your attention to God. Purity of heart means just this. "Keep yourself free," Surin repeats again and again, "in order to love and fear God Himself. You will find all in Him who is all."

> Sometimes when good and pure souls have had a long apprentice-ship in love, and have made frequent efforts to find Our Lord in all things, He will actually let them feel His presence and the workings of His grace within them. This feeling is so strong that we can call it the testimony of the Holy Spirit, who assures them that theirs is the good fortune to be numbered among the children of God. This recalls the saying of St. John in his epistle "He who believes in the Son of God has the testimony of God in himself."[5]

The interior presence of the Holy Spirit is the source of all spiritual life. It reveals itself gradually to those who lose themselves in order to lay themselves open to the activity of divine life, and is manifest in that cry which takes possession of our whole being, "Abba, Father." "With this testimony we are certain, in the darkness of faith here below, that our soul belongs to God and resides in God."[6] It is not that this conviction claims to anticipate the end of our existence in time nor God's definitive

[1] *Lettres* I, 202.   [2] *Ibid.*   [3] *Dialogues* I, II, 3.   [4] *Lettres* I, 204.
[5] *Questions* I, 2.   [6] *Questions* I, 2.

judgment. It is rather a deepening faith that experiences mutual love in a spirit of filial piety.

The final degree of this "continual and vital communication between God and the soul"[1] becomes substantial in the mystical alliance of the Eucharist, the *Mysterium fidei*.[2] But even in its higher levels this is not so much a direct experience of God as the rapturous awareness of His approach. It is a "divine experience," but not an experience of God. "The divine touch spoken of by the mystics is a supernatural *notion* through which the soul grasps what God is like, not as a result of seeing, but of touching Him." More precisely, "as a result of this divine experience, which is the chief fruit of purity, the soul receives an impression of God and also of the gifts of this purity to which He has raised it."[3] The soul is drawn powerfully towards God, altogether captivated by the feeling of His infinite and overflowing presence. The "divine purity" which defines this outburst of love is the inexpressible echo of the divine visitation. "I should not have desired Thee, hadst Thou not first found me." These words, in a context of immediate awareness, sum up the soul's experience which is founded on the Incarnation of the Word and the descent of the Holy Spirit; in short, on the approach of God.

Mystical theology for Surin consists in this experimental knowledge of God. It is a tasting and perception of His "interior presence" awakened by His conversing with the soul. Surin often refers to it as a "universal and confused notion." By "notion" he means not a communion with the act of God, for this would involve complete identification with God Himself, but a welling-up of the spirit after it is brought face to face with Him. A completely novel experience, it is human in character, yet is connected with the engulfing presence of God.

A reference at this point to Origen's "Image" or to the "Eternal Idea" of St. Augustine may help to explain Surin's "notion." It is a source of knowledge rather than its object. It represents a movement towards a goal rather than its attainment; it is not a particular idea, because this awareness of "divinisation" is the very "form" of the experience. Hence its claim to be "universal." "It is like a jet directed from the heart of God on to the tiny heart of man and completely engulfing it"[4]—a "confused" notion

---

[1] *Questions* 3, 7.   [2] *Questions* 3, 8.   [3] *Questions* 3, 6.   [4] *Questions* 3, 10.

precisely in that it has no definite content, but is the basic principle of all religious knowledge. At the same time it is also a "clear" notion to the extent that it is the original datum of every religious intuition. One can regàrd it as the Idea of Infinity seized in the very movement that leads to God.

Surin also speaks of it as an immediate perception of the *coincidentia oppositorum* in God—for instance His Power and His Meekness. "When these two qualities come together in a point, they form a lightning flash that fills the soul with brightness."[1] But the clash of two ideas will not produce such a flash. It is the obscure yet somehow dazzling perception by the creature of its relation to God, or, to be more exact, of that relation between God and himself which shines through the spiritual condition of mankind. It is the "disproportion between the soul's lowly being and the divine Being of God, pursuing and consuming it with majesty and love."[2] This ontological experience recognises God through man's worth in God and for what God can make of him. The existential experience of this relation to God coincides with knowledge of God. Alongside the divine Being the mystic is a being faced with death (*être-pour-la-mort*), yet a being who is loved. At the level of existence he acquires an immediate and in some sort *a priori* knowledge of this "harmony of extremes."[3] God's majesty and mercy; in a word, His infinity. From now on this "universal and confused notion" will set a permanent seal on the life of the mystic. It is the interior form, the fundamental category of that life.

Surin's own philosophical formation and the general state of scholasticism in his day explain the vigour with which he defended this essential and immediate knowledge against the attacks of those he depreciatingly calls "the philosophers."[4] With a violent shading off at times into indignation and irony he assails those closed minds who admit as true knowledge only that which proceeds from distinct ideas and from successive conclusions. To their syllogisms and ideas of "understanding" (*entendement*) he opposes his interior awareness and the notions of the "intellect" (*l'intelligence*). This opposition is not merely the characteristic of Surin's whole conception of religious knowledge. It must also be attributed to the type of philosophy he had studied. For the

---

[1] *Questions* 3, 10.   [2] *Ibid.*   [3] *Ibid.*
[4] This is the main theme of the *Guide Spirituelle.*

opponents of mysticism, like the Carmelite Chéron, wanted to retain from their master St. Thomas only his theory of abstract ideas derived from sensation. They neglected certain key passages in the *De Veritate* which deal with interior illumination and the treatment Thomas gives of the gift of Wisdom and of the Beatitudes. It seems that Surin never read the works of any theologian who understood the nature of the problem with which he was dealing. These shortcomings in his theological background show themselves in the over-psychological character of his analyses. But this does not prove that his critics were right. He was up against "doctors who can believe something only if it has first been through the mill of their syllogisms,"[1] who could see in mystics only incoherent praters, writers of nonsense fit merely for ignorant women, devotees of enthusiasm and melancholy whom a good bowl of porridge would soon cure of their hallucinations. Looking back on this one-sided dialogue, one is left wondering, a little wistfully, what would have been the outcome of a meeting between Surin and Malebranche.

It is obvious that the problems raised by the corpus of Surin's writings cannot be settled within the limits of an article. One thing is clear. Surin's work must not be judged in terms of its author's mental illness. To suspect a man's writings *a priori* because he was unwell mentally would be both unjust and mistaken. For one thing, Surin had recovered by the time he wrote the greater number of his books. Also, in spite of his illness, he received an abundance of the highest graces, while in passing judgment on his own condition he always remained perfectly lucid. Finally, his work forms an objective whole whose truth must be considered on its own merits. Only when this has been done does it become possible to assess the consequences of the writer's misfortune. A number of clues to the nature and history of Surin's case are to be found in his writings. But the writings themselves, which were examined minutely before publication, do not appear to be tainted with any doctrinal deviation.[2]

The trenchant character of his teaching is the aspect which

[1] *Questions* 3, 6.
[2] The Italian translation of the *Catéchisme Spirituelle* was later in 1687 put on the Index because of the use made of it by the Quietists of Naples.

seems most to recall his illness. At first sight he appears to leave out of all account the slow passage of time. "I find that God places the soul outside the bonds of time."[1] Although this expression is used in an offhand manner in one of his letters, it seems to bring out a leading idea of Surin's. We have seen how the "first step" must be instantaneous; the heart must remain fixed in a purity which is the mysterious forerunner of future happiness. The "universal and confused notion" is the perception of a union with God which remains the unique foundation for all spiritual life. Throughout his writing the absolute is regarded as outside time. But this is surely always the case when questions are raised about being. For Surin, whose mystical passion inevitably reminds one of Pascal's metaphysical passion, the temptation was to confound the perception with the nature of the absolute. But as his destiny unfolds itself, he was led to embrace anew the common "order" which God had made his own. The logic of the *coincidentia oppositorum*, the glowing content of his "mystical theology," recalled him to the "simplicity of the common way"[2] in which the highest coincides with the lowest. As a country missioner, who fostered devotions which we would think childish, he came to insist more and more on the state of faith which "does away with the impress of anything that could be called extraordinary, to lodge us in the common usages and run of life."[3]

In all this he was impelled by the depth of his mystical experience. His humility is part of the mystery surging over him. "Although these waters roar mightily when one is in them, they flow for all that in secret channels."[4] Thus it is that the interior mystery re-enacts to the full the mystery of God. The voice of the mystic enters into the silence of the Presence which is beyond reach, yet granted to all.

[1] *Lettres* 2, 197.   [2] Letter 11 April 1662.   [3] *Ibid.*   [4] Letter 7 May 1662.

25. JEAN PIERRE DE CAUSSADE

George Scott-Moncrieff

ALTHOUGH HE DIED only two hundred years ago, Jean Pierre de Caussade has left us practically without detailed information about his life. Only the barest facts are recorded. He was born in 1675, entered the Jesuit novitiate for the province of Toulouse when he was eighteen, taught classics, did his theological studies, was ordained in 1705 and took his final vows three years later. For the next six years he taught grammar, physics and logic, and was thereafter preacher and confessor in various parts of France before returning to Toulouse in 1740. The following year saw the appearance of the only book that he wrote as such, and even this was published anonymously so that it was commonly supposed to be the work of his fellow-Jesuit Paul-Gabriel Antoine, well known as a writer on Moral Theology. In the same year Caussade became Rector of the College of Perpignan. In 1744 he was Rector at Albi. In 1746 he returned to Toulouse and was director of the theological students there until his death in 1751.

Active and useful as it was, it is a life that remains lost in the obscurity of daily duties, a personal immolation entirely in keeping with Caussade's own teaching. Yet he lived at a time of painful disputes that had begun to disrupt the Christian world before his birth and that were still active sources of contention at the time of his death.

Even in the great days of the Spanish mystics anxiety over tendencies to quietism, an oriental inactivity passively awaiting the divine direction, had stirred an opposition that, whatever its justification, could become hysterical to the point of malevolence. St. John of the Cross himself was flung into prison by the Calced Carmelites of Toledo, and all he had written by that date, 1577, destroyed. Thereafter his writings were subject to suppression, destruction and to lavish interpolation, the addition of material that sometimes made nonsense of his whole thesis, in order to place it beyond suspicion. Nor could the writings of St. Teresa of Avila be published until after her death. The gifted Augustinian author, Luis de Leon, spent five years in the prisons of the Inquisition for an inoffensive exposition of the *Song of Songs* and was thereafter tragically inhibited in what he wrote. Even the *Spiritual Exercises* of St. Ignatius were under suspicion for illuminism, and the savagely anti-mystical Inquisitor, Melchior Cano, tried his best to have them condemned. Indeed, it was hardly safe for St. Ignatius to revisit his own country.

It was rather later, and from rather a different direction, that the wave of anti-mysticism hit France, although it received stimulus from the condemnation in Rome of the Spaniard Molinos in 1685 (although Molinos' *Spiritual Guide* was not actually published in France until later, under Protestant auspices). The main disputes were of course between the Jansenists, who in their antipathy to contemplation exploited the condemnation of Molinos, and the Jesuits, and between Fénelon and Bossuet. The development of Cartesian thought, with its emphasis upon rational introspection, was detrimental to the mystical approach to religion. This more psychological consideration of human motivation might usefully disperse much that was mere ignorance, but at a certain point it was liable to treat religion itself as ignorance. St. Francis de Sales illustrates in his development first the psychological approach, admirably exemplified in the *Introduction to the Devout Life*, and then, after he had been influenced, although not without initial misgivings, by St. Jane Frances de Chantal, the more mystical approach of *The Love of God*.

Madame Guyon, the wealthy widow whose undoubted proficiency in mystical forms of prayer influenced Fénelon, was a somewhat over-ardent type of lay missionary whose excesses, coupled with the jealousies and suspicions of others, finally brought the whole quietist dispute to a head. Fénelon, Archbishop of Cambrai, a profounder and more impressive person altogether, supported her, and laid himself open to the attack of the powerful and brilliant Bishop of Meaux, Bossuet. Their dispute has become a matter of history. Whatever justice may have been on the side of Bossuet, the moralist, it is Fénelon, the mystic, who comes out of the affair better, for Bossuet certainly acted unscrupulously in publishing private documents and being prepared to indulge in defamation if not even calumny. But it should not be hard for us to realise today the dangers that he was opposing: dangers of illuminism, private revelation, and all the squalor and hysteria of false mysticism.

He attacked these in a long and very learned treatise on prayer. This proved effective against the quietists, but it could also be used as a weapon against truly mystical prayer. There was a tendency amongst the moralists to segregate the mystics formally recognised and canonised by the Church and to treat them as a people apart, a people granted special graces by God whose teaching and way of life were not for everyman. At its worst this attitude could become tinged with Pelagianism; but even short of that it tended to discourage any intimate prayer of surrender to God. Behind it lay the fear that Christians might "bypass" the Incarnation, and allow certain self-induced states to dominate their spiritual lives. Yet it is plain that such mystics as St. John of the Cross, even without the editing of his writings, never departed from essential Christian doctrine for all his particular emphasis upon the nothingness that man can bring to the divine union.

Jean Pierre de Caussade's one deliberate entry into print was directly inspired by, indeed based on, Bossuet's great controversial treatise on the various states of prayer. But Caussade's contribution was not controversial. It was an effort to correct some of the stigma that overflowed from the vehemence of Bossuet's attack on false mysticism to the prejudice of truly mystical prayer. As Fr. Louis Cognet puts it, "Rightly observing that in his practice of direction the bishop of Meaux had proved far more favourable to mysticism than might have been expected, Fr. de Caussade drew from the Instruction of 1697 a complete theory of the interior life, of a type on the whole very like Fénelon's." But he adds, "This ingenious and paradoxical plea does not seem to have met with great success."

Caussade maintains that he himself learnt from Bossuet not only to detest false mysticism but also to value true mysticism. At the same time, in eighteenth-century France when the Jesuits were the object of attack from many bitter enemies, it was certainly shrewd of him to put forward his ideas under the umbrella of Bossuet. If his book met with no great success at the time, at least it was spared attack or suppression.

Besides his treatise *On Prayer* Caussade left a considerable number of letters, almost all addressed to nuns, which have been collected and published; but his masterpiece is the little book *L'Abandon à la Providence Divine*. Even this was not written by him for publication but compiled by a nun of the Visitation from letters and conferences. Here, it may be argued, we only have Caussade's teaching at secondhand; but much the same might be said of the treatise of Fr. Augustine Baker, *Sancta Sophia*, which is in fact compiled by another hand. Nor were the *Dialogues* of St. Catherine of Genoa actually written by her. We may properly credit the authorship of *Abandon* to Caussade, with due credit to the nun who compiled it and to Fr. P. H. Ramière, S.J., who, in the last century, reassembled the material in the form in which we now know it.

The late Dom John Chapman, Abbot of Downside, himself a much-revered director of souls, had the profoundest admiration for Caussade and refers to him in many of his letters, collected and published under the title *Spiritual Letters*. Writing the Introduction to the English edition of Caussade's book *On Prayer*, Abbot Chapman refers in particular to *L'Abandon à la Providence Divine* and traces Caussade's thought back to that of his spiritual father. He defines it thus:

The whole rule of our life is God's Will. At the last day we shal be judged according to our works. Our good works are those in accordance with God's Will at the moment we do them. They are our renunciation of self, they are the gift of ourselves to God. It is right to desire our own salvation and our own perfection, for this desire is a part of our nature. But we ought to desire it not only for our own sake, but still more for God's sake, because he wishes it, and made us for himself. Charity is not the love which wants to get (although that is good), but the love which wants to give, which is better; God's love can never want to get, but is always giving, always charity.

So our love is to be—a love which consists in giving ourselves to God. The active side is obedience to all God's commands, counsels, and inspirations; the passive side is the acceptance of all God does by *abandon*.

There is no English word for *abandon*, for "abandonment" is only just coming into use in this transferred sense. The doctrine is mere Christianity, and even Natural Religion; but it was formulated in a special way by St. Ignatius, who chose the word "indifference."

St. Francis de Sales took up St. Ignatius's teaching; he rejects such words as "conformity" (used by Scaramelli and others), or "resignation" (used by Fr. Baker), as less expressive than "indifference." St. Francis is perhaps ignorant of the word *abandon*, but this admirable word was used by the French writers of his generation and the next. De Caussade takes it from his master, Bossuet: *Abandon à la divine Providence*.

The doctrine, however, he has derived not so much from Bossuet as from his Father St. Ignatius, who begins and ends his exercises with this simple and sublime teaching: in the Foundation he lays it down dryly, with irresistible logic; in the final *Contemplatio ad amorem* he spiritualizes it as the conclusion of the whole retreat: *Sume et suscipe, Domine, universam meam libertatem. . . .*

In *Abandon* Caussade assumes his reader to have graduated by meditation to the need for a more intimate prayer and with it a more immediate practice of the life it inspires. What Caussade illustrates is not necessarily an exalted mysticism, it is simply that element of quiet in the Presence of God that must in greater or lesser degree become an integral part of man's personal approach to his Creator. It is the shedding of worries and of all worldliness which, even if only passingly realised, enables him to speak in silence, and thereby sometimes to apprehend the peace that passes understanding. Worries are rooted in past and future, we can only be liberated from them by accepting what Caussade has so tellingly defined as "the sacrament of the present moment." It is plain that if a man could live his life in constant reference to God's will the whole of that life would be sacramental. We sometimes get glimpses of what this could mean in the lives of the saints. To Caussade the old question whether the mystical approach is for everyone does not present difficulties if we see mystical prayer as not confined to the exaltation of the great mystics but simply as a necessary, often unconscious element; mystical in the proper sense of being the *hidden* part of our speaking to God. Although he stresses the need for an arduous preparation during which "God instructs the heart not by means of ideas, but by pains and contradictions," he declares "I wish to show all that they may lay claim, not to the same distinct favours, but to the same love, the same self-abandonment, the same God . . . and to eminent sanctity."

These and the following passages are quoted from Algar

x

Thorold's translation of *l'Abandon*, entitled in English *Self-Abandonment to Divine Providence*. To this translation another Benedictine writer, Dr. Knowles, contributed a valuable introduction in which he traces the influence of St. Francis de Sales and of St. John of the Cross upon Caussade's thought. Indeed, he considers Caussade's distinctive achievement to lie in making a synthesis of the Salesian and Carmelite traditions. Just as the effect of his association with St. Jane Frances de Chantal is evident in the development of Francis de Sales' thought, so Caussade's work amongst her spiritual daughters must as certainly have influenced him. If Caussade seems to have had little direct contact with the Carmelites, Dr. Knowles considers that "he alone of the great French spiritual writers superimposes on the Salesian teaching of self-abandonment and simplicity the typically Carmelite emphasis on grace as a dynamic force, enlightening and cleansing the soul." And Dom Roger Hudleston, in his Memoir of Abbot Chapman, defines it thus:

> The development peculiar to Caussade consists in this: that, while every soul which is really trying to live an interior life endeavours to do God's holy will always, everywhere and in all things, de Caussade insists that it best achieves its end, *not* by anxious search after God's "signified will" (*voluntas signi*), not by deliberate acts of resignation to his "will of good pleasure" (*voluntas beneplaciti*), but by simply receiving what comes to it, moment by moment, and abandoning itself thereto; accepting and *willing* everything because it comes as God's will for that soul *hic et nunc*, in this actual moment of time, which is the only moment in the soul's control.

Because of distrust of a suspected passivity in Caussade's advocacy of "abandon" he has been accused of encouraging a tendency to quietism. This was cogently refuted by Abbot Chapman who pointed out that Caussade's "abandon" to God's will was essentially active, not a form of resignation but an active willing, therefore an uniting of our own will with God's will. In Caussade's own words "the soul is active as far as concerned with her present duty, but passive and abandoned as regards all the rest, where her only action is to await in peace the divine motion." Abbot Chapman summarised this by saying that while we may never know God's will for us at any future moment of time, we may learn to discern His will for us for the present moment, the one and only thing of time that we can ever possess and make our own for good or evil. We may plan for the future, but our planning must be relaxed so that our knowledge that we have no certainty of its outcome may still be a happy acceptance.

Caussade's teaching, indeed, seems particularly well adapted to those living an active life, a life in the world. He carries asceticism the necessary stage further when he defines as a double process the reduction of all created things "First to nothing, and then to the point that they have to occupy in God's Order," for, "Since God is in all things, the use we make of them by His Order is not use of creatures but rather enjoyment of the divine action which dispenses its gifts through different channels."

This is intrinsically the same ideal as that of those who live their lives withdrawn from the world; of the anchoress, Julian of Norwich, who prayed: "God, of thy goodness, give me thyself: for thou art enough to me, and I may nothing ask that is less, that may be full worship to thee, and if I ask anything that is less, ever me wanteth,—but only in thee I have all."

For those in the world Caussade's definition makes it clear that to pray thus is not to aspire beyond anything they might ever hope to approach in their own lives, but simply to express the essence of the Christian longing. At the same time it controverts the approach of the Jansenists and of all who would make Christianity a cold, negative and puritanical creed in which creatures are of their nature a detraction from God, for it restores love of creation to its true place as part of the love of the Creator who himself loves the world divinely.

Such love, everlastingly exemplified in the Redeemer, entails suffering. With many beautiful and penetrating turns of phrase (and he is a recognised master of French prose) Caussade emphasises our need to accept the suffering incidental to our own lives, to strive for perfection through that acceptance lovingly made rather than to devise extraneous mortification. This, he says, is a true humility, the one-ing of ourselves with the Divine Will. And here he warns the soul against being "determined to action by ideas or tumults of words which by themselves merely inflate her." Purely natural reason must give way before faith, "the light of time," since "our understanding" which "wishes to take the first place among the divine methods . . . must be reduced to the last." Here we recognise in another context those nights and those clouds of unknowing of the great mystics, and we see them, as it were, brought within our own sphere of experience. Paradoxically, it can give us some understanding of what is happening to us when we have lost faith in our own understanding of ourselves, teaching us that, in Caussade's words, "The divine action ... can only take possession of a soul in so far as she is empty of all confidence in her own action."

There is in Caussade's doctrine a gentleness not enervating but stimulating, not concealing the rigour of the demands made upon us but presenting them with a sweet reasonableness. There is no escaping the burden of our humanity: the difference between the good man and the bad is simply that where one accepts what has happened to him and uses it for the enrichment of his soul, the other resents it and tries to change it by arbitrary action or by taking refuge in the pride of imagination. The life of faith as advocated by Caussade

consists of joy in God's gift and a confidence founded on the expectation of his protection which makes everything harmonise and makes us receive everything with a good grace. It produces a certain indifference of soul and prepares us for all situations, all states and all persons we may meet. Faith is never unhappy, even when the senses are in a state of desolation. The soul ever maintains a living faith in God and in his action beyond the contrary appearances that darken the perceptions of the senses.

The proud man, on the other hand, "is an enigma incomprehensible to himself, but very intelligible to a simple soul enlightened by faith."

This acceptance or "discovery of the divine action in all that passes within us and around us is the true science of things," and Caussade goes on to say:

Quand Dieu se donne ainsi, tout le commun devient extraordinaire; et c'est pour cela que rien ne le paraît; c'est que cette voie est par elle-même extraordinaire; par conséquent, il n'est pas nécessaire de l'orner de merveilles qui ne lui sont point propres. C'est un miracle, une révélation, une jouissance continuelle, à de petites fautes près; mais, en soi, son caractère est de n'avoir rien de sensible et de merveilleux, mais de rendre merveilleuses toutes les choses communes et sensibles.[1]

[1] When God gives himself in this way, the ordinary becomes extraordinary, and this is why nothing seems extraordinary. For this path in itself is extraordinary and it is quite unnecessary to adorn it with irrelevant marvels. It is itself a miracle, a revelation, a continuous joy, apart from our trifling venial faults, but it is a miracle which, while it renders marvellous all our everyday life of the senses, has nothing in itself that is marvellous to the senses.

There is a rare sense of integration in *l'Abandon*. To Caussade prayer is something increasingly to be lived. Fr. Ramière, in editing the papers that compose it, made an effort to separate what he considered the instructions for acquiring the virtue of *abandon* from the material primarily intended for those proficient in it. The second part opens: "There is a time when the soul lives in God and a time when God lives in the soul. What belongs to one of these periods is unsuitable for the other. When God lives in a soul, she should abandon herself completely to his Providence." But many souls far from proficient in the life of faith may gain a much more profound understanding of its demands and of that transcendent element in it that is offered to all who even feebly seek the Kingdom: the element that makes our faith not just an ethical system on which the spiritual life is a mere gloss used partly to cover up what cannot be readily explained, but a unity concerned simultaneously with body and soul, verily a wholeness in Christ. To see the present moment as a sacrament, for our part in which we are immediately answerable, is to see the utter necessity for the integration of the spirit in our daily life, and to apprehend the joy that would ensue from the transformation of that life into a state of prayer. Abandon means just that to Caussade, a constant acceptance, not in any sense one that discards necessary activity but rather absorbs it into its place in the spiritual life, so that the humblest and most obscure tasks may be transformed by gaining a sacramental significance.

There is an academic approach to spiritual writings by which theologians may decide the soundness of their doctrine, and here Caussade's orthodoxy is beyond dispute. There is inevitably a more subjective approach, more strictly practical and one that must remain primarily a matter of personal predilection. We commonly experience the curious way in which a book that seems to us personally to cast great light upon the dark places of the soul, makes hardly any impression upon another even when that person is one with whom we feel we have much in common. Tastes, and therefore needs, in the matter of spiritual reading seem to be as varied, perhaps as unpredictable, as tastes in aesthetics or humour. Nor would it be possible, even were it seemly, to judge the spiritual progress of another simply by the books that he finds pertinent, for there are many approaches to the many mansions. But it is certain that numerous souls, in the words of Dr. Knowles, "have found in Caussade their greatest stay—perhaps their only resource—at a particular period in their spiritual life. How many others have found, not this, but—sure token of a classic—a steady friendship to which they can return again and again, not at a period of crisis but during the ordinary flow of life." Abbot Chapman aligned himself with these unequivocally when he wrote, "I have found no writer so helpful to myself as Fr. Jean Pierre de Caussade. . . . He speaks from experience and from the heart. His words are lighted up with a magic splendour by his enthusiasm and zeal."

26. GREGORY OF NYSSA

Jean Daniélou

IF THE IMPORTANCE of St. Gregory of Nyssa in the history of spirituality has now been established,[1] the part he played in the history of monasticism is only just being brought to light. In order to clarify Gregory's· role in the development of monasticism certain preliminary problems concerning the chronology of his life and the authenticity of some of his works have to be resolved. But the researches involved are, it must be admitted, still insufficiently advanced. Definite progress has, however, been made by Werner Jaeger's discovery of the authentic text of the *De Instituto Christiano* and by his demonstration that this work is Gregory's.[2] Together with what was previously known, this evidence now makes it possible to form some estimate of Gregory's writings on monasticism.

Gregory first appears in the history of monasticism with his treatise *De Virginitate*; this is also the first of his works which we possess. It is important to define the circumstances under which it was written as far as we can ascertain them. Jaeger has fixed the date of this work as 371. Gregory does in fact here use the term *episcopus* of his brother Basil (249, 4).[3] Basil did not become bishop of Caesarea until 370, and Gregory's reference to his brother implies that he was himself not yet a bishop. He was made a bishop in 372. What was his position in 371?

The problem of Gregory's personal situation with regard to monastic life is made considerably more difficult by this preliminary question. In 357 Basil abandoned his profession as a rhetorician and withdrew to the solitude of Annesi. According to a letter he wrote to Gregory Nazianzen he seems to have tried

---

[1] Cf. Jean Daniélou, *Platonisme et Théologie mystique. Essai sur la doctrine spirituelle de Saint Grégoire de Nysse*, 2nd edition, Paris, 1952.

[2] *Two Rediscovered Works of Ancient Christian Literature*, Leiden, 1954.

[3] References are given to page and line of the editions of the *De Virginitate* by J. P. Cavarnos and the *De Instituto Christiano* by Werner Jaeger in *Gregorii Nysseni Opera*, ed. Werner Jaeger, Vol. viii, pars. 1, Leiden, 1952.

to take Gregory with him. But he did not succeed. Gregory married and became a rhetorician.

Meanwhile Basil had become the reformer of Cappadocian monasticism. From 359 to 361 he wrote the *Moralia*. He visited the Cappadocian communities and the replies to the questions he was asked constitute the *Little Asceticon*.[1] Ordained priest in 364, made bishop of Caesarea in 370, he continued to be occupied with monastic organisation. At first he was a disciple of Eustathius of Sebaste, but he became more and more independent, rejecting the excessive asceticism of Eustathius and at the same time opposing his theology of the Holy Spirit.

It is at this point that he turned to his brother Gregory to ask him to write the manifesto of monasticism he desired. This was the treatise *De Virginitate*. Gregory's prologue exactly explains the relationship of his work to Basil's rules. He is writing a proclamation. It is therefore not necessary to dwell in detail on the rules or treat individual questions. But it is clear that his work presupposes the rules, that is, evidently, the *Moralia* and the *Little Asceticon*. This is a valuable testimony to the existence of these works unnoticed by Dom Jean Gribomont.

At the end of the *De Virginitate* Gregory returns to the question, "The particular prescriptions concerning the practice to be followed by him who chooses to live in this philosophy, the rules he should follow, the exercises he should adopt, the moderation to be kept in ascetical matters, the way of filling the time and everything concerning the purpose of this life, each one can study these things in detail: there are written documents which teach them." Jaeger remarks that this certainly refers to the *Moralia* of Basil, but there is no reason to exclude the *Little Asceticon*. And the word "documents" does not therefore refer exclusively to Scriptural texts, as Dom Jean Gribomont believed when discussing the use of the word in Basil.

Therefore, and this point is of great interest for us, Gregory wishes to complement the writings of Basil as they existed at this date. But the text contains more than this. Gregory declares explicitly that he himself does not practise the ideal which he praises, "Blessed are those to whom the choice of the better is still possible and who are not excluded from it by having

[1] Cf. Jean Gribomont, *Histoire du texte des Ascétiques de Saint Basile*, Louvain, 1953.

previously adopted an ordinary state of life, as in our own case, we who are separated as by a gulf from the glory of virginity."

From these different pieces of evidence we can gauge the circumstances in which the work was written. Gregory is married. But he has been slowly won over to the reforming work of his brother. This work has met with obstacles. Primitive Cappadocian monasticism, that of Eustathius of Sebaste, contained excesses and abuses which gave rise to the well-founded criticism of pagans and even, one supposes, of certain Christians. The echo of these criticisms is to be found some years later in the *Dion* of Synesios.[1] Basil is trying to establish a more balanced form of monasticism, capable of appealing to the *élite*. Looking for someone able to present it to the cultivated world of the time he naturally enough thinks of the brilliant rhetorician, his brother. In this way Gregory becomes engaged in the service of the monastic ideal without himself being a monk.

The contents of the work confirm its importance in the history of monasticism. Its composition is in fact somewhat disjointed. But if it is evident that Gregory used different sources, it is this fact which enables us precisely to discern his own originality. The first part derives from the traditional treatises on virginity and contains in particular an account of the inconveniences caused by marriage which recalls the homilies on virginity of Eusebius of Emesa.[2] The Virgin Mary, Elias, John the Baptist, Mary the sister of Moses are proposed as models.[3] Then come chapters on virginity and purity as a condition of the vision of God which certainly derive from Plotinus and are a new contribution. After this Gregory develops the idea dear to Basil that the simultaneous possession of different virtues is necessary, and there are two very fine chapters on spiritual marriage in the tradition of the *Symposium* of Methodius of Olympus.

The last chapters are the most important for the historical significance of the work. Chapters twenty-one and twenty-two criticise the excesses of certain forms of asceticism and José Janini Cuesta has established that they are directed immediately against the treatise on virginity of Basil of Ancyra. Basil of Ancyra belongs to the same generation and the same theological back-

[1] Cf. K. Treu, *Synesios von Kyrene, Ein Kommentar zu seinem Dion*, pp. 63–6.
[2] Cf. D. Amand, *La virginité chez Eusèbe d'Emèse* (*Revue d'Histoire ecclésiastique*, 50, 1955, pp. 790–6).
[3] Cf. St. Athanasius, *Sur la virginité* (Muséon, 42, 1929, pp. 243–9).

ground as Eustathius of Sebaste; both were founders of Cappadocian monasticism.

In the preceding generation Eusebius of Emesa had represented the same background, and the existence of a whole tradition, deriving from Syrian monasticism, is therefore apparent. Basil encountered this tradition and at first accepted it though finally he abandoned it. His break with Eustathius of Sebaste began about 372 and Gregory of Nyssa's treatise is an expression of the rupture.

In the last chapters Gregory expounds the necessity of a sure guide in the monastic life, comparing it to those remedies which can become poisons if the doctor's prescriptions are not followed. He then describes the various aberrations which can befall those who wish to guide themselves by their own lights. There are those who refuse to work and "make of idleness a way of life"; there are the illuminated who mistake their imaginations for revelations instead of following the "doctrine of the Gospels"; there are those who "confuse virtue with a solitary and savage life and who know nothing of patience and humility."

These are not merely the extreme ascetical tendencies of the disciples of Eustathius alone. The relationship of our text to the remarks of Epiphanius and Theodoretus show that the tradition described is that of Messalianism,[1] whose followers rejected all work and even all activity in favour of devotion to prayer alone. They conducted themselves according to the revelations received in prayer. This tradition is known to have been condemned by the synod of Side about 384 and to have been fought by Amphilochius of Iconium and Letoios of Melitene in Asia Minor. Gregory's text shows that as early as 371 it constituted a danger in Cappadocia, and it was partly in opposition to it that Basil defined the main components of his own ideal: manual labour, recourse to the Gospel teaching alone, communal life.

After becoming bishop of Nyssa in 372 Gregory, according to Basil, more or less successfully assisted his brother in the struggle against Arianism. When Basil died in 379 Gregory tells us that he inherited his work. He strove to continue and to complete it in the spheres of theological controversy and ecclesiastical affairs. But until about 390 we find in his works only

[1] Cf. Jean Daniélou, *Grégoire de Nysse et le Messalianisme* (*Recherches des sciences religieuses*, 48, 1960, pp. 119–34).

isolated allusions to monasticism. In 381 he wrote, for instance, to three nuns whom he had met in Palestine. In the same year he published, at the request of the monk Olympios, the life of his sister Macrina, including a description of the female community she founded. The homilies on the Canticle of about 388 contain two brief allusions to the life of the monks.

But at the end of this period there is a change and in Basil's monastic work Gregory begins to play a part analogous to that which he had already assumed in his brother's other work. He contributed certain finishing touches which had been lacking. How can one explain Gregory's lengthy delay in assuming this role? Possibly his episcopal activity had completely occupied him until this time. He had, in particular, been frequently obliged to live at Constantinople where he was retained by the confidence of Theodosius. When Theodosius established himself at Milan in 386 it was Ambrose who took over the part hitherto played by Gregory. Gregory himself was therefore freed.

But there is certainly another reason. We must not forget that Gregory was married. It is not certain that he separated from his wife on accession to the bishopric, and we know that in Cappadocia at this time bishops could be married, as was bishop Gregory, father of Gregory Nazianzen. Also we know from a letter of Gregory Nazianzen that Gregory of Nyssa's wife, Theosebia, had just died. This letter, addressed to Gregory of Nyssa, must have been written about 386. In view of the nostalgia for the monastic life to which the *De Virginitate* bore witness we may wonder whether, having become a widower, Gregory might not have given himself more completely to the monastic ideal. At any rate the monastic period is the last in his life.[1] He remained, of course, a bishop, but henceforward he dedicated himself much more completely to the monasticism whose ideal he could now share.

A first expression of his activity with the Cappadocian monks is to be found in the *Vita Moysis*. This work is addressed to a certain Caesarius, whom some manuscripts mention in the title where he is called a monk. In his preface Gregory alludes to the obedience of his correspondent, apparently referring to one of the specific features of Basil's monasticism. Gregory speaks of

---

[1] Cf. Jean Daniélou, *Le mariage de Grégoire de Nysse et la chronologie de sa vie* (*Revue des études arméniennes*, 2, 1956, pp. 71-3).

himself as "established in the place of a father over so many souls," and appears in this way to refer to the spiritual direction of Basil's monasteries which he now assumed.[1] The treatise is designed as an introduction to the life of perfection, an expression which Gregory had used to designate monastic rules in the *De Virginitate*. The success of the *Vita Moysis* in monastic circles is attested by the discovery of extracts from it found on papyri in Egypt.

In the *Vita Moysis* Gregory speaks explicitly of monastic life. He sees in the bordered coverings of goats' hair on the Tabernacle a symbol of "the austere life of continence which is the Church's finest adornment" and of "the virginal-life which mortifies (literally 'presses lightly on') the life of those who practise it." The variant reading here seems preferable on account of its relationship to the bordered coverings, although the authentic text of St. Paul, referring to the athletes' combat, has "mortifies" (1 Cor. ix, 27)[2] and Gregory certainly had this text of St. Paul in mind.[3] It should be noted, too, that in his homilies on the Canticle, Gregory similarly presented the monastic life as constituting a privileged part of the Church.[4]

But these partial indications are not all. The *Vita Moysis* belongs to monastic literature by its very purpose, which is to present an Old Testament saint as model of the monastic life. This idea comes from Basil. Basil wrote to Gregory Nazianzen, "He who strives to perfect himself in all the parts of virtue should turn his eyes to the life of the saints as to statues which move and act." But Gregory writes in the *Vita Moysis*, "Is not the reason for which the life of these holy souls has been written in detail to direct in the way of good, by the example of the just of ancient times, the life of their successors?" The saints referred to by Basil were Joseph, Job, David and Moses; Gregory speaks of Abraham and Sara.

There are, in addition, sketches of such lives in Gregory's work before the *Vita Moysis*. In the *De Virginitate*, for example, Elias is shown to be a model for those who live in the desert and for virginity. The seventh homily on the Canticle takes up the same theme:

---

[1] This is in the body of the work itself where Moses is shown to be the figure of spiritual guides.

[2] Literally this means "to strike under the eye." St. Paul uses the word metaphorically in the sense of "mortify."

[3] Ho. Cant. 2; P. G. xliv, 1213A.   [4] P. G. xliv, 1104D.

Elias, who led the monastic life for a long time in the mountain of Galaad, was the founder of the life of continence. And all those who model their lives on the example of this prophet become the ornament of the Church, practising virtue together according to the form which at present determines monastic life.[1]

The end of this passage makes a clear allusion to Basil's reform. The same theme recurs a little further on in the fifteenth homily.[2] Still more precise sketches for the life of Moses are to be found in the commentaries on the Psalms, Gregory's first exegetical work, probably written in 379 and 380[3] and in the homilies on the Canticle.[4]

In this way the *Vita Moysis* appears as the achievement of a project which had long been latent in Gregory's mind. It corresponds also to the idea expounded in the *De Virginitate*, that along with written teaching living examples are necessary. These living examples are the spiritual masters under whom the candidate for monastic life should seek instruction. But Gregory does not separate them from the exemplars offered by the Old Testament saints, and this recourse to Scripture is a feature of Basil's background. It is also worth remarking that when Gregory praises Basil he compares him to Elias[5] or to Moses.[6] The *Vita Moysis*, in so far as it is an attempt to find an archetype of the life of perfection in the Old Testament, appears therefore as an expression of Basil's monasticism.

It is not only by its literary genre, but still more by its contents that the *Vita Moysis* is epoch-making in the history of Cappadocian monasticism. Basil had already laid the foundations. He had organised the disparate tendencies and composed the charter of monastic life. But his was primarily a work of organisation. In 390, ten years after Basil's death, Gregory is confronted by a well-organised monasticism, but one which lacks a spiritual doctrine. Gregory is himself a person of great spiritual gifts and is therefore quite prepared for the task before him. In the *Vita Moysis* he gives Cappadocian monasticism a mystical theology. Just as he had completed the theological and exegetical work of his brother, he now completes Basil's work in the sphere of the monastic life.

If Gregory belonged to the history of monasticism only by the

---

[1] P. G. xliv, 924A.   [2] P. G. xliv, 1104A–1105C.   [3] *Ibid.*, 456D–457C.
[4] *Ibid.*, 1025B–D.   [5] P. G. xlvi, 796D–806A.   [6] 789B; 809A.

De Virginitate and the *Vita Moysis*, his contribution would certainly not have been negligible, but it would have remained secondary. A recent discovery allows us to give him a much more important place. This is the *De Instituto Christiano*, a treatise formerly known only in a series of extracts. Werner Jaeger was the first to find and edit the complete text. The hesitations shown by several critics on the subject of its authenticity have thereby been overcome, so that one need no longer be afraid to draw on it for studies of Gregory. It is certainly a treatise of Gregory's and, for our subject, one of the most important, since it is nothing less than a little compendium on the cenobitic life.

Gregory begins by explaining that he is writing this treatise to satisfy the desires of those who "practise in common the form of apostolic life." This is a clear allusion to the cenobitic life as organised by Basil. The monks had asked Gregory to give them "not only orally, but in writing, a treatise to serve as a guide in their way of life, so that they could refer to it at need." It seems therefore that this treatise is the echo of teaching at first given orally and that the monks had asked Gregory to edit it. Gregory expounds the leading principles of his spiritual doctrine such as it is to be found in his earlier works. He bases it on texts of Scripture which serve both as a justification and an explanation and, briefly, he undertakes to draw up for the monks a small compendium of his spirituality.

Gregory himself announces in his introduction the plan he will follow. He will first deal with the end of monastic life and of the means of attaining this end. Then he will show why it is fitting that those who follow this life should live in common. Finally he exposes "how the superiors should direct the monasteries" and "what practices should be assumed by those who aim at the perfection of virtue and desire to dispose themselves to receive spiritual gifts." The work does in fact consist of clearly distinguished parts with well-marked divisions.

In the first part Gregory begins by laying down the end of monastic life. Its principle is faith and baptism. But the spiritual man must achieve adult status, and this is attained through the effects of grace and liberty together. God aims in this way to cleanse the soul of its impurities in order to render it capable of seeing the intelligible and ineffable light. The soul must free itself from shame to acquire spiritual liberty. In this way the soul becomes the spouse of Christ by virginity, and it must become like Christ. Gregory insists above all on humility, supporting his doctrine with long quotations from St. Paul. He emphasises that the soul should never be satisfied with any progress that has been achieved, but should always proceed further according to the principle enunciated in Phil. iii. 13, which recurs constantly throughout Gregory's works.

Gregory now starts the second part, concerned with common life. He emphasises first the necessity of renouncing one's own will by means of "obedience to him whose mission it is to direct the community of the brethren to the harbour' of the divine will." Nothing except clothing should be considered as belonging to individuals, and each should dedicate himself to the service of the community according to the prescriptions of obedience, considering himself in the service of all. This is particularly true of superiors on whose role Gregory specially insists. Their conduct with regard to their subjects should be that of tutors to whom parents have entrusted their children and "who undertake their education with a mixture of punishments, counsels and praise."

These pages on common life are remarkable. They summarise the whole substance of Basil's reform. The last part is no less striking and it consists of Gregory's personal contribution. He is dealing with the practices which lead to perfection. Gregory puts the emphasis essentially on prayer, which he makes the summit of the scale of virtues. He describes in a concrete manner its effects in the soul, "He who applies himself to prayer, having taken the Spirit for guide and support, burns with the love of the Lord and is enkindled with desire, not finding satiety in prayer but being always enflamed with the desire of the Good." Prayer gives spiritual joy. It is the Kingdom of God. By it the Spirit dwells in the soul. The remainder of the brethren should allow anyone attracted to prayer to devote himself to it, and they themselves will benefit from it. Superiors should consider the souls of prayer as the flower of their monastery and should support them in every possible way.

The whole of Gregory's mystical experience, as it had been expressed in the homilies on the Canticle and the *Vita Moysis*, bears fruit here, but he prescinds from the structure of symbols which had enveloped it in these works. He retains only what is essential. It has been suggested that in this part of the work Gregory was influenced by Messalianism. But we have seen that Gregory fought against such a tendency as early as 371. What is true is that he appears here as the defender of contemplation, perhaps against those who, reacting excessively against Messalianism, had come to mistrust him.

The influence of this treatise of Gregory's was considerable, as we are now beginning to discover. As we have already mentioned, an epitome, which we possess, was made from it. There is also a *Great Letter* in the name of Macarius which derives directly from this treatise and is a paraphrase of it. This text seems to belong to the early fifth century and emanates from the monastic background whose charter is constituted by the *De Instituto Christiano*. A whole group of homilies which are also attributed to Macarius, but which are certainly not by the same author as the *Great Letter*, also testify to Gregory's influence, and particularly to that of the *De Instituto Christiano*. Dom Alphonsus Kemmer has also established the influence of the *De Instituto Christiano* on Cassian.[1] And recently Dom Adalbert de Vogüé, in a still unpublished thesis, has shown that certain differences between the *Regula Magistri* and the Rule of St. Benedict concerning the importance attached by Benedict to common life and obedience derive doubtless from the influence of our treatise.

When St. Gregory of Nyssa is compared to his brother Basil it is often emphasised, and not without reason, that whereas Basil was above all a man of action and an organiser, Gregory was a thinker and a mystic. But this contrast is true only if it is not interpreted in too absolute a fashion. Basil, it is generally agreed, was also a theologian and had great spiritual gifts. But it is true, too, that Gregory of Nyssa played a part in the history of the Church, although this fact is less widely recognised. In a commentary of the Oxford Society of Church History I have shown how from 381 to 386 he played an important role with Theodosius at the court in Constantinople. This part ceased when, in 387, Theodosius established his court at Milan. From this time it was Ambrose who took over Gregory's role. But another form of action now awaited Gregory, the task of completing Basil's work in the organisation of Cappadocian monasticism. This is what we have tried to show in the course of these pages.

[1] *Gregorius Nyssenus estne inter fontes Jo. Cassiani numerandus?* (*Orientalia Christiana Periodica*, 21, 1955, pp. 454–5).

NOTES ON CONTRIBUTORS

FR. CHARLES BOYER, S.J., was born at Pradelles, Haute-Loire, France, in December 1884, and entered the Society of Jesus in 1907. He was ordained priest in 1916. Most of his priestly life has been spent at the Gregorian University, Rome. He was professor of philosophy there from 1922–26, of theology from 1927–62, and he was in charge of all studies from 1935–55. Since 1932 he has been general secretary of the Roman Academy of St. Thomas Aquinas, and president of the International Association, *Unitas*, since 1945. He is director of the Review *Doctor Communis* and of the various editions of *Unitas*. He is a member of the Secretariate for Christian Unity, and *a peritus* of Vatican Council II.

His publications on St. Augustine include: *L'idée de vérité dans la Philosophie de St. Augustin* (2me éd. 1941); *Christianisme et Néoplatonisme dans la Formation de St. Augustin* (2me éd. 1953); *Essais sur la Doctrine de St. Augustin* (1933); "St. Augustin," dans la collection *Les Moralistes Chrétiens* (1932). All these works have been "recognised" by the *Académie française*.

Fr. Boyer has also published manuals of philosophy and theology for seminary students.

DAME ANSELMA BRENNELL, O.S.B., was educated in England and in Belgium and then entered the University of Liverpool, where she read her degree in History. After a year of postgraduate research she taught for a few years. In August 1925 she entered religion at Stanbrook Abbey. In 1950 she published *British Mediaeval History* in the Ashley Historical Series, in 1954 *Mediaeval Mystical Tradition and St. John of the Cross* and in 1958 *Life of the Servant of God, Daniel Comboni*, for the Verona Missionary Society.

FR. ODO BROOKE, O.S.B., was educated at Eton and New College, Oxford, then joined the Prinknash Benedictines. Sent to Farnborough, he took the course in philosophy under Fr. Bede Griffiths as Prior. He studied theology at Saint' Anselmo, Rome, where he took the Licentiate and Doctorate. His thesis under Fr. Cyprian Vagaggini was on William of St. Thierry's doctrine of the Trinity. He has published articles on this subject in the *Révue de Théologie Ancienne et Médiévale*. At present he is teaching theology at Prinknash Abbey.

MOTHER MARIA CARITAS, S.H.C.J., is Assistant Professor of History at Rosemont College, a university college conducted by the Sisters of the Holy Child Jesus in Pennsylvania, U.S.A. In 1960 she received a Doctorate of Philosophy at the Catholic University of America.

Her dissertation, *The Rule for Nuns of St. Caesarius of Arles: A Translation with a Critical Introduction* (Vol. XVI of Catholic University of America Studies in Mediaeval History), will be re-published shortly in the *Fathers of the Church* series. She is currently preparing several articles for *The New Catholic Encyclopedia* on the beginnings of monasticism in Egypt. She has written several articles on the Society of the Holy Child Jesus and on its foundress, Cornelia Connelly; and has published *Cornelia and Pierce Connelly: New Perspectives on Their Early Lives* in *Records of the American Catholic Historical Society of Philadelphia.*

FR. MICHEL DE CERTEAU, S.J., who was born in 1925, and ordained a priest of the Society of Jesus in 1956, is the co-editor of the French review of spirituality, *Christus,* and of the series *Collection Christus.* He has spent several years in studying the history of spiritual experience and its expression. This study has led him to edit and publish the *Memoriale* of the Jesuit *Beatus,* Pierre Favre (1960), and monographs on the Carmelite Maurus of the Infant Jesu (in *Révue d'Ascétique et de Mystique, 1959*) and the Jesuit Jean-Joseph Surin (Collection *Christus,* 1963). These works and other articles in *Révue d'Ascétique et de Mystique* form part of the background for a major work now in preparation, *Expérience et langage,* which deals with experimental knowledge in the French mystics of the seventeenth century.

JAMES M. CLARK, who died in 1961, was Emeritus Professor of German at Glasgow University. His main publications are *Meister Eckhart* and the *Great German Mystics.* He is also the author of *The Abbey of St. Gall* (1926) and *The Dance of Death* (1950).

EDMUND COLLEDGE, O.S.A., has specialised in the study of the devotional literature, Latin and vernacular, of England, the Low Countries and the Rhineland in the later Middle Ages. He is the author of studies and modern English translations of Ruysbroek, Tauler and Suso; he published in 1957, in collaboration with Joyce Bazire, a critical edition of *The Chastising of God's Children,* and, in 1961, an anthology, *The Mystics of Medieval England.* He taught English language and philology at Liverpool University from 1937 until 1963, when he resigned his Readership there, and entered the English novitiate of the Augustinian Friars Hermit. He made his simple profession in September 1964.

FR. HENRI CROUZEL, S.J., was born in Toulouse in January 1919. Educated at the Jesuit College in Toulouse he entered the Society of Jesus in December 1936. After three years of military service during World War II, he was ordained priest in 1950. He received his doctorate in Theology at the University of Strasbourg in 1954, and became a Doctor of Letters of the Sorbonne in 1959. He now teaches moral theology at the Faculty of Theology in Toulouse. He is the author of several studies on Origen.

Fr. Jean Daniélou, S.J., was born on the 14th May 1905. Before entering the Society of Jesus in 1929 he took his doctorate in philosophy at the Sorbonne. He is a doctor in theology, a "doyen" of the Faculty of Theology at Paris, and a director of the series *Sources Chrétiennes*. He is also *a peritus* at the Second Vatican Council. His principal published works, most of which have been translated into English, are *Platonisme et Théologie Mystique: Essais sur la doctrine spirituel de St. Gregoire de Nysse; Sacramentum Futuri; Bible et Liturgie; Théologie du Judeo-Christianisme; Origéne; Les Symboles Chrétiennes Primitifs*. His most recent work is a *History of Christianity in the First Three Centuries*, written in collaboration with H Marrou, which is to appear in French, English, German and Dutch.

Fr. Jean-Marie Déchanet, O.S.B., is a native of the Vosges (France). After studying at the Diocesan Seminary of Mattaincourt, he entered the Benedictine Abbey of Saint-André, Bruges, in 1927. From 1930 he has devoted himself to the study of medieval spirituality, and in 1935 began to publish in *Vie Spirituelle* a first series of articles on William of St. Thierry and his famous *Golden Epistle;* and in 1941 he published *Guillaume de Saint-Thierry, l'homme et son œuvre*. During these years, he taught Patristic Theology at Saint-André. In 1958 Fr. Déchanet was sent by his superiors to the Belgian Congo, to be novice-master at the African Monastery of Kansénia (Katanga); he has been there ever since, and is now the Monastery's superior. His *Exposé de Guillaume de St. Thierry sur le Cantique des Cantiques* appeared in 1961; and he is now preparing a critical edition, with a new translation and notes, of the *Golden Epistle*.

Fr. Bede Griffiths, O.S.B., was born in December 1906 and was baptised and brought up in the Church of England. Educated at Christ's Hospital School, and at Magdalen College, Oxford, he returned to the Christian faith whilst at Oxford, partly influenced by C. S. Lewis, and was eventually received into the Catholic Church in 1932. He entered Prinknash Abbey in 1933, and was ordained priest 1940. Sent as Prior in 1947 to the new Benedictine foundation at St. Michael's Abbey, Farnborough, he was later transferred to Pluscarden Priory, Scotland, as novice-master. In 1955 he went to India to assist in the foundation of a contemplative monastery at Kerala. (This foundation is an Eastern monastery of "eparchial" rank, under the Syrian Bishop of Tiruvalla in the Syro-Malankara rite, under Eastern Canon Law and subject to the Oriental Congregation, though the monks observe the rule of St. Benedict, interpreted according to the strict Cistercian observance.)

Fr. Griffiths published his autobiography, *The Golden String*, in 1954. He writes frequently on the ecumenical approach to Hinduism and Eastern religion, and was awarded the Gold Medal of the Catholic Art Association in America for "ecumenical understanding". He is at present planning a work on the "New Creation" which he hopes to complete this year.

PROFESSOR THE REV. DAVID KNOWLES was born on the 29th September 1896, in Warwickshire. He was educated at Downside school, and entered the Abbey novitiate in 1914. He read classics at Cambridge from 1919 to 1922, and was ordained priest at Downside in July of that year. He made further studies in theology after his ordination at Sant' Anselmo in Rome. He taught at Downside from 1923 to 1928 and was editor of the *Downside Review* from 1929 to 1933. It was at this time that he began to study the sources of English monastic history, and his book *The Monastic Order in England* was published in 1940. During the war years he was working on the continuation of his history of English monasticism, the *Religious Orders in England*, the first instalment of which came out in 1948, the second in 1955 and the third in 1959. In 1944 he was made a Fellow of Peterhouse, Cambridge, and in 1945 a University Lecturer. He was elected as Professor of Medieval History at Cambridge in 1947, and in 1954 was appointed Regius Professor of Modern History. He has served as Chairman of the History Faculty at Cambridge, and has influenced historical studies in Cambridge in a number of ways: by supervising postgraduate research, and by reviving the series of monographs published under the title of *Cambridge Studies in Medieval Life and Thought*. He was Ford's Lecturer in English history at Oxford in 1949, Raleigh Lecturer (British Academy) in 1949, and Creighton Lecturer in the University of London in 1956. He received the honorary degree of Doctor of Letters at Oxford in 1952, at Bristol in 1956 and at Leicester in 1962. He has been a Fellow of the British Academy since 1947 and has served as a Vice-president and as a member of its Council. He was President of the Royal Historical Society from 1956–60. On his recent retirement as Regius Professor of Modern History at Cambridge he has been made an Honorary Fellow of Peterhouse. His most important work in the history of spirituality is his *The English Mystical Tradition*.

FR. ANTHONY LEVI, S.J., was born in 1929 and entered the Society of Jesus in 1949. He studied philosophy in Germany and took a first-class honours degree in modern languages at Oxford University. He has presented a doctoral thesis at the same university, which is to be published by the Clarendon Press under the title *French Moralists: The Theory of the Passions*, 1585–1649. He was ordained priest in 1962.

MOTHER MARY DENIS MAHONEY, O.S.U., was born in 1921 in Brooklyn, New York. She took her Bachelor's degree at the College of New Rochelle in 1941, and then worked in a publishing house for a few years. Later she entered the Ursuline Novitiate in New York. After receiving her Master's degree from Fordham University, she taught English at the College of New Rochelle. She received her doctorate at the Catholic University of America in 1958. At present she is Associate Professor of English at the College of New Rochelle, and hopes to see her biography of Mary of the Incarnation published by Doubleday in the autumn of 1964.

FR. ELMER O'BRIEN, S.J., is chairman of the Department of Theology, Loyola College, Montreal, Canada. He was formerly Professor in the Graduate school of Fordham University, New York. He has been a regular contributor to Theological journals for several years, and has published, amongst other works, *The Essential Plotinus* and *Varieties of Mystic Experience*.

FR. HUMPHREY PAWSEY is a Carthusian monk at St. Hugh's Charterhouse, Parkminster, Sussex.

KATHLEEN ELIZABETH POND was born in October 1898, at King's Heath, Birmingham, of Presbyterian parents. Educated at King Edward VI's Grammar School, Birmingham, she became a Catholic in 1917. In 1929 she founded the Society of the Magnificat for the recitation of the Divine Office by the laity, and took an Honours degree in Modern Languages, University of London, 1946. She has since been engaged in university and general tutoring in Spanish, French and Latin. She is unmarried. Her published works include: *The Spirit of the Spanish Mystics* (1958); translations of: Marcelle Auclair: *St. Teresa* (1952); Louis Bouyer: *Meaning of the Monastic Life* (1955); Arintero: *Stages in Prayer* (1957); Crisógone de Jesús: *Life of St John of the Cross* (1958); Hugo Rahner: *St. Ignatius' Letters to Women* (1960); Lefebvre: *The Well-Springs of Prayer* (1960); Du Buit: *Biblical Archaeology* (Faith and Fact Series, 1960).

FR. GABRIEL REIDY, O.F.M., D.D., B.A., born in Dublin in 1906, was educated in London at St. Antony's, Forest Gate, and St. Bonaventure's Grammar School. He entered the English Province of the

Friars Minor at Chilworth, Surrey, in 1924, and in addition to the normal course of ecclesiastical studies, took a degree in history at London University in 1931. Ordained priest in 1932, he studied theology at the Antonianum, Rome, specialising in Mariology under Fr. Charles Balic, O.F.M. From 1936–39 he was a research student in history at Christ's College, Cambridge, specialising in the religious movements of the fourteenth century under the direction of the late J. G. Sikes of Jesus College. He taught Dogmatic and Patristic theology at Forest Gate and Buckingham (1939–42) and after a period of parochial and missionary work in the archdiocese of Liverpool (1942–45) returned to the teaching of theology and Church history at Forest Gate and East Bergholt in Suffolk. His main interest latterly, apart from teaching and occasional retreat-giving, has been aspects of the theology of the religious life and other forms of dedicated Christian life, particularly that of the Secular Institutes and of "solitaries". In 1962 he published *The Secular Institutes* in the Faith and Fact series, and has also written or translated several articles on the same subject.

GEORGE SCOTT-MONCRIEFF was born in Edinburgh in 1910. He has lived most of his life in Scotland, and has written topographical books on different aspects of the country. He is also author of plays, including *Fotheringhay*, a verse play about Mary Queen of Scots. His latest works include *This Day* and *The Mirror and the Cross*, a study of Catholicism in Scotland.

ANN STAFFORD is the pseudonym of Mrs. Anne Pedler. She was educated at the Universities of Cambridge and London, where she took a doctorate in Philosophy. She was received into the Church in 1950. She earned her living for many years as a novelist, journalist and lecturer. Her recent novels include: *Blossoming Rod, Seven Days Grace, It Began in Bangkok*. Non-fiction: *Saigon Journey* (the record of a lecture tour in the Far East), *A Match to Fire the Thames* (appearing shortly: *The Age of Consent*). Her special interests are social problems, Welfare Work and the study of St. Thomas Aquinas; her recreations, grandchildren and riding.

FR. ANSELM STOELEN is a Carthusian monk at St. Hugh's Charterhouse, Parkminster, Sussex.

DR. P. G. WALSH is a graduate of Liverpool University, formerly Lecturer in Ancient Classics at University College, Dublin, and now Lecturer in Humanity at the University of Edinburgh, where he lectures on classical and medieval Latin. He has published *Livy, His*

Historical Aims and Methods (Cambridge, 1961), as well as articles and reviews in classical journals. At present he is co-operating with Fr. Anthony Ross, O.P., on an edition of Aquinas' *De Fortitudine* in the new Blackfriars series. He hopes eventually to produce a study of Paulinus of Nola.

FR. WILLIAM YEOMANS, S.J., was born in Leeds on the 10th May 1925, and was educated at St. Michael's College there. He entered the Society of Jesus in September 1942. He made his theological studies at the Jesuit theologate in Fourviére, Lyons, and was ordained there in July 1956. He studied spiritual theology at Innsbruck, Austria (under Father Hugo Rahner), in Spain and at the Institut Catholique, Paris. He has contributed articles to the *Dictionnaire de Spiritualité* and has translated and edited the autobiography of St. Alphonsus Rodriguez. He is co-editor of the English Jesuit review of spirituality, *The Way*.

BIBLIOGRAPHY

This is only a brief selection. Many of the books listed contain exhaustive bibliographies.

A. REFERENCE

ALTANER, B., *Patrology*, Edinburgh, 1960.

Dictionnaire de Spiritualité. 36 fascicules have appeared covering A–François.

Dictionnaire de Théologie Catholique.

The Oxford Dictionary of the Christian Church, London, 1957.

B. GENERAL

BOUYER, L., *Introduction to Spirituality*, London, 1964.

BOUYER, L., *The Spirituality of the New Testament and the Fathers*, London, 1964. The first volume of a three-volume history of spirituality. The two remaining volumes covering the Middle Ages and the modern period have yet to appear in English.

CAYRÉ, F., *The First Spiritual Writers* (Faith & Fact), London, 1959.

COGNET, L., *Post-Reformation Spirituality* (Faith & Fact), London, 1959.

POURRAT, Pierre, *Christian Spirituality*, I–IV, Westminster, Md, 1953–8.

SITWELL, G., *Medieval Spiritual Writers* (Faith & Fact), London, 1961.

C. INDIVIDUALS

The writings of the first twelve authors can be found in one or more of the great collections of the Fathers. The most complete collections of original texts are those of the Abbé Migne: *Patrologia Graeca* (PG) in 168 volumes and *Patrologia Latina* (PL) in 222 volumes. Two important series which are not yet complete are *Die griechischen christlichen Schriftsteller der ersten drei Jahrhunderte* (GCS) and the *Corpus Scriptorum Ecclesiasticorum Latinorum* (CSEL). More recent are the *Corpus Christianorum* (CC), and the *Sources Chrétiennes* (SC) which print the original texts with a French translation. Three collections of English translations were published in the nineteenth century: *The Ante-Nicene Christian Library* (ANCL), *The Nicene and Post-Nicene Christian Fathers* (NPNCF) and *The Library of the Fathers* (LF). Three modern series are still in course of publication: *Ancient Christian Writers* (ACW), *Fathers of the Church* (FC), and *The Library of Christian Classics* (LCC).

ORIGEN

Texts: PG 11–17; GCS 2, 3, 6, 10, 22, 29, 30, 35, 38, 40, 41, 49; SC 7, 16, 29, 37, 67, 71, 87.

Translations:
Various works in ANCL 10, 23, 25; LCC II; ACW 19, 26.
Contra Celsum, ed. and trans. by H. Chadwick, Cambridge, 1953.
Studies:
CROUZEL, H., *Théologie de l'image de Dieu chez Origène (Series Théologie, 34),* Paris, 1956.
CROUZEL, H., *Origène et la connaissance mystique,* Paris, 1961.
DANIÉLOU, J., *Origen,* trans. by W. Mitchell, London, 1955.

ST. AUGUSTINE
Texts:
PL 32–47; CSEL 12, 25, 28, 33, 34, 36, 40–4, 52, 53, 57, 58, 60, 63, 74, 77, 80; SC 75.
Bibliothèque Augustinienne: this will eventually comprise the complete works accompanied by a French translation, introduction and notes. 29 volumes have already been published as well as volumes of *Études.*
Translations:
Works, ed. by Marcus Dods, 15 vols., Edinburgh, 1871–6.
NPNCF 1–8; Various works in LF 1, 16, 20, 22, 24–6, 29, 30, 37, 39; ACW 2, 3, 9, 12, 15, 22, 29, 30; FC 2, 4, 5, 8, 11, 12, 14, 16, 18, 20, 21, 24, 27, 30, 32, 35, 38, 45.
Studies:
GILSON, E., *The Christian Philosophy of St. Augustine,* trans. by L. E. M. Lynch, London, 1961.
PORTALIÉ, E., *A Guide to the Thought of St. Augustine,* London, 1960. (English trans. of the article on St. Augustine in DTC).
VAN DER MEER, F., *Augustine the Bishop,* London, 1961.

JOHN CASSIAN
Texts: PL 49–50; CSEL 13, 17; SC 42, 54, 64.
Translations: NPNCF II, 11; LCC XII.
Studies:
CHADWICK, O., *John Cassian; a Study in Primitive Monasticism,* Cambridge, 1950.
GUY, J. C., *Jean Cassien, vie et doctrine spirituelle,* Paris, 1961.
CRISTIANI, L., *Jean Cassien, ou la spiritualité du désert* (2 vols.), Paris, 1946.

ST. GREGORY OF NYSSA
Texts: PG 44–6; SC 1, 6. 8 volumes have appeared of a critical edition ed. by W. Jaeger and H. Langerbeck, Leiden, 1952–
Translations:
Selection in ACW 18; NPNCF II, 5 and LCC 3.
From Glory to Glory: Texts from Gregory of Nyssa, selected by J. Daniélou, trans. and ed. by H. Musurillo, London, 1963.

Study: DANIÉLOU, J., *Platonisme et Théologie mystique. Essai sur la doctrine spirituelle de St. Grégoire de Nysse (Series Théologie, 2),* Paris, 1944.

CAESARIUS OF ARLES

Texts:
PL 67.
Opera Omnia, ed. by G. Morin, O.S.B., in 2 vols., Maredsous, 1937–42.
The Sermons have appeared in a second edition as CC 103, 104.
Translations:
FC 31.
The Rule for Nuns of St. Caesarius of Arles: A translation with Critical Introduction by Mother M. Caritas McCarthy, Washington, D.C., 1960.
Study: DORENKEMPER, M., *The Trinitarian Doctrine and Sources of St. Caesarius of Arles,* Freiburg, 1953.

ST. BENEDICT

Texts:
PL 66; CSEL 75.
Critical edition by C. Butler, O.S.B., 3rd ed., Freiburg, 1935.
Translation: The Rule of St. Benedict in Latin and English, ed. and trans. by J. McCann (Orchard Books), London, 1952.
Studies:
BUTLER, C., *Benedictine Monachism,* London, 1924.
LINDSAY, T. F., *St. Benedict, His Life and Work,* London, 1949.
MATT, Leonard von, and HILPISCH, Stephan, *St. Benedict,* trans. by E. Graf, London, 1961.
VAN ZELLER, H., *The Holy Rule, Notes on St. Benedict's Legislation for Monks,* London, 1959.

VENANTIUS FORTUNATUS

Texts:
PL 88.
Critical edition in *Monumenta Germaniae, Auctores Antiquissimi,* 4, Pts. 1 and 2, 1881–5.
Study: TARDI, D., *Fortunat,* Paris, 1927.

JOHN SCOTUS ERIGENA

Text: PL 122.
Translation: Selections in MCKEON, R., *Selections from Mediaeval Philosophers,* Vol. 1, London, 1930.

Studies:

Bett, Henry, *Johannes Scotus Erigena*, Cambridge, 1925.

Cappuyns, Dom M., *John Scot Érigène, sa vie, son œuvre, sa pensée*, Louvain, 1933.

ST. BRUNO

Texts: PL 152, 153; SC 88.

Study: Gorse, M. M., *Saint Bruno, son action et son œuvre*, 1902.

ST. BERNARD

Texts:

PL 182–5.

A critical edition in nine volumes is being published in Rome under the general editorship of J. Leclercq, O.S.B. Volumes 1 and 2 have already appeared.

Translations:

The Letters of St. Bernard of Clairvaux, trans. by Bruno S. James, London, 1953.

Of conversion. Text with trans. and notes by Watkin Williams, London, 1938.

Concerning Grace and Free Will, trans. by Watkin Williams, London, 1920.

Studies:

Dumontier, P., *St. Bernard et la Bible*, Paris, 1953.

Gilson, E., *The Mystical Theology of St. Bernard*, trans. by A. H. C. Downes, London, 1940.

Leclercq., J., *St. Bernard mystique*, Bruges, 1948.

Luddy, A. J., *Life and Teaching of St. Bernard*, Dublin, 1927.

WILLIAM OF ST. THIERRY

Texts:

PL 180 and, among works of St. Bernard, 182 and 184: SC 61, 82.

Text with French trans. by M. M. Davy of: *Meditativae Orationes*, 1, 1934; *Commentaire sur le Cantique des Cantiques*, 1958; *Epistola ad Fratres de Monte Dei*, 2 vols., 1940; *Deux Traités sur la Foi, Enigma Fidei, Speculum Fidei*, 1959.

The Epistle to the Brethren of Mont Dieu, trans. by Walter Shewring and ed. by Justin McCann, London, 1930.

In the *Fleur de Lys* Series: *On Contemplating God*, 1955; *On the Nature and Dignity of Love*, 1956; *The Mirror of Faith*, 1956.

Studies:

Déchanet, J.-M., *Aux sources de la Spiritualité de Guillaume de S. Thierry*, Bruges, 1940.

Déchanet, J.-M., *Guillaume de Saint-Thierry: L'homme et son œuvre*, Bibliothèque Médiévale, 1942.

GUIGO THE ANGELIC

Texts:
Scala Claustralium in PL 40 and 184.
Meditations, text with Fr. trans. published in *La Vie Spirituelle,*
suppl., 1932–34.
Translation: A Ladder of Four Rungs, ed. J. McCann, Stanbrook Abbey,
1953.

ST. CLARE OF ASSISI

Text: THOMAS DE CELANO, *Legendae Sanctae Clarae,* ed. by F. Pennacchi,
Assisi, 1910.
Translations:
The Life of Saint Clare ascribed to Fr. *Thomas of Celano,* trans. and
ed. by P. Robinson, O.F.M., London, 1910.
The Life and Legend of the Lady Saint Clare, trans. from the French
by Charlotte Balfour, London, 1910.
Study: GILLIAT-SMITH, E., *Saint Clare of Assisi, Her Life and Legislation,*
London, 1914.

MECHTILD OF MAGDEBURG

Text: The original Low German text is no longer extant.
Translations:
Offenbarungen der Schwester Mechtild von Magdeburg, ed. by G. Morel,
Ratisbon, 1869.
The Revelations of Mechthild of Magdeburg or the Flowing Light of the
Godhead, trans. by Lucy Menzies, London, 1953.
Study: ANCELET-HUSTACHE, J., *Mechtilde de Magdebourg,* Paris, 1926.

ST. BONAVENTURE

Texts: Opera Omnia, 10 vols., Quaracchi, 1882–1902.
Translations: Works of St. Bonaventure, trans. by J. de Vinck: Vol. I.,
Mystical Opuscula, Paterson, N. J., 1960; Vol. II., *Breviloquium,*
Paterson, N. J., 1963. The first volumes of a projected complete
translation.
Studies:
BOUGEROL, J., *Introduction to the Works of Bonaventure,* Paterson,
N. J., 1964.
GILSON, E., *La philosophie de St. Bonaventure,* 3e ed., 1953.
QUINN, Sister M. B., *To God alone the glory, A life of St. Bonaventure,*
Westminster, Maryland, 1962.

ANGELA OF FOLIGNO

Texts:
Le livre de la bienheureuse Angèle de Foligno: Documents édités par

P. Doncoeur avec le concours de F. Pulignani (Bibliothèque d'Ascetique et de Mystique, II), Paris, 1925.

Le livre de l'experience des vrais fidèles. Texte latin publié par M. J. Ferré, traduit avec la collaboration de L. Baudry (Collection de Textes Franciscains), Paris, 1927.

Translation: *The Book of Divine Consolation,* trans. from the Italian by M. G. Steegman, London, 1909.

Studies:

LECLEVE, L., *Sainte Angele de Foligno, sa vie-ses œuvres,* Paris, 1936.

THOROLD, A., *An essay in aid of the better appreciation of Catholic mysticism illustrated from the writings of Blessed Angela of Foligno,* London, 1900.

JOHN RUYSBROEK

Text: *Opera* in 4 vols, published by members of the Ruusbroec-genootschap at Tielt, 1944–48.

Translations:

The Spiritual Espousals, trans. by Eric Colledge, London, 1952.

The Chastising of God's Children, by Eric Colledge and Joyce Bazire, Oxford, 1957, contains versions, made in England, *c.* A.D. 1400, from Latin translations of *The Treatise of Perfection of the Sons of God* and parts of the *Espousals.*

The Seven Steps of the Ladder of Spiritual Love, trans. by F. S. Taylor, London, 1944.

Studies:

UNDERHILL, E., *Ruysbroeck,* London, 1915.

WAUTIER D'AYGALLIERS, A., *Ruysbroeck, the Admirable,* trans. by F. Rothwell, London, 1925.

JOHANN TAULER

Texts: *Johannes Tauler Predigten.* Vollstandige Ausgabe Übertragen und herausgegeben von Dr. George Hofmann, Freiburg, 1961.

Translations:

Signposts to Perfection. Sermons, selected, ed. and trans. by Elizabeth Strakosch, London, 1958.

Spiritual Conferences, trans. and ed. by Eric Colledge and Sister M. Jane (Cross and Crown Series of Spirituality, 20), St. Louis and London, 1961.

Study: CLARK, James M., *The Great German Mystics: Eckhart, Tauler, and Suso,* Oxford, 1949.

DENYS THE CARTHUSIAN

Text: *Opera Omnia,* 43 vols., Montreuil-sur-Mer, 1896–1913.

Study: MOUGEL, D. A., *Denys le Chartreux,* Montreuil-sur-Mer, 1896.

BERNARDINO DE LAREDO

Text: In *Misticos Franciscanos Españoles II*, Madrid, 1949.
Translation: The Ascent of Mount Sion, ed. by E. Allison Peers, London, 1952. [A translation of the third part only.]
Study: FIDÈLE DE ROS, O.F.M. Cap., *Un inspirateur de S. Thérèse, le frère Bernardine de Laredo*, Paris, 1948.

ST. IGNATIUS LOYOLA

Text: The best editions are in the *Monumenta Historica Societatis Jesu*, published at Rome.
Translations:
The Spiritual Exercises of St. Ignatius, a new trans. by Louis J. Puhl, S.J., Westminster, Maryland, [Revised] 1963.
The Spiritual Exercises, trans. by Thomas Corbishley, S.J., London, 1963.
St. Ignatius Loyola, Letters to Women, ed. by Hugo Rahner, S.J., Edinburgh, 1960.
St. Ignatius' Own Story as told to Luis Gonzalez de Camara, trans. by William J. Young, S.J., Chicago, 1956.
Studies:
BRODRICK, James, S.J., *St. Ignatius Loyola: The Pilgrim Years*, London, 1956.
BRODRICK, James, S.J., *The Origin of the Jesuits*, London, 1949.
RAHNER, Hugo, S.J., *The Spirituality of St. Ignatius Loyola: An Account of its Historical Development*, Westminster, Maryland, 1953.

ST. ALPHONSUS RODRIGUEZ

Text: Autobiografia, ed. by Vicente Segarra, S.J., Barcelona, 1956.
Translation: The Autobiography of St. Alphonsus Rodriguez, trans. by William Yeomans, S.J., London, 1964.

ST. FRANCIS DE SALES

Text: Oeuvres, 26 vols., Annecy, 1892–1932.
Translations:
Introduction to the Devout Life, newly trans. by Michael Day (Orchard Books), London, 1956.
The Love of God: A Treatise, trans. and introduced by Vincent Kerns (Orchard Books), London, 1962.
Study: DE LA BEDOYERE, M., *François de Sales*, London, 1960.

VEN. MARY OF THE INCARNATION

Text: Écrits spirituels et historiques, réédités par Dom A. Jamet, 4 vols., Paris, 1929–39.
Study: RENAUDIN, P., *Une grande mystique française au XVIIe siècle*, 1935.

JEAN-JOSEPH SURIN

Texts:

Lettres spirituelles, Édition critique par Louis Michel et Ferdinand Cavallera, 2 vols., Toulouse, 1926–28.

Les Poésies spirituelles, suivie des Contrats Spirituels (Études de théologie et d'histoire de la Spiritualité XV). Critical text with introduction and notes by E. Catta, Paris, 1958.

Guide Spirituel pour la perfection. Texte établi et présenté par Michel de Certeau, S.J. (Collection Christus, 12), Paris, 1963.

Translation: Spiritual letters, trans. by Sister M. Christopher, London, 1892.

Study: KANTERS, R., *Vie du Père Surin,* 1942.

JEAN PIERRE DE CAUSSADE

Text: A complete edition is being prepared for the Collection Christus by Fr. Olphe-Galliard. The first volume, *Lettres Spirituelles,* I (Christus 8), appeared in 1962.

Translations:

Abandonment to Divine Providence, trans. by E. J. Strickland, 7th impression, Exeter, 1961.

Self-Abandonment to Divine Providence, etc., trans. by A. Thorold (Orchard Books), London, 1959.